Career Paths in Psychology

Career Paths in Psychology

Where Your Degree Can Take You

Second Edition

Edited by

Robert J. Sternberg

American Psychological Association
Washington, DC

Second Printing, September 2007

Published by
American Psychological Association
750 First Street, NE
Washington, DC 20002
www.apa.org

To order
APA Order Department
P.O. Box 92984
Washington, DC 20090-2984
Tel: (800) 374-2721; Direct: (202) 336-5510
Fax: (202) 336-5502; TDD/TTY: (202) 336-6123
Online: www.apa.org/books/
E-mail: order@apa.org

In the U.K., Europe, Africa, and the Middle East, copies may be ordered from
American Psychological Association
3 Henrietta Street
Covent Garden, London
WC2E 8LU England

Typeset in Meridien by World Composition Services, Inc., Sterling, VA

Printer: Victor Graphics, Inc., Baltimore, MD
Cover Designer: Naylor Design, Washington, DC
Technical/Production Editor: Pamela McElroy

The opinions and statements published are the responsibility of the authors, and such opinions and statements do not necessarily represent the policies of the American Psychological Association.

Library of Congress Cataloging-in-Publication Data

Career paths in psychology : where your degree can take you / edited by Robert J. Sternberg.—2nd ed.
    p. cm.
  Includes bibliographical references and index.
  ISBN-13: 978-1-59147-732-7
  ISBN-10: 1-59147-732-8
  1. Psychology—Vocational guidance. I. Sternberg, Robert J.

 BF76.C38 2007
 150.23'73—dc22   2006021146

British Library Cataloguing-in-Publication Data
A CIP record is available from the British Library.

Printed in the United States of America
Second Edition

Contents

III

A VARIETY OF ORGANIZATIONS   201

IV

DIVERSE AREAS OF PSYCHOLOGY   279

Contributors

Daniel J. Abrahamson, PhD, Traumatic Stress Institute, Center for Adult & Adolescent Psychotherapy, South Windsor, CT

Jane Annunziata, PsyD, independent practice, McLean, VA

Mary Barringer, PhD, Bryan Independent School District, Bryan, TX

Judith S. Blanton, PhD, RHR International, Los Angeles, CA

Bruce L. Bobbitt, PhD, LP, United Behavioral Health, Golden Valley, MN

Marc H. Bornstein, PhD, Child and Family Research, National Institute of Child Health and Human Development, Bethesda, MD

Sharon Stephens Brehm, PhD, Indiana University, Bloomington

Ronald T. Brown, PhD, College of Health Professions, Temple University, Philadelphia, PA

Kelly D. Brownell, PhD, Yale University, New Haven, CT

Robert Calfee, PhD, School of Education, Stanford University, Stanford, CA

Wayne J. Camara, PhD, College Board, New York, NY

Paul L. Craig, PhD, ABPP-CN, School of Medicine, University of Washington, Seattle

Brian P. Daly, PhD, College of Health Professions, Temple University, Philadelphia, PA

Debra L. Dunivin, PhD, ABPP, Walter Reed Army Medical Center, Bethesda, MD

Christine H. Farber, PhD, Traumatic Stress Institute, Center for Adult & Adolescent Psychotherapy, South Windsor, CT

Elena L. Grigorenko, PhD, Yale University, New Haven, CT

Tamara M. Haegerich, PhD, Institute of Education Sciences, U.S. Department of Education, Washington, DC

M. Victoria Ingram, PsyD, ABPP, Walter Reed Army Medical Center, Bethesda, MD

Marc Nemiroff, PhD, Washington School of Psychiatry, Potomac, MD

Lynn Okagaki, PhD, Institute of Education Sciences, Washington, DC

John J. Pass, PhD, Iona College, New Rochelle, NY

Henry L. Roediger III, PhD, Washington University, St. Louis, MO

Adam Saenz, PhD, Bryan Independent School District, Bryan, TX

Peter Salovey, PhD, Yale University, New Haven, CT

Robert J. Sternberg, PhD, Tufts University, Medford, MA

Melba J. T. Vasquez, PhD, ABPP, independent practice, Austin, TX

Victor H. Vroom, PhD, Yale University, New Haven, CT

Acknowledgments

thank Cheri Stahl for her editorial assistance in the preparation of this book. I also thank Gary VandenBos at the American Psychological Association for his support of this project.

Career
Paths in
Psychology

Robert J. Sternberg

Introduction

F ew fields of study offer more career opportunities than does psychology. This book is about those career opportunities. They are diverse. They are challenging. They are fun. And, for the most part, they pay well. They are also flexible: People can switch, often fairly easily and with a minimum of adjustment, from one career within psychology to another. Moreover, even within a single career, the variety of challenges and activities will interest even the most easily bored individuals.

This is the second edition of this work. The first edition was published 10 years ago. Since then, the complexion of the field of psychology has changed. This book contains five more chapters than the first edition. Moreover, all chapters have been either very substantially updated or, in most cases, completely rewritten to reflect current trends. Some chapters have been deleted and others added to reflect changes in the field.

In a randomly chosen week, I may fly across the country to give a departmental colloquium, teach courses to both undergraduate and graduate students, work on an article for a professional journal, work on an article for a popular magazine, work on a chapter of a textbook for undergraduates, consult with an educational or business organization, write part of a grant proposal, meet one on one with students

I supervise, review an article for a journal, answer several calls from parents whose children are having problems in school, correspond with collaborators on other continents about how our joint research enterprises are going, attend a faculty meeting, meet with a job candidate and attend the candidate's talk, have an informal dinner meeting with members of my research group during which we informally discuss research, and also see my wife and children. I love the amazing variety of activities I do in my job, and mine represents only one of many possible careers in psychology—that of an academic psychologist (and now, also a dean). Other psychologists combine clinical practice, research, teaching, and administration. How could anyone ever be bored?

Psychology is not only one of the most interesting fields of study but also one of the most diverse: Few fields offer a greater number and variety of career opportunities. College students who decide to major in psychology, therefore, open up a world of possibilities for themselves. Graduate students can be confident of diverse kinds of careers, and practicing psychologists often can change the kind of work they do or the setting they work in while remaining within the field of psychology.

Psychology is one of the most rewarding fields a person can enter. Psychology can be fun. It helps people, advances scientific and clinical understanding, and pays relatively well. Most psychologists earn well above the median salary in the United States. Few earn stratospheric wages, but some do—generally highly successful psychologists in private practice, organizational psychologists, or writers of textbooks or books for the popular press. Realistically, chances are you will neither go broke nor live in a palatial mansion if you choose a career in psychology. What you will do is help people improve their lives, help students learn to understand themselves and others, and perhaps advance the state of the field's knowledge—and have a great time while you are doing it.

This book will help you start on a career path in psychology, or perhaps continue on one or even change the path you are on. The chapters in this book tell you about 19 different graduate-level careers in psychology (i.e., those achieved with a PhD, EdD, or PsyD). Each chapter discusses what the career is, how to prepare for the career, typical activities people pursue while they engage in the career, the approximate range of financial compensation for the career[1], the advantages and disadvantages people typically find in the career, personal and professional attributes desirable for success in the career, and opportunities for employment and advancement in the career.

---

[1] The level of information provided on financial compensation varies from chapter to chapter according to the availability of data in each subfield.

The authors of the chapters were chosen for their distinction in their chosen careers. They all have achieved a level of prominence and a depth of experience that any budding graduate student should seek to emulate. They were asked to write about their careers not only because of their stature in their respective fields but also because of their ability to convey the excitement of their careers to readers of this book.

Of course, a book of this length cannot cover every possible career, but the careers that are covered are fairly representative of the range of work psychologists do and the range of careers that a substantial proportion of psychologists have chosen. The book is divided into four main parts, each of which considers a different facet of career paths in psychology: careers in academic organizations; careers in clinical, counseling, and community psychology, usually through private practice; careers in nonacademic organizations; and careers that cut across these various kinds of settings. Of course, this organization of the chapters is only one of many possible, but it does seem to capture a way in which many people organize the field.

I hope readers find in this volume a series of examples that will both inspire and enthuse them. Psychology is a field that offers many possibilities, and I wish you well on your journey of discovery.

I

Academia

Henry L. Roediger III

Teaching, Research, and More: Psychologists in an Academic Career

1

W riters of this book make one fact abundantly clear: Psychologists work in many different settings at many different occupations. However, virtually all were trained in colleges and universities, and therefore almost everyone in the field is familiar to some degree with psychology in an academic setting. Most students reading this book are also in an academic setting and so have some appreciation for what their professors do. However, my experience from talking with students over the past 35 years indicates that whereas they understand some of the prominent aspects of careers in academic settings, they do not know about parts of the profession that are less apparent from their own vantage point. I discuss some of these more hidden features in this chapter.

Henry L. Roediger III, BA, PhD, is the James S. McDonnell Distinguished University Professor of Psychology at Washington University in St. Louis. He received his BA from Washington and Lee University and his PhD from Yale University. Roediger previously taught at Purdue University, the University of Toronto, and Rice University before moving to Washington University in 1996. His research has been concerned primarily with human memory. This chapter benefited from the comments of Lyn Goff, Jane McConnell, Kathleen McDermott, Kerry Robinson, Rebecca Roediger, and Dave Schneider.

Writing about the academic career in psychology is difficult because academia affords a number of different types of careers. The psychologist teaching in a community college, for example, may be a part-time professor who has another job outside academia. Professors in liberal arts colleges may devote much of their time to teaching, often three or four courses a semester. Whereas the teaching loads in community colleges and other liberal arts colleges may leave little time for research or other activities, faculty at larger universities with graduate programs (often called *research universities*) are expected to conduct research and publish it in scholarly journals. Typically, faculty at these institutions teach one or two courses a semester at either the graduate or undergraduate level.

Although the careers in academic psychology are different in the various academic settings, all share certain features, such as teaching and counseling students. In this chapter, I cover the common features while touching on aspects of the job that vary among academic settings. I draw on my experiences in teaching at Purdue University, the University of Toronto, Rice University, and Washington University and my own education at Washington and Lee University and Yale University. All of the schools at which I have taught are research universities, but two (Purdue and Toronto) are public (i.e., supported by government) and two (Rice and Washington) are private (i.e., supported largely by privately raised funds). Enrollment at these schools varies widely, from around 33,000 students at Purdue (when I was there) to about 4,000 at Rice.

The Nature of the Academic Psychology Career

The nature of one's career in academia depends, as I have noted, partly on the kind of academic institution. The most obvious characteristic of a career in academia is teaching, the common thread at all institutions of higher learning. Anyone devoting his or her life to an academic career should have a love of teaching as well as a love of learning and a desire to instill that love of learning in others. Teaching, in its broadest sense, occurs on many levels and may take place in several settings. Besides teaching formal courses, professors interact with students in small seminars, private consultations, research meetings, and sometimes (depending on the school) settings outside the classroom, such as dining halls.

One of the most delightful benefits for faculty members of being in an academic setting is the opportunity to learn from students. Students new to psychology often have different and interesting viewpoints. Also, faculty learn new information when students pick novel topics for term papers or research papers or when they do an outstanding job reviewing what is known.

It is wrong (or, at best, only partly right) to think of a college professor as someone who learned about his or her field in graduate school and who then went out to teach that knowledge. Education only begins the process of learning, which continues throughout the career of teaching in academia. Professors must continually keep up with their fast-changing fields to keep their courses current. Of course, no one can master all aspects of every field one teaches, but being a professor causes one to keep up with at least the broad sweep—the main ideas and major new developments—in the topics one teaches.

In sum, the primary features of devoting oneself to an academic career are the love of learning and the desire to instill that love in others. But what does one do in academic settings besides teach? I turn to this issue next.

Activities of College Professors

What do professors do besides teach? Lots of things! They conduct research, write, and serve on committees, to mention a few activities. College professors are often criticized because, the way some outsiders see it, they teach so little. What people mean by that is that the number of hours professors actually spend in the classroom is relatively small when compared, say, with high school teachers' hours. However, this difference in time spent teaching does not mean that college professors are not in a demanding profession or that they do not work hard. They do. But most people outside the profession are unaware of the range of demands professors face. The illustrations in the following sections are somewhat personal because I do all these things, but all professors perform most of the same activities at some point in their careers.

PREPARING COURSES

Before a professor actually walks into a classroom, he or she has undertaken a huge amount of preparation. Preparing for a lecture that lasts an hour may take several hours of background reading, note taking, preparation of slides, or other activities such as arranging a classroom demonstration. The professor must know what is in the assigned text but must also consult other books and research articles in preparing the lecture because the lecture usually goes far beyond the text material. Students sometimes complain about the workload or amount of reading in a course, but typically the professor is doing much more. College professors who are just beginning teaching often spend most of their time in course preparation. Beginning professors often teach large lecture courses, and preparing material for 40 or so lectures for each course over the period of a semester takes huge amounts of time. Even experienced professors who have been teaching for years must continually update their material. And if they decide to teach a course on a new topic, they must begin preparation from scratch. For professors who teach three or four courses a semester, course preparation may take virtually all their time in their early years in the profession.

Recent advances in technology have changed course preparation somewhat. Many publishers of college textbooks offer supplemental packages that include traditional aids (e.g., books of adjunct readings for the course, acetate transparencies) or the latest in video technology and other materials to help professors prepare. These aids can be wonderfully helpful in making large lecture courses more interesting, but in a way they increase the demands placed on the professor to learn more about these new technologies, to preview the materials, and to integrate them into the course.

TEACHING

Professors may teach in lecture courses, in small seminars that combine lecture with discussion, or in reading groups in which everyone has read the material and discusses it. Although the lecture method of teaching has been under attack for years, it is probably still the most common form of teaching. However, much has been written to instruct professors on converting standard (i.e., noninteractive) lectures into experiences in which the students participate more fully (e.g., small break-out discussions among groups, class exercises or experiments, demonstrations). Everyone reading this book knows that there are huge individual differences in teaching: Some people are gifted teachers because of some combination of personality, knowledge, eloquence, humor, and skill in presentation. But probably everyone can be a more effective teacher by working at it. (See Bernstein and Lucas's [2004] chapter "Tips for Effective Teaching.")

As I noted previously, the time professors spend in the classroom often appears to be limited. During much of my career, I have taught two courses a semester, usually one undergraduate and one graduate course, so I spend about 6 hours a week in the classroom. However, I usually work 60 to 70 hours in a typical week because my time is occupied with all the other activities listed in this section.

MAKING AND GRADING TESTS

Composing and grading tests is part of teaching but is separate from course preparation and time spent in class. Depending on the number of courses taught, the number of students in the course, and the type of tests and assignments given, these activities can take large amounts of time. Multiple choice tests (and other "objective" tests, such as true–false or matching tests) are easy to grade, but they often require considerable time to compose. Designing essay and short-answer tests is often quicker, but then these tests take much longer to grade.

In my own case, I dislike giving only objective types of questions. Evidence indicates that these sorts of tests cause students to focus on learning isolated facts rather than drawing material together to see the larger picture and the overarching themes (e.g., Schmidt, 1983). So I prefer to give tests that require students to write essays to encourage them to look for interrelated themes when studying. When I teach introductory psychology, I give four tests composed of a mixture of essay and objective questions. In addition, all students write an essay on a book and take a cumulative final examination. In my other undergraduate course, which is on human memory, students take two 2-hour essay tests, write two essay papers, and take a cumulative (essay) final examination. The time required for test construction and grading for these two courses, which usually have enrollments of about 150 and 35 students, respectively, is not trivial; luckily, although I do some grading myself, I have teaching assistants in both courses who help with these chores. When I teach graduate courses, I usually require the students to write a few shorter essays on various topics during the course of the semester and then to write a long paper reviewing a body of research pertaining to any topic of the course that they find of interest. At the end of the paper, they are required to write a proposal for future research that would add to knowledge in the field.

CONSULTING WITH STUDENTS

Most professors enjoy meeting with students outside of class. Depending on the type of institution, students feel varying degrees of freedom to visit with faculty and to talk about problems in a course, ask for advice about courses or careers, learn more about the material, or discuss ideas. For universities with graduate programs, a considerable amount of faculty time is devoted to advising graduate students on their research and discussing research with them. I estimate that I spend 4 to 5 hours a week consulting with graduate students and undergraduate students about their research projects. In addition, once a week I hold a lab meeting that includes both students working directly with me and others who also want to attend (even though they primarily work with another professor). The lab meeting functions like an informal course, but with topics shifting across a range of topics from week to week

CONDUCTING RESEARCH

Many faculty members conduct psychological research. This activity is especially common in research universities, but psychologists in all types of schools have programs of interesting and important research. Planning this research takes time, although it usually occurs in the natural course of other activities, such as consulting with students, reading articles, and writing proposals for research. Research may seem a mysterious process at first, but it is the lifeblood of every academic discipline because the discoveries and advances in every field all come from new research. Scientists know the state of knowledge in their fields, and their curiosity about the unexplained leads them to push forward the frontiers of knowledge. The motivations for future research are many—exploring unexplained past findings, testing implications of theories to see if they hold true, seeing if findings obtained in one setting generalize to another, and many others. The researcher usually works from a theory to generate hypotheses and then collects data to evaluate the hypotheses. When students first come into a field, they often wonder about the source of all the ideas that generate the research they are reading about and about whether they will be able to generate their own ideas. Later, after being immersed in the field, most researchers lament the lack of time and resources to conduct all the research they would like to do.

When students first enter graduate school, a professor often guides them in their initial research projects. No one expects students just beginning in a field to design and conduct cutting-edge research because the process of becoming a researcher is a gradual one. Collaboration is critical as the student learns to conduct research. Typically, students who are beginning to work with me will take on part of a project, which might already be ongoing, to get their feet wet and to immerse themselves in the problems and procedures of the field. However, throughout the 4 or 5 years that I work with the student, he or she gradually becomes more independent and begins designing, conducting, and writing about research, needing less consultation with me.

Students often learn about conducting research in one-on-one meetings with their major professors. Students who work with me meet in our weekly lab meeting. Sometimes a student will present his or her research or plans for future research, but often I select a recent research article or chapter for all of us to read and to discuss. Many ideas for future research come out of these meetings. (I cover other aspects of research elsewhere in this chapter.)

WRITING LETTERS OF REFERENCE

Surely, you might think, this activity does not deserve a separate listing. Yes, it does. During certain times of the year, writing letters of reference takes a great deal of time. Undergraduate students need letters of reference for applications to graduate school and for jobs. Graduate students need employment letters of reference, perhaps for 20 or more applications. Former students and colleagues in the field need letters for jobs to which they apply. Also, as one becomes more senior in the field, other universities request letters about candidates being considered for promotion and tenure. (Tenure is the award of lifetime job security to faculty so that they may investigate any topic freely, without fear of reprisal for investigating taboo topics.) Often these requests are accompanied by a selection of the candidate's relevant writings, a statement of his or her research accomplishments and plans, and curriculum vitae. Processing all this information before writing the letter can take several hours. I estimate that in a given year I write letters of reference for 10 or so students and colleagues and for 5 to 7 seven candidates for promotion at other universities. All these letters take time, especially during the fall and winter. Writing letters of reference is seasonal labor.

ATTENDING FACULTY MEETINGS AND COMMITTEE MEETINGS

A university is, among other things, a large organization with a hierarchical structure. Organizations need the various groups that deal with particular matters to run smoothly. Within the typical psychology department, there may be

- a space committee to assign research space to people,
- a committee for subject use to oversee proposals for testing human and animal subjects,
- an animal care committee to oversee the care and housing of animals,
- a promotion and tenure committee composed of senior professors,

- a graduate committee to oversee the graduate program, and
- an undergraduate committee to perform the same service for the undergraduate program.

Of course, an individual professor might be assigned to only one or two of these committees, but the assignments do take time. In addition, there are general faculty meetings of the department and of the university faculty as a whole.

There are also committee meetings for students. In undergraduate programs with honors degrees, a professor may be a part of a two- or three-member committee that advises and examines the research of an honors student. In universities with graduate programs, each student typically has a committee both for the master's degree and for the PhD. Professors may meet with students to discuss the proposal that deals with the research the student is planning and how it is to be carried out. Then, eventually, faculty must read the thesis or dissertation that the student has written, and the student must defend it at another meeting. Some universities also require preliminary or qualifying examinations of students before they embark on the PhD, which necessitates faculty attendance at other committee meetings.

There are other committee meetings in addition to those I have listed. Professors may need to staff search committees when their department is hiring a new faculty member; these take a large amount of time, first to review the numerous applications, then to interview three or four candidates, and then to decide whom to recommend for the position. Professors may also be involved with any of the other committees that exist for the entire university, such as search committees for a new dean, provost, or president. Most universities have still other committees to advise on such matters as athletics and admissions. At certain times during the academic year, committee work can require considerable time. Sometimes it is not fascinating work, but it is critical to the overall good of the department and the university.

Serving on professional committees can also take large chunks of time. Every national and regional organization of psychologists has a program committee, an executive committee, and often many other committees. University psychologists are frequently asked to serve on these committees.

COMMUNICATING WITH OTHER SCHOLARS WITH SIMILAR INTERESTS

One curious fact about universities is that individual faculty members may be intensely interested in one topic, whether it is the history of ancient Rome, the poetry of Wordsworth, the stars of the Orion nebula, or how people form and change beliefs and attitudes. Often no one with your particular scholarly interest exists at your university, and yet you want to maintain contact with others in the specific field to share ideas and to learn of late-breaking developments. A century ago, scholarly communication was largely confined to reading others' books and articles, when they appeared, or writing letters. Communication is much faster now, and e-mail permits people to stay in constant contact and to learn of new developments almost instantaneously, either through informal contact or through formal bulletin boards. Many professors are now finding themselves glued to their computers, communicating with others with like interests. Many research collaborations blossom by e-mail; this mode of communication can especially aid professors at smaller colleges and universities by allowing them to communicate with almost anyone in the field. Although fascinating, this activity takes time, and it seems likely to become increasingly important.

ATTENDING PROFESSIONAL MEETINGS

Professional meetings are another activity that permits academics to keep pace with their fields. People go to professional meetings to present their own research findings by giving papers or displaying posters and to hear about cutting-edge research by many others in their field. In psychology, there are national meetings of large organizations like the American Psychological Association and the Association for Psychological Science, of regional groups (e.g., the Midwestern Psychological Association), and of more specialized groups interested in particular topics (e.g., the Society for Research in Child Development). Years ago, the big national meetings dominated the scene, but now many professors choose to go to more specialized meetings concerned with their area of interest instead of or in addition to the large conventions. The meetings usually last 2 to 3 days. Attendance at such meetings is optional; some professors go to many, and others go to practically none. Attending at least some meetings is a good idea because it allows academics to become acquainted with people with interests similar to their own. Networking is important in academia, as in other spheres of life.

WRITING

For psychologists active in research, technical writing is a critical skill, one that must continually be honed. The greatest research ever conducted would never have been known if it had not been effectively communicated. Psychologists in research universities must be skilled in writing research articles to communicate their findings clearly. There are also opportunities to write chapters for scholarly books (like this one), and some write monographs (treatises written by one author, usually on specialized areas of learning) to communicate their research to interested scholars. Technical and scholarly writing can be difficult skills to learn, but several useful guides exist (see Bem, 2004; Sternberg, 2003). In addition, researchers seeking support for their research usually write grant proposals to federal agencies and to foundations.

Some professors write textbooks in their areas of interest (e.g., developmental or social psychology) or general textbooks (e.g., on research methods or introductory psychology). Writing textbooks can be lucrative and is also a critical part of the educational process. An outstanding teacher at one university, no matter how brilliant, has a limited impact: He or she will affect only the students attending those classes at that campus. But a professor who writes an outstanding textbook can literally help teach an entire generation of students about a given topic and entice those students further into this field of study. It is curious that textbook writing is often not professionally rewarded within university settings; colleagues and administrators do not see this kind of publication as the scholarly equal of other kinds of works (Roediger, 2004). However, with the great emphasis on the importance of teaching now reinvigorating universities, perhaps this attitude will be relaxed. After all, a textbook writer is a teacher of thousands of students, and the text is the main course contact for many students. In my own case, I have coauthored two textbooks—*Research Methods in Psychology* (Elmes, Kantowitz, & Roediger, 2006) and *Experimental Psychology: Understanding Psychological Research* (Kantowitz, Roediger, & Elmes, 2005)—that have both gone through eight editions and have been used in courses for several generations of students. In addition to the satisfaction I have obtained from having these books used widely over the past 25 years and from educating many students, I have learned much about psychology while researching material for the books.

REVIEWING AND EDITING

Another task in academia that can take significant amounts of time is the evaluation of scholarly publications. Publishing in scholarly journals occurs by a process of peer review. If I submit an article for publication to a journal, the editor sends it to several experts in the field of inquiry (the peers), who are asked to read the article and to write evaluations of the research, answering such questions as, Does the paper deserve to be published? Does it make a significant contribution to knowledge?

Serving as a referee on an article entails considerable work. Every manuscript deserves a careful and thoughtful reading and a fair and unbiased review. Reviewing a manuscript properly can take hours, and some researchers are called on by several journals and therefore get many manuscripts to review. This activity can place a large burden on already overworked scholars, but there are rewards. A person learns about the latest findings in his or her field by reviewing manuscripts. In some cases (usually after a trial period during which the editor of the journal finds the person's reviewing especially good and insightful), reviewers become consulting editors for a journal. Psychologists who serve as editors or associate editors of journals make the final decisions about the publishability of articles in that journal. Some journals receive hundreds of manuscripts a year, which means that editors must find time to read the articles, read the reviews of consultants, and then write letters of acceptance or rejection to the authors. The editorial process is critical in every field and requires great amounts of time from editors and reviewers.

Other types of reviewing may be required of the academic psychologist. For instance, textbooks are reviewed by many teachers both before they are published and during the revision process. In addition, many scholars evaluate books in book reviews published in scholarly journals or in the popular press.

CONSULTING

Some psychology professors consult with organizations in industry or the legal profession about their areas of interest. This is not an activity I participate in very often, but many others do. Human factors psychologists may consult on the design of equipment to make the product easier to use. Industrial/organizational psychologists may consult with companies on personnel selection or on ways to improve the morale of the organization. Clinical and counseling psychologists in academia may have a small private practice. Indeed, virtually every area of psychology has something to offer some industry or occupation. Psychologists in academia often step outside the academy to offer advice on more practical matters of the world.

PERFORMING COMMUNITY SERVICE

Psychologists may also be called on for various kinds of community service. For example, they may be asked to educate the general public through lectures to civic and religious groups. In addition, they may work with community groups, such as Alcoholics Anonymous or a local crisis center, on various social or personal problems. Some psychologists appear on radio and television programs to explain psychological issues to wider audiences. Academics differ widely in how much time they spend in community service, but it can be rewarding because the teaching involved extends the traditional forums.

SUMMARY OF COLLEGE PROFESSORS' ACTIVITIES

The dozen or so activities listed in this section include most of the activities in which psychologists in a psychology department might be involved. Of course, the list is not exhaustive. Professors can and do participate in other activities, but this sample constitutes a reasonable range of the usual activities. After reading the foregoing account, your opinion might have swung from "College professors don't do much; they only teach a few hours a week" to "How can anyone do all these things?" Keep in mind that this section includes activities that occur over the course of a year; not all are done every day. One important feature of being a professor is that there is considerable time (i.e., summers and holidays) when teaching requirements are reduced or absent altogether. Yet these are not times of relaxation for professors. Most professors work as hard or harder during the summer months and vacations, but they work on different activities from those that occupy them when classes are in session: writing research reports, conducting research, attending meetings, preparing courses for the next year, among others.

Academic Settings

Psychology departments appear in all kinds of institutions of higher education. Almost every city or town of any size has a community college to—as the name implies—serve the members of the community. Professors in these settings usually devote most of their time to teaching (rather than research). There are also hundreds of relatively small private and public colleges and universities in the United States that offer undergraduate education in psychology culminating in a BA or BS degree. Each of these colleges and universities has a psychology department. Larger public and private schools provide both graduate and undergraduate education in psychology, so usually they have larger departments with faculty who specialize in various fields in psychology.

Students aspiring to an academic career in psychology may seek a position in any of these types of schools or in others, such as the independent schools in clinical psychology that give graduate degrees. Each type of school has its benefits, and all can be very attractive places to work. For example, community colleges often have adult students who have worked and experienced more of life before they decided to return and further their education. Often these students are very eager to learn and appreciate the opportunity to learn in a way that 18- to 21-year-old undergraduates may not. Other professors love teaching in small liberal arts colleges. The student–faculty ratio is often low, which promotes good interactions with students. Similarly, faculty at larger schools or research universities may enjoy interacting with graduate students, conducting research, and publishing in scholarly journals. The demands and rewards of the various academic settings are different, and some may appeal more to one type of person than to another. If you are considering a career in academia, you should carefully consider which type of setting might suit you best.

Preparing for the Academic Career

The standard preparation for a career in a psychology department is usually fairly straightforward. Typically, a person should have an undergraduate degree in psychology or a degree in some related field such as biology, anthropology, or neuroscience and a considerable amount of psychology coursework. Next, a student interested in an academic career in psychology should apply to graduate school. Students do not apply to graduate school in the general area of psychology, but rather to a specialized field in which they are interested (e.g., cognitive psychology, social psychology, clinical psychology). If you intend to pursue a graduate degree in psychology, you should find out from your advisors and from other sources which schools have good programs in your area of interest and then apply only to those schools.

Graduate school training usually takes from 4 to 6 years, although longer periods are not unheard of, depending on what other duties a student may have (e.g., heavy teaching requirements, a part-time job for financial support). Typically, students receive a master's degree in 2 or 3 years and then begin working on a PhD. Students receiving a PhD in clinical psychology need to complete an internship if they want to be licensed to practice, which most do. Students receiving PhDs in other areas may take a postdoctoral fellowship following completion of their degree to further their research training.

While in graduate school, the student learns about the subject matter of psychology in general and his or her field in particular. Doing coursework, reading, attending talks and colloquia, and participating in discussions with advisors and other faculty are the usual means of learning. Students usually receive their research training through an apprentice system in which they work closely with one or more faculty members to learn how to conduct research. Many other professional aspects of psychology are learned almost by osmosis (or observational learning) and from watching how successful people in the profession operate. Two books that help people prepare for academia are *The Compleat Academic: A Career Guide* (Darley, Zanna, & Roediger, 2004) and *Psychology 101½: The Unspoken Rules for Success in Academia* (Sternberg, 2004). Again, graduate education in a field should be considered only the beginning. Psychologists continue learning their entire lifetimes, and in academia they do so from continual course preparation, students, research, reading, and professional meetings.

My Interest in Psychology: How Did I Choose This Career?

The story of how one comes to choose a career in academic psychology is different for everyone. But because you (or at least the editor of this volume) asked, my story starts in high school. I attended Riverside Military Academy, which had two campuses at that time. In the fall and spring we were in Gainesville, Georgia, but from January to March we were in Hollywood, Florida, which is located between Miami and Fort Lauderdale. I suspect that everyone is interested to some degree in human behavior, in what makes people tick. Being in a military school for my tender high school years increased my curiosity because of experiences that I need not relate here. (Strange things happen in military schools, and the conditions, which are harder than those in other high schools, can make life interesting. Some of these conditions can be glimpsed in Pat Conroy's [1980] *The Lords of Discipline*, although my experiences were not as severe as those recounted in that novel.)

During January or February of 1964, my guidance counselor, a man named Jerry Sullivan, approached me with a letter and packet of material from Stetson University in DeLand, Florida. That university offered a special program for selected high school juniors from Florida: They could enroll at Stetson in summer school between their junior and senior years in high school, and if they did well in three regular college courses, they could skip their senior year in high school and go right on to college at Stetson. Stetson apparently wanted to capture some of Florida's bright high school students rather than have them head north to attend other private colleges, so they tried to attract them with this program. I liked the idea of spending the summer at college, my parents agreed to foot the bill, and off I went.

I had to take English and mathematics and was given one elective. I chose psychology, knowing nothing about it except that it sounded vaguely interesting and different. I loved it. I had a fine professor (a Dr. Jones), and we used a good book, which I still have: *Scientific Principles of Psychology* by Lewis (1963). Although we were assigned only half the book, I read the whole thing and thought all the material was fascinating. I recall being especially struck and enlightened by material on classical and operant conditioning—here was how to control behavior!—and about the measurement of intelligence. Wonderful knowledge was available in this field, and I had known nothing about it before this course. In addition, even though the book was in its second printing, it was filled with small errors. When students bought the book, they were given three pages of errata and had to piece together the correct information from the misprints in the book. Through this experience, I learned that the printed word in books was not immutable truth. Someone actually wrote these books, and he or she, and the publisher, made errors. (Yes, I should have known that, but I didn't.) I got As in English and psychology that summer and a B in mathematics—the story of my life. I was admitted to Stetson, but (after long thought) went back to Riverside.

The next year I faced the question of where to go to college. Again, psychology intervened in an important way. I had received an appointment to the U.S. Military Academy at West Point, passed the physical and mental examinations, and was admitted. Did I really want to go? The Vietnam War was just heating up in 1965, but this did not much permeate my thinking. Instead, I looked at the psychology offerings in the various college catalogs I had because I thought I wanted to study psychology. At West Point the offerings were slim; as I recall it now, the closest courses to psychology were those such as military science and hygiene. I decided against West Point and went to Washington and Lee University.

My freshman year I was required to take many courses and could not work psychology in, but I did take a course in my sophomore year (from Joseph Thompson) and continued on that path by taking almost all the courses available in psychology (from David Elmes and William Hinton, as well as Thompson). Elmes got me interested in research, and I spent several summers there conducting research. I was also near to completing a major in sociology and anthropology. There was no course in social psychology at Washington and Lee during my era, but one of my professors told me that a great textbook in this area was *Social Psychology* by Roger Brown (1965). I read it and decided to go to graduate school in this area, despite my relative ignorance of the topic. (Although I also was admitted to graduate school in two anthropology departments, social psychology seemed a good blend of my interests in sociology, anthropology, and psychology.) It is surprising (in retrospect) that my lack of credentials or research experience in social psychology did not prevent me from being admitted to the social psychology graduate program at Yale, but I was and so off I went. However, I switched into the cognitive psychology program during my 1st year there.

So that is how I wound up in psychology. It is more than you wanted to know, perhaps, but I imagine that every psychologist has a story like it: What we wind up doing is determined in large part by the various accidents of life.

Financial Compensation

I write in July 2005. The range of salaries for full-time university professors in psychology is quite great. For those interested in looking into the salary ranges of psychologists, the American Psychological Association publishes figures based on surveys of its membership. Salary differences occur between types of schools, geographic regions, small-town versus large-city location, and the various specialty areas within psychology. The 2004–2005 figures are shown in Table 1.1 and are from a report by the Research Office of the American Psychological Association (Wicherski, Frincke, & Kohout, 2006); the mean salary for all ranks at universities with doctoral programs was $65,539 for that year.

Psychology professors will never be accused of entering their profession to become rich. Professors can usually live comfortably, but not opulently. However, professors can augment their academic salaries

TABLE 1.1

2005–2006 Salaries for Full-Time Faculty in U.S. Doctoral Departments of Psychology by Rank and Years in Rank

	Median	10%	25%	75%	90%	Mean	SD	N
Full professor								
24 or more years	101,200	76,011	86,987	130,900	158,352	109,570	31,741	303
18–23 years	101,538	74,387	85,453	120,500	151,650	107,829	31,514	369
12–17 years	98,914	72,108	83,031	116,478	140,070	102,320	26,257	402
6–11 years	87,953	67,264	75,886	104,000	125,920	92,808	24,277	471
3–5 years	82,218	64,282	71,259	96,794	124,248	87,729	25,528	251
Less than 3	75,014	60,251	66,734	89,908	107,450	79,845	19,978	264
Not specified	92,804	71,717	83,122	130,000	151,747	101,801	28,176	15
All years	91,500	67,416	77,000	111,703	137,678	97,571	28,730	2075
Associate professor								
11 or more years	64,984	51,633	58,262	73,505	82,383	66,973	13,497	334
6–10 years	64,731	54,346	58,854	73,114	80,211	66,918	11,486	249
3–5 years	64,951	52,463	57,603	74,803	84,236	66,654	12,862	324
Less than 3	63,249	51,974	57,218	71,316	79,010	65,160	12,366	416
Not specified	59,586	50,520	57,750	66,280	70,852	60,859	6,394	10
All years	64,375	52,540	57,852	72,757	81,726	66,274	12,609	1333
Assistant professor								
3 or more years	56,013	47,439	51,195	61,350	68,082	57,011	9,067	583
Less than 3	55,215	45,086	50,000	60,000	65,000	55,150	7,763	653
Not specified	50,036	39,654	45,750	60,501	68,200	52,950	9,568	22
All years	55,622	46,410	50,403	60,257	66,005	55,974	8,478	1258
Lecturer/Instructor								
3 or more years	48,292	40,525	42,967	55,769	64,912	50,416	9,147	57
Less than 3	44,000	30,000	35,874	52,148	62,062	44,535	11,049	43
All years	46,312	35,000	40,889	55,000	63,947	47,887	10,377	100

Note. Included in this table are only those faculty who are full time, who hold the doctoral degree, and who are in departments of psychology that award the doctoral degree (e.g., psychology departments, educational psychology departments, and schools of professional psychology). All salaries are 9–10-month salaries. No statistics are provided where the *N* of faculty is less than 10. From *Faculty Salaries in Graduate Departments of Psychology* (p. 15), by M. Wicherski, J. Frincke, and J. Kohout, 2006, Washington, DC: American Psychological Association. Copyright 2005 by the American Psychological Association.

by consulting, writing textbooks, reviewing textbooks for publishers, obtaining research grants (which pay summer salaries), and doing extra teaching (e.g., during summer sessions or at night). In addition, most colleges and universities offer good benefit packages in the form of health care and the like, as well as good retirement programs. So although no one is likely to become extraordinarily wealthy by teaching in a college or university, professors are usually able to afford a comfortable lifestyle.

Advantages and Disadvantages of the Career

Some people contemplating a career in academia consider the range of salaries the major drawback. A person could probably make more money over his or her lifetime by becoming a physician, lawyer, or engineer or by obtaining a master's degree in business administration and going into business. If you definitely have personal wealth as the major goal in life, then an academic career may not be appropriate for you. But most professors have other goals in mind. The benefits of an academic career are many, but they have more to do with the quality and style of life and less to do with money. First, there is considerable freedom and flexibility in arranging one's time. Besides giving classes and attending some mandatory meetings, one is often free to manage one's time as needed, so long as the work gets done. I write this section of this chapter after 11:00 p.m. However, I am free during the day to attend to personal matters, if need be. I sometimes play squash during my lunch hour, which is stretched to more like an hour and a half. Unlike the working conditions in other large organizations, no one is paying much attention to my comings and goings, as long as I get my work done. I do much of my writing at home, in fact. Academic positions offer great freedom in arranging what one does and when and where one chooses to do it. In addition, no one tells me what research I should be doing, what books and articles I should be reading or writing, and (within some limits) what courses I have to teach. It is rare in the world of work to be permitted to decide what you want to do and then have someone pay you to do it.

Another advantage of a university atmosphere is continued education. Professors in psychology often know professors in other disciplines and can discuss interesting topics in, say, anthropology or astronomy or history. Universities are abuzz with activities like colloquia, concerts, plays, sporting events, public addresses, and debates. There is always something interesting happening, and the difficulty is usually in being able to go to events and still get one's work done. Professors usually love to interact and to work with students. (If they don't, they are in the wrong field.) The best students are lively, probing, challenging, and fun. They keep the faculty informed and teach the faculty new things as they are being taught by the faculty. The faculty member ages, but the student body stays at about the same age, so students help keep the faculty young, to some degree.

The detriments of being a professor are, in my opinion, not great. Some faculty complain about bureaucracy, but every large organization has a bureaucracy. Faculty politics and political bickering can sometimes break out and, in some cases, can achieve legendary proportions. (A famous academic law is Sayre's Third Law of Politics: "Academic politics are most bitter, because the stakes are so small.")

The life of a college professor is, in my opinion, a wonderful one. I have never for a moment regretted my career choice. I never want to retire, although of course I may change my mind in 15 more years.

Attributes Needed for Success in the Career

Some of the required attributes for success in the academic psychology career are obvious. A certain level of verbal and mathematical intelligence is required. However, beyond some required level of intelligence, sheer IQ probably does not account for much in academia (or in any other demanding job). Graduate schools have already selected for intelligence because a person must have good grades in college and reasonably good scores on standardized tests to be admitted to graduate school. And several factors in the 4 to 7 years in a graduate school program further eliminate people along the way, for better or for worse. Many people who enter doctoral programs drop out before obtaining the PhD. Anyone who receives a PhD has the intelligence to be a psychologist in academia or elsewhere.

Besides intelligence, what else matters? As the editor of this volume has maintained (Sternberg, 1988), there are other types of intelligence, too. Practical intelligence (i.e., "street smarts"), social intelligence, and what is informally called "common sense" can all make an important difference. So can the desire to learn, creativity, and communication skills. All of these help and the stereotype of the brilliant but absentminded professor did not arise from nothing. Universities do seem to acquire more than their fair share of eccentrics, who excel in their fields but seem barely able to cope with life outside. That helps make universities interesting places, even if the presence of a few unusual people does sometimes strain university administrations that try to manage faculty, who, at the best of times, are an independent and sometimes fractious lot. Faculty are often resistant to change within the university—try changing the required curriculum for students to see this quality come out—even while they profess to like change as a general principle.

If I had to put my finger on two characteristics that predict academic success, the two would be achievement motivation (how much you really want to do this and how hard you are willing to work) and persistence (whether you will keep coming back even if you have suffered setbacks and rejection). Most of the really successful academics have these qualities, in my opinion, although I cannot point to empirical studies to show this.

Range of Opportunities for Employment

It is no secret that the academic job market is relatively poor today. Although there are about 4,000 junior colleges, colleges, and universities in the United States, the 150 to 200 research universities that produce most of the PhD students still produce them in greater numbers than the academic job market requires. The reasons for this state of affairs are complex. On the supply side, graduate departments have not much reduced the number of graduate students they admit, even though everyone recognizes that the job market in academia is weak. This may be because faculty at research universities enjoy working with graduate students and simply seek students interested in conducting research with them. In addition, many universities (especially large state universities) need graduate students to help teach undergraduates, either in the capacity of teaching assistants or as undergraduate instructors. So the fact that there are fewer jobs for doctoral-level graduates does not necessarily serve as a disincentive to the admission of new graduate students at most universities.

Why aren't there more opportunities to obtain positions? Again, the causes are complex. Just 25 years ago predictions were made that there would be an undersupply of candidates for professor positions in the 1990s and into the new century. However, the federal government has banned compulsory retirement at age 70 (as age discrimination) in universities, so some professors are staying on, which prevents openings for younger people just out of graduate school. State governments, which support state universities, colleges, and community colleges, have generally reduced aid to higher education. Many private colleges and universities feel similar financial pressures. Consequently, given that few universities are growing significantly—many are not even replacing faculty who leave—and with fewer professors retiring (or retiring later), the result is that the many students receiving PhDs are chasing too few jobs in academia.

That is the bad news. The good news is that there are still many jobs available in higher education. These differ across the specialty areas in psychology and change from year to year. But for those students who establish outstanding records in graduate school, job opportunities are available. In addition, in many fields in psychology, it is possible and even desirable to seek an appointment as a postdoctoral fellow after receiving a PhD to continue conducting research before entering the job market and embarking on a career. Taking a 2- to 3-year postdoctoral fellowship permits a young psychologist to gain additional valuable research experience (usually in a different environment from that in which he or she received the PhD), to build a stronger publication record, and therefore to be in a much more favorable position when he or she enters the job market later (see McDermott & Braver, 2004, for a discussion of postdoctoral fellowships in academia).

The other bit of good news about receiving a PhD in psychology (rather than, say, English or history) is that a wide range of job opportunities exists outside academia. The other chapters in this volume attest to the range of possibilities for a career in psychology outside of an academic setting. Good advice for graduate students in this day and age is to take a wide variety of courses in graduate school and to keep a broad perspective on career opportunities. Many exciting possibilities exist outside university teaching and research.

A Day in the Life

Contributors to this volume were asked to write about a typical day in their lives. One problem with this requirement for me is that no day is really typical. Given the many different activities a college professor engages in, my activities also differ dramatically from day to day. I wrote this chapter for the first edition in 1995, and I am leaving this section as I wrote it then, while teaching at Rice University.

I am up at 6:30 a.m. this Wednesday morning and, with no more than the usual commotion and bother, leave with my children for their school at 7:35 a.m. I get them deposited and make it to my office by 8:00 a.m.

I have a lecture at 9:00 a.m. for my introductory psychology course, for which I must first prepare. Fortunately, the lecture is on visual illusions and the constructive nature of perception. I like to think it is one of my best lectures, but I review my notes, because it has been 2 years since I last gave this version of the lecture, and I go over some 20 slides that I will use. I add two new ones that I have collected. I finish preparing for class in half an hour and decide to see what new messages have come overnight by e-mail. (Telephoning and correspondence by regular mail is becoming obsolete for me and others in academia; most important news is delivered via e-mail.) I read and respond to most of the 13 new messages that have appeared before I leave for class.

The lecture seems to go successfully, and several students ask questions during and after class. On the way back from class, I pick up my mail. I receive considerable mail from a journal that I edit—*Psychonomic Bulletin & Review*, published by the Psychonomic Society—as well as other kinds of mail. I sort the journal mail and discover several reviews of manuscripts and one new manuscript that has been submitted. I go to the journal office and talk about various matters with the secretary for the journal, and then I examine the new submission, which looks quite promising. I assign the manuscript reviewers who will evaluate it for the journal and provide advice that will help me decide on its acceptability. I get back to my office at 10:45 a.m. and finish my e-mail correspondence.

It is now shortly after 11:00 a.m., and I realize that the meeting of my lab group is looming at noon. We are to discuss the draft of a manuscript by Endel Tulving that is being submitted to a journal. I had wanted to read it and thought it would be good for my graduate students to read, too. Now the meeting is less than an hour away, and I have not finished the manuscript. So off I go to a hiding place in the basement (it has no telephone), which I use when I need to read in a quiet environment. (There are too many interruptions in my office.) I finish the manuscript, wolf down some lunch, and go off to my noon meeting. The session is quite lively, with some students suggesting items for further research. We spend some time analyzing statements or passages that seem ambiguous or unclear. One student, in particular, picks up what seems to be a weak point in the logic. I raise some points of my own, which the group discusses. I am jotting down notes, because I promised Dr. Tulving I would respond with comments based on the group's discussion.

After the lab meeting, I have an appointment with a student to discuss her master's thesis. That lasts about 20 minutes, so it is now 1:20 p.m., and I begin to prepare the afternoon lecture for my course on human memory. We are discussing the issues of the malleability of memory and of eyewitness testimony and the possibility of false memories occurring in therapy. The students are reading *The Myth of*

Repressed Memory by Elizabeth Loftus and Katherine Ketcham (1994) at this point in the course, and they seem to be enjoying it. I am discussing evidence for various memory illusions in class. However, I need to prepare some slides to display some recent results, so this chore occupies me until my class begins. After the lecture, two students come by to ask (rather nervously) about the nature of the test to be given the following week. They ask questions about material in one of the textbooks in paralyzing depth, much more than I would ever expect on the test, and we cover the intricate topics they have asked about. I suspect that they have little to worry about if they know the material in such detail, but I keep my suspicions to myself.

When the afternoon mail, which includes two journals, arrives, I scan the journals' contents and zip through one article that is of particular interest to me. Then it is 4:00 p.m. and time for me to meet with a PhD student about his dissertation. He has some of the first results of a test of nearly 700 subjects in a large-scale project. He lays out the preliminary findings, and the news is exceedingly good: The part of the research that had to work out a certain way for the rest to make an interesting contribution did come out as expected. He is very encouraged, and so am I. He leaves to embark on the additional analyses.

Now it is 4:30 p.m. and I deal with half a dozen e-mail messages that arrived during the day. Finally, I turn to a manuscript that I need to evaluate for my journal. The reviews of the manuscript are mixed, so it looks as if a difficult decision will be required. I read until 5:20 p.m. and head for home. That night, after the children are safely asleep, I finish the manuscript and dictate a letter.

This is a reasonably typical weekday, which includes about 10 to 11 hours of work. However, most of my teaching is confined to Mondays, Wednesdays, and Fridays, so on Tuesdays and Thursdays I work more at my own research, writing, and editing. The activities those days would be quite different.

Conclusion

The life of a college professor may not be rich and glamorous, but it has its own rewards: being a part of the continual search for knowledge; being surrounded by young, inquisitive minds; being in an academic setting with people interested in every imaginable topic; and having a great degree of personal freedom and autonomy, among others. Most professors I know would not trade their occupations for any other. Indeed, most do not think of themselves as having a "job" in the traditional sense. They are doing what they most want to do and getting paid for it, which is a happy bargain.

References

Bem, D. J. (2004). Writing the empirical journal article. In J. Darley, M. Zanna, & H. L. Roediger III (Eds.), *The compleat academic: A career guide* (2nd ed., pp. 185–220). Washington, DC: American Psychological Association.

Bernstein, D. A., & Lucas, S. G. (2004). Tips for effective teaching. In J. Darley, M. Zanna, & H. L. Roediger III (Eds.), *The compleat academic: A career guide* (2nd ed., pp. 79–115). Washington, DC: American Psychological Association.

Brown, R. (1965). *Social psychology.* New York: Free Press.

Conroy, P. (1980). *The lords of discipline.* Boston: Houghton-Mifflin.

Darley, J. M., Zanna, M. P., & Roediger, H. L., III (Eds.). (2004). *The compleat academic: A career guide* (2nd ed.). Washington, DC: American Psychological Association.

Elmes, D. G., Kantowitz, B. H., & Roediger, H. L. (2006). *Research methods in psychology* (8th ed.). Belmont, CA: Wadsworth.

Kantowitz, B. H., Roediger, H. L., III, & Elmes, D. G. (2005). *Experimental psychology: Understanding psychological research* (8th ed.). Belmont, CA: Wadsworth.

Lewis, D. J. (1963). *Scientific principles of psychology.* Englewood Cliffs, NJ: Prentice Hall.

Loftus, E. F., & Ketcham, K. (1994). *Myth of repressed memory: False memories and allegations of sexual abuse.* New York: St. Martin's Press.

McDermott, K. B., & Braver, T. S. (2004). After graduate school: A faculty position or a postdoctoral fellowship? In J. Darley, M. Zanna, & H. L. Roediger III (Eds.), *The compleat academic: A career guide* (2nd ed., pp. 17–30). Washington, DC: American Psychological Association.

Roediger, H. L., III. (2004). Writing textbooks: Why doesn't it count? *American Psychological Society Observer, 17,* 5, 42.

Schmidt, S. R. (1983). The effects of recall and recognition test expectancies on the retention of prose. *Memory & Cognition, 11,* 172–180.

Sternberg, R. J. (1988). *The triarchic mind: A new theory of human intelligence.* New York: Viking.

Sternberg, R. J. (2003). *The psychologist's companion: A guide to scientific writing for students and psychologists* (2nd ed.). Cambridge, England: Cambridge University Press.

Sternberg, R. J. (2004). *Psychology 101½: The unspoken rules for success in academia.* Washington, DC: American Psychological Association.

Wicherski, M., Frincke, J., & Kohout, J. (2006). *2005–2006 faculty salaries in graduate departments of psychology.* Washington, DC: American Psychological Association.

Robert Calfee

Learning About Learning: Psychologists in Schools of Education

2

P sychology is the study of the individual in context. Education is the collection of institutions through which a society transmits its cultural heritage to children and young adults. Educational psychology stands at the intersection of these two domains. Educational psychologists study how people think, behave, and learn as individuals and in learning communities. A century ago, psychologists' work ranged from armchair philosophizing to laboratory research to real-world situations; today's activities span much the same range. Practical applications were important when psychology developed in the United States, and the improvement of school learning was often at the top of this list (Glover & Ronning, 1987; James, 1899/1983).

Since the launching of Sputnik in 1957, improvement of the nation's public schools has been a hot political topic,

Robert Calfee, PhD, is a cognitive psychologist with research interest in the effects of schooling on the intellectual potential of individuals and groups. He served as a professor in Stanford's Committee on Language, Literacy, and Culture and the Committee on Psychological Studies. His theoretical efforts are directed toward the nature of human thought processes and the influence of language and literacy in the development of problem solving and communication. He has written critical articles in recent years on the effects of testing and educational indicators, ability grouping, teacher assessment, and the psychology of reading.

and educational psychologists have played critical roles in reform efforts (e.g., Marzano, 2003; Schlechty, 2005; Zimmerman & Schunk, 2003). Psychologists handle a broad range of issues, including individual differences, instructional design, and assessment, to name a few. Educational psychologists seek to apply this understanding to the processes of schooling and learning: how students learn; how teachers instruct; how motivation affects achievement; the influence of social contexts; and the interplay of curriculum, instruction, and assessment (Berliner & Calfee, 1996; Winne & Alexander, 2006).

Educational psychologists are interested in how people learn from birth to adulthood, but their attention centers most frequently on education in public schools. Because they are interested in understanding what they investigate, theory development is an important goal they share with other scientific psychologists. Because educational psychologists are often located in universities, they conduct and publish empirical research. Because they study children as they move through the years, they have connections with developmental psychologists and with the study of how individuals differ from one another. Because they focus on schools, they often involve themselves in practical applications, like the construction and evaluation of educational programs. But because home, family, and community have strong influences on school learning, educational psychologists also look at the bridges between home and school. And although they frequently take the individual student as their point of departure, students are connected to classrooms and teachers, who in turn belong to schools and districts. In the United States, these social systems are quite complex and interactive, so that educational psychologists often have to deal with practicalities and politics. Finally, because of a long history of constructing and validating testing instruments, they have taken leadership in quantitative methods, but much of their work relies on qualitative methods.

Several themes have emerged in the work of educational psychologists during the past century (Berliner, 2006). Near the top has been the measurement of individual differences, including the development of reliable and valid tests of various human characteristics such as learning and achievement (Linn, 1989). Another significant theme is the study of the child in school environments, which was the focus of the forefathers (who all were men) of American psychology in the first half of the 20th century: William James, G. Stanley Hall, John Dewey, and E. L. Thorndike. In the 1940s and 1950s, as part of their involvement in World War II and its aftermath, educational psychologists played a vital role in the design of instructional programs (e.g., operating a radar system, repairing an aircraft engine), many based on behavioral principles. In the 1960s, educational psychology was at the forefront of the cognitive revolution (Bransford, Brown, & Cocking, 1999), in the development of curriculum programs that promote thinking and problem solving in social situations (Resnick, 1987), and in the preparation of teachers to handle new concepts of reflective instruction (Richardson, 2001).

Educational psychologists are a diverse group. This chapter describes opportunities for the profession in a university setting, but the doctorate in educational psychology opens the way to a range of positions in academia (schools of education but also schools of other social sciences), in schools and other educational organizations (curriculum development, evaluation, and assessment), and in business (design of training programs and client-interface programs). In fact, you can find educational psychologists employed in virtually every field represented by the chapters in this entire volume.

Preparing for a Career in Educational Psychology

Preparation for the discipline of educational psychology starts with an understanding of basic psychological principles, mastery of research skills, and connection with the worlds of schooling. Within these constancies are a diversity of concrete tasks and personal styles. Some educational psychologists commune with computers, conducting large-scale surveys to explore the relations among home background, teaching practices, and student achievement. Others develop and analyze tests and instructional materials, assisting with implementation and evaluation in school settings. There are also those who spend their time working directly with schools, teachers, and students. They are researchers, but they do more "people work" than paperwork. What binds the discipline of educational psychology together is a commitment to the scientific method for understanding individual human beings, with particular emphasis on the institution of schooling.

Therefore, because the discipline of educational psychology falls toward the research end of the continuum rather than the clinical or counseling end, it requires an analytic frame of mind. Research methods are the core of graduate training in educational psychology. Not too many years ago, this preparation emphasized experimental design and statistical techniques, but the past decade has seen the emergence of qualitative methods—observations, interviews, case studies, and even ethnographies—as significant parts of the researcher's toolbox.

Educational psychology has always had an interdisciplinary flavor, and that tendency has increased in recent decades (Shavelson & Towne, 2002; Towne, Wise, & Winters, 2004).

A doctorate is usually required for positions both in an academic setting and in research organizations such as the Rand Corporation or American Institutes for Research (AIR) or federal agencies (e.g., Department of Education, National Science Foundation). Doctoral training involves 4 to 6 years of postbaccalaureate study. Fellowships and assistantships are available in many universities to cover tuition costs and some living expenses. The studies require hard work, especially in the methodological areas: research design, statistics, surveys and interviews, and qualitative techniques like ethnographies and case studies. Evaluations of schools of education and psychology departments appear regularly in national publications, and graduates of highly rated institutions have better prospects in the job market. So start with the highest ranked, and then look over the bulletins to see how well each program matches your interests. Once you have identified several prospects, write or phone for additional information, or check the Web site if one is available. Don't hesitate to call the institution for additional information and counsel. Talk with the department chair and the secretary.

Whether in a university setting or any other workplace, educational psychologists have to be willing and able to write. Research matters only when it is published in archival journals like the *Journal of Educational Psychology* or as technical reports for client agencies. Educational psychologists must also be effective in group presentations like conventions and conferences. Many educational psychologists teach in universities and colleges, where they are expected to set the standard for instructional quality.

So if you're a newcomer to the field of educational psychology and want to learn more, what's the best way to start? Introductory books on educational psychology are designed to provide beginning teachers the fundamental principles of the field: learning and development; cognition and motivation; individual differences and social–cultural styles; models of curriculum, instruction, and assessment; and basic principles of educational research. These introductions range from the theoretical and "researchy" to the very practical. A visit to the library will allow you to sample the variety of publications available, which is a useful way to survey the field. For more in-depth information, there are handbooks (Berliner & Calfee, 1996; Winne & Alexander, 2006) that offer comprehensive descriptions of the field. They are designed as resources for graduate students and professionals and are not easy reads. Other sources offer a glance at the more practical aspects of the field (e.g., Lambert & McCombs, 1997; McCombs & Pope, 1994;

Sternberg & Spear-Swerling, 1996). Another strategy is to skim a few of the leading journals in the field: *Journal of Educational Psychology, Educational Psychologist, Cognition and Instruction,* and *Educational Psychology Review* are among my favorites. Start with a few recent issues to see what looks interesting.

As important as coursework is when preparing for a career in educational psychology, personal contacts also play an essential role. People with experience in the field can give you advice and perspectives that textbooks and research projects cannot, so you can only improve your prospects by seeking them out and getting to know them. To be sure, when approaching someone for advice, it helps to have some concrete ideas about your interests and job aspirations.

My Own Professional History (Especially the Past 10 Years)

I didn't really know what I wanted to do during my senior year in college, but I was fortunate. Along the way, one professor conveyed his excitement about perceptual adaptation (Parducci), another stalked his classroom portraying multiple regression as the "patina on the plane" (Gengerelli), a young assistant professor challenged us to explore "finite math" equations (Atkinson), and an insomniac insisted that everyone fully understand and appreciate the marvels of analysis of variance (Anderson). These individuals had each mastered demanding domains and insisted that students also strive for mastery. The lesson is that you should grasp every opportunity to search for tough instructors who can help you find out what you can learn. Do this when applying to an institution, while you are in the program, and after you graduate.

It's in this spirit that I offer a personal sketch of my career as an educational psychologist. My experiences may not seem typical, but that's the point; ask any two educational psychologists about their professional histories, and you will uncover incredible variability, with many ways to move from "here" to "there."

What do I do? Where and how do I do it? How did I wind up in my present situation? How do I like it? Why would I recommend it to young people thinking about a career in this field? In the first edition of this book, I described my career path, which led me from doctoral work in experimental cognitive psychology at the University of

California, Los Angeles (UCLA) along a winding path that included a stint as a research assistant at Stanford, an academic appointment in psychology at the University of Wisconsin at Madison, and then a return to Stanford, where I joined the faculty in the School of Education. Along the way, experience in research methods and laboratory investigation provided the foundations that have allowed me to approach the challenges that confront anyone who seeks to understand the "blooming, buzzing confusion" found in most classrooms (James, 1890, p. 488). (Also in the first edition, I sketched "a week in my life" to illustrate the variety of activities that can fill the days of an educational psychologist. Although my routine is much different now, some readers may still find that blow-by-blow account of interest and may want to refer to the first edition.)

My story has changed substantially over the past 10 years, and the lessons are different. I have retired, twice, once from a position at Stanford University and more recently following a stint as dean of the Graduate School of Education at the University of California, Riverside (UCR). Both positions included responsibilities in teaching, research, and service. In addition, my role as dean meant spending time on administration and leadership. For whatever reasons, psychologists in general and educational psychologists in particular often wind up as administrators in colleges and universities, and so I spend a few paragraphs reflecting on this experience. A second change in the past decade centers on my role as an educational advisor to LeapFrog Enterprises, a top-ranked maker of educational toys. Many of my colleagues serve as consultants to publishers, as well as to school districts and state or federal agencies, and so it makes sense to say a little about this activity. Finally, I'm not sure what I imagined retirement to be, but it has turned out to be quite an experience and worth a few reflections.

Psychologists seem to move to the top of academic institutions. Among my acquaintances who have pursued administrative tasks are David Pearson at the University of California Berkeley, Aimee Dorr at UCLA, Deborah Stipek at Stanford, Kenji Hakuta at the new University of California campus at Merced, and, until recently, Richard Atkinson as president of the University of California system. These positions bring with them the burdens of administrative work, and they can displace both teaching and research; your life is taken up with service. Why would anyone volunteer for such positions? It may seem the easy answers are prestige, power, and money, but the aggravations are seldom worth it in these settings—far better to stay on as a plain old professor.

The deeper answer is the opportunity to make a difference, to provide leadership. This was certainly the case for me. When I became dean at UCR, Chancellor Raymond Orbach had committed the university to a far-reaching program of outreach to educational institutions throughout the region. It is interesting to note that he relied on a developmental psychologist, Executive Vice Chancellor David Warren, to advance these ideas. California's budget crises cut short a rather ambitious program, but for several years the school and the university collaborated with local school districts in a variety of reform projects. It was an exciting time, and I felt privileged to be part of the effort.

My background as an educational psychologist helped in several ways in my role as dean. For example, it provided me with ways to connect with colleagues across a variety of disciplines, including curriculum, administration, and the other social sciences, a capacity that had developed during my years at Stanford. The education schools at both Stanford and UCR were relatively small, so people had opportunities to talk with one another. This helped in discussions with local school people, both teachers and administrators, that I knew something about hot topics like literacy and testing.

More directly, the knowledge and skills that I developed as a psychologist contributed directly to my leadership responsibilities. In one of his marvelous monographs, Gardner (1990) offered insights into the tendency for psychologists to migrate to leadership positions. In *About Leadership*, Gardner wrote the following:

> [They say that] "leaders are born not made." Nonsense! Most of
> what leaders have that enables them to lead is learned.
> Leadership is not a mysterious activity. It is possible to describe
> the tasks that leaders perform. And the capacity to perform
> those tasks is widely distributed in the population. (p. xv)

Leadership is an obligation that most people can learn to fulfill. To the degree that psychologists subscribe to this proposition, it makes sense that they seek out positions of responsibility. In his monograph Gardner lays out the skills and knowledge one needs to learn—how to understand and communicate with individuals, promote group cooperation, and build capacity for self-reflection—to serve effectively as a leader.

The second change in my life over the past 10 years occurred when I was approached in 1995 by Mike Wood, a lawyer who was developing a device to help his 4-year-old son become a reader—more precisely, to learn phonics. Wood was dissatisfied with the products he found on the shelves of toy stores, and he decided to construct a system of his own. He called the Stanford School of Education looking for an advisor and was referred to me. I had been conducting research on early reading for 30 years and offered some suggestions (e.g., think about short words as sandwiches, with vowels gluing together the consonants). The ideas clicked with Mike, and 10 years later LeapFrog Enterprises led the nation in the sales of educational toys. In my role as chair of the LeapFrog educational advisory board, I continue to offer advice, working along with a team of top-flight colleagues who meet biannually.

LeapFrog employees tend to be techies with an entrepreneurial bent, and they often are idealistic. A few have classroom experience and others come from publishing. My contributions have tended to center on cognition and learning in unusual environments. For example, the PhonicsDesk was LeapFrog's first product, a plastic box with letters of the alphabet and a collection of word cards. Punch a letter, and it would say its name and then its sound. Slide a word card into a slot, place the corresponding letters into the cutouts, and it would spell and sound out the word and provide encouragement—"Wow, that's great!" My role was to analyze the learning situation, to look for ways to encourage interest and sustain efficient learning. An important finding from cognitive psychology is the KISS principle—"Keep it simple, sweetheart!" Our short-term memory capacity is quite limited to no more than half a dozen chunks of information. So the challenge is to teach a few things well, to find ways to identify the few things, and to present them most effectively. My recommendation was straightforward—"teach the vowels." The letter blocks for vowels were colored red, and the curriculum elements were built around primary vowel patterns: short vowels, long (final-*e*) vowels, and digraph (two letters, as in *lean*) vowels. This strategy was a gamble because most preschool phonics programs promise to teach hundreds of spelling objectives, and parents want to be sure that their little ones know everything before they go to school. But the advice was solid, and the gamble paid off. The PhonicsDesk was an instant hit, and LeapFrog was off and running.

This story highlights the opportunities for educational psychologists serving as consultants to business and industry. Virtually all universities allow faculty to spend a few days per month in such activities, which typically provide additional income but, more important, open doors to making a practical impact—and along the way, to having a great deal of fun. I travel a fair amount, and it's not unusual to be stopped by a stranger who asks, "Aren't you the LeapFrog guy? My kid really likes those toys!"

Finally, I have retired—twice. But I remain active, and probably will for the foreseeable future because my career continues to be so rewarding. I have more freedom now to choose what I do and when I do it. But the moral of this story is the long-range satisfaction I have obtained from my job. To be a psychologist invested in education blends the theoretical and the practical, and the results can be immediate, as when a young child looks up from a book and says, "I get it! Vowels are like glue letters."

Mine has been a zigzag path, typical in its atypicality, that illustrates important themes but also demonstrates the variations. My bottom line is an enthusiastic recommendation of an academic research career in the field of educational psychology to today's young people.

What are the downsides? One is the workload. The modern university does not allow the opportunity for quiet reflection that many people imagine, and most of us occasionally resent and resist the stress of continuing and overlapping commitments. Another is the financial payoff; although most academic salaries allow a satisfying lifestyle, other careers might have put much more money in my bank account for the same time and effort.

The upsides have been personally significant for me. I grew up during the Great Depression, worked on an assembly line, and was unemployed for a while. The stability of a tenured academic position lets a person take risks and wrestle with new problems where there is no answer at the back of the book, where research poses nonroutine challenges, and where teaching means that last year's lectures won't work for this year's students. Some view tenure as a sinecure—"without care"—but responsible teachers care continuously, and tenure carries responsibilities as well as securities and freedoms.

All of my academic appointments have been in research universities, but teaching has also been a priority, even during my tenure as dean. Faculty in such settings have limited courseloads, and classes are small. However, expectations are high, and advisement is intensive. In my courses, students submit a succession of papers during each quarter, and I typically prepare a two- to three-page critique for each draft, an investment of an hour per week for each student beyond class time. It is an intensive apprenticeship program and impossible to automate. The teaching costs are high, but the teaching rewards are substantial.

Like many educational psychologists, I have spent a great deal of time working with schools, conducting workshops, and consulting with curriculum directors and administrators. This is my choice; I could write more, specialize in teacher preparation, or invest more effort in administrative and committee activities. Virtually all educational psychologists confront such choices, because we are prepared for all of them. Cronbach once remarked, "Nothing is worth teaching unless learners can use it in a new situation. Teaching is about transfer (personal communication, 1981)." This advice applies to both teachers and students, and the best educational psychology programs provide graduates with generalizable skills and knowledge. To be sure, you have to figure out how to use what you already know to tackle each new problem. But never throw away a learning opportunity: You never know when you might need it later on.

Range of Opportunities for Employment

What is the future likely to hold for those interested in educational psychology? You can find general information about careers in psychology on the American Psychological Association (APA) Web site (http://www.apa.org/students), but in this section I offer a few specific suggestions tailored to the educational psychology profession. Not long ago, some observers reviewed the situation for educational psychologists, finding cause for both optimism and concern (Salomon, 1992; Wittrock & Farley, 1989). The increased national attention to public education has led to a renewed set of opportunities, which are likely to increase during the next decade or two.

Educational psychologists often find a place in research universities, but they also play major roles in research organizations like AIR, the Rand Corporation, Educational Testing Service, and SRI International to name a few. Teacher preparation programs in universities and colleges rely on educational psychologists for foundation courses in learning and motivation that provide novice teachers the skills and knowledge they need for the practicalities of classroom instruction. State, district, and federal organizations hire large numbers of educational psychologists to develop, implement, and evaluate instructional programs. Industries hire educational psychologists directly or as consultants to handle similar tasks.

Times have changed since I began my career in the 1960s. At that time, the federal government was broadly committed to research and development, including the behavioral, social, and educational sciences. Two ideals were leading the nation to world leadership in higher education: (a) cutting-edge college instruction enlightened and enlivened by cutting-edge scholarship and (b) university contributions to basic research that affected all facets of national life. The 1980s and 1990s saw substantial reductions in these commitments, in both the "hard" and the "soft" sciences (real funding in social and psychological research has declined by 30% during that time; Smith & Torrey, 1996). The creation in 2001 of the Institute for Educational Sciences within the Department of Education has been accompanied by increased funding, along with efforts to build interagency collaborations at the federal level.

The 1960s was also a time of increased opportunity for college education, which meant more academic jobs. Economic policy was a driving force; a "smarter" nation would be more competitive in the world market. Social policy also entered the equation; the civil rights movement focused attention on inequities in educational opportunity from preschool through graduate work, for women as well as for ethnic minorities. This confluence was propitious for educational researchers. The job market flourished, and research funding was available for a broad range of projects.

By the mid-1970s, graduates found fewer openings in the job market. Many colleges, especially those in the public sector, came to rely on temporary and part-time positions to fill teaching slots—no employment benefits, no promise of tenure, and little expectation that the individual would conduct research. Graduates who located tenure-track positions have found opportunities for research restricted by heavy teaching loads and limited funding opportunities.

At the turn of the new millennium, this tide appeared to be turning, with increased support for educational research and development bringing greater opportunities for educational psychologists. One reason for hope will come from the nation's continuing search for an appropriate role for the federal government. Another is the emerging demographic profile; after years of declining birth rates, schools are now bulging from kindergarten through college. From 1985 to 1995, the K–8 public school enrollment increased from 27 to 32 million and was projected to reach 35 million in 2005. College enrollment rose from 12 million in 1985 to 15 million in 1995 and should exceed 16 million by 2005. More students mean more teachers, and more teachers mean more professors.

The third factor is research funding. Although research support from the Department of Education has been relatively flat over the past decade, agencies like the National Science Foundation and the National Institute of Child Health and Development increased funding to support basic and applied research on student learning and classroom instruction. The point is that one should aggressively explore future possibilities.

Educational psychology has made significant conceptual break-throughs in the past 50 years (Berliner & Calfee, 1996; Bransford, Brown, & Cocking, 1999; Winne & Alexander, 2006). Scientific psychology applied to education is a significant discipline in its own right. Many in the field immerse themselves in laboratory studies of human learning and motivation. But others explore applications in a variety of real-world settings—schools, of course, but many other situations as well, including business, out-of-school programs, and even homes. For readers especially interested in the applied side of educational psychology, I strongly urge you to search out opportunities to connect with practice during your graduate program. Here my story has more to offer a posteriori: It was only during my visit to Israel in 1970 that

I was able to immerse myself in the genuine study of schools and could appreciate the enormous influence of contextual factors in shaping the experiences of students, as well as of teachers and all the other individuals who inhabit schools (e.g., principals, parents, and secretaries). For me, this occasion was accidental, but given limited funding, today's newcomers may need to be more foresightful.

THE AVAILABLE JOBS

What kinds of jobs are available once you have completed the course of study, and what are the salaries like? In 2003, 39% of recent doctoral graduates in educational psychology were located in universities and colleges throughout the country in departments of educational psychology, curriculum, and teacher education—reading and language arts, science and mathematics, and special education (Wicherski & Kohout, 2005). This category includes positions in state universities and colleges, where the emphasis is focused less on research and more on teaching, especially courses in teacher preparation. The latter offer opportunities for research, but the demands of working with novice teachers, especially for intern programs that demand school-based activities, mean that time is at a premium, and opportunities for reflection and writing can be limited. Additionally, 30% were employed in elementary and secondary schools and district offices, and 9% were found in other academic settings.

About 21% of the educational psychology graduates in the APA survey were in nonacademic settings. Several of my former students hold positions in major industrial settings, including Hewlett Packard and Apple. Their jobs include corporate training, the design of systems for learning to use computers, and personnel evaluation and education. Other business opportunities are found in companies producing educational software for home and school, a burgeoning industry for individuals with skill in the design and development of computer learning programs. Other graduates can be found in federal and state programs managing support activities and developing testing and assessment systems; some are assistants in policy positions. One of my former advisees joined the research department of the Sacramento County Office of Education several years ago and now heads a multimillion-dollar enterprise providing professional development services for hundreds of schools throughout California.

As I noted earlier, educational psychologists often move into administrative positions, reflecting their combination of analytic skills and knowledge of human relations. Private consultancies attract the more entrepreneurial persons, who survive through their talents in acquiring federal and state grants for surveys and evaluations of educational programs. The risks are greater in industry than in academia, but the rewards can be substantial. Education has its own industries, including organizations like the Educational Testing Service, AIR, and the Rand Corporation. Closely related are semigovernmental institutions like the network of educational laboratories funded by the Department of Education. In these organizations, educational psychologists conduct applied research, but the agenda tends to be driven by external contracts and demanding timelines, leading to a frenetic pace.

SALARIES

Monetary compensation varies widely across the different positions, and information is sketchy for jobs in private business. The 2003 Doctorate Employment Survey reported an overall median starting salary of $52,556, with an average of $54,814 and a standard deviation of $16,889 (Wicherski & Kohout, 2005). The APA conducts an annual survey of graduate departments of psychology. In 2005–2006, the starting 9- to 10-month salary for new doctorates in doctoral departments was a median of $53,500, and their colleagues who were full professors reported a median salary of $91,500. Doctoral faculty in master's departments who were full professors reported a median of $70,250 in 2005–2006 (Wicherski, Frincke, & Kohout, 2006).

These faculty positions typically lead to tenure, along with good benefits and retirement packages. Civil service positions also carry job security, sometimes subject to the vagaries of politics and changing budgets. Salaries vary substantially depending on the organization, but they are typically stable, with increases based on time in the job. The salary schedules are public information, but you have to ask the organization. Positions in business and industry, as well as private consultancies, entail much less security, of course, and it is harder to find out what people are paid. There is no guarantee of stability, and although salaries appear to be higher than in academic and civil service positions, the bottom can always drop out because of business slumps or program changes.

Conclusion

The real rewards of a career in educational psychology go beyond financial return for individuals who value the opportunity to do people work, especially when the ultimate clients are learners. For example, textbook publishers play a major role in setting the stage for classroom curriculum and instruction, and the publishing industry employs many educational psychologists. My conversations with colleagues in textbook publishing, although revealing a practical side ("Whatever we do, it has to sell!"), also reveal a concern and caring for the ultimate clients—students, teachers, and parents—along with attention to issues of learning and motivation. My experience with LeapFrog certainly exemplifies these features of the publishing business.

This combination of hardheadedness and softheartedness, of science and practice, perhaps best characterizes the field of educational psychology. The individual with this preparation can move across a spectrum from statistical analysis to classroom narratives, from evaluating the effectiveness of a science curriculum to developing a program for character education, from investigating eye movements in reading to inquiring about how children's literature fosters empathy. Our field has a distinguished past, and the future promises even more.

References

Berliner, D. C. (2006). Educational psychology: Stability, change, and improvement during a century of improvement. In P. Winne & P. A. Alexander (Eds.), *Handbook of educational psychology* (2nd ed., pp. 3–28). Mahwah, NJ: Erlbaum.

Berliner, D. C., & Calfee, R. C. (1996). *Handbook of educational psychology*. New York: Macmillan.

Bransford, J. D., Brown, A. L., & Cocking, R. R. (Eds.). (1999). *How people learn: Brain, mind, experience, and school*. Washington, DC: National Academy Press.

Gardner, J. W. (1990). *About leadership*. New York: Free Press.

Glover, J. A., & Ronning, R. R. (Eds.). (1987). *Historical foundations of educational psychology*. New York: Plenum Press.

James, W. (1890). *The Principles of Psychology*. Cambridge, MA: Harvard University Press.

James, W. (1983). *Talks to teachers on psychology and to students on some of life's ideals*. Cambridge, MA: Harvard University Press. (Original work published 1899)

Lambert, N. M., & McCombs, B. L. (Eds.). (1997). *How students learn: Reforming schools through learner-centered education*. Washington, DC: American Psychological Association.

Linn, R. L. (Ed.). (1989). *Educational measurement*. New York: Macmillan.

Marzano, R. J. (2003). *What works in schools: Translating research into practice*. Alexandria, VA: Association for Supervision and Curriculum Development.

McCombs, B. L., & Pope, J. (1994). *Motivating hard to reach students*. Washington, DC: American Psychological Association.

Resnick, L. B. (1987). *Education and learning to think*. Washington, DC: National Academy of Education.

Richardson, V. (2001). *Handbook of research on teaching* (4th ed.). Washington DC: American Educational Research Association.

Salomon, G. (1992). The nature and mission of educational psychology. *Educational Psychologist, 27*(Whole No. 2).

Schlechty, P. C. (2005). *Creating great schools: Six critical systems at the heart of educational innovations*. Cambridge, MA: Wiley.

Shavelson, R. J., & Towne, L. (Eds.). (2002). *Scientific research in education*. Washington, DC: National Academy Press.

Smith, P. M., & Torrey, B. B. (1996, February 2). The future of the behavioral and social sciences. *Science, 271*, 611–612.

Sternberg, R. J., & Spear-Swerling, L. (1996). *Teaching for thinking*. Washington, DC: American Psychological Association.

Towne, L., Wise, L. L., & Winters, T. M. (Eds). (2004). *Advancing scientific research in education*. Washington, DC: National Research Council.

Wicherski, M., Frincke, J., & Kohout, J. (2006). *2005–2006 faculty salaries in graduate departments of psychology*. Washington, DC: American Psychological Association.

Wicherski, M., & Kohout, J. (2005). *2003 doctorate employment survey*. Washington, DC: American Psychological Association.

Winne, P., & Alexander, P. A. (Eds.). (2006). *Handbook of educational psychology* (2nd ed.). Mahwah, NJ: Erlbaum.

Wittrock, M. C., & Farley, F. (1989). *The future of educational psychology*. Hillsdale, NJ: Erlbaum.

Zimmerman, B., & Schunk, D. (Eds.). (2003). *Educational psychology: A century of contributions*. Mahwah, NJ: Erlbaum.

Victor H. Vroom

Teaching the Managers of Tomorrow: Psychologists in Business Schools

3

The enlightened management of organizations is of monumental importance to society. The quality of managerial leadership in organizations has a strong influence both on their effectiveness as organizations and on the extent to which their members experience their lives as satisfying and fulfilling.

Historically, business schools have played a key role in the development of tomorrow's managers, and there is no reason to believe that this role will diminish in the years to come. The scientific discipline of psychology has much to contribute to an understanding of the interplay of people, groups, and organizations and can help future leaders meet the challenge of unleashing the human potential in the workforce. In addition, confronting and studying real-world problems, such as those involved in the management of complex organizations, can lead to the development of more viable and more applicable theories of human behavior.

Victor H. Vroom, PhD, holds the John G. Searle Professorship in Organization and Management at Yale University. He received his PhD in psychology from the University of Michigan, after which he taught at the University of Pennsylvania and Carnegie Mellon University before moving to Yale.

Although I now find these arguments compelling, I did not always feel this way. Let me digress to reveal a little bit about my professional background to show how I came to be an enthusiastic supporter of the role that psychologists can play in business schools.

I studied organizational psychology at the University of Michigan and received my PhD there in 1958. Because academic job opportunities for organizational psychologists were not abundant that year, and because my spouse had another year or more to finish her dissertation in clinical psychology, I elected to stay at Michigan as a study director in the Survey Research Center and a part-time lecturer in Michigan's psychology department. Two years later I was offered an assistant professor position in the department of psychology at the University of Pennsylvania. For the next 3 years I occupied myself with teaching large undergraduate sections of introductory psychology, teaching doctoral courses in motivation and social psychology, and writing a book that subsequently was titled *Work and Motivation* (1964). My career path was set. I intended to spend the rest of my academic life in a psychology department.

While at Penn, I had only limited contact with the Wharton School of Finance and Commerce. I had some friends there in the economics and sociology departments, but I never taught a course or offered a seminar there. Then in 1963, for reasons that I expand on later, my telephone began to ring with requests to consider moving to a business school. Among the most interesting were Columbia Business School, Stanford Business School, the Graduate School of Industrial Administration at the Carnegie Institute of Technology, and Yale's Department of Industrial Administration. There were some apparent advantages to this kind of career move. All talked of an immediate promotion to associate professor, a substantially higher salary, and contacts with field sites in which I could carry out my research.

Despite the economic advantages, I was ambivalent about a change in career. My conception of business education was that it was crassly commercial and that its students were professional rather than academic. I had been trained as a psychologist and was unprepared for what I felt would be a wrenching change in my identity required by moving to a business school.

To reduce the risks involved, I made it clear to those who sought to induce me to move that I would consider only a joint appointment with a psychology department. This, I felt, would afford me easy access to colleagues who shared my discipline and a safe exit in the event that I found business school life unpalatable. That requirement proved unacceptable to Columbia and Stanford but manageable at both Yale and Carnegie. After a protracted decision process that reflected my ambivalence, I decided in 1963 to accept Carnegie's offer and moved to Pittsburgh as associate professor of industrial administration and psychology.

Now I have logged over 40 years teaching in business schools. I do not argue that all of these years have been fun or that a career in a business school dominates other choices on all dimensions. It is clear to me that business schools are a palatable home for psychologists and a reasonable alternative for newly minted PhDs with relevant interests and capabilities. At least part of my change in heart has come about as a result of changes in the business schools themselves. Although the discipline of psychology spans more than a century, the role of psychology in formal education in business and management began in the late 1950s. Its inception can be traced to a pair of reports prepared for the Ford Foundation and the Carnegie Corporation (Gordon & Howell, 1959; Pierson, 1959). Both reports were highly critical of the existing university programs designed to prepare people for careers in business. At that time, such education was largely conducted at the undergraduate level. Courses included secretarial science, bookkeeping, and office management. Academic standards were low, and the students were among the least able in the entire university. The course content was uninformed by the concepts and tools that were being developed in the social sciences. Business school faculty members were frequently part-time managers, and fewer than half of full-time faculty had doctoral degrees. Curriculum content emphasized *institutional knowledge*, which involved describing existing managerial practices rather than the applications of methods of science to determine what the practices should be.

The Ford Foundation not only characterized the unhappy state of business education but also set out to rectify it with a major infusion of funds designed to alter significantly the academic and research underpinnings of business education. Between 1954 and 1966 the Ford Foundation awarded more than $35 million primarily to seven selected business schools, including Stanford and Carnegie. The funds were to be used not just for the benefit of these highly select institutions but for spreading the "gospel" to other universities around the country. Ford gave research grants to faculty, sponsored an annual doctoral dissertation competition, and financed courses and workshops for faculty around the country. In the late 1960s, the Ford Foundation extended its reach to management education in Europe.

The landscape of management education today is, in substantial part, a reflection of the vision portrayed in the Ford and Carnegie reports. These reports ushered in the conditions for psychology in business schools, and many distinguished psychologists have moved their base of operations from psychology departments to business schools. Faculty seminars in many business schools are undistinguishable in rigor and sometimes in content from those in psychology departments. Research is a major factor in faculty hiring and promotion, and the subjects chosen for research are often theory driven rather than motivated by managerial relevance.

The movement instigated by the Ford and Carnegie reports has been very successful in integrating business schools into their universities. In fact, some critics have argued that they have been too successful. Recently, business schools have been criticized for being too academic, doing research of little relevance to management, and producing graduates who are ill equipped to deal with the complex, unquantifiable issues involved in managing a global organization (Bennis & O'Toole, 2005; Mintzberg, 2004). It is too early to know whether or how far the pendulum will swing. However, there is little doubt that business schools will continue to be a comfortable home for psychologists interested in exploring the applications of their discipline to making organizations more effective and humane.

Business schools are inevitably different from psychology departments, but the differences are seldom ones of academic standing or quality of scholarship. To be sure, faculty in psychology departments may look askance at the "extravagant" facilities or less rigorous research methods found in the business school, and business school faculty may criticize the "lack of relevance" of much of what is taught and studied in psychology departments. These two parts of the university must be different from one another because they serve different functions in the larger university of which they are a part. The socialization patterns in both are strong and support the prevailing epistemology and values of each setting. Someone pursuing doctoral work in psychology and contemplating a career in a business or management school should be cognizant of such differences and carefully weigh the characteristics of both against their own interests and propensities.

Structure of Business Schools

The field of management education has been compared to a three-legged stool. The legs of the stool correspond to the three academic disciplines on which management is based: economics, management science, and the behavioral sciences. These three fields provide many of the concepts and tools on which management education and practice rest. The top of the stool represents the functional areas of management, including marketing, production or operations, finance, accounting, and human resources. Many business school professors come from backgrounds and teach in the areas represented by the legs of the stool and include economists, management scientists, political scientists, and sociologists. Others, whose training was in marketing, finance, production, accounting, or human resources, are more appropriately represented by the top of the stool.

If I were to revise the metaphor of the stool, I would add another, cross functional level that corresponds not with the functions of management, such as marketing and human resources, but with those areas of managerial practice that represent a synthesis of managerial functions and depend on knowledge from each of the underlying disciplines. This level includes areas such as general management, leadership, and strategy, which are of increasing importance to managerial education as corporations abandon functional silos in favor of cross functional teams at lower levels of management.

Students in Business Schools

Business schools serve a wide range of students. Although faculty members in many universities teach undergraduates, the major degree offered is the master of business administration (MBA). The MBA curriculum is usually a 2-year, full-time program but can be a longer program when offered during evenings. In addition, many universities offer an executive MBA to students who are middle- to high-level executives and are typically sponsored by their firms. Such programs are typically conducted on Fridays and Saturdays, when classrooms are available. Many business schools also conduct nondegree programs for executives ranging in length from short courses on particular topics to longer programs lasting 4 to 6 weeks. Finally, the major business schools offer doctoral programs leading to PhD or doctor of business administration degrees.

A common characteristic of students in all of these programs (with the possible exception of the PhD) is a principal interest in knowledge that is useful and that can be directly translated, in the short or long run, into managerial practice. They are a demanding lot and will be insistent on getting value for their money. Many MBA students have left high-paying jobs in industry and are likely to be intolerant of education they do not perceive as being relevant to their career goals.

Young assistant professors trained in psychology (or, for that matter, any academic discipline) frequently have a difficult time adapting to teaching students who are less interested in their professors' academic credentials than in their general knowledge and practical experience.

The challenges of teaching students in a business school are perhaps greater than those found in other professional schools. The principal reason for this is that in most other schools, the faculty have been trained, and in many cases practice, in their professions. Most faculty in medical schools are MDs. Most faculty in law schools have been trained as lawyers. Most faculty in schools of architecture are architects, and so on. However, in schools of business or management, many faculty members have been trained in social science disciplines. They are economists or mathematicians or statisticians or psychologists or sociologists. Others have done their doctoral work in fields like finance, marketing, or accounting. There are relatively few with MBA degrees, and as a consequence, faculty find it more difficult to understand the perspectives that their students bring into the classroom.

Effectiveness in teaching MBA students and experienced managers requires more than simply repeating the teaching methods one was exposed to in graduate study in psychology. The issue is not only one of content but also one of process. Your goal as a psychology instructor in a business school is not simply the transmission of knowledge but, rather, the development of skills in applying the knowledge to specific cases or to managerial issues.

It may be helpful to coteach with or observe a more experienced colleague. If you do, you will probably see many pedagogical methods that have not been a part of your doctoral education. I refer to such devices as role-playing, films, simulations, and case studies that involve students in thinking about how to deal with challenging managerial issues. The essence of such methods is that they are inductive rather than deductive; they start with specific events observable by all and move from there to theory or concepts. In that way, students can see the concepts as useful in making sense of their immediate experience in a case or simulation and generalizing from the case to a broader range of situations.

Although management students may require a different pedagogy, they bring a great deal to the learning process. They are typically very culturally diverse and come from a vast variety of backgrounds and work experiences. Individually and collectively, they have broad practical experience and often a high degree of social and political awareness. Management education can provide a unique forum for testing theoretical ideas against a world of practical experience and cultural differences.

Courses Psychologists Teach

The courses that you would teach would vary with where you are in the departmental structure and, of course, with your own interests and competence. Psychologists are most frequently found in the management, organizational behavior, or (less commonly) marketing departments.

One of the courses most frequently assigned to a psychologist, particularly in smaller schools, is a survey course on the principles of management. This course might include some topics that you learned while studying psychology but would cover other disciplines and functional fields, albeit at a general level. Alternatively, you might be asked to teach a course entitled Introduction to Organizational Behavior, which typically includes material on topics such as perception, learning, motivation, and decision making, which are, of course, familiar to psychologists. This course might also include material on teams, group dynamics, diversity, and leadership, which are perhaps more familiar to those trained in social psychology. In addition, the course might focus on organizational design and organization theory, which are somewhat less familiar to psychologists but are more familiar to those with training in sociology.

Advanced courses typically expand on the topics within the core courses. It is very common to find a course on interpersonal skills. Courses on managing organizational change and organization theory are also commonplace. Perhaps less common are courses on race and gender, diversity, power and influence in organizations, and consumer behavior. Historically, social and organizational psychology have been the areas within psychology most useful in business school teaching. In recent years, business schools have also attracted psychologists with backgrounds in cognition, decision making, and emotion. They might be found working alongside economists and finance professors on behavioral theories of choice or with marketing professors on consumer choice problems.

Psychologists are also frequently involved in teaching courses on negotiations, a field they share with game theorists and economists. They are also involved in teaching courses on the management of human resources. *Human resources* is a contemporary term for what used to be called *personnel,* and it is a field in which economists, particularly labor economists, stake some claim.

Research Opportunities

The opportunities to do research are different in a business school than in a psychology department. There are advantages and disadvantages in both settings. If your research requires dedicated laboratory space, you are better off in a psychology department. A few business schools have research labs, but they tend to be shared among many faculty rather than to be the province of an individual professor. Furthermore, access to subjects may be more difficult in a business school. You are unlikely to have access to a pool of subjects who are required to take part in an experiment as part of their course requirement. I know of no business school that requires MBA students to serve in experiments.

Many business school faculty do collect data from their MBA students or even conduct experiments as part of their teaching, but the experiment must have direct pedagogical value, or students will march directly to the dean's office to complain. However, if students see the personal value of the project, it can be quite easy to get them to participate willingly, either in their limited free time or in courses. In addition, being a professor in a business school is more likely to open opportunities for field research in organizations in the local community or those that employ your graduates.

In short, if your research interests involve answering important questions about the real world or organizations, you should have little or no difficulty in getting the research subjects you need. Conversely, if your interests are purely academic and deal with questions of relevance only to the discipline of psychology, you would be better off in a psychology department.

Career Paths

The structure of positions in a business school is not unlike that found in academic departments in the arts and sciences. Although most people start as assistant professor, there are a relatively small number of post-doctoral positions that might be attractive to those with little familiarity with business schools or with a desire to collaborate with senior faculty and publish research in business journals. Such positions are for 1 or 2 years and are likely to be found at the leading schools such as Harvard,

Northwestern, and Stanford. They require minimal teaching and provide maximum research opportunity, along with a reasonable stipend.

Following the postdoctoral position, one would expect to secure an assistant professorship at the same or a different university. Promotion to associate professor for those who meet the institution's standards for promotion typically occurs after 5 or 6 years. The final step on the promotional ladder is professor, which typically follows several years of successful performance as an associate professor.

Moving up the promotional ladder is dependent on a thorough review of performance. Such reviews begin with a committee appointed within the department or, in smaller schools without a departmental structure, within the school. The committee is likely to be made up of faculty members at or above the level to which promotion is being considered. The committee reads your research publications, assesses the evidence of your teaching effectiveness, and evaluates the quality of your citizenship within the school, the university, and the broader academic community. The relative weights placed on these three factors vary across universities. Major research universities such as Harvard, Stanford, Chicago, and the Massachusetts Institute of Technology place a much heavier emphasis on research than do colleges dedicated to teaching. More attention is likely to be paid to teaching in business schools than in psychology departments. Particularly during the past decade, the heightened competition among business schools for the best students as well as for higher rankings in surveys such as that conducted by *Business Week* has resulted in greater attention to teaching quality among faculty.

Tenure is imperfectly related to one's level on the promotional ladder. Most frequently, it is granted at the associate professor level, but a school may have associate professors with and without tenure. Occasionally, I have heard of tenured assistant professors, and I have known professors who were brought in from the outside without the immediate promise of tenure. Departmental committees seldom, if ever, make the final decision regarding promotions and tenure. They make recommendations to be voted on by the faculty of the business school. When promotion involves tenure or a professorship, as is often the case in promotions at lower levels, a committee solicits views from distinguished scholars in the candidate's field whose letters must attest to the impact of the person's scholarship outside the institution. Obviously, such letters are more likely to be informative about the quality of the candidate's research than about his or her teaching or citizenship.

In many educational institutions, the promotional review does not end with the business school. The ultimate decision may be made by the university president, the provost, or a university committee set up for this purpose. In rare instances, candidates who have passed all of the hurdles within the business school are turned down at this higher level.

My description of the multiple steps on the ladder and multiple hurdles in each review may suggest that teaching in a business school, or indeed academia in general, leads to a very uncertain and hazardous career path. The probability of successfully climbing the ladder obviously varies with one's talent and commitment and depends also on the nature of the institution. For example, public universities have more certain promotional ladders than do the private Ivy League schools. The latter are highly protective of tenure, and successful candidates for tenure must demonstrate that they are competitive with all the cohorts in their field who might be available.

Financial Rewards

It is a fact of life that psychologists in business schools get paid more than their counterparts in psychology departments. I would estimate the difference to be as much as 100%, and that difference remains relatively stable over the academic career. It is also likely that as a psychologist, you might be paid less than a faculty member at a comparable stage in a career in finance or accounting. Academic salaries, like salaries in other fields, reflect market forces of supply and demand.

Salaries other than those for faculty who hold administrative positions are for 9 months. You can get compensated for the summer months (usually for two ninths of your salary) through extra teaching or research funded either internally or through external grants or contracts. Most schools finance travel expenses to professional meetings, particularly to present a paper or perform some administrative function. Another practice that is increasing in popularity is providing each faculty member with an annual budget to be used at the faculty member's discretion for professional expenses, including books, travel, society memberships, and computers.

Business schools also allow faculty to use up to 1 day per week for outside consulting. Although faculty at all levels on the academic ladder have this benefit, those at more senior levels are more likely to take advantage of it. Junior faculty find that they need all of their time to begin their research program and are less likely to have made the contacts necessary for consulting.

Professional Associations

A critical component of any academic career is membership in one or more professional associations. These organizations sponsor annual meetings in which colleagues present papers, discuss their experiences, and share the latest gossip. They also reward academic and professional achievements.

Psychologists tend to join either or both the American Psychological Association (APA) and the American Psychological Society. More directly relevant to the research and professional interests of psychologists in business schools is the Society of Industrial and Organizational Psychology (SIOP). This organization has come a long way in the past 25 years. It was originally the Division of Industrial Psychology of the APA. "Organizational Psychology" was added to its name in the late 1970s, and a few years later it was incorporated as an independent society. At this time, in 2005, it has about 4,000 full members and 3,000 student members. It holds an annual meeting in April of each year.

SIOP is increasingly addressing managerial issues in its professional meetings, but it is much less likely to be a source of interdisciplinary exchange around management concerns than is the Academy of Management. In 2006, the Academy is much larger than SIOP, with 16,000 members, including 5,000 in the Organizational Behavior division. In addition to the Organizational Behavior division, there are divisions of organizational theory, organizational development, conflict management, business policy, marketing, and the like. The Academy of Management has its annual meeting in August. Furthermore, there are regional academies of management (e.g., Eastern, Western, Southwestern), each of which holds its own meeting. Other organizations of potential interest, all of which hold annual meetings, are the Organizational Behavior Teaching Society, the Decision Sciences Institute, and the Institute for Operations Research and the Management Sciences.

Attributes Needed for Entry to a Business School Career

I began this chapter noting the role of the Ford Foundation in promoting the movement of eminent psychologists and other social scientists into business schools. Naturally, such individuals need access to PhD students to further their own research programs. The predictable result was the establishment of PhD programs totally within the business school. Now, newly minted PhDs from psychology departments seeking to enter a business school find themselves competing for entry-level positions with their counterparts who were trained in business schools.

More than 2 decades ago, Miner (1984) noted that the most valid and useful theories of behavior in organizations were authored by psychologists and involved the process of motivation. However, Miner also expressed doubt that psychology would continue to be the influential discipline that it had been in the past:

> Yet, by its nature, this source cannot be relied upon to produce the successful theories of the field in the future. There are too many areas that need attention, areas in which psychologists have not done as well as with motivation. . . . In short, the legacy of the Gordon and Howell and Pierson reports is drying up. It cannot be relied upon to fuel the organizational theories of the future. (p. 303)

Miner recommended the establishment of doctoral programs in *organizational science*. Although that term has not caught on as much as the terms *organization theory* and *organizational behavior,* his recommendation is reflected in many high-quality PhD programs that exist in business schools. However, even today, PhD students trained in psychology tend to be better trained in the quantitative aspects of research design and in statistics. They also have the advantage of a fairly coherent academic discipline with a shared language and terminology that they can bring to bear on problems in many different institutional settings.

PhD students trained in psychology may also have certain disadvantages. They may be totally unprepared for life in a business school and for the teaching responsibilities they will be expected to pursue. Over the years in hiring new faculty at Carnegie or Yale, I have quickly passed over the applications of many young PhDs or PhD candidates who looked as though they were capable of outstanding work in experimental psychology, cognitive psychology, or even industrial psychology, but who appeared to have no conception of what life in a business school would be like.

In reviewing applications from psychologists, I look for membership in the Academy of Management and for evidence that the candidate has taken courses in or had contact with professors or students in the business school. Of course, I look for a good background in psychology—particularly social psychology or cognition, because those fields are more closely linked to business applications. Probably the best preparation available within a psychology department for life in a business school can be found in a good program in industrial/ organizational psychology with a strong emphasis on organizational psychology. Extensive training in industrial psychology—that is, job analysis, job evaluation, personnel selection, merit rating, and so on— is not, for me, a strong positive indicator. Such training would be conducive to teaching a small part of a course in human resources management but would be too technical and too specialized to interest many students of management.

Among the other attributes helpful in getting a job at a good institution is some evidence in your academic vita of research activity before the PhD This could take the form of published papers but, failing that, could include papers that have been submitted for publication that would be available to be read by the selection committee. Furthermore, the content of the papers should manifest an interest in exploring the connections between the discipline of psychology and the problems of organizations and their management. The search committee would also look for enthusiastic letters from professors with whom you have worked. It is always helpful if the endorsers are known to members of the selection committee, which typically means that they have a visible research productivity record themselves. The committee is also likely to look for evidence of your success in teaching, and because some universities do not permit teaching by nonfaculty members, it may be necessary for them to rely on your experience as a teaching assistant. It would also be helpful to your case if you had presented papers at academic conferences and, even better, if those papers had received some kind of award or acknowledgment within the profession.

Of course, the nature of the papers themselves has a great deal of weight in the decision. If your record is otherwise attractive, you can expect that your papers—those that have been submitted as part of your application—will be critically read by members of the committee, who in turn will discuss the suitability of your candidacy. Typically, the selection committee chooses a short list of three to five candidates who are invited to come to the university and be interviewed. As part of the interviewing process, you will be asked to give what is often called, colloquially, a "job talk." This talk, essentially on the subject matter of your doctoral research, is given before the faculty in the host institution and lasts about an hour. It is a very critical step in the process and should not be taken lightly. It is a good idea to rehearse your job talk well before giving it and to conduct a dress rehearsal before members of your own faculty who can help you improve your performance. If you are invited to several institutions, it is always useful to visit those in which you are most interested toward the end of the process, so that you have had some practice before you make your presentations there.

You should be aware of the fact that the audience for your job talk may not be restricted to people in your own discipline. You may get questions from economists, from management scientists, and from those in functional areas whose perspectives and whose language and terminology may be quite different from your own. It is always helpful if your topic is, or can be made to be, relevant to some real-world issue and not solely driven by a problem relevant to the discipline of psychology. Thus, a problem-centered focus is very helpful to establishing your suitability for a position in a business school.

Some Advantages and Disadvantages of the Career

Let us assume that after reading everything in this chapter, you are still interested in a business school career. Is there anything else that you need to know before committing to that career path? In this section, I offer a few observations of a less formal nature based on more than four decades as a psychologist working in a business school. Some of these are geared to academic life in general, and others are more specific to business schools.

One benefit that deserves special attention is the amount of freedom that faculty members enjoy, not only in business schools but also in all parts of academia. You will never be asked to punch a time clock. As long as you meet your teaching obligations, attend faculty meetings, make yourself available to meet with students (usually during set office hours), and meet other committee obligations, you're free to work at home and schedule your life around your own priorities. In many institutions, no one will question your decision to do large amounts of work at home, should that be your preference. The significance of this freedom for meeting child-care obligations with a dual-career family should be apparent.

I should point out that this freedom is a two-edged sword. No one will tell you what to do until it is too late. You must be a disciplined self-starter, or you will find yourself at the end of your contract without having met the promotional standards in your institution. The moral is clear: Learn from your colleagues what it takes to climb the promotional ladder, assuming that this is in fact your goal. Set specific objectives for each time period of your contract, and focus on these objectives. Don't get sidetracked by the many potential distractions of the university until you are sure that you have more than met the standards to which you will be held accountable.

Another benefit is the opportunity to learn from a diverse set of colleagues. Working with other faculty who do not share your concepts or theories can be unsettling and the source of politically motivated disharmony. But it can also prove to be an enriching experience leading to fruitful collaborations in both teaching and research.

One source of potential concern for a psychologist in a business school is the difficulty in "replicating" oneself. Although doctoral programs exist in many business schools, and certainly in those at large or prestigious universities, they don't produce psychologists. They are likely to produce PhDs in management, industrial administration, human resources management, or organizational behavior. But they do not train future professors of psychology. Furthermore, these doctoral programs are likely to play a smaller role in your life than if you were teaching in the psychology department. Your primary responsibility is to educate students interested in management, not professionals in your own discipline. Accordingly, opportunities to teach doctoral seminars may be less abundant in business schools than in psychology departments.

Another frequent complaint that I hear from psychologists in business schools is the political bent of faculty who staff these institutions. Because of the diversity in training of business school faculty, turf wars can be a frequent occurrence as groups seek to enhance the numbers and influence of their respective fields. Intergroup conflict can certainly be found in any academic department. In psychology departments, for example, one can find experimental psychologists "at war" with the clinicians and, neuroscientists looking down on their colleagues in social psychology, and so on. Skilled leadership can minimize or even avoid such conflicts, but unfortunately, not all business schools have been successful in this regard. It is my view that the leadership challenge of creating a shared vision among faculty is even greater in business schools. It is all too common to find faculty members bonding with their parent academic discipline in the competition for resources. Thus, faculty in economics and finance have been known to make life difficult for those in organizational behavior, and vice versa. Such forces are likely to be maximized when disciplines or functional areas find that they can expand only at the expense of other disciplines or functional areas. I hope the fairly recent trends for business schools to compete with one another for *Business Week* rankings, students, and in some cases survival as an institution, will result in more cooperative behavior and an awareness of shared goals and responsibilities within the department.

A final consideration is that in a business school, you are likely to experience significant changes in your identity away from that of a psychologist toward that of a scholar with broad interests in the potential contribution of the social sciences to management. The interdisciplinary and multidisciplinary endeavors that are frequently discouraged within psychology departments are encouraged and rewarded in business schools. I have observed countless young scholars gradually shifting their academic interests away from the theoretically driven to the problem driven and from being psychologically relevant to being relevant to the world of managerial practice. So if you move into a business school, be prepared to be socialized and to have your interests changed.

Conclusion

The motivation for selecting a career does, and indeed should, rest not only on the intrinsic properties of the career but also on the broader social context to which that career contributes. Although it is true that business education has rarely been the most glamorous part of the academic world, events of the past decade have brought it closer to center stage in the public consciousness. The United States's position as the world's economic leader has been clouded by revelations of ethics scandals. The business leaders of tomorrow must possess not only sound technical skills but also a vision that includes responsibility for the environment and the communities in which their businesses operate.

The education of tomorrow's leaders is too important to be left solely to economists. Psychology and the other behavioral sciences have much to contribute to understanding the determinants of productivity (Campbell, Campbell, & Associates, 1988). Such issues as the sources of the motivation to work, the dynamics of effective leadership, and the bases of teamwork and collaboration are all important to productivity and relevant to the conceptual and methodological lens of psychology. They represent the kinds of topics to which psychologists can make important contributions and, at the same time, will strengthen the underlying discipline of psychology.

From my perspective, teaching in a business school is a noble profession—one filled with personal rewards and only a modicum of frustration. It is a career in which one's research and teaching can make organizations more productive and more satisfying places to work.

References

Bennis, W. G., & O'Toole, J. (2005). How business schools lost their way. *Harvard Business Review,* May 2005, 95–104.

Campbell, J. P., Campbell, R. J., & Associates. (1988). *Productivity in organizations: New perspectives from industrial and organizational psychology.* San Francisco: Jossey-Bass.

Gordon, R. A., & Howell, J. E. (1959). *Higher education for business.* New York: Columbia University Press.

Miner, J. B. (1984). The validity and usefulness of theories in an emerging organizational science. *Academy of Management Review, 9,* 296–306.

Mintzberg, H. (2004). *Managers not MBAs.* San Francisco: Berrett-Koehler.

Pierson, F. C. (1959). *The education of American businessmen.* New York: McGraw-Hill.

Vroom, V. H. (1964). *Work and motivation.* New York: Wiley.

Elena L. Grigorenko

Working as a Psychologist in a Medical School

4

The career of a psychologist in a medical school has three distinct features. First, everyday activities are primarily determined by either the services offered by or the research profile of the department of the particular medical school. Second, there is typically no "hard money" supporting one's salary; that is, one is usually responsible for generating one's own funding, often through grants or other funding. Third, teaching is typically not a part of the job description or is, at best, a minor part. The next few paragraphs describe each feature in more detail.

First, the range of medical school departments employing psychologists is rather broad. Psychologists are typically found in departments of pediatrics and psychiatry, but I have encountered psychologists in neurosurgery, orthopedics,

Elena L. Grigorenko received her PhD in general psychology from Moscow State University, Russia, in 1990 and her PhD in developmental psychology and genetics from Yale University in 1996. Currently, she is associate professor of child studies and psychology at Yale and associate professor of psychology at Moscow State University. Dr. Grigorenko has published more than 200 peer-reviewed articles, book chapters, and books. She has received awards for her work from five different divisions of the American Psychological Association (APA; Divisions 1, 7, 10, 15, and 24) and the APA Distinguished Award for an Early Career Contribution to Developmental Psychology.

radiology, public health, and obstetrics and gynecology. In fact, if one examined medical schools across the country, one would probably find psychologists in pretty much every department. However, psychologists are disproportionately frequent in clinical departments in medical schools; they are rarely employed in basic science departments (e.g., a department of genetics, if it is housed in a medical school rather than a school of arts and sciences). This phenomenon can be explained, I believe, by the fact that many, if not most, academic positions for psychologists in medical schools are opportunistic and are mostly the result of the departments' openness to new opportunities and emerging collaborations, rather than the outcome of systematic developments in the field. For example, such opportunities often emerge from funded collaborations between medical professionals and psychologists. Many medical grants have behavioral assessment components to them, and often psychologists carry out these assessments. In addition, many grants have data analytic components; as a result, medical schools employ psychologists as data analysts. Often what starts as a single collaboration turns into a chain of collaborations, so that full salaries are pieced together from multiple grant-funded projects.

Another major source of opportunities for psychologists is in medical departments that provide certain services. Many clinics in medical school departments are staffed by psychologists who contribute to clinical assessments. For example, a clinic in a neurology department might have a psychologist on staff whose responsibility is to collect family history, conduct a neuropsychological evaluation, and carry out IQ testing or some other evaluation requiring high-level professional involvement. Sometimes a number of clinics in a department of a medical school form an assessment center; such centers are often staffed with psychologists who conduct assessments for a number of clinics or grants. Often these responsibilities are not limited to assessment issues and extend to contributions to treatment. Once again, a particular arrangement may vary, but the profile of responsibilities includes leadership and team-based activities shaped around research and clinical activities within a particular department of a medical school.

This profile of responsibilities determines the second feature of psychology positions in medical schools—what is typically referred to as the "soft money" salaries of such psychologists. Often, there is no department or school budget line for these positions; they are available within the financial, space, and political constraints of a particular department. A psychologist at a medical school often must generate, through grants and clinical services, the salary for his or her own position. Although specific arrangements vary widely from group to group and from department to department, the spirit of a medical school position is that the psychologist is responsible for generating a budget line for his or her salary. Unlike self-employed psychologists, however, psychologists at medical schools, although responsible for generating funding for their salaries, do not determine their pay scales; they must follow the regulations of their department and school. These regulations typically are quite constraining, and even if a psychologist has a multimillion-dollar grant, his or her salary is likely to be capped at a certain level. Conversely, if a psychologist is not able to generate enough grants to support his or her salary, medical schools usually have a responsibility to cover only a certain percentage of this salary (e.g., up to 50%).

Fortunately, there are many opportunities for psychologists in medical schools. Many medical school departments are committed both to providing high-quality clinical services and to conducting high-quality research. With these two commitments in place, there is a strong demand for psychologists who can contribute to both lines of activity simultaneously. Correspondingly, if one is interested in providing clinical services and conducting research simultaneously and can handle the uncertainties of funding and flow of clinical and research cases, working as a psychologist in a medical school is an exciting career path, providing freedom to conduct both academic and applied professional development.

The third distinct feature of the career path of a psychologist at a medical school is a rather limited set of training and teaching responsibilities. In fact, the majority of psychologists who work at medical schools do not teach formal classes, unless they wish to, and their supervisors (e.g., principal investigators on the grants that support them, directors of clinical services, or their chairs if psychologists are the principal investigators themselves) believe that teaching would fit well with their other activities. Similarly, because clinical departments of medical schools do not typically admit graduate students studying for the PhD (although there are notable exceptions, such as the Sackler School of Graduate Biomedical Studies at Tufts University), psychologists on the faculty at medical schools do not typically have easy access to graduate students. Moreover, because of a lack of explicit requirements for teaching undergraduate, graduate, or medical students, access to students of all kinds is rather limited. However, many students look for part-time employment at medical schools, and many of them decide to work on their theses with psychologists who do not make initial admission decisions.

What is typically present in abundance in medical schools is the need for supervision of other young psychologists and social workers who are in training. Because many medical departments have trainees, a portion of the responsibilities regarding these trainees rest with psychologists on the faculty.

Professional Activities of Psychologists at Medical Schools

Medical schools employ psychologists from a variety of backgrounds. However, psychologists who are interested in finding a home at a medical school are usually interested in atypical, rather than typical, human functioning. Specifically, of the many subdisciplines of psychology, five areas—clinical, health, developmental, cognitive, and biological (neuroscience)—contribute the largest portion of their graduates to medical schools.

Because the main thread of work in clinical psychology is to help people with specific conditions or disorders (e.g., cancer, dementia, learning disabilities), many clinical psychologists seek employment at medical schools to gain access, through the schools' clinics, to these populations to offer their expertise, knowledge, and skills to those who need them. Clinical psychologists employed by medical schools often work hand in hand with medical doctors to provide both diagnostic and treatment services.

Developmental psychologists often decide to engage in clinical practices as well, seeing patients and providing developmental consultations and evaluations. The placement of developmental psychologists in medical schools is especially prevalent in departments that run clinics for children, adolescents, and older people. However, although quite a few clinical psychologists working in medical schools limit their responsibilities to clinical services, many developmental psychologists contribute to and design research projects. In my experience, the majority of clinical psychologists in most medical schools contribute to services, the majority of cognitive and biological psychologists contribute to research, and developmental psychologists usually contribute to both.

Health psychologists who work in medical settings are most often employed in schools of public heath, which often have their own programs for master's- and doctoral-level students. Typically, health psychologists in such departments contribute to both research and teaching.

Work Settings for Psychologists at Medical Schools

Three features of the atmosphere of medical schools are especially important for a psychologist seeking employment in such an arena: (a) the structure of the body of the faculty in the department and the school, (b) the atmosphere of competitive collaboration, and (c) the always-problematic issue of space. In this section I provide a glimpse into the statistics on faculty at medical schools across the United States. These data are based on 2004 statistics; more detail and statistics for other years are available through the Web site of the Association of American Medical Colleges (AAMC, 2006; Pate & Kohout, 2004).

First, unlike traditional academic departments of psychology, the colleagues of a psychologist employed as faculty members at a medical school are primarily MDs, mostly male, and predominantly White. To illustrate, the AAMC faculty roster listed about 114,000 faculty members at medical schools across the United States. Of these, 68% were medical doctors (24% had a PhD or other high-level degree, and 8% had a master's or other comparable degree or an unknown degree), 69% were male, and 72% were White. These disproportions are even more pronounced in the senior ranks of the faculty: Among full professors, 67% were MDs, 85% were male, and 84% were White.[1] This demographic profile of medical school faculties, in combination with the funding factors I discussed in the previous section, create a particular atmosphere that I refer to as "competitive collaboration."

The atmosphere at medical schools is characterized by much higher levels of collaboration between faculty members than in traditional academic departments for at least three reasons. First, the main line of research support coming to medical schools is from the National Institutes of Health (NIH). NIH grants are very competitive and traditionally multidisciplinary, calling for teams of basic scientists and clinicians to work together. Correspondingly, faculty members at medical schools often pool their efforts to form collaborations that are not as prevalent in typical academic departments.

---

[1] It is important to note that over the past 20 to 25 years, the number of full-time women faculty members has nearly tripled and the number of non-White faculty has increased more than 2.5 times.

Second, the concept of tenure at medical schools is different from that in schools of arts and sciences. Unlike the latter, tenured professors in medical schools often contribute to their salaries, and the medical school guarantees only an agreed-on portion of the salary if a person loses his or her research support. Thus, the drive for collaboration is often supported not only by overlapping scientific interests but also by an objective need to ensure that one's full salary is paid. Third, professional acknowledgment and rewards (e.g., endowed chairs) at medical schools are rare and very competitive. Moreover, the ladder system of promotion for faculty is different from that in schools of arts and sciences, and often decisions are made in such a way that current or former junior collaborators compete for the same promotion. Thus, collaborations in medical schools are often competitive: Senior faculty compete for the time and attention of junior faculty, and junior faculty compete for the time and attention of senior faculty. Yet because interdisciplinary team efforts are essential for success in medical schools, collaborations are almost always in place and are essential to success. This environment of competitive collaboration is something that one deals with on an everyday basis, apparently, not an easy task: For a number of years now, the attrition, in absolute numbers, of PhD clinical faculty has steadily increased.[2]

The recent national trend in medical training is to require medical students to devote significant time to scholarly and research activities. This trend is expressed not only in the constantly increasing number of joint degrees obtained by students while in medical school (e.g., MD and MPH or MD and PhD) but also in the redistribution of time in regular curricula for future medical doctors (e.g., Stanford University School of Medicine, n.d.). This redistribution has resulted from the growing emphasis on research and, therefore, on the increasing demand for all kinds of researchers, psychologists among them.

The third distinct feature of the medical school environment is the chronic shortage of space. Like almost any department in academia, medical schools employing psychologists provide them with office and laboratory space. However, given the dynamic nature of funding for research operations, space commitments are typically more fluid in medical schools than in traditional academic departments. Medical schools often rent space outside of their immediate premises for specific research operations, so medical school faculty members may have office and laboratory space away from the main department building.

---

[2] However, because of hiring, the attrition rate (e.g., the ratio of attrition count to increases in faculty size) has decreased.

Academic and Other Preparation Needed for the Career

The trajectory of a psychologist at a medical school is somewhat distinct from that of psychologists in other careers. Indeed, psychologists in medical schools fill a demand for special skills and qualifications and respond to special concerns and unique challenges.[3] The "typology" of psychologists at medical schools is rather extensive and representative of a number and variety of departments that employ psychologists. Although each particular setting might differ in terms of the professional expectations for psychologists employed there, the types of jobs psychologists hold at medical schools can be subdivided into three tracks: clinical, research, and mixed.

A clinical track calls for all the qualifications of an excellent practitioner because most working hours are spent in interactions with patients (e.g., performing clinical evaluations, participating in research studies). Working in this track also necessitates familiarity with the department's major research agendas and an ability to contribute to the overall life of the department and its applied and scientific objectives.

A research track calls for qualifications related to the design and conduct of research within a particular area of expertise. Medical schools often hire psychologists with neuroscience backgrounds, especially psychologists interested in the application of neuroimaging techniques in both healthy individuals and patients. These psychologists

---

[3] To stress this distinctness and to form a network of support for psychologists at medical schools, in 1982 members of the American Psychological Association established the Association of Medical School Psychologists. In 2005, the organization became the Association of Psychologists in Academic Health Centers (APAHC), an advocacy group for academic health center psychologists. The organization wanted to extend its outreach to psychologists working in teaching hospitals, academic health centers, schools of health professions, dental schools, and other medical settings. The current leadership of the APAHC believes that the new name of the association is more consistent with the association's stated purpose of promoting the discipline and profession of psychology in academic health centers and encouraging and supporting psychologists' participation in institutional governance, research, educational programs, administration, leadership, and policy development (see APA Division 12, 2006)

The APAHC is part of the Society of Clinical Psychology of the American Psychological Association and is a member of the Council of Academic Societies of the Association of American Medical Colleges. This dual affiliation reflects the uniqueness of an association created for psychologists who work at the intersection of psychology and medicine. The APAHC also publishes the *Journal of Clinical Psychology in Medical Settings*.

spend most of their time doing research, leading research units, and contributing to research collaborations. Common denominators for research-oriented psychologists employed by medical schools are their ability to generate financial support for their own research and their contributions to team efforts on behalf of their departments.

A mixed track is typically occupied by individuals who are interested in and qualified to carry out both clinical work and research. Thus, qualifications for both the clinical and the research tracks are applicable to this track.

Financial Compensation

Typically, the rate of compensation for faculty members in a medical school is comparable to or somewhat higher than that for faculty members in a traditional academic department of psychology (see http://chronicle.com/stats/aaup/aaupresults.php for an online salary tool; see also Pate & Kohout, 2004 for faculty salaries in psychology and Wicherski, Washington, Kohout, & Bohacik, 2005). Although, to my knowledge, no comprehensive analyses of faculty salaries in medical schools versus traditional departments are publicly available, the analyses conducted by APA's Research Office in 2003 are quite interesting. In these analyses, efforts were made to survey a sample of psychologists employed by medical schools (for details, see previously listed URL) and a sample of psychologists employed by a variety of institutions and self-employed (Pate, Frincke, & Kohout, 2005). Although these two surveys have a variety of weaknesses, they illustrate the range of salaries within the profession as a whole, within traditional academic departments of psychology, and within medical schools.

Here I present some numbers that are indicative of the situation, although these numbers should be interpreted with caution. The 2002 median base salary for psychologists with 2 to 4 years of experience employed full-time in medical schools was $63,500 (mean $73,144). At 5 to 9 years of experience, the median base salary was $65,000 (mean $67,244). It is not uncommon for psychologists in medical schools to have other sources of income beyond the base salary, such as clinical income or income from grants. For psychologists with 5 to 9 years of experience, the additional income raised the median salary by more than $12,000 and the mean increased by more than $2,000 (Pate & Kohout, 2004). When funding is not easily obtainable, these numbers can drop dramatically as salaries revert to the level established between a psychologist and the department administration at the contract sign-ing; this level can be quite low (50% or less of the base salary). Also, medical school salaries tend to be for 12 months, and arts and sciences salaries for 9 months. Arts and sciences faculty can thus supplement their salaries by up to 3 months of summer salary.

Advantages and Disadvantages of the Career

Pursuing a career as a psychologist at a medical school has its pluses and minuses, as everything does. As I stated earlier, this career path affords a great deal of freedom for pursuing one's passion, whether it is practice or research. However, it also offers less security and more instability. In times when funding is tight, the appeal of these careers decreases, understandably. Similarly, when insurance companies are not willing to cover the costs of psychological assessments and therapies, the appeal of practice, whether in a medical school, privately, or else-where, also decreases.

So what are the pluses of being a psychologist at a medical school? They are a tight connection to the applied work; a close link to research, especially health issues–driven research; an ability to focus on research questions that are of great interest; an opportunity to work with repre-sentatives of many disciplines related to patients' well-being; and rela-tive financial and time independence. And what are the minuses? They are a relative lack of security, especially when funding is not readily available; the fact that not being an MD puts one a bit outside the mainstream flow of collegial interactions; and a relative clinical bias in the research questions one pursues.

Attributes Needed for Success in the Career

A career as a psychologist in a medical school calls for all the attri-butes necessary for success in any domain of practicing psychology—commitment to the profession, a solid knowledge base, and the capacity to stay in touch with a developing field. Yet there are three additional dimensions of professional qualifications that, from my point of view, are critical. One is an ability to work in an environment where you and your colleagues are in the minority, always the case for psychologists in a medical school, where MDs far outnumber PhDs. The second characteristic is related to risk taking: Although psychologists at medical schools develop all kinds of arrangements to maximize the security of their employment, in general it is a higher-risk enterprise than the relative safe haven of teaching in a traditional academic career. The third important quality is resilience. Because medical school faculty tend to write more grants, they also tend to experience failure more often.

Why I Chose to Work at a Medical School

Psychologists end up working at medical schools for a variety of reasons, some professional and some personal. From talking to my colleagues and thinking about this issue myself, I think the main reason psychologists end up at medical schools rather than in traditional academic departments is their commitment to patients, their interest in certain disorders, and the nature of academia. Traditional academic psychology departments are mostly structured around specific psychological problems, and faculty members—even in areas of clinical psychology—rarely have as much access to patients as do faculty members at medical schools. Accepting a job in a traditional academic department of psychology typically means committing oneself primarily to teaching and only secondarily to research and practice. Accepting a job in a medical school typically means committing to research or practice (or both), and then to teaching. It is this balance of priorities that may help determine which psychologists choose a position at a medical school.

In my case, deciding on a medical school position was a natural thing to do. An affiliation with a medical school allowed me to maintain close contact with its clinics for various neuropsychiatric conditions from which I recruit my study participants; set up a genetics wet lab, where I do most of my research; establish a close connection with the world of applied psychology (i.e., aspects of developmental and clinical psychology that are relevant to the mental health of children); enjoy a highly rigorous academic atmosphere (a medical school is still an academic department, with all necessary qualifications); and do as much teaching as I care to (one or two courses per year) for joy, pleasure, and the transmission of knowledge. So the decision to be at a medical school, in my case, was obvious.

Range of Opportunities for Employment

Although I am not aware of any systematic research on specific place-ments of psychologists in medical schools, the APA has listed the following departments as primary "homes" of psychologists at medical schools: psychiatry and behavioral sciences, pediatrics, neurology/ biology, physiology/anatomy, family/community/health/prevention, and rehabilitation/pain management (Pate & Kohout, 2005, para. 7). Consistent with the earlier discussion of pay, the distribution of the source of income varied, depending on home department, and the proportions of salary ranged from 27% to 94% for clinical work and from 64% to 89% for research for 12-months salary.

A Day in the Life of a Psychologist at a Medical School

I conclude this chapter with brief descriptions of a typical day for three psychologists at a medical school. These 1-day portraits describe people I know, and each is an example of the three tracks I discussed previously: primarily clinical, primarily research, and mixed.

DG, A CLINICAL PSYCHOLOGIST

A typical day for DG consists of three parts: seeing patients (e.g., to conduct assessments or provide therapy), writing reports, and partici-pating in the life of the department (e.g., going to presentations and meetings). The number of patients DG sees in a day varies but averages around two to three. DG is part of a team that evaluates and treats each patient. DG also supervises trainees and regularly participates in feedback and discussion sessions with them. DG works across a number of clinics in the department (e.g., autism clinic and learning disabilities clinic), administering the same instruments or evaluating patients within a particular domain of functioning.

MC, A COGNITIVE EXPERIMENTAL PSYCHOLOGIST

A typical day for MC is focused on research. MC was hired to work on particular experiments (e.g., eye-tracking experiments, evoked potential experiments, neuroimaging experiments) and to design, individually or as part of a team, collaborative experiments within these various paradigms. MC works with a number of collaborators within and outside of his department and spends 100% of his time on research and research-related activities.

AK, A CLINICAL PSYCHOLOGIST

AK came to work in a medical school because she was interested in a particular clinical population (e.g., children with autism) but wanted to develop further her own research interests and agendas. AK combines her clinical and research agendas by running a clinic through which she recruits participants for her studies. AK subdivides the week into clinical and research days. In other words, she typically sees patients only 1 or 2 days a week, committing her other time to research (e.g., writing and carrying out grants, analyzing data, writing manuscripts).

Conclusion

A career as a psychologist in a medical school is a career at the junction of psychology and medicine. It naturally attracts professionals interested in atypical rather than typical functioning and in applications and basic science that can have a direct impact on applications. These careers are generally characterized by a small training and teaching load and a heavy clinical and research load. They are also usually characterized by more dependency on soft (i.e., practice, services, and research) funds. Psychologists in medical school careers assume a higher commitment to generating funds to support their own careers. A great deal of freedom is inherent to the profession, as is a great deal of uncertainty—so it is not for the faint of heart.

References

American Psychological Association, Division 12, Section VIII. (2006*). Association of Psychologists in Academic Health Centers web page.* Retrieved September 27, 2006, from http://apa.org/divisions/div12/sections/section8/

Association of American Medical Colleges. (2006). *U.S. medical school faculty, 2004.* Retrieved September 27, 2006, from http://www.aamc.org/data/facultyroster/usmsf04/start.htm

Pate, W., Frincke, J. L., & Kohout, J. L. (2005). *Salaries in psychology: 2003 report of the 2003 APA salary survey.* Retrieved July 10, 2006, from http://research.apa.org/03salary/homepage.html

Pate, W., & Kohout, J. (2004). *Report of the 2003 medical school/academic medical center psychologist employment survey.* Retrieved July 10, 2006, from http://research.apa.org/amsp/2003/index.html

Stanford University School of Medicine. (n.d.). *Medical education: Mission and goals.* Retrieved July 10, 2006, from http://medstrategicplan.stanford.edu/fullreport/medical_education.html

Wicherski, M., Washington, T., Kohout, J., & Bohacik, J. (2005). *2004–2005 faculty salaries in graduate departments of psychology.* Retrieved September 27, 2006, from http://research.apa.org/facsal2004 2005.pdf

Sharon Stephens Brehm

Coming Full Circle: From Academe to Administration to Academe

5

When I went to college at Duke in 1963, I felt right at home, and, over the ensuing decades, I figured out how to never leave the halls of academe. But this doesn't mean that I stayed in one place—quite the contrary. I have lived in many different places, working in many different positions. This kind of vagabond life, moving from one university to another, is fairly typical of those who go into academic administration.

Most of the other chapters in this book address careers that are strongly and specifically connected to being a psychology major. This is not the case with academic administration, which draws people from many different disciplines. Nevertheless, it seems to me that psychologists are particularly well suited for administration, with their strong skills in analyzing problems, crunching data, and understanding

Sharon Stephens Brehm, PhD, is professor of psychology in the clinical and social programs at Indiana University Bloomington. Dr. Brehm has been an Intra-University Professor at the University of Kansas, a Fulbright Senior Research Scholar at the École des Hautes Études en Sciences Sociales, a visiting professor in Germany and Italy, and was inducted into the University of Kansas Women's Hall of Fame. Her empirical research has examined the effects of psychological reactance, empathy, and self-focus. She is currently president-elect of the American Psychological Association.

interpersonal relations. In fact, many academic administrators come from a background in psychology. This may reflect the size of the field, however, rather than the match between skills and job responsibilities. Significant numbers of administrators are also drawn from other large academic fields, such as chemistry and English.

Despite this pipeline between academe and administration, the vast majority of students and even many faculty[1] do not know much about what administrators do. However, even without specific information, faculty and students often perceive administrators as being somehow different. For example, administrators are sometimes referred to as "the suits," alluding to the attire that distinguishes them from faculty and students, who prefer more casual clothing. This combination of a lack of detailed knowledge and a sense of cultural divide reduces the like-lihood that faculty members will develop an interest in academic administration.

On one hand, in 16 years as an academic administrator, I never met a student or a faculty member who said that his or her goal in life was to be a provost (i.e., the vice president for academic affairs, with some additional responsibilities that vary across institutions). On the other hand, I have met a fair number of students (but no faculty) who said they wanted to be a college or university president. Students aspiring to a presidency are always a bit startled when I tell them that to want to be a president is equivalent to wanting to be a basketball player after spending several decades as a figure skater. Because most presidents in higher education have a doctoral degree and initially are employed full-time as a professor, their original motivation was to teach and contribute to their discipline through scholarship, research, or creative activity. Surely there are some individuals who decide early on that they want to be a president (or provost or dean), but typically academic administration is an unantici-pated, often accidental diversion from one's original academic career path.

Because there are no general models for this transition, I begin this chapter with an account of my own experiences. By providing you with some details about my personal and professional life as an academic, I hope to give you some understanding of the complexities of personal and professional development that can lay the foundation for an interest in academic administration.

---

[1] When I refer to "faculty," I mean faculty who do not hold senior level academic administrative positions (i.e., dean, provost, chancellor, president). However, I do include department chairs.

My Academic Life

Although I knew from my midteens that I wanted to major in psychology, this strong interest did not immediately dictate my eventual career path. At first, I assumed that I would be a psychiatrist. However, it took just one semester of chemistry to convince me that premed was not my destiny. Looking around for other possibilities, I thought about becoming a lawyer. But when I took the LSAT, I performed miserably on those items that (I presume) are intended to measure law-specific capabilities—of which I apparently have none. Fortunately, my love for psychology stayed secure and stable. I just didn't know how I could make use of it after college.

Fortunately, I soon found out from my professors that I could continue in psychology and be able to treat patients. In other words, I could be a practicing clinical psychologist. This was amazing to me. I had never realized that it was possible, but once informed of this option, I pursued it. I applied to several clinical psychology programs and was accepted at Harvard, which was my first choice, even though all the applicants had been informed that the clinical program was in transition. David McClelland was going to step down as director of the clinical program, and Norman Garmezy had agreed to come from the University of Minnesota as the new head of the program.

No one could have anticipated in that spring of 1967 how difficult the coming year would be. More students had accepted admission in the Harvard program than had been anticipated, which complicated research and clinical supervision arrangements. Then, late that summer, we were informed that Garmezy was not coming to Harvard; McClelland would continue in the directorship. So there we were: an oversized class, an unsettled program, and a country that seemed to be coming apart—riots in Detroit, New York, and Birmingham that summer; the Tet offensive in January, 1968; the My Lai massacre in March; and the assassinations of Martin Luther King Jr. and Robert F. Kennedy in April and June. Our professors were extremely helpful and supportive, but by the end of the year, some of us, for many different reasons, had decided to leave the program.

My own decision was purely personal. Jack Brehm and I were married in the fall of 1968, and we lived on Long Island that year. He was a visiting professor at Stony Brook, and I worked in the female adolescent ward of a state psychiatric hospital. In 1969, we returned to North Carolina. Jack resumed his faculty position at Duke, while I worked for Eric Schopler in his Child Research Project at the University of North Carolina. Then, in 1970, I was admitted into the Duke clinical psychology program. Because I was living with a social psychologist and hanging out with clinical psychologists, it wasn't surprising that I became interested in the ways in which these subdisciplines had much to offer each other. My integrative interests were given strong and consistent encouragement by Robert Carson and Philip Costanzo, both members of the Duke clinical faculty.

It was wonderful to be back at Duke, enjoying the perfect match between personal and professional interests. But it was not to last. Clinical programs require a yearlong clinical internship, and I realized that I would learn more in a new setting than if I were an intern in either the Duke or University of North Carolina university hospitals, which I knew so well. Fortunately, Jack was able to take a sabbatical, and off we went to Seattle. He was a visiting professor in the University of Washington's department of psychology, and I was a clinical psychology intern with rotations on the rehabilitation ward and in (what is now known as) the Center on Human Development and Disability. At the end of that year, Jack went back to Duke and I became a visiting assistant professor of psychology at Virginia Tech.

At the end of that year, Jack and I moved to Lawrence, Kansas, where both of us had faculty positions, Jack in social psychology and I in clinical psychology with an emphasis on child clinical. My research interests continued to bridge both clinical and social psychology, but over time I focused more on social and personality topics, including psychological reactance, empathy, self-awareness, and Type A personality. I was very fortunate to be able to work with wonderful colleagues and extremely talented graduate students. Although Jack and I were divorced in 1978, we have continued (even to this day) to be close friends and colleagues, and we wrote a book together—on psychological reactance—soon after the divorce. After a sabbatical in Paris in 1981–1982 studying social influence with Serge Moscovici, I came back to Lawrence and somehow got the itch to write an undergraduate textbook.

This unexpected inclination came about through a very circuitous route. In my early years at The University of Kansas, I often taught introductory psychology to a large class (500 students) early in the morning. It was not easy to keep the students engaged. But I discovered that if I used relationship examples (e.g., love, jealousy, attraction, conflict), the students were much more attentive. So I found myself reading and thinking more about the psychology of relationships than I had ever done before. At some point, I decided to try to write a textbook on intimate relationships, emphasizing social psychological theory and research and including work from clinical psychology, sociology, communications, and developmental psychology. When I contacted publishers about the book, I encountered great difficulty. Quite reasonably, publishers wanted to know about the possible market for this book. Where were the courses that would adopt such a textbook? Fortunately, Judith Rothman, who was with Random House at the time, recognized that this was "a chicken-and-egg book" (her exact phrase): You have to have the textbook in order for faculty to want to teach the course, and once the courses are taught, the books will be bought. To my amazement (and I think to hers), Judy convinced the powers that be that the book should be published. The first edition came out in 1985, and thanks to Rowland Miller, who has now become the lead author of the text, the fourth edition was published this year (Miller, Perlman, & Brehm, 2007).

Having written one textbook and enjoyed it, I thought perhaps I'd like to write another. Fortunately, Saul Kassin thought this was a good idea, and together we published our *Social Psychology* text (Brehm & Kassin, 1990). Steve Fein joined Saul for the fourth edition, and the two of them have continued regular revisions through the current sixth edition (Brehm, Kassin, & Fein, 2005).

Entry Into Administration

In 1987, when Saul Kassin and I had just signed a contract for the publication of *Social Psychology*, I took my first major step into academic administration as director of the college honors program. No one had recruited me for this position, and no one had sought me out; I just saw the job ad in the *Daily Kansan* and applied. It was then, and still is, a wonderful administrative assignment: working with many of the university's brightest undergraduates, helping select and prepare these students for prestigious national and international scholarship competitions, and trying to convince many of the university's best professors to teach honors courses while begging their department chairs to find a way to cover the large enrollment classes left without a teacher when the professor taught the much smaller honors section.

Having expected to like the director's job, I was startled to find that I loved it. My only previous major administrative experience, as cochair of my department for 1 year during a time of considerable discord in the department, had been quite stressful. Moreover, as an active participant in faculty governance and a member of the University Senate Executive Committee, I had assumed that my role was to ask tough questions and, overall, make life difficult for college and university administrators. It was therefore quite startling, to me and to my faculty friends, to discover that I had (at least formally) joined the enemy.

My responsibilities expanded—and my new identity as "a suit" strengthened—when the new dean of the college asked me to be the associate dean of graduate studies in addition to my honors program role. I welcomed this opportunity to be involved in both undergraduate and graduate education. In addition to my administrative duties, I was also teaching one course each semester, conducting and publishing research, and working with Saul Kassin on the first edition of our social psychological textbook. It was a very busy time. In retrospect, however, these may have been the best years of my professional life. I was a true hybrid, faculty member *and* administrator.

But perhaps such a state is inherently unstable. If I could be an associate dean, then couldn't (and shouldn't) I be a "real" dean? Just as there is an academic ladder (assistant professor, associate professor, full professor, distinguished or named professor), there is an academic administrative ladder (department chair, associate dean, dean, provost, chancellor or president).[2] You do not have to step on each rung, but many administrators step on most of them.

Because I was divorced and didn't have children, it was fairly easy for me to consider moving to another university. "Movability" is a major factor in academic administration. After all, the dean who had hired me had left for another university, and the new dean had come from yet another university. Moving is by no means an absolute rule. A significant number of senior academic administrators are appointed from within, with some institutions having a strong tradition of internal appointments to such positions. However, many—perhaps most—senior academic administrators are appointed from the ranks of external candidates.

So I began to look around for a deanship and thereby discovered the world of search committees and search consultants. This process differs sharply from searches conducted for academic positions. In essence, academic searches are conducted within a "family," whereas administrative searches are conducted by a crowd of strangers. When you are a candidate for an academic position, you usually would not

---

[2] *Chancellor* and *president* are often interchangeable terms. For example, in the State University of New York system, the head of each campus is a president, and the head of the system (to whom the presidents report) is a chancellor. In the University of California system, these titles are reversed: The campus head is a chancellor; the head of the system is a president. In this chapter, I use the term *president* to denote the chief executive officer of a relatively autonomous campus.

know everyone in the department. However, you probably would know some or all of the faculty in your specialty area, and you would be part of a complex set of interlocking networks—for example, one of your potential colleagues may have had the same mentor that you did, your mentor may have gone to graduate school with one of your potential colleagues, or your mentor or your best friend from graduate school may once have worked in the same department as one of your potential colleagues. Indeed, if you're being recruited as a full professor, it's likely that you would know many or perhaps all of the faculty in your area quite well—certainly professionally, and perhaps personally.

In contrast, candidates for academic administrative positions often have no known connections with any member of what is typically a very large search committee. And although you will have been asked to prepare a letter indicating why you would be a good fit for this institution, you may well have no direct knowledge about the college or university. So how do you write that letter? How do you prepare for that interview? The answer is, you do your homework. You read the materials they send to you, explore the institution's Web site, search through the data (e.g., salaries, endowments, graduation rates of athletes) collected by the *Chronicle of Higher Education*, go over the "America's Best Colleges" and "American's Best Graduate Schools" editions of *U.S. News and World Report*, ask your administrative friends what they know about this institution, and search Google—a lot.

Academic and administrative searches also differ in what knowledge is being sought by whom. As a candidate for an academic position, you want to tell the faculty and students in the hiring department what you know they might be interested in learning. As an external candidate for an administrative position, you want to show them how much you've learned about the institution that they know so well. The search committee members will, of course, want to hear about your administrative accomplishments at your home institution. However, you have to be careful not to be seen as too eager to apply what you learned at your institution to their institution. The words "Well, at my university, we do it this way" should never be uttered in an interview, or even after you get the job. Every college and university believes that its way is the best way.

Although each administrative search is unique (reflecting the institution and the individuals on the search committee), there are typically four basic steps in the search process:

1. Your name is in the pool. Typically, you apply, or someone nominates you. I believe it's better to be recommended than to apply. You are then contacted and asked if you would

like to submit materials. If you express interest, the search committee will send you a position description and other information about the institution and the search process.

2. In response to these materials, you send in your curriculum vitae, indicating your academic and administrative experience and accomplishments. Preparing a CV for an administrative position is an art in itself and it helps to have the advice of individuals with administrative experience.

3. Most searches then proceed to what are called "airport interviews." These are confidential interactions, not on campus (and not necessarily at an airport!), with some 8 to 12 candidates being invited. Usually, you meet with the full search committee for an hour or so.

4. The next step is the selection of finalists, usually three to five, for campus visits. After these interviews, the search committee reports its recommendations to the administrator who will make the final decision.

In academic job searches, there tends to be a very strong relationship between the level of the candidate and the number of searches in which the candidate participates. Those seeking their first full-time academic position typically strive to be involved in a number of searches, whereas senior academics (i.e., full professors) usually participate in very few job interviews. The hit rate varies according to the degree of competition: The chances of being offered the job at the junior level are usually much lower than at the senior level. In contrast, the relationship between level of position and the number of searches in which individuals participate is much weaker for administrative jobs. For example, some individuals seeking a dean's position may be in fewer searches than some people who are candidates for a presidency.

In general, however, candidates for administrative positions are involved in more searches than candidates for academic positions. When I was a candidate for the position of dean of arts and sciences, I was involved in at least four searches (I say "at least" because I can only recall four; there may have been some others that I have forgotten or repressed). Indeed, participating in many searches is one of the most unpleasant features of administrative life. To do well in the interview, you have to fall in love with the institution. But for most candidates, most of these love affairs turn out to be unrequited, and although the courtship is wonderful, the rejection hurts. The stresses and strains of administrative searches take a heavy toll, and many people who would make wonderful administrators are simply not willing to go through this ordeal.

Administrative Life

As a senior academic administrator, I held three positions: dean of the Harpur College of Arts and Sciences at the State University of New York at Binghamton, provost and vice president for academic affairs at Ohio University, and chancellor of Indiana University Bloomington and vice president for academic affairs at Indiana University. Although these universities and jobs varied enormously, there are some core characteristics of such positions, and in the rest of this chapter, I give an overview of what it's like to have a career in academic administration.

SCHEDULES AND ROUTINES

The single biggest shock for an academic who becomes an academic administrator[3] is the mail, which these days means electronic as well as paper. During my first semester as a dean, I wondered if I could possibly survive the daily chore of going through my mail. I did, and I have since learned that most new deans have similar panic attacks. It seems overwhelming, but over time, I figured out a system to make sure I read and answered what needed to be read and answered. The other stuff just piled up and, at some point, was thrown away or deleted.

The daily routine of an administrator is vastly different from that of the faculty. A relatively small portion of faculty time is tied to a fixed schedule, such as giving classes, holding scheduled meetings with undergraduate and graduate students, participating in departmental meetings, giving talks, and attending talks by others. Other tasks and responsibilities are usually more flexible in terms of timing, including preparing for classes, grading papers and tests, talking with colleagues (both locally and at a distance) and students, reading articles and books, analyzing data, writing, developing grant proposals, and most important—thinking. In contrast, there is little, if any, flexibility in a senior administrator's schedule. Most of one's life is spent in one's office, and typically, every weekday hour from 8:00 a.m. (sometimes

---

[3] Because I was never a full-time chair of an academic department, I do not have a good understanding of the similarities and differences between being a chair and being a college or university academic administrator. Furthermore, size and complexity affect all administrative positions. Thus, if the chair of a large and complex department becomes the dean of a smaller and less complex college, the level of administrative responsibilities would decrease with this movement "up" the administrative hierarchy. Typically, however, one moves from smaller, less complex units to larger, more complex ones.

7:00 a.m.) to 5:00 p.m. is scheduled for meetings and phone calls. Administrators also attend a significant number of events in the evening or over the weekend. This schedule is directly connected to the mail panic I experienced: If you're booked solid, when can you read? The answer is, anytime you're free—between meetings, late at night, and whenever you can grab some time over the weekend.

Many administrators have a frazzled look much of the time. That's because they're having such a hard time finding enough time to do everything they need to do. During the regular academic year, the time pressure is severe. And typically, administrators remain very busy for at least a month after graduation, trying to catch up on all the projects they could not take care of during the regular school year. The remaining 2 months of summer are much slower, and most administrators welcome them as a time to relax and to think more broadly about the institution's goals and challenges.

BUDGETING

As an academic administrator, much of one's time and energy is spent on money. For most—perhaps all—colleges and universities, concerns about funding are constant and never ending. No funding source is ever fully secure over time. Endowments can lose their value depending on market fluctuations and investment choices; student enrollments can decrease; state funding can decline; grants and contracts can diminish. As an academic administrator, I experienced both horrendous cuts and stable budgeting. Unfortunately, I never had the pleasure of rolling in dough.

The challenge of budgeting in times of either scarcity or stability is to decide how much, if any, reallocation of funds among units will occur and to develop a process that will determine the reallocations to be made. As an academic administrator, I always took a strong position on this issue: To stay still is to wither and die. If you fail to reallocate when a surplus is not available, you will fail to make the necessary strategic investments, and the institution will decline in quality and effectiveness. In each of the three institutions in which I was an administrator, I developed ways to make strategic investments by reallocation of existing funds or by allocation of new funds through a process that was administered separately from the existing budgetary system. Because money well spent is the fuel of all enterprises, I believe that my focus on strategic investments benefited the universities that I served. I am also aware that my decisions in this area were highly controversial. The politics of money are complex, intense, pervasive, and the bane of most academic administrators' lives.

TENURE AND PROMOTION OF FACULTY

The tenure and promotion of faculty is another major responsibility for senior academic administrators. Newly hired assistant professors can usually expect to have a job for 7 years. During this time, they work very hard to earn tenure. In their 3rd year, the assistant professor's progress is reviewed by the tenured faculty of the department. If this review does not go well, some assistant professors leave. Early in the 6th year, assistant professors submit their record of accomplishments (e.g., student evaluations of teaching; expert evaluations of scholarship, research, and creative activity; publications; grants and contracts) to a series of reviewers (both internal and external) who recommend for or against tenure. This process takes most of an academic year.

If tenure is not granted, the individual has only 1 more year of employment in the institution. If tenure is granted, the individual has obtained what amounts to lifetime job security, so long as he or she meets standards of competence and professional behavior. The rationale for the tenure system is the importance of academic freedom: Professors must be free to speak the truth as best they see it and not risk their jobs for voicing unpopular opinions. Senior academic administrators participate in all promotion and tenure cases. Deans are very involved, provosts review all cases in the institution, and presidents make the final decision for the institution or make recommendations to the board of trustees.

GOVERNANCE

Academic administrators also work closely with faculty governance. American colleges and universities emphasize shared governance, which refers to the collaboration and cooperation between the board of trustees and academic administrators, on the one hand, and the faculty's elected representatives, on the other. This is a complicated arrangement that varies somewhat from institution to institution and that can present significant challenges to both constituencies. For example, the conversation often takes place at two different levels. Academic administrators are immersed in the details of institutional issues, whereas faculty governance officers are often more concerned with broader values and principles. Both are necessary for good policy and practice, but getting on the same wavelength can sometimes be difficult. One of the greatest obstacles to true collaboration is cultural in nature. Most faculty stay at an institution for many years, often for their entire career. Many senior academic administrators, however, stay at an institution for a shorter period (e.g., 5 years). Thus, in general, the faculty's commitment to and knowledge of the institution is much greater than the administrators'.

As I noted earlier, most senior academic administrative positions are filled by external candidates. And yet, given the cultural divide between faculty and administrators, wouldn't it be better for the institution to have an administration that shares the faculty's long-term connection and commitment to the institution? In other words, why are internal candidates for deans, provosts, chancellors, and presidents not more numerous and more successful? Part of the reason may have to do with the fact that internal candidates are known quantities, having both strong friends and at least a few enemies, whereas the external candidates come with glowing letters of recommendation (usually from individuals outside the institution) and are on their best behavior during the interviews. Most of us do look better from afar. Moreover, too much reliance on internal candidates does have it's dangers. Psychological inbreeding can foster the status quo, fail to perceive serious weaknesses, and prevent needed change.

Administrative Positions

So far, I've focused on academic administration in general, but there are, in fact, many differences among specific positions. I have always regarded being a dean as the most "romantic" of the senior academic administrative positions. One is close to one's academic roots and has extensive contact with faculty and students. These factors nourish the individual's academic identity and enhance the psychological significance of one's work. Even the title itself has great resonance, with its origins in both educational and religious organizations. Indeed, the dean's position is similar in many respects to the president's position. The organizational structure is straightforward: The dean works with the department chairs, who work with the faculty and students; the president works with the vice presidents, and the vice president of academic affairs (aka, provost) works with the deans. Furthermore, both deans and presidents are expected to be actively engaged in fundraising. Private colleges and universities have always depended heavily on private donations (in addition to tuition) to support the institution. Public institutions, however, vary in this respect. For example, many midwestern public universities have been raising private funds for many years. In the northeast, however, many public institutions began serious private fund raising only in the 1990s. Today, all institutions seek private funding, and such efforts are a major responsibility for deans and presidents.

The president works closely with the institution's board of trustees and has the unique responsibility of representing the institution as a whole. Presidents of public institutions interact with state legislators and the governor. Presidents of both public and private institutions often discuss specific bills affecting higher education with congressional representatives and senators. Deans may have such conversations on occasion, but typically this is a presidential responsibility. Presidents engage in even more ceremonial and social functions than deans. Like deans, presidential days are long, their weekends often filled, and their summer break is eagerly anticipated.

Now, let's look at the provost's position. This is a fairly new title in the United States but is now commonplace in universities. Many colleagues have also adopted this title, usually in conjunction with the more traditional term of Dean of the College. Since my administrative experience has been entirely in universities, I will focus on the role of the university provosts only. As far as I know, all university provosts (at least in U.S. institutions) are also vice presidents for academic affairs (in assignment, even if not in title). It has long been the tradition that the vice president for academic affairs is first among equals, relative to the other vice presidents, and serves in the president's absence if necessary. However, as institutions grew larger and more complex, and as the pressure on presidents to raise external funds and work with government bodies grew stronger, some presidents in some institutions wanted a provost who could be, in effect, the chief operating officer of the institution, coordinating the work of all the other vice presidents. In a few universities, all the vice presidents report to the provost.

There are, in my view, a number of problems with the provost position and with its role in the career advancement of academic administrators. For example, the public at large doesn't know what a provost is. One can argue that this lack of understanding isn't a problem, but I think it is. It is unsettling to always have to explain what you do or to use your other title (vice president for academic affairs). Actually, the general public doesn't understand what a vice president for academic affairs is either, but at least they can guess. When one says "provost," most people don't know how to even begin to guess. There are several dictionary definitions of provost, among them "important university administrator" and "senior dignitary of a cathedral" (*MSN Encarta Dictionary*, 2006a). A related term, provost marshal, is defined as "army officer with police duties" (*MSN Encarta Dictionary*, 2006b). It's understandable why there is confusion about the term.

But the provost problem isn't confined to the title; the role of the provost is the real issue. First, as mentioned earlier, the official job responsibilities vary. Some provosts are basically vice presidents of academic affairs with few, if any, other responsibilities or authority; some provosts have significant budgetary planning responsibilities not only for the academic units but for the entire university; some have significant authority for coordination of the other the vice presidents; and some have direct reports from some or all of the other vice presidents. Second, regardless of what the formal job description says, the president defines the role of the provost, and different presidents want different kinds of provosts. Third, it has become increasingly likely that when a new president is appointed, he or she will want a new provost. My own view is that greater acceptance of the third item can resolve some of the difficulties presented by the first two. A new president should have his or her own provost so that he or she can define the role in whatever way is best for his or her administration. This should be a standard practice, with no blame or hard feelings on either side.

Even under the best of circumstances, however, many provosts would continue to face one other challenge. As I indicated earlier, the most typical path to a presidency is to be a dean and then to be a provost. The usual rationale is that individuals interested in being a president need to have a broad understanding of university functions, and experience in the provostship provides this education. What gets left out of the equation, however, is that the number one job of a president and, increasingly, of a dean is external fund-raising, whereas most provosts engage in relatively little fund-raising. Perhaps even more important, many people who are psychologically very well suited to being a dean or a president are not well suited to being a provost and vice versa. Chief executive officer and chief operating officer positions are very different jobs. I was pleased that my alma mater hired as its new president Richard Brodhead, who was previously dean of Yale College but had never been a provost.

Nevertheless, the current practices and preferences continue in most colleges and universities. Thus, deans who seek a presidency would be well advised to think carefully about whether they need to be a provost before applying for a presidential position. Furthermore, candidates for a provostship should determine whether the president views fund-raising as a significant part of the provost's responsibilities.

The greatest challenge for all senior academic administrators is to make it possible for changes to be made that will benefit the institution and help it fulfill its mission. This is a challenge because we all love the changes we initiate, but we almost always hate the changes that others create. And so the script is written well in advance. The new dean, or provost, or president, who has perhaps never been on the campus before his or her on-campus interview, has come to town and moves into his or her office. Typically, the first few months are quite positive. There's an air of excitement, and everyone is on his or her best behavior.

But at some point, perhaps in the first year, perhaps a bit later, the new administrator makes it clear that he or she would like some changes made on campus. The typical reaction from the faculty (and often from other administrators) is not wholly positive. Sometimes it's possible to find common ground; sometimes it's not. Sometimes change is made; sometimes not. But the roles are cast. From the perspective of many of the faculty, the changes are not necessary: Many other things are more important, the administrator doesn't know the institution well enough, and besides, the administrator is simply trying to pad his or her CV in order to be successful in moving to another, higher-level, better-paying position. As for the administrator, he or she is convinced once again that most of the faculty cannot tolerate any change, no matter how beneficial, and looks forward to the upcoming conference of academic administrators, where people gather to console each other that all the faculty on all their campuses are uniformly resistant to change. Obviously, this is not a productive dialogue and skillful administrators are usually able to avoid it by developing the mutually respectful relationship with the faculty necessary for a healthy and productive institution.

Up to this point, as you may have noticed, I have deliberately refrained from using the L-word: leadership. I have done so because I believe the term has been debased. It has acquired a kind of magical status such that everyone strives to be a leader of something. Personally, I think we would be better off if we concentrated more on doing good work than on being a leader. However, as I consider the effective senior academic administrators I have known, I am forced to admit that there is something called leadership and that those who have it (no matter what role or position they occupy) often make lasting contributions to their colleges and universities. From my perspective, the essential characteristics for effective leadership as an academic administrator include working very hard over long periods of time, accurately identifying important changes that need to occur in the institution, listening carefully to criticism yet not being devastated by it, being exceptionally skillful in interpersonal relations, and having the courage to do the right thing.

Conclusion

If after reading this chapter, you find at least some elements of academic administration to be of interest, it's important to consider the advantages and disadvantages of such positions. The greatest reward of academic administration is easy to identify: the opportunity to help make the college or university a better place. You can get things done that will benefit students, faculty, the academic mission, and the greater good of humanity. You will also meet many interesting people, both on campus and off. Although exact salaries and benefits vary depending on the size and type of the institution, academic administrators are typically well paid.

Of course, like any line of work, there are some risks and challenges in being an academic administrator. Disagreements can become very intense, sometimes involving personal animosities and damaging your future prospects. But now that I am back on the faculty again, I realize how much I learned from being an academic administrator. Perhaps that's the greatest attraction of such positions. The tasks are so varied, the problems so complex, and the personal interactions so complex that it's simply impossible to stop learning. As it turns out, being an academic administrator is a great way to continue being a student.

References

Brehm, S. S. (1985). *Intimate relationships*. New York: Random House.

Brehm, S. S., & Kassin, S. M. (1990). *Social psychology* (6th ed.). Boston: Houghton Mifflin Company.

Brehm, S. S., Kassin, S. M., & Fein, S. (2005). *Social psychology* (6th ed.). Boston: Houghton Mifflin.

Miller, R. S., Perlman, D., & Brehm, S. S. (2007). *Intimate relationships* (4th ed.). New York: McGraw-Hill.

MSN encarta dictionary. (2006a). Retrieved July 27, 2006, from http://encarta.msn.com/dictionary_/provost.html

MSN encarta dictionary. (2006b). Retrieved July 27, 2006, from http://encarta.msn.com/dictionary_/provost%2520marshal.html

II

Clinical and Counseling Psychology

Christine H. Farber and Daniel J. Abrahamson

Clinical Psychologists in Independent Practice: Infinite Opportunities

6

C linical psychology is the branch of the discipline that is concerned with the assessment, diagnosis, and treatment of psychological issues, including maladaptive thought patterns, problematic behaviors, distressing feelings, learning difficulties, and interpersonal problems. Clinical psychologists are health care providers who attend to psychological health and its intersection with physical health at the individual, community, and societal levels. They ask questions such as how people act in certain situations, what motivates them to act the way they do, and what they need to

Christine H. Farber, PhD, is a clinical psychologist in private practice in South Windsor, Connecticut. She received her PhD in clinical psychology from Duquesne University and worked with Dr. Abrahamson at the Traumatic Stress Institute for about 6 years.

Daniel J. Abrahamson, PhD, is the assistant executive director for state advocacy with the Practice Directorate of the American Psychological Association. He received his PhD in clinical psychology from the State University of New York at Albany, after which he spent 20 years with the Traumatic Stress Institute in South Windsor, Connecticut, before moving to Washington, DC.

We are grateful to the scores of colleagues with whom we worked and collaborated while at the Traumatic Stress Institute. They very much shaped our shared vision of independent practice in psychology. We also thank Dr. Allison Ponce and Nan Hayes for their thoughtful comments on this chapter.

accomplish their goals or heal from emotional pain. Clinical psychologists seek to understand how behaviors, thoughts, and feelings are adaptive and how and when they are not; in an effort to promote health among the individuals and groups with whom they work, they are interested in factors that contribute to resilience.

In their work to assess, diagnose, and treat psychological issues, clinical psychologists seek to understand context. They look to the past of both individuals and groups to explicate how their experiences have shaped who they are. They examine the present family, social, and cultural influences that affect individuals and groups. And they adopt a future orientation, seeking to understand how goals, aspirations, and motivations influence behavior and mental processes. Clinical psychologists also need to understand the context of group identities and the meaning of such identities for a particular individual or group. For example, in an effort to make sense of the depression experienced by a young, Latino, male client who recently became disabled, one would need to explore what it means to be young, to be Latino, and to be male—in general, and for this specific individual. One would also need to understand what it is like to have a disability in this culture and what this individual's experience of living with disability has been like. In short, clinicians know that group identities help to construct people's experiences: Any individual is affected by multiple group identities, and an infinite variety of experiences exist within any one group.

As the discipline of psychology matures, clinical psychologists have become more and more attuned to context and culture, realizing that individuals exist not in isolation but, rather, in relationship to others and to their worlds. This development points to the excitement inherent within the discipline. As the existing body of psychological research and theory grows to incorporate more diverse perspectives, clinical psychology too will expand, leading to new ways of promoting health; fresh avenues for understanding growth, change, and resilience; and unique solutions to age-old problems.

In this chapter, we describe the practice of clinical psychology in a private setting in more detail. We discuss the range of activities that clinical psychologists conduct, the settings within which they practice, and the range of compensation they earn. We provide information about the preparation, motivation, and attributes needed for a successful career in this field and about the advantages and challenges of pursuing this line of work. We also describe a typical day in the life of a clinical psychologist. Our hope is that you will gain a richer knowledge of and appreciation for this discipline that we value so much.

Activities Pursued in Independent Clinical Practice

If one were to call to mind a picture of a clinical psychologist, one might imagine an individual sitting across from another individual in a private psychotherapy session. Psychotherapy is perhaps the most recognized of the many activities clinical psychologists in private practice pursue. They conduct psychotherapy with children, adolescents, and adults; couples and families; and groups of individuals who share a common concern. As psychotherapists, they work in collaboration with clients to address issues that are causing distress or interfering with well-being. Such issues include interpersonal difficulties; depression, anxiety, and other clinical entities; life changes such as marriage, a job loss, or a move; and day-to-day stress. Psychotherapy can also work toward increasing a client's self-knowledge and self-acceptance. A course of psychotherapy can be brief, ranging from several sessions to several months, or long-term, taking place over the course of several years.

Psychotherapy is not the only activity clinical psychologists pursue in independent practice. They can work as case managers, connecting clients to available resources and teaching psychological skills and coping strategies. They might work in conjunction with physicians and their patients to enhance treatment compliance, foster coping with medical illnesses, and improve overall well-being. They also work in communities, addressing issues such as violence, homelessness, and disasters that affect groups of people. Recently, specially trained psychologists in some states have been granted prescriptive authority for psychotropic medications.

Clinical psychologists in independent practice also conduct assessments. For example, a psychologist might conduct an assessment to determine the presence of brain damage in an individual. A school may refer a child to a psychologist who specializes in learning disabilities to assess whether the child has such a disability. A criminal attorney might ask a psychologist to assess a client in an effort to determine whether psychological issues may have had some bearing on the alleged crime or whether psychological treatment is warranted. In each of these activities, the clinician is asked to answer a specific question by performing an assessment of the person or persons being evaluated. The clinician then consults with the appropriate party about findings, opinions, and recommendations. An assessment often includes the administration and scoring of intelligence and psychological tests, the review of records or reports by other professionals, and meetings with the person who is being evaluated. Such assessments are like psychotherapy insofar as they involve an understanding of the context and dynamics that influence behaviors, feelings, and attitudes of individuals or groups. Many of the skills required by a psychotherapist also apply to conducting assessments. An assessment, however, is usually more circumscribed and short term. Furthermore, it can involve a third party and require a level of objectivity that psychotherapy does not. Both demands have implications that separate assessment from the work of psychotherapy.

Clinicians conduct consultations in which they share their knowledge about a specific case or issue. A couple might consult with a psychologist about whether and how their parenting style and relationship might be contributing to their child's difficulties in school. An organization might hire a psychologist to consult about the psychological needs of its staff. Psychologists also consult with one another to broaden their perspective and approach or to gain clarity about a case or an issue. Consultations often involve psychoeducation, some assessment work, and recommendations.

One of the advantages of working in independent practice is that it allows for a diversity of activities. Clinical psychologists who practice independently can also pursue activities that fall within other subdisciplines of the field. For example, they might teach and train, write, conduct research, and provide consultation to organizations. They also perform administrative work, such as tending to the business aspects of private and group practices: paying expenses, maintaining paperwork, and communicating with insurance companies and other third-party payers. Administrative work might also involve applying for and managing grant funds.

Clinical psychologists often engage in professional organization activities. Being involved with a professional organization such as the American Psychological Association allows one to gain support from colleagues, connect with ongoing study and research, and advance psychology through collective efforts to define the field and gain political, financial, and community resources. Clinicians might find themselves in the role of advocates for themselves, their clients, and the profession. For example, they might meet with politicians to fight for legislation that benefits the discipline of and the populations served by psychology; write editorials to the local paper to clarify concepts or correct misconceptions about issues to which psychological study is relevant; and provide public education through community talks, brochures, or press releases. For the authors, being involved in professional organizations and advocacy efforts has allowed us to give back to our profession and to society, to be a part of the collective force that shapes the discipline, and to experience renewed interest and passion in the field through our connection with colleagues.

Potential Work Settings

The variety of tasks psychologists pursue allows for a tremendous amount of diversity in day-to-day activities that are determined in part by the work setting. A survey of more than 1,600 recent doctorate recipients in psychology revealed that approximately 42% of clinical doctorates were employed full-time in direct human service settings (Wicherski & Kohout, 2005). Of these, approximately 5% were working in some type of independent practice, 15% were in other human services settings (including nursing homes and college counseling centers), and 14% were in hospital-based employment. Eight percent worked in managed care settings. The remaining 58% were employed in a variety of educational settings and in business and government workplaces.

According to the U.S. Department of Labor's Bureau of Labor Statistics (2004) *Online Occupational Outlook Handbook,* employment of clinical psychologists is expected to grow faster through 2012 compared to all occupations. This growth is expected to result from increased demand for psychological services in hospitals, social service agencies, mental health centers, schools, consulting firms, private companies, and substance abuse treatment centers.

As psychologists gain experience working in these various settings, a larger percentage over time gravitates toward some type of independent or private practice as their primary or secondary employment option. Most clinical psychologists in private practice spend some of their time providing individual, marital, family, or group psychotherapy within their private practice offices, offices that also may serve as a base from which to offer a variety of other services. For example, a clinical psychologist in private practice may serve as an expert witness in court, consult with management on personnel matters in a corporate setting, or teach at a local college or university. Independent practice also affords the flexibility to work part-time and to maintain flexible hours.

Financial Compensation

How much one earns as a clinical psychologist depends on the work setting and the number of years one has been in the field. Many clinical psychologists who have been in private practice for 20 or more years earn in excess of $100,000 per year. Those at the 75th percentile reported salaries of $130,000 (Pate, Frincke, & Kohout, 2005). At the other end of the continuum is the recent graduate who has taken a position at a university or college counseling center and who earns an average salary of $39,000.

A survey of 333 recent clinical psychology doctoral graduates working in a range of direct service settings found a mean annual salary of about $50,900 (Wicherski & Kohout, 2005). It is interesting to note that recent graduates in group private practices reported somewhat lower income levels, with a mean of $47,900. This discrepancy is likely due to the fact that it takes most clinical psychologists in private practice several years to establish a full caseload. Factors that can help clinical psychologists build up a busy private practice relatively quickly include having a specialization that is in high demand and serving as a provider on managed care panels that generate a high volume of referrals in their geographic region.

Clinical psychologists also work in state psychiatric hospitals, general hospitals, college counseling centers, and as university professors, to name just a few options. Each of these settings has its own income range and other benefits. For example, a clinical psychologist with 10 years of experience working for the state department of mental health might make a salary of $60,000, whereas a colleague with the same amount of experience might earn a total of $75,000 in private practice with no benefits. However, when the value of benefits such as health insurance, pension, and time off are added into the equation, the total compensation of the state employee might be closer to $80,000.

Flexibility and diversity of professional options have been emphasized as a hallmark of a career in clinical psychology, a factor that is relevant when considering the range of compensation available. For example, an individual who values the stability of working in an organizational setting with a regular salary and benefits can also start a part-time private practice to supplement income and create an opportunity to work independently as a therapist or consultant. If this psychologist had a steady flow of referrals and saw clients two evenings per week and on Saturday mornings, it would be possible to generate an additional $25,000 to $35,000 per year after expenses.

Clinical psychologists who obtain training and develop a high level of competence in a number of specialized areas can command high hourly fees. For example, a psychologist who is able to conduct evaluations for the courts and to serve as an expert witness in matters related to civil and criminal litigation can receive fees of $250 per hour or more. Consultants to private corporations sometimes receive fees as high as $5,000 per day. Although these examples reflect only a small proportion of clinical psychologists' fees, they do illustrate that the field offers rewarding income potential.

Of course, although income potential is one reason to consider a career option, it is important that it not be the primary reason for pursuing a career as a clinical psychologist. The work requires a high level of education and training and, as discussed in more detail later in this chapter, it can be personally demanding. Financial compensation alone will not sustain most people in a career that requires such a deep investment of time and energy. It is best to pursue this field on the basis of a budding passion for certain aspects of the work and a belief that the career possibilities will be motivating through the years of study and training.

Preparation Needed for a Career in Clinical Psychology

Pursuing a career in clinical psychology requires extensive study and training. You must first receive a doctorate and then become licensed in the state in which you plan to practice. In this section we will give you a brief overview of how you get from here to there.

The journey to a career as a clinical psychologist involves a number of stages. Many high school students begin with a single course in psychology. This early glimpse into the field leads some to select psychology as an undergraduate major. Others discover psychology when they take an introductory course early in their college studies. They might then major in psychology with either a vague or a clearly defined sense of what they want to do with the degree. Regardless of individual motivation, psychology continues to be an extremely popular undergraduate major, just behind business and education (Institute of Education Sciences, n.d.). Of course, although an undergraduate major in psychology can be very beneficial when applying to a clinical psychology doctoral program, it is not the only route. Given the competitive admission requirements for these programs, it is important to know before applying what prerequisite courses you need to have taken.

About 14% of undergraduate majors in psychology enroll in doctoral study, and about one third of that group pursue a degree in clinical psychology (National Science Foundation, n.d.). More than 2,000 doctoral degrees in clinical psychology are granted each year (Hoffer et al., 2005). It is thus a relatively difficult field to enter; only about 17.4% of applicants are accepted into doctoral programs in clinical psychology each year (American Psychological Association, 2005).

There are two major types of doctorate in clinical psychology, the PhD and the PsyD. Both degrees are structured to be completed in 5 years, although it is common for people to take 2 or 3 years longer to complete all of the program requirements. Although the two degrees have similar coursework and training requirements, students enrolled in PhD programs experience more emphasis on conducting original research as part of their academic training. Doctoral candidates in PsyD programs typically find a greater focus on applied aspects of clinical psychology, such as psychotherapy and mental health services administration. Additionally, all doctoral programs in clinical psychology include an internship component. The internship is usually a 1-year full-time commitment, although part-time internships are also available to a more limited degree. Because of the competitive nature of internship programs, it is common for students to move to another state for this part of their training.

Upon completion of the doctoral degree in clinical psychology, individuals are ready to start accumulating postdoctoral work experience. This experience is a requirement for licensure as a psychologist in almost every state. Each state has its own criteria for the postdoctoral experience. Typically, it involves a year of full-time supervised employment in an organized mental health setting that employs psychologists. If you know which state you plan to settle and start your career in, it would be a good idea to check on the postdoctoral requirements for licensure in that state before accumulating your postdoctoral hours. To be licensed in some states, your postdoctoral setting need employ only one psychologist on staff, whereas another state may require at least two psychologists on staff. The licensing process in most states is regulated by the state's department of public health or its equivalent. The American Psychological Association recently adopted a policy statement recommending the equivalent of 2 years of full-time training ("a sequential, organized, supervised professional experience") that can be completed before or after the doctoral degree is granted (American Psychological Association, 2006, p. 53). Over time, this recommendation may change requirements related to postdoctoral training, which is another reason for checking the most current requirements in your state before you begin accumulating hours. The licensing process will also go more easily if you attend a doctoral program that is accredited by the American Psychological Association and one of the six regional educational accrediting bodies in the United States.

After completing all training requirements and meeting a state's credential review, an aspiring clinical psychologist is ready to take the licensing examination. All states require that one pass a national examination, and many also include a state-specific component. Mobility from one state to another has been simplified in recent years through licensure portability mechanisms such as the Certificate of Professional Qualification in Psychology (CPQ) granted by the Association of State and Provincial Psychology Boards (ASPPB). ASPPB issues the CPQ to psychologists licensed in the United States and Canada who meet standards of educational preparation, supervised experience, and examination performance and who have practiced a minimum of 5 years and have no history of disciplinary action (ASPPB, n.d.). If a licensed psychologist then moves to another state that accepts the CPQ, he or she will not have to go through the complete credentialing process again. This transferability can be extremely beneficial in those states that have idiosyncratic credentialing requirements.

Preparation for the career continues even after you have begun working. Psychology is a broad and ever-evolving field. Ethical practice requires one to keep up with developments in the field by reading research journals, attending workshops and conferences, and collaborating with colleagues. In addition, some aspects of clinical psychology in a private practice setting involve on-the-job training. For example, most graduate programs have not offered extensive coursework in business management, yet working in private practice is tantamount to owning your own business. Management, financial, and more general administrative skills are often required to run a practice. Many psychologists receive this training on the job, learning from their own successes and failures. Professional associations are beginning to pay attention to this aspect of private practice preparedness, providing resources, tips, and strategies for successful business management. Some doctoral programs have also incorporated a business-related course or workshop into their training programs. Pursuing opportunities within and outside of the field to supplement your training is one way to remain prepared for a long-term career in the field.

Reasons for Choosing a Career in Clinical Psychology

Individuals choose to enter the field of clinical psychology for a variety of reasons. Many cite wanting to help others as a primary reason for choosing this career. Some find that their family histories and dynamics played a role in steering their career path. For example, if you have a relationship with a younger sibling who needs a lot of emotional support, or if you play another helping role within your family, you may have developed intuition, counseling skills, or a desire to help others. If you were raised in a family that valued kindness and social responsibility, you may find that you have an interest in the human service professions, including clinical psychology. Likewise, a lack of family support or a traumatic childhood might also lead toward an interest in helping others to heal from past hurts.

Exposure to the career is another influential factor in career choice. Whether it is personal experience with a clinical psychologist; a high school or undergraduate course in clinical psychology; or the example of television personalities such as Bob Newhart, Frasier, or Dr. Phil, most individuals who enter the field have had prior exposure to some aspect of clinical psychology. As you decide whether this is a career that you would like to pursue, it may help to know that clinical psychology is much broader than one's initial exposure is likely to indicate and often very different from how the practice is portrayed in the media. Reading introductory texts such as this one, exploring the Web site of the American Psychological Association, and interviewing a practicing clinical psychologist are all ways to gain a broader perspective on what clinical psychology has to offer.

Recognizing that one's own skills and talents lend themselves to clinical work may also steer an individual toward such a career. Individuals with good listening skills, critical thinking skills, problem-solving abilities, and a knack for negotiating with others might find themselves drawn to the discipline as a place to develop, enhance, and use those skills and talents.

In addition to these personal reasons, individuals choose this career for reasons related to the nature of the day-to-day activities of a clinical psychologist. Both the range of opportunities and the variety of activities available to clinical psychologists allow for a great deal of flexibility and diversity within this career. We both are grateful for the opportunities we have had to combine psychotherapy with administrative work, writing, and teaching. We are also grateful for the professional auton-omy that our work permits. We have flexibility in the hours we set for ourselves and in the balance of activities that define our jobs. This flexibility means that our jobs are more likely to fit with who we are as people.

Individuals also choose this career path because the theory, re-search, and other intellectual aspects of the discipline fascinate them. Clinical psychology is a field that operates according to the Boulder model, which means that it combines research, theory, and practice (Benjamin & Baker, 2000). One might choose to focus primarily on one of these areas, but the nature of the field is such that each area contains the others within it. Clinical practice, for example, draws heavily on research and theory and, in turn, influences them. This dialectic or back-and-forth relationship among research, theory, and practice generates intellectual excitement and opportunities for contin-ued learning and discovery throughout one's career, keeping the work fresh and thereby reducing the risk for burnout.

Attributes That Contribute to Success in the Field

Although there is no formula for a specific mix of traits needed to succeed as a clinical psychologist, there are a variety of attributes that can help foster professional success and growth. A strong skill set can help you develop a career in clinical psychology. One of the main staples of this skill set is the ability to problem solve. Problem-solving abilities entail a dual vision, meaning that you must keep an eye on the big picture and the details at once. It is a skill that involves gathering data and being able to think about options based on the information you have at your disposal, and it can be enhanced by collaboration with others. Whether you are performing psychotherapy, clinical as-sessment, consultation, or administrative work, your ability to problem solve will serve you well in this profession.

Related to problem-solving abilities are critical thinking skills. Criti-cal thinking helps one to recognize the complexity of a given issue, the interpersonal and contextual factors at play, and the ways in which these factors are interrelated. As experts in human behavior, psy-chologists should be able to think critically about the complexity of interpersonal and intrapersonal dynamics and to conceptualize such dynamics into a meaningful whole.

Negotiation and diplomacy skills are assets for clinicians as well. Perhaps the most obvious context in which negotiation skills come in handy is in couples, family, or group work, where the clinician must recognize and respond to the needs of multiple individuals. Being able to negotiate such needs while remaining respectful of all individuals can be challenging, effective, and rewarding. Negotiation is also an important aspect of conducting individual psychotherapy, whether in helping an individual to resolve internal conflicts or negotiating aspects of the therapy relationship between therapist and client. Likewise, case management, assessments, consultations, and personnel administration all require sensitivity to conflicting needs among individuals or groups of people.

Business aptitude can be an advantage to the person who pursues a career in clinical private practice. As mentioned previously, private practice often means being self-employed, which entails attention to financial, managerial, and administrative details. Financial skills include understanding budgets and cash flow and are often enhanced by familiarity with database software programs that allow one to track and organize one's professional finances. Managerial skills include managing employees and working with and within organizations. Psychologists in private practice may be vulnerable to viewing managerial and personnel matters as an extension of their clinical or supervisory work, when in fact effective management requires a different mindset (J. Mehm, personal communication, April 16, 2006). Other, administrative skills that can help one succeed in clinical practice include organization, problem solving, and the ability to multitask.

Basic listening and empathy skills are among the attributes that foster success in the field. Many of the activities that characterize clinical private practice entail connection with others who are experiencing a great deal of vulnerability. These connections offer comfort and healing, in part because psychologists are able to appreciate and respect what they are hearing while acknowledging that they can never fully understand another's experience.

Although sometimes touted as abilities that come naturally, these skills can be enhanced, developed, and nurtured throughout one's training and career. This is the value of doctoral training. During your graduate work, you will not only learn the content of clinical psychology by studying specific theories and approaches to the discipline but also develop the capacity to think critically and conceptually about human behavior, to solve problems in collaboration with others, to actively listen with empathy, and to negotiate challenging conflicts.

You may find, as well, that strategies such as self-knowledge, collegial support, and a sense of humor can enhance your success in the profession. These strategies can be developed and nurtured throughout your training and career and can be thought of as ongoing commitments that become part of a professional development plan for long-term success.

Knowing yourself—through psychotherapy, journaling, and clinical supervision, for example—helps you acknowledge limits, take responsibility for dynamics you introduce into relationships, and find ways to meet your own needs so that they do not interfere with your clinical work. Seeking out social and collegial support and good mentors is one way to meet the needs that arise from challenging clinical work. Supportive connections can be an antidote to burnout. The ability to allow a place for humor within the work setting is also an important long-term strategy for success in the field. One of the gifts of humor is that it offers perspective, helping you (and your clients) to take a step back from whatever feels irritating or overwhelming so that a new perspective can open up.

Humility, comfort with one's own vulnerability, and tolerance for the unknown are also assets within this profession. Psychology, especially for the clinician in private practice, is an art as much as it is a science. As an art, the practice of clinical psychology is inexact and leaves room for interpretation, creativity, and intuitive responses. This aspect can be anxiety provoking as well as exciting, and the individual who can be humble in the midst of not knowing is likely to experience more comfort than one who cannot. Likewise, clinical practice requires confrontation with your own vulnerability. Developing strategies that help you to achieve comfort in the face of vulnerability will foster your growth and success in the field and will increase your capacity to have empathy for your clients and for yourself. Finally, attention to self-care and maintenance of balance between the personal and professional realms and within the professional realm are key to long-term success in the field.

Advantages and Disadvantages of Pursuing Independent Clinical Practice

As with any career, clinical psychology has its advantages and challenges. Some of the advantages have been mentioned previously and include the diversity of activities, flexibility in one's schedule, and potential autonomy in the workplace. Clinical psychology is an intellectually rich field, providing constant opportunities for learning. Working with a wide range of individuals, including clients and other professionals, can be a benefit of the career as well. Other advantages include connection with oneself and the discovery of meaning in one's work and life. It is ironic that many aspects of the career can be thought of as both advantages and disadvantages.

Clinical work can be emotionally challenging; interviewing an incarcerated individual for a forensic evaluation, providing individual psychotherapy, or heading up a domestic violence program all can take an emotional toll. Hearing about difficult stories and witnessing the suffering of others produce changes to one's sense of self, sense of meaning, and ways of viewing the world. Such changes can be experienced as highly valued benefits of the career and/or as unwanted challenges. *Burnout* is the experience of emotional exhaustion, disconnection from one's clients, and lack of a sense of competence or success, all of which can result from work in the helping professions over time (Maslach, Jackson, & Leiter, 1996). A related term, *vicarious traumatization,* refers to the negative transformation in the self of the helper that results from engaging with clients who are survivors of trauma and wanting to help them (McCann & Pearlman, 1990). Implicit in this concept is a sense of hope: The pain one experiences, like that of one's clients, can be transformed, leading to deeper meaning and enhanced connection with oneself and others.

One way of transforming the pain that can accompany clinical work is through relationships with supportive colleagues. Connection with colleagues who do similar work allows one to feel less alone and to transform distress through sharing, meaning making, understanding, and humor (Pearlman & Saakvitne, 1995). We both are clinical psychologists who have worked at the Traumatic Stress Institute/Center for Adult & Adolescent Psychotherapy (TSI), an organization cofounded by the second author in 1986. During our years at TSI, we dedicated several hours per week to staff meetings, which became a space for connections to develop and grow. One of these hours was dedicated to sharing our feelings about the work. As a result of this type of sharing and mutual support, staff members developed valued relationships with one another.

Connections with clients, too, can bring about unexpected gifts, such as increased compassion and a deepened sense of meaning in one's own life. Witnessing the suffering of others brings with it the witnessing of others' resilience and resourcefulness. One glimpses a picture of suffering and resilience, pain and kindness. Connections with clients offer pain, healing, and inspiration—sometimes all at once.

In addition to the challenges associated with burnout, vicarious traumatization, and the emotional toll of the work, other aspects of a career in clinical psychology are challenging, and you should consider them before embarking on such a career. Working in clinical psychology generally requires about 6 to 8 years of coursework and training after college. An internship follows the coursework, which is then followed by a postdoctoral position and a challenging licensing exam. It is important to prepare for the necessary, long-term training by having a financial and personal plan that can support it. This might entail taking out student loans or moving across the country to be placed at an internship site. These are not insurmountable challenges, but you should appropriately consider them when deciding on a career in psychology.

Other challenges involve the day-to-day activities and level of involvement in one's job. Working with clients on a daily basis, which most clinicians in private practice do to some degree, brings with it a great deal of responsibility and requires consistent attention to clients' welfare and the ethical responsibilities inherent in this task. Most clinicians need to develop strategies over time for establishing boundaries between their professional and personal life. This is difficult to do when one's professional activities affect who one is on a personal level.

Independent clinical practice is a career that brings challenges as well as great benefits. It is a field that requires extensive preparation and ongoing training. Working with clients and their clinical material will affect you, and ethical practice requires attending to your own experience. At times, this career will be difficult and perhaps even painful. At other times, your work will engender an attitude of gratitude and joy. Awareness of both sides of the coin will help you take care of yourself and grow as an individual and as a professional.

A Typical Day in the Life of a Clinician in Independent Practice

Throughout this chapter, we have discussed the career paths of clinical psychologists in independent practice. In doing so, we have interwoven statements and reflections about our work in this field. In our years working at the Traumatic Stress Institute, our primary area of focus was working with individuals who had experienced psychological trauma to restore meaning and wholeness to their lives. One of our goals at TSI was to pay special attention to the impact of clinical work on the clinician, a focus that allowed us to support each other in our mission to provide clinical services of the highest quality. In concluding this chapter, we offer a description of a typical day in the life of the primary author to bring to life what we have discussed thus far; we remind readers that there are infinite possibilities regarding practice within this field.

It is 10:30 a.m., and I have just arrived at work. I notice that Dan (the second author) is out of the office and then remember that he is fulfilling his contractual work with the Connecticut Psychological Association (CPA), as he does every Wednesday morning. On the basis of my own experience with CPA, I imagine that Dan is having a lot of fun as he works with the staff of CPA to develop a strategic plan for the organization, puts the final touches on the most recent newsletter, and addresses legislative issues that require the association's attention. The fact that Dan's office light is on suggests that he was in earlier that morning, probably meeting with a client or two for psychotherapy before heading out to CPA. Meanwhile, I check my voice mail and e-mail before meeting with my first psychotherapy client at 11:00 a.m.

At 12:00 p.m. I knock on the door of my colleague to ask if she has some time to consult with me about a client. The consistent presence of colleagues who offer support and consultation, as well as opportunities for learning and laughter, is what I value most in my practice. My colleague and I are able to talk for 20 minutes, and the consultation provides me with very useful information about how I am relating with this psychotherapy client. It is not surprising that I learn something about myself that strengthens my clinical work.

At 2:00 p.m., our nine clinical psychologists and two administrative staff members gather for a staff meeting, which doesn't really get off the ground until about 2:15 p.m., as individuals slowly trickle in with their lunch in hand. Someone has brought in cookies for the rest of us, a gesture that is always appreciated. As the staff meeting gets under way, I remember that I have a question about a forensic referral that I want to raise with my colleagues in an effort to formulate an informed answer. Another colleague requests that we brainstorm ideas for a community project that he is currently undertaking. Someone else shares information about a textbook that she has been using to teach her course in Diversity and Psychology. And Dan recounts his experience in giving a television interview earlier this week: The local program was featuring a show about psychological trauma in the wake of natural disasters.

A call comes in during the meeting for one of our colleagues. It is a psychiatrist with whom she has been playing phone tag for some time, and so she excuses herself to take the call. It is not unusual for a staff member to be in and out of the staff meeting, given how busy our schedules are and how difficult it can be to reach other mental health professionals by phone. It would be unusual for this to happen, although, in the next meeting, which is dedicated to our feelings about the work. For 1 hour, we sit together with virtually no interruptions in an effort to support one another, to laugh or cry, and to explore what we might not otherwise have an opportunity to acknowledge. It is one of our most valued times of the week, and we leave feeling lighter and more connected, just in time to meet with our late-afternoon and evening clients.

Between sessions with clients, we respond to e-mails related to our professional affiliations, take phone calls from individuals who need help locating resources, and prepare lectures for upcoming classes or workshops. Dan leaves at 6:00 p.m. after his last session of the day. I wish him well, knowing that he will be testifying as an expert witness in a case the following day. I leave about an hour later, making sure to bring the brochures I need for the workshop I will conduct the next morning. As I walk to my car, I find myself smiling, reflecting on the amazing if sometimes challenging work we do.

References

American Psychological Association. (2005). *Graduate study in psychology*. Washington, DC: Author.

American Psychological Association. (2006). *Report of the Board of Directors Work Group on the Recommendations of the Commission on Education and Training Leading to Licensure in Psychology* (Policy statement approved by the APA Council of Representatives). Washington, DC: Author.

Association of State and Provincial Psychology Boards. (n.d.). *What is the CPQ?* Retrieved January 13, 2005, from http://www.asppb.org/mobility/cpq/what.aspx

Benjamin, L. T., & Baker, D. B. (2000). The affirmation of the scientist–practitioner: A look back at Boulder. *American Psychologist, 55*(2), 241–247.

Bureau of Labor Statistics, U.S. Department of Labor. (2004, May 14). Psychologists. In *Occupational outlook handbook, 2004–05 edition*. Retrieved February 1, 2005, from http://www.bls.gov/oco/ocos056.htm

Hoffer, T. B., Welch, V., Jr., Williams, K., Hess, M., Webber, K., Lisek, B., et al. (2005). *Doctorate recipients from United States universities: Summary report 2004*. Chicago: National Opinion Research Center.

Maslach, C., Jackson, S. E., & Leiter, M. (1996). *Maslach Burnout Inventory manual* (3rd ed.). Palo Alto, CA: Consulting Psychologists Press.

McCann, I. L., & Pearlman, L. A. (1990). Vicarious traumatization: The emotional costs of working with survivors. *The Advisor: Newsletter of the American Professional Society on the Abuse of Children, 3*(4), 34.

National Center for Education Statistics. (n.d.). *Fast facts.* Retrieved June 26, 2006, from http://nces.ed.gov/fastfacts/display.asp?id=37

National Science Foundation. (n.d.). *Detailed statistical tables.* Retrieved June 26, 2006, from http://www.nsf.gov/statistics/nsf05310/pdf/tables.pdf

Pate, W. E., Frincke, J. L., & Kohout, J. L. (2005). *Salaries in psychology 2003.* Washington, DC: American Psychological Association.

Pearlman, L. A., & Saakvitne, K. W. (1995). *Trauma and the therapist.* New York: Norton.

Wicherski, M., & Kohout, J. (2005). *2003 doctorate employment survey.* Washington, DC: Author.

Jane Annunziata and Marc Nemiroff

Careers in Child Clinical Psychology 7

A *child clinical psychologist* is a clinical psychologist who specializes in work with children in a variety of settings. As you probably already know from other chapters in this book, a clinical psychologist has specific training and experience in doing psychotherapy with people who have a full range of emotional problems. A child clinical psychologist works with children, their parents, and sometimes their whole families to handle the variety of developmental and emotional problems that children may have. Most child clinical psychologists are also trained in psychotherapy with adults. In fact,

Jane Annunziata, PsyD, is a clinical psychologist with a private practice specializing in children and families in McLean, Virginia. She has taught at the University of Bergen (Norway), Mary Washington College, and George Mason University. As a writer, she has contributed parent guidance sections to children's books on such topics as shyness, parental depression, ambivalence, touching and boundaries, and a new baby in the family.

Marc Nemiroff, PhD, is cochair of the Infant/Young Child Mental Health program at the Washington School of Psychiatry and maintains a private practice in Potomac, Maryland. He has written and presented papers on various topics related to the mental health issues of children. He is an affiliate member of the Baltimore–Washington Society for Psychoanalysis and a fellow of the American Orthopsychiatric Association.

Dr. Nemiroff and Dr. Annunziata are the authors of *Sex and Babies: First Facts; A Child's First Book About Play Therapy; Help Is On the Way: A Child's Book About ADD;* and *Why Am I an Only Child?*

we find that many of the best adult psychotherapists have specific training in working with children. Most adult patients have difficulties stemming from childhood, and child clinical training enhances the ability of the therapist to fully understand the adult patient's childhood experience.

Child clinical psychologists also have specialized training and expertise in psychodiagnostic assessment of children using both clinical and developmentally based instruments. Such assessment is often referred to as "psychological testing." Although clinicians in other disciplines are trained in psychotherapy, only psychologists are trained and authorized to administer psychological tests.

Some child clinical psychologists pursue academic careers. Many of those who work in an academic setting also engage in research specifically related to child psychology. These psychologists might teach and do research in areas such as child development, behavior problems of childhood, treatment outcomes, and child psychopathology. Child clinical psychologists also engage in professional writing and consultation.

The field of child clinical psychology is really quite broad and offers important and diverse opportunities that are both intellectually stimulating and personally rewarding. In essence, child clinical psychologists devote themselves to the improvement of children's lives. One of the pleasures of the field is the variety of ways to help bring about this improvement.

What Do Child Clinical Psychologists Do?

Child clinical psychologists engage in a variety of therapies. They assess children using diagnostic clinical evaluations such as playroom interviews and formal psychological testing instruments. They also may choose to focus their careers on teaching, conducting research, and providing consultation to a variety of agencies involved directly in the provision of services to children. Many child clinical psychologists choose to engage in several of these activities to provide themselves with a varied and stimulating career.

Children most often come to a child clinical psychologist with problems such as anxiety, phobias, depression, difficulty with peer relationships, acting-out behaviors at home or school, academic underachievement, and parent–child attachment problems. Many child clinical psychologists develop an interest in particular populations and specialize in their treatment. For example, some are interested in adoption, children with pervasive developmental disorders, adolescents, very young children, children with attention-deficit disorders, or children with alcoholic parents.

CHILD THERAPIES

There are numerous treatment modalities for children. Play therapy is a common form of treatment with younger children, who naturally express themselves through their play. Play is the preferred language of childhood. Play therapy is most typically used with children between the ages of 2 and 10. Older children can be engaged in a combination of talk therapy with adjunctive "play" activities such as crafts, games (e.g., chess), or self-expression through art. The basic assumption of play therapy is that the children's symptoms are really only surface manifestations of underlying conflicts that need to be understood to bring about lasting improvement. The play therapy approach to treatment also entails active, ongoing child guidance sessions with parents. The goal of such sessions is to help the parents better understand and learn new ways of responding to their child. Often the child clinical psychologist is in contact with the child's school to facilitate school adjustment and to receive information regarding the child's school functioning.

Dyadic therapy is a variation of play therapy. It is often used in the treatment of parent–child attachment problems. Usually the parent and child play together in the presence of the child clinical psychologist, who helps facilitate an improved relationship between the two. The psychologist may join in the play as a way of directly supporting stronger attachment, improving communication, and encouraging better mutual reading of each others' cues. The psychologist may provide demonstrations, interpret the interactions, and directly teach the parent how to play with the child at the child's developmental level.

In family therapy, all members of the family are treated together. Family therapy is based on the belief that problems in a family often result from the patterns of interactions among its members. In other words, family problems are not the responsibility of just one person; problematic behaviors by an individual family member are seen as a form of communication that needs to be understood on a family level before change is possible. Family therapy provides family members with an opportunity to learn new and effective ways to communicate and relate to each other. Some child clinical psychologists use "flexible family therapy," in which various family members are seen in different combinations. For example, if sibling rivalry has become the most obvious problem, the therapist may see just the brothers and sisters for several sessions before reuniting the whole family in their ongoing treatment.

In group therapy, children are seen together to help them learn and receive feedback about their problems and ways to handle them from peers and from the child clinical psychologist. Child clinical psychologists usually receive specific training in the theory and practice of group psychotherapy with children. In this modality, usually six to eight children of approximately the same age are seen together, occasionally by two cotherapists. The children are usually preselected for types of problems, such as children experiencing a parental divorce, children with serious peer relationship problems, or children who are developmentally delayed in similar ways. Group therapy can be a powerful form of treatment for children who are uncomfortable in an individual setting, who need feedback directly from peers under the guidance of the therapist, or who need to understand how they affect other children. Sometimes children respond to treatment better in the presence of other children.

Behavior therapy focuses specifically on the child's problematic behavior. The psychologist intervenes by providing parents and teachers with systematized reinforcement strategies to help children develop alternative and constructive, more appropriate behaviors. Specific problems a behavior therapist might address include social inhibition, acting-out behaviors, or poor work habits. Child clinical psychologists who use behavior therapy techniques seek to understand the function of problem behaviors so that they can target those behaviors for modification. Behavior therapists might also focus on the child's cognitions, or faulty ideas that contribute to behavioral or social problems.

Child clinical psychologists who are behavior therapists often work actively with parents to teach them methods of reinforcing positive behaviors, such as sticker charts or praise, and ways to help their child rethink negative thought patterns and engage in positive self-talk. Parents are also taught appropriate responses to their child's negative behaviors, such as the use of logical consequences, time-outs, and ignoring. Behavior therapists tend to be actively involved with the child's classroom teacher so that the child's problem behaviors at school are addressed. In addition to facilitating better school adjustment, working with the school also ensures consistency between the home and school environments—that is, that teachers and parents are both on the same page in addressing the child's behavior problems.

TESTING

In addition to providing psychotherapy for children, child clinical psychologists also perform psychological testing evaluations (often called "psychodiagnostic evaluations"). Psychological testing of children (and adults) is the exclusive domain of psychologists. Psychological testing of children involves the use of a series of assessment instruments designed to evaluate intellectual and social–emotional functioning. Testing provides information that cannot be obtained through face-to-face interviews with children or parents. It is, in its way, an X-ray into a child's emotional inner world and cognitive functioning.

The testing instruments include intelligence scales to determine intelligence quotient, cognitive strengths and weaknesses, and potential problems in learning, including formal learning disabilities and emotional factors that may be affecting a child's learning. Many projective instruments, such as the Rorschach inkblot technique, are also included in the child clinical psychologist's battery of tests. Projective assessment techniques yield information about the child's unconscious functioning, personality, areas of underlying conflict, and social and emotional strengths and vulnerabilities. Often psychopathology is revealed on projective instruments rather than on cognitive tests.

Other psychologists, such as school psychologists and neuropsychologists, engage in psychological testing and evaluate similar aspects of a child's functioning. However, it is the child clinical psychologist who focuses on psychopathology and the complexities of the inner emotional life of the child.

OTHER ACTIVITIES

In addition to engaging in psychotherapy and psychological testing, many child clinical psychologists use their training in other ways. They might teach child-related courses, such as child psychopathology and child development, in a college or graduate school setting. They might perform research on topics pertinent to childhood, such as the effects of day care on development, the effects of TV violence, attention deficit disorder, or treatment outcomes. Child clinical psychologists may also work as consultants to agencies that provide services to children other than psychotherapy, such as school systems, preschools, day care centers, and pediatric departments in hospitals. Child clinical psychologists may engage in several of these activities simultaneously; they might, for example, practice psychotherapy and also do research and consultation.

Some child clinical psychologists enjoy professional writing as a component of their careers. They write journal articles and books reporting on their research. Child clinical psychologists also write textbooks pertaining to psychopathology in children, assessment and treatment, psychodiagnostic testing, and child development. They may write books or journal articles on specific child clinical populations, such as those with Asperger syndrome, attention deficit disorders, reactive attachment disorders, or childhood depression. Or they may focus on the purely theoretical aspects of child development, assessment, and treatment in their writing.

Child clinical psychologists are also qualified to write books for the public, particularly for parents. They write parenting books on such topics as helping a child adjust to a new baby in the family, adoption, or raising a child with a specific disorder. They also write general parenting books that guide parents through the various developmental stages. These books are sometimes written as a series that discusses what children are like and what they need from their parents at different ages. Parents look to such books to help them successfully raise a well-adjusted and well-behaved child. Lastly, child clinical psychologists (such as the authors of this chapter) write bibliotherapy books for children. Bibliotherapy books focus on normative aspects of child development such as dealing with bullies, adjusting to a new baby, being an only child, being adopted, or experiencing a death in the family. They may also address topics of concern for children and their parents, including helping a child cope with learning disabilities, attention deficit disorders, anxiety, depression, and anger. Some bibliotherapy books are even more specific and deal with such topics as having a parent with a major illness or having an alcoholic parent. Many bibliotherapy books include a separate section for parents in which the authors explain the book's topic from a psychological perspective and provide specific parental guidance on the issue or problem discussed in the book.

Many child clinical psychologists serve as consultants in a variety of settings. They may work with the staffs of child treatment centers, or they may provide clinical case consultation to other individuals in the field on an individual or group basis. Child clinical psychologists also serve as consultants to public and private preschools and elementary and secondary schools. They might work directly with teachers concerning specific children, classroom issues, or group dynamics, or they may consult with an admissions office regarding a child's developmental level and appropriate placement. They are often asked to provide child-related presentations to parent groups at schools, churches, and other organizations. These presentations may cover a wide array of topics, including ways to build self-esteem in children, discipline issues, early sex education, and adoption.

Child clinical psychologists may also consult with the media on a variety of topics of concern to children and their parents. These topics may be of general interest to parents or a specific response to a crisis in the community or the world—for example, a series of community abductions or the terrorist attacks of September 11, 2001. Sometimes an unusual opportunity for consultation may arise. For example, a child clinical psychologist might be asked by a novelist to review the writer's portrayal of a child character for the accuracy of the depiction.

Work Settings

One of the benefits of being a child clinical psychologist is the variety of settings in which one can use one's training and skills. Most child clinical psychologists do at least some amount of direct clinical service, including psychotherapy and psychological testing. When most people think about child clinical psychology as a career, they picture having a private practice. Although this is certainly the most common setting in which child clinical psychologists work, it is far from the only one. There are also rewarding and fascinating opportunities for clinical work in public mental health centers, short- and long-term psychiatric inpatient treatment facilities, juvenile detention and other court-related facilities, and various medical settings.

A private practitioner may have a solo practice or work independently within a group setting. Solo practitioners enjoy the independence and flexibility that come with having one's own office. Other child clinical psychologists enjoy the diversity of a group practice, where they have the opportunity to work with psychiatrists, social workers, and adult as well as child clinical psychologists. They enjoy the professional contact with colleagues and the opportunity for sharing and discussing clinical cases.

Public mental health settings are another common venue for child clinical psychologists. In community mental health centers (CMHCs), for example, they provide direct clinical service to children and parents, supervision, psychological testing, and consultation to community agencies. Many child clinical psychologists enjoy the diversity of the patient population seen in public settings and feel a commitment to serve families who otherwise could not afford mental health services. They also enjoy the fast-paced work environment that most CMHCs provide and the opportunity to be surrounded by a large group of colleagues.

Inpatient treatment facilities (psychiatric hospitals) provide support, safety, and short-term intensive treatment to patients who are severely emotionally disturbed, at high risk of self-harm, or in an acute psychological crisis. One of the reasons to hospitalize a child is so that he or she and the family can receive multiple modalities of treatment and psychopharmacological intervention quickly and concurrently to meet the urgency of their situation. Children are also admitted to an inpatient facility for observation and extended diagnostic evaluation in a controlled environment.

Forensic-related work includes child custody evaluations (which involve separate assessments of each parent, each child, and each child together with each parent), ability-to-parent assessments, forensic psychological evaluations of juvenile offenders, and court testimony in criminal and domestic proceedings. Child clinical psychologists may have the opportunity to provide psychotherapy with these populations.

Medical settings offer another venue for practice. A child clinical psychologist may work in a pediatrician's office, where he or she functions as a consultant to parents regarding developmental and social–emotional concerns about their children. Within that setting, the child clinical psychologist might see the child directly, in addition to the parents, to determine possible treatment needs and to facilitate appropriate referrals. Some child clinical psychologists work in the pediatrics department of a general medical center or a specialized hospital department such as pediatric oncology. There they can work directly with children with a range of medical problems, from anxiety about a routine tonsillectomy to the challenges of battling cancer. The treatment performed in this setting is necessarily short-term, focused therapy centered on the medical issue. Child clinical psychologists also do testing for emotional readiness for difficult medical interventions, provide differential diagnoses (i.e., rule out an emotional basis for an apparent physical symptom, assess level of depression and anxiety while undergoing difficult treatments), consult with medical staff regarding the psychological issues of hospitalized children of differing ages, and do consultative and supportive work with parents. Work with parents may be as simple as helping them talk with their child about an impending surgical intervention or as complex as working with parents whose child is dying.

Many child clinical psychologists work in academic settings. They seek an academic environment because it enables them to teach, do research, write, and mentor students who are interested in a career in psychology. Many child clinical psychologists particularly value the mentoring role. Of course, child clinical psychologists in academic settings may also have a private practice.

Child clinical psychologists teach at both the undergraduate and the graduate levels. They may teach such topics as child psychotherapy, child development, child psychopathology, psychodiagnostic assessment and testing, and other related courses. In undergraduate courses, they may provide an introduction to child psychopathology and child development and a broad survey of relevant child-related issues. Undergraduate coursework is not intended to train students to be child clinical psychologists; rather, it provides the building blocks for graduate work in clinical psychology to students who want to become child clinicians. Child clinical psychologists are also employed in graduate school settings, providing formal training to students who seek to function autonomously as child clinical psychologists.

Academic settings also afford an excellent venue for performing research in areas related to children. Child clinical psychologists who work in academic settings are formally encouraged to engage in research projects relevant to their specific interests. Psychology students are often helpful in assisting their professors in conducting their research. This is not only a mutually beneficial arrangement but also a way in which professors can actively mentor students who are particularly interested in child clinical research. Participation in research provides students with an invaluable opportunity to learn about designing, conducting, and analyzing clinical research. They also learn the essential tools for differentiating well-designed studies from poor ones. Unfortunately both are reported in the literature.

Child clinical psychologists also engage in research in nonacademic settings. Child-oriented nonprofit organizations, government agencies, and public interest and social policy groups are examples of such settings. Child clinical psychologists might study such issues as the effects of different types of day care on children's social, emotional, and academic development; factors that affect the development of self-esteem in children; effectiveness of different types of treatment; effectiveness of different forms of discipline; effects of exposure to violence in the media; development of attachment disorders; and effects of parental trauma, substance abuse, depression, and domestic violence on children's psychological and social functioning.

Academic and Clinical Preparation

Training to become a child clinical psychologist requires 3 years of formal graduate-level academic preparation (coursework), successful completion of comprehensive examinations, practicum (externship) placements, a full-time year-long clinical internship, and the writing and defense of a doctoral dissertation.

ACADEMIC PREPARATION

In most states, to call yourself a "clinical psychologist," it is necessary to have a PhD or PsyD in psychology, most commonly in clinical psychology. Although it is possible to have a specific degree in child clinical psychology, most child clinical psychologists have a clinical psychology doctorate with specialized training in psychotherapy and assessment with children and their families. Some clinical psychologists have a doctorate in another area of psychology and then go on for specialized training in the clinical field. In particular, there are child clinical psychologists whose original doctoral degree in psychology was in human development, child development, or personality development. After they received their degree, they realized that they were most interested in working clinically with children, and they pursued formal specialized training in the assessment and treatment of children.

Academic courses cover the entire age range from infancy through late adolescence and usually include core areas such as child development and theory, child psychopathology, intellectual and cognitive assessment, personality assessment, and theories and techniques of psychotherapy with children and their parents. Academic training also includes courses about the child's role in the family system. It is important to understand the child's social and emotional development within the context of the family, as well as the family dynamics that have an impact on the child.

The academic culmination of clinical psychology training is the completion of a doctoral dissertation. In most programs, this requires a research study, although a comprehensive clinical dissertation is sometimes substituted. The doctoral dissertation is an intensive, usually lengthy, closely mentored project, and the student must defend his or her work before a number of faculty members.

CLINICAL PREPARATION

Clinical training includes both the practical experience (practicum) undertaken concurrent with the first 3 academic years (or sometimes just the 2nd and 3rd years) and a clinical internship after the successful completion of formal coursework, practicum placements, and comprehensive academic examinations. Practicum placements provide students with a variety of supervised clinical experiences, usually with both children and adults. Students can be placed in many different settings, including CMHCs, hospitals (both medical and psychiatric), therapeutic nurseries, geriatric treatment settings, prisons, university counseling centers, and a variety of public and private treatment-focused agencies. Practicum placements are usually about 20 hours per week and may last one to two semesters before the student is rotated to another placement setting. Internship settings are quite similar to practicum settings; the difference is that they require a full-time (at least 40 hours per week) commitment and are always 1 full year in length. Internships are generally a more intense and comprehensive experience in that students work with more difficult patients, a significantly larger caseload, additional seminars, and a greater number of intensive (and sometimes personal) hours of individual supervision. During the internship year, students are usually strongly urged to begin their own treatment. Early internship experiences are closely supervised, but by the end of the internship, the student begins to function more autonomously in preparation for beginning a career.

Personal Attributes Needed for Success

Anyone pursuing a graduate degree in clinical psychology needs to have compassion, empathy, the ability to absorb intense emotions, and skill in relating comfortably to people. Intellectual curiosity and a twofold interest are required: an interest in alleviating the distress caused by psychological problems as well as an interest in the intellectual challenge of "figuring people out."

Certain characteristics are particularly necessary in the child clinical psychology field. The first and most obvious is an interest, even a delight, in children and in the multitude of ways they make sense of the world and express themselves. Children know when someone is really interested in them and are more likely to respond in psychotherapy when they sense a genuine connection with the therapist.

In addition, child clinical psychologists must have the following characteristics:

- They must be comfortable with their own sense of playfulness without falling into the trap of becoming a playmate. Child clinical psychologists need to be able to be in the moment and involved with the child's play but at the same time not get overly caught up in it so that they can analyze the material with perspective. In other words, a tea party is not just a tea party with therapist participation; it is an act of communication from the child to the psychologist. It is just the same when playing war with action figures: It's not just a war between toys; it is *about* something. It has a meaning beyond what is visible. Thus, the child clinical psychologist must be able to work with play as a metaphor.

- They must have a sense of humor and the ability to adapt it across the age span and across different types of personalities. Similarly, a lack of self-consciousness and a comfort with fantasy play are essential. You might find yourself being a talking truck, or having a conversation with a misbehaving dog, or acting like a crying baby. You need to be able to do this without feeling foolish or uncomfortable.
- They must be quick-witted and flexible, because children think fast and are fluid in their style of relatedness. No two children are alike, and they are always clinically challenging us.
- They must be able to empathize and work with parents and not blame them for their children's problems. In our experience, some clinicians are too prone to see parents as the bad guys, whereas in reality, most parents have their children's best interests at heart and are doing the best they can. Despite this, some children do have difficulties and need professional help, and their parents are in need of guidance as well.

Financial Compensation

Careers in clinical child psychology are obviously diverse, and so is the financial compensation these professionals receive. Private practitioners typically earn the highest incomes and can have a quite comfortable lifestyle. The amount they earn depends on the number of hours they work, the location and type of their practice, whether they choose to have junior clinicians working for them, and other factors. The salary range in public agencies, community mental health centers, and medical settings tends to be somewhat lower (as for many other careers in those settings). Don't forget, however, that there are many other benefits in public sector employment, including health insurance and paid leave. Clinical and other professional benefits include the following: working with a diverse population of clients; having greater access to colleagues for peer supervision, support, and personal connections, and having a sense of professional community rather than the isolation of private practice. Child clinical psychologists working in other settings, such as academia, research, and consultation, generally fall somewhere in the middle of the salary range. Again, this depends on the particular university, the funding sources of the research, or the level of consultation in which one engages. (And if you should write that million-seller self-help book for parents, one never knows!)

Choosing to Be a Child Clinical Psychologist: Our Personal Stories

Although our backgrounds are quite different in many ways, we had remarkably similar reasons for deciding to become child clinical psychologists. We have both, from early in our lives, been interested in understanding why people do what they do. In high school, this interest deepened, and we realized that it had a name: psychology. We both took high school courses in psychology and found them quite interesting. At this time, during our adolescence, we both did volunteer work with children. Nemiroff worked with mentally retarded children in a residential facility, and Annunziata worked in a pediatric play program in a medical setting. Our volunteer experiences, along with our abiding interest in what makes people tick and our high school psychology classes, led us to enter college as psychology majors.

For 4 years in college, we took an array of courses in the various fields of psychology. It became clearer to us that children were our primary interest and that we wanted to pursue advanced education and ultimately a career in child clinical psychology. We went to graduate programs where we could specialize in clinical work with children, but of course we were trained extensively in work with adults as well. Within our programs, we were able to emphasize psychotherapy and psychological testing as opposed to research and teaching. We also both chose to pursue our interest in insight-oriented theoretical and technical approaches to psychotherapy. We were fortunate to have excellent practicum and internship placements that focused on work with children and provided excellent experience with adults across the age span as well. Thus, although we concentrated on children, the age range of our patients was $2\frac{1}{2}$ to 83 years old. We were grateful at the time for our training and supervision, and we continue to feel grateful for it on an almost daily basis.

After graduate school, we were both lucky enough to find positions that allowed us to continue our focus on children while also working actively with adult patients. We both began in community mental centers; serendipity, in fact, led us to the same CMHC, which is where we met. Now we both work in separate private practice settings and also teach, supervise, consult, and write.

A Typical Week in the Life of a Child Clinical Psychologist

People often ask us, "What is a typical day like for you as a child clinical psychologist?" A typical week, rather than a day, is a better representation of the variety of our activities.

In a typical week we might do the following:

- spend several days seeing a variety of patients; our patients are diverse in both age and type of problem; within any given day, we might sit on the floor in a playroom with a 3-year-old or enjoy the comfort of our ergonomic office chairs while talking with a 33-year-old; we might also see the parents of the children and teenagers whom we treat, as well as a couple experiencing marital difficulties and an entire family in formal family therapy; we also treat diverse problems in our patients, ranging from very high-functioning patients with mild anxiety and depression to children and adults who are significantly more disturbed;
- spend time on professional writing (such as the writing of this chapter), although generally we write books for children and parents (i.e., bibliotherapy);
- spend time preparing and delivering a lecture for students, other professionals, or postgraduates; we might also give a talk to a community parent organization, school, or church or synagogue group on a topic pertaining to children;
- engage in the supervision of less-experienced clinicians;
- participate in our own continuing education, including formal presentations and peer supervision groups; and
- consult with an agency that provides services to children to help staff deal with particularly problematic clients and develop their clinical skills.

As you can see, our week is quite full, meaningful, and wonderfully varied. This is one of the advantages of being a child clinical psychologist.

Pros and Cons: Advantages and Disadvantages of the Career

Like any career, child clinical psychology has both positive and negative aspects. We, of course, believe that the advantages far outweigh the disadvantages. Given that the disadvantages are so few, we're going to start with them. Don't be dissuaded!

One of the hardest things about being a clinical psychologist is the burden of listening to and absorbing the pain and suffering of our patients. It is no different in work with children, although it is sometimes harder to see a little one suffer, whether it is from extreme anxiety and depression or from the horrors of child abuse. Thus, burnout is an unfortunate hazard of our profession. Burnout can be prevented, however, if one takes proper self-care steps.

Child clinical psychology is different from other clinical work because it involves the added challenge of working with each child's parents. Although most parents are extremely supportive of their children's treatment and are open to the parent guidance that we always provide as part of the child's treatment, there are times when work with parents can be the most frustrating aspect of child psychotherapy. It is particularly difficult when parents won't make the necessary changes, either in the family or in themselves, to facilitate the child's emotional growth. The final disadvantage is that child clinical psychologists often need to spend much time outside of psychotherapy sessions on the phone in case coordination with schools and parents and may occasionally need to make a school visit for observation or for clinical staffing on a student.

The advantages of being a child clinical psychologist, again, far outweigh the disadvantages. This is very meaningful life work, and it is most gratifying to help people with their problems and to make a difference in the lives of children and their families. Work with children is uniquely satisfying because you have the opportunity to make a difference early in a child's life and thus to prevent considerable later suffering and hardship.

The work is intellectually stimulating, emotionally engaging, and financially rewarding. Work with children is unique because you can influence the whole system that surrounds a child, including schools, parents, and child-care providers. Thus, you can make a huge impact on a little person's development that helps him well into his adult life. Sometimes a child's therapy alters the entire course of his life.

We've saved the best for last: Work with children is just plain fun. It engages our sense of playfulness and creativity as we sit with a child and participate in his or her emotional growth and psychological development.

Suggested Readings

Carroll, J., Schaefer, C., McCormick, J., & Ohnogi, A. (Eds.). (2005). *Children talk about play therapy*. Northvale, NJ: Jason Aronson.

Drotar, D. (Ed.). (2000). *Handbook of research methods in pediatric and child psychology*. New York: Kluwer Academic/Plenum Publishing Corporation.

Mikeshell, R. H., Lusterman, D. D., & McDaniel, S. H. (Eds.). (1995). *Integrating family therapy: Handbook of family psychology and systems theory*. Washington, DC: American Psychological Association.

O'Dessie Oliver, J. (1997). *Play therapy: A comprehensive guide*. Northvale, NJ: Jason Aronson.

Sweeney, D. S., Homeyer, (Eds.). (1999). *Group play therapy*. San Francisco: Jossey-Bass.

Walker, C. E., & Roberts, M. C. (Eds.). (2001). *Handbook of clinical child psychology* (3rd ed.). New York: Wiley.

Watson, T. S., & Gresham, F. M. (Eds.). (1998). *Handbook of child behavior therapy*. New York: Plenum Press.

Melba J. T. Vasquez

Diverse and Intriguing Career Opportunities for Counseling Psychologists

8

P sychologists spent the first 50 years of the profession's history building a scientific knowledge base (Fowler, 1990). Before World War II, almost all psychologists were employed in academic settings. After World War II, thousands of students were attracted to applied fields in psychology, including counseling, clinical, industrial, organizational, and school psychology. In 1979, the number of psychologists employed in academic settings still exceeded the number employed in all other settings, but 10 years later, although educational institutions were still the largest single employer of psychologists, they employed fewer than all others combined (Fowler, 1990). Psychologists are now employed in business, government, and consulting and in various service delivery settings. Ray Fowler (1990), former president and later chief executive officer of the American Psychological Association

Melba J. T. Vasquez, PhD, ABPP, is a psychologist in independent practice in Austin, Texas. She is coauthor, with Ken Pope, of *Ethics in Psychotherapy and Counseling: A Practical Guide* (Jossey-Bass, in press) and of *How to Survive and Thrive as a Therapist: Information, Ideas, and Resources for Psychologists in Practice* (American Psychological Association, 2005a). She has served as president of the American Psychological Association's Divisions 17 (Society of Counseling Psychology) and 35 (Society for the Psychology of Women) and of the Texas Psychological Association.

(APA), stressed that the academic science foundation of psychology has continued to grow even as U.S. psychology has developed as part of the health care system.

The undergraduate degree in psychology is a wonderful and popular liberal arts degree that allows graduates to be employed in any number of jobs. Obtaining a bachelor's degree is an important accomplishment; only 27% of the U.S. population has a bachelor's degree (National Center for Education Statistics, 2003). However, the doctorate (PhD, EdD, or PsyD) in one of several applied fields in psychology is required to practice independently as a professional psychologist. According to the U.S. Census Bureau (J. R. Gonzalez, personal communication, May 20, 2005), only about 9.5% of the U.S. population has obtained a graduate or professional degree (i.e., master's, professional, and doctorate degrees). Those who obtain master's degrees are part of only 6.5% of the population in the United States age 25 years and older (the data include degrees such master of arts, master of science, master of education, master of social work, and master of business administration). Only 1.9% of the U.S. population obtain a professional degree (e.g., medical degree, dental degree, legal degree), and only 1.2% obtain a doctorate (e.g., EdD, PsyD, PhD). Attending graduate school is thus a special opportunity and privilege.

Although several counseling and clinical psychology programs provide master's degrees, the APA and most states recognize only the doctorate in psychology in licensing psychologists to practice independently. A master's degree in a mental health field such as social work, counseling and guidance, and marriage and family therapy may allow one to practice as a clinical social worker, counselor, or family therapist, depending on state licensing laws. But only the PhD in one of the applied psychology specialties allows one to obtain a state license to practice as a psychologist.

This chapter focuses on the varied career opportunities in counseling psychology, including both the academic and applied professional practice of counseling psychology. A doctorate in counseling psychology provides an interesting and diverse number of career opportunities. This chapter defines counseling psychology, including how it is similar to and different from clinical psychology, and describes the varied career opportunities in counseling psychology as well. Potential work settings include academia, university counseling centers, independent practice, business and industry, medical settings (e.g., Veterans Administration [VA] settings), community mental health centers and clinics, and schools. Counseling psychologists may take the role of teachers or trainers, researchers, or providers in any of these settings, but some settings require more of some activities than others. I also describe a day in the life of a counseling psychologist.

What Is Counseling Psychology?

The Executive Committee of APA Division 17, Society of Counseling Psychology, provided a definition of counseling psychology that describes the values and goals of the specialty:

> Counseling psychology is a specialty in the field of psychology whose practitioners help people improve their well-being, alleviate their distress, resolve their crises, and increase their ability to solve problems and make decisions. Counseling psychologists utilize scientific approaches in their development of solutions to the variety of human problems resulting from interactions of intrapersonal, interpersonal, and environmental forces. Counseling psychologists conduct research, apply interventions, and evaluate services in order to stimulate personal and group development, and prevent and remedy developmental, educational, emotional, health, organizational, social, and/or vocational problems. The specialty adheres to the standards and ethics established by the American Psychological Association. (Division of Counseling Psychology, 1985, p. 141)

In their preface to the second edition of the *Handbook of Counseling Psychology*, Brown and Lent (1992) further defined the field:

> Counseling psychology is a field notable for its diversity and vigorous evolution. Influenced by diverse political and social forces as well as by developments from within mainstream psychology, it has expanded from an initial concern with educational and vocational guidance to the remediation and prevention of personal, interpersonal, vocational, and educational concerns. Further reflecting counseling psychology's growth is the great diversity in work settings, types of services performed, and theoretical orientations that characterize today's counseling psychologists. (p. xi)

Walsh (1999) described how psychology is not only the study of weakness and fixing what is broken but also the study of human strength and well-being, including the study of fulfillment, enjoyment, and productivity. Following World War II, psychology as a whole was guided by the medical model of focusing on personal weaknesses. This focus developed primarily because those services were what got reimbursed, through the creation of the VA, the emergence of third-party payments, and the establishment of the National Institute of Mental Health, which funded grants for research on mental illness. The recent recognition of "positive psychology" (Seligman, 1998) reflects the shift in psychology's focus to what makes people's lives meaningful and satisfying.

The professional practice of counseling psychology has been characterized as providing personal counseling as well as career and educational specialization (Brown & Lent, 2000; Norcross, 2000). It is one of the few disciplines (with community psychology) that has continued to focus on the value of fostering strength and well-being (Walsh, 1999). A focus on human development across the life span in research has led to the development of interventions that are preventive and developmental as well as remedial. This focus requires counseling psychologists to study the normal, predictable life cycle, including predictable life changes and transitions, of individuals within a culture and to identify issues and experiences that add to or detract from their sense of well-being in that process. They then develop interventions to facilitate their clients' development. Counseling psychologists see themselves as educators; they emphasize the empowerment of individuals, and work toward increased quality of life for all people. They bring a unique set of lenses for viewing and understanding human behavior and the factors they believe are necessary for psychologically healthy functioning.

NATURE OF THE CAREER

Counseling psychology is unique in its historical focus on preventive and developmental interventions. Preventive interventions are those that help people recognize and deal with issues before they become problematic. For example, a preventive intervention may involve consulting with members of a community to prevent gang involvement and providing seminars in the schools for parents and teachers to discuss and prevent bullying. Developmental interventions are educative in nature and are designed to help people understand the issues, factors, and skills involved in normal human development. For example, a developmental intervention may involve communication skills training or a death and dying seminar. Remedial interventions are those designed to remedy problem areas and usually, but not always, involve psychotherapeutic services.

Inherent in the philosophy of counseling psychology is a nonpathological focus on normalcy and day-to-day problems in living, with emphasis on strengths and adaptive strategies and resilience in clients (Fassinger & Schlossberg, 1992; Heppner, Casas, Carter, & Stone, 2000). A major theme in counseling psychology for the past two decades has been an awareness of the need to view people and their behavior within a sociocultural context influenced by such variables as culture, ethnicity, gender, sexual orientation, and age (Heppner et al., 2000). Because counseling psychologists view these environmental and societal factors as important in human development (in addition to individual or familial factors), they tend to be leaders in the profession in attending to research, training, curriculum development, and interventions involving human diversity (Brown & Lent, 2000; Vasquez, 2003).

COUNSELING VERSUS CLINICAL PSYCHOLOGY

One of the first questions most frequently asked of academic advisors is, "What are the differences between clinical psychology and counseling psychology?" Norcross (2000) provided a summary of similarities and salient differences. The distinctions between clinical psychology and counseling psychology may have become more minimal in recent years, and there may be more similarities than differences between the two specialties. For example, graduates of doctoral-level clinical and counseling psychology programs are generally eligible for the same professional benefits, such as psychology licensure, independent practice, and insurance reimbursement. Norcross noted that the APA no longer distinguishes between counseling and clinical psychology internships, which usually consist of a full year of supervised practice at the end of one's doctoral program before receiving the doctorate. Only one list of accredited internships exists (see http://www.apa.org/ed/accreditation/ or the latest December issue of the *American Psychologist*). Accreditation serves as quality control and is described more fully later in this chapter. As of May 2005, there were 871 accredited programs (applied doctoral academic programs are accredited as well), including 368 doctoral programs, 468 internship programs, and 35 postdoctoral programs (APA, 2005a).

However, several differences between counseling and clinical psychology exist, and perhaps one of the most important is the unique perspective of counseling psychology, as I described in the previous section. Kagan et al. (1988) summarized the contributions of counseling psychology, as well as the increasingly diverse settings in which counseling psychologists' unique perspective is applicable and valued. Counseling psychology's unique perspective has evolved from an exclusive focus on working with and studying the developmental and interpersonal needs of the relatively normally functioning person. This history is wedded to a developmental perspective focusing on factors that are necessary for normal, psychologically healthy functioning. The approach of seeing the health and strengths of a person, of being concerned with adaptation in social systems, and of valuing the importance and centrality of work in persons' lives comes out of counseling psychology's heritage in the schools, in business and industry, and in university counseling centers. Because the majority of counseling psychology programs are housed in colleges of education, the historic emphasis of this specialty has been on developmental issues, skill training, and cultural diversity and on affecting the lives of large numbers of persons (Kagan et al., 1988). This unique perspective positions the profession of counseling psychology to more easily expand work in business and industrial settings and in other diverse settings.

Another difference has to do with the number of programs and thus the number of students each specialty produces. In December 2004, there were 230 accredited doctoral programs in clinical psychology and 72 in counseling psychology (K. Kirkpatrick, personal communication, May 18, 2006)). Other applied doctoral programs accredited by the APA include accredited programs in combined professional–scientific psychology (11 programs) and school psychology (56). Clinical psychology programs produce some 2,500 psychologists per year (about 1,200 PhD and about 1,300 PsyD), and counseling psychology programs graduate about 370 new psychologists per year (APA, 2007).

Congruent with its emphasis on human diversity, counseling psychology programs tend to accept a significantly higher percentage of ethnic minorities (25%) than their clinical counterparts (18%; Norcross, 2000; Norcross, Sayette, Mayne, Karg, & Turkson, 1998). For both types of programs, Norcross et al. (1998) noted that two thirds of the entering doctoral students were women. Because of counseling psychology's respect for diversity and flexibility, the faculty of counseling psychology programs have been in the forefront in valuing the importance of increasing the preparation of ethnic minority psychologists as well as those from other diverse groups. Since the 1980s, significant strides have been made in integrating diversity issues into the counseling psychology curriculum, and counseling psychology has been recognized as leading the field (Heppner et al., 2000; Kagan et al., 1988).

Norcross et al. (1998) also explored research areas in clinical and counseling psychology doctoral programs. For all programs, the most frequently listed areas were behavioral medicine/health psychology, minority/cross-cultural psychology, psychotherapy process and outcome, family therapy and research, child clinical/pediatric psychology, neuropsychology, mood disorders, anxiety disorders, eating disorders, and assessment. The largest differences occurred in minority/cross-cultural psychology (69% of counseling psychology programs listed this research area, compared to 32% of clinical psychology programs) and vocational assessment (62% of counseling psychology programs listed this research area, compared to 1% of clinical psychology programs). Counseling psychologists have been pioneers in career development across the life span by providing research and theory in the areas of work and career and developing vocational tests and measures.

Although clinical and counseling psychologists are employed in similar settings, counseling psychologists are more often employed in university settings and clinical psychologists more often in hospital settings (Norcross, 2000). However, both counseling and clinical psychologists work in universities, independent practice, business and industry, hospitals, community mental health centers and clinics, school settings, and medical settings.

Career Paths

In 1988, the Georgia Conference Work Group Task Force on Professional Practice concluded that counseling psychologists have demonstrated that they have been able to practice anywhere they have the competence to practice including academia, university counseling centers, independent practice, business and industry, medical settings (e.g., Veterans Administration [VA] settings), community mental health centers and clinics, and schools (Kagan et al., 1988). Counseling psychologists are able to make unique contributions affecting a wide variety of diverse client populations, ages, and issues (Fretz & Simon, 1992). At the beginning of this chapter, I emphasized the importance of science as a foundation in psychology. The integration of science and practice has a long and important history in counseling psychology as well. Special efforts have been made to ensure the integration of science and practice throughout the doctoral training curriculum, including the thorough training of students in both qualitative and quantitative research methods and the development of more critical thinking and writing by students (Heppner et al., 2000). The linkage between science and practice is critical in the training, curriculum, journals, and work settings of counseling psychologists. In the past 2 decades, more and more graduates in counseling psychology have found employment in the private sector, and the changing face of psychology, especially in psychology practice, means that bridging the gap between training and the diverse needs of practicing counseling psychologists will be a challenge. New practice applications are difficult to incorporate into the training curriculum. Alternatively, it is sometimes a long period of time before psychologists who are practicing are able to obtain information about new discoveries in psychology.

ACADEMIC POSITIONS

An academic counseling psychologist may serve as a professor in either a counseling psychology doctoral program, usually housed within a psychology department, or a department of education or educational psychology. Counseling psychologists may also teach undergraduate psychology or educational psychology courses in 2- or 4-year institutions. They may teach, conduct research, or serve as administrators in academic settings.

Teaching

Counseling psychologists may teach undergraduate courses such as introductory psychology, personality, human adjustment, abnormal psychology, marriage and family, or human relations. They may also teach in master's-level counseling courses, as well as in other related departments such as health psychology, marriage and family, and social work. Doctoral programs often require faculty not only to teach graduate courses but to serve on student master's or doctoral research committees, as well as to engage in a number of other university-related activities. APA's Division 2, Society for the Teaching of Psychology, has promoted a scholarly activity, "the scholarship of pedagogy," which involves ways to improve teaching and learning across all levels of education through research, evaluation, and the creation of textbooks, workshops, and software (Walsh, 1999).

Research

Counseling psychologists who teach in graduate institutions and at research-oriented institutions are expected to have a program of research, and promotions and tenure are partly if not largely based on the psychologist's productivity in that area. Walsh (1999) encouraged counseling psychologists to respond to the urgent need for education and research in the following areas:

- cost-effective preventive health care,
- reduction of drug and alcohol abuse,
- nurturance for children who lack stable families,
- strengthening of families,
- better and more effective schooling,
- school-to-work transition,
- welfare issues and work,
- retirement issues and work,
- more productive business practices,
- alternatives to violence of all kinds,
- reduction of discrimination against all marginalized groups,
- prevention of depression and anxiety,
- prevention of other mental illnesses, and
- prevention of sexual and other forms of abuse.

Administration

Some counseling psychologists in academia serve in administrative roles, including as training director, head of the counseling psychology faculty, head of the department (which may include various other subspecialties of psychology), or dean or even provost, chancellor, or president of a university. Because of the emphasis on work and career in the field of counseling psychology, counseling psychologists have the knowledge, skills, and attitudes to serve effectively in administrative roles. The emphasis on prevention and development in the workplace in counseling psychology (Hesketh, 2000) helps counseling psychologists in all settings, not only academia, promote healthy organizational climates.

UNIVERSITY COUNSELING CENTER

University counseling centers are usually part of student services at public and private colleges and universities, and they offer a wide range of services. Sometimes these centers are housed within student health services; occasionally, they are related to a clinic operated by the graduate program in psychology on campus. Counseling center psychologists provide remedial services such as assessment, individual and group psychotherapy, and crisis intervention services. Psychotherapy services at university counseling centers have instituted time limits, because of the high demand for services and funding limitations, that can range from a couple of sessions to 6 or 8 or 10. Students are sometimes referred to the independent practice community for long-term therapy. Sometimes, practicum or intern trainees are able to see long-term clients for training purposes.

Counseling psychologists also provide preventive and developmental services and serve as consultants and program specialists. Prevention programs include psychoeducational programs such as date-rape workshops, alcohol and drug abuse prevention seminars, and suicide prevention programs, all offered to students, faculty, and staff. Counseling psychologists may also serve as consultants to faculty, administrators, student groups, or staff regarding any number of organizational issues and challenges.

Because most university counseling centers also serve as training sites for practicum and intern students from various doctoral programs, counseling psychologists also serve as supervisors and trainers. They also engage in research and sometimes hold appointments in academic departments such as psychology or educational psychology. In addition, counseling psychologists serve in administrative roles, such as training director, director of the counseling center, or vice president of student affairs.

INDEPENDENT PRACTICE

Since the 1980's, external forces and changes in the health care market have resulted in a significant increase in the job market for the practice of psychology, including for counseling psychologists, particularly in independent practice (Heppner, Casas, Carter, & Stone, 2000). The vast majority of counseling psychologists in independent practice offer psychotherapy services to individuals, couples, and families and group psychotherapy. Some offer services to adults only, or even to older adults; others serve only adolescents and children. Many counseling psychologists in independent practice offer psychological testing and may also provide consultation, workshops, and seminars. Forensic services, including testifying as an expert witness and providing psychological evaluations for use in the court system (either criminal or civil courts), are other services that counseling psychologists provide. The counseling psychologist may be self-employed or may join other professionals in group practices or partnerships.

Business is an important aspect of independent practice in which most graduate students are typically not trained, but more and more graduate programs are providing some information in this area, including business management skills, marketing and advertising skills, and guidelines for obtaining relevant consultant services (e.g., accountants, attorneys). Other counseling psychologists acquire this crucial information through training after graduation, including continuing education workshops and classes, consultation, or reading; *How to Survive and Thrive as a Therapist: Information, Ideas, and Resources for Psychologists in Practice* (Pope & Vasquez, 2005) is a valuable resource.

New Directions in Independent Practice

The changing face of independent psychology practice is largely driven by the changing needs of society. Traditional practitioners have begun to diversify, mainly by integrating psychological and medical care. Understanding the landscape of reimbursement policies is important. APA Executive Director of Professional Practice Russ Newman (2005) described how managed care techniques became a popular method for employers and insurers in the context of private market reform since the mid-1980s. Legislated health care reform has not been successful in this country. Instead, with the goal of stimulating market-driven health care and increasing competition to control costs, for-profit investor-held managed care companies "paid more attention to Wall Street than to patients" (Newman, 2005, p. 51). In addition, Newman described how information technology advances have also begun to exert an influence on the health care industry. The result is "an integrated, primary health–oriented, market-driven, employer focused, information technology–assisted, health-care delivery system" (Newman, 2005, p. 51). Newman encouraged psychologists to diversify into primary care settings so they can more easily integrate psychological and medical care and to offer services beyond traditional psychotherapy and assessment for mental health patients. In fact, psychology identified itself as a health care profession and codified this change in the bylaws of the APA (Barlow, 2004). The research supporting the efficacy of psychological interventions in health care systems is "more than sufficient for their inclusion in health care systems around the world" (Barlow, 2004, p. 869). Indeed, the biggest trend to shape the discipline of applied psychology has been the growing demand for and use of integrated, comprehensive health services that blend health and behavior, prevention, health promotion, and disease management (Clay, 2005).

Newman (2005) also observed that psychologists have expanded their practices into sports psychology, forensic psychology, executive coaching, and gerontology. He agreed that the growing societal awareness and attention to the effects of lifestyle and behavior on health and illness is creating important roles for psychologists in prevention, health promotion, and disease management. Counseling psychologists have the skills, training, and perspective to provide services, whether psychotherapy, consultation, or training, to solve behavioral problems with individuals, groups, organizations, systems, or even the population at large. Learning how to apply those abilities and knowledge in new settings is a lifelong strategy for success.

Training other providers is also an activity that independent practitioners with unique skills may specialize in. For example, one colleague provides training for employee assistance program counselors who provide telephone services for employees of a major international corporation. One recent training program involved skill development in dealing with anger management issues for couples who called in for telephone services. Independent practitioners may provide a wide variety of preventive and psychoeducational topics to various groups in the community.

Prescription Privileges for Psychologists

One of the newest roles for psychologists in independent practice is that of obtaining prescriptive authority. Former APA president Pat DeLeon saw prescriptive authority for psychologists as part of promoting the health care system's ability to be more responsive to consumer needs (Heiby, DeLeon, & Anderson, 2004). The APA has approved this goal and developed a model of training for prescription privileges. A

Department of Defense project that involved 10 psychologists demonstrated success in this endeavor, and as of 2006 two states, New Mexico and Louisiana, have passed legislation allowing for the prescription privileges of licensed psychologists who obtain the appropriate postdoctoral training. Psychologists in various other states have taken the postdoctoral training in anticipation of their states granting prescription authority for psychologists.

Counseling and clinical psychologists with prescriptive authority are in a unique position to improve the quality of medication utilization for clients. They may modify previously ordered dosage levels, substitute more appropriate medications, and ensure that the "all-important psychosocial aspects of therapy are incorporated into the treatment regime. They often take patients off inappropriate medications. In essence, they effectively utilize their psychological expertise" (Heiby et al., 2004, p. 337).

OTHER HUMAN SERVICE AGENCIES

Community health agencies or clinics employ counseling psychologists as providers and administrators. Some are federally, state-, or county-funded community mental health clinics; others are privately funded agencies (usually, but not always, nonprofit settings), such as a women's agency focusing on rape, domestic violence, or related issues. Community agencies often offer psychotherapy services; some provide preventive and developmental services, although probably to a lesser extent. Assessment services and forensic work may also be involved.

DeLeon, Giesting, and Kenkel (2003) described federally funded community health centers that provide comprehensive primary health care, such as that found in a family medicine practice, and highlighted the unique opportunities for the expansion of mental health services, creating the need for psychologists and other mental health providers. The specific skills involved are those consistent with primary behavioral health care approaches and the provision of services to an entire community. Usually, community health centers provide services using a sliding fee schedule that adjusts for family income and ensures that low-income patients make only nominal payment for care. The public sector has seen cuts in government funding, leading to decreased availability of health care services (Newman, 2005). The privatization of parts of the public sector has also had a significant impact on health care professionals, as well as consumers. Yet federal funding in 2003 increased the availability of oral health, mental health, and substance abuse services, thus creating opportunities for psychologists to help health centers comply with these new service mandates (DeLeon et al., 2003).

As I indicated previously, one of the significant thrusts in the professional practice of psychology is for psychologists to provide services in primary behavioral health care settings (Gray, Brody, & Johnson, 2005; Newman, 2005). Traditionally, the existing mental health system has provided specialized, intensive services to a minority of clientele with behavioral health problems, and the rest have received treatment from their physicians or not at all. In the recognition that psychological services benefit the whole person, various models have been proposed for training and practice to facilitate better integration and collaboration. Greater integration occurs, according to Dobmeyer, Rowan, Etherage, and Wilson (2003), when the mental health providers are placed directly in primary care facilities, such as in a community health center.

HOSPITAL SETTINGS AND MEDICAL CENTERS

Typically, hospitals and medical schools hire counseling psychologists to provide skills and knowledge that supplement the services provided by other professionals in these settings and to design and teach courses in patient counseling and patient education (Kagan et al., 1988). In such settings, the counseling psychologist may provide direct counseling services to either the patient or the patient's family. Counseling interventions may include stress management for heart patients, support groups for families of terminally ill patients, adjustment following changes in physical appearance due to amputations or burns, or lifestyle issues with conditions such as diabetes or chronic pain. Counseling psychologists in medical settings may also serve as consultants to treatment teams regarding the psychological well-being of patients and provide recommendations for psychiatric or psychological treatment. They may also fill the role of psychoeducator to teach medical students and residents to increase interpersonal sensitivity and to recognize patients who should be referred for psychiatric or psychological services.

Research is another activity that counseling psychologists may conduct in hospital settings. Research-related activities may include writing applications for grants, evaluating programs for funding purposes, or gathering data in such settings as rape and sexual abuse trauma units, children's units, or other settings where sensitivity to the persons or knowledge of family or family dynamics is critical (Kagan et al., 1988).

Since the end of World War II, the VA has hired counseling psychologists, and the VA continues to be a major employer of these professionals. Duties, according to Kagan et al. (1988), typically involve career development for former military personnel, intervention with problems such as posttraumatic stress disorder and other effects of war trauma, and treatment of disorders that the general population exhibits, including alcohol and drug abuse, depression, and anxiety.

SCHOOLS

Kagan et al. (1988) observed that the roots of counseling psychology are in educational settings. A primary function of the counseling psychologist in the school is to create and maintain a psychologically healthy climate within a school system. Usually, he or she serves as a consultant to administrators, teachers, parents, students, and the community. The counseling psychologist may also provide preventive services such as parent effectiveness classes, suicide prevention for the community, behavior management seminars for teachers, and personnel management for school principals and other school administrators. Development of a counseling curriculum might involve designing courses for students grades K–12 that focus on healthy development and the key psychological issues at each age (e.g., basic impulse control, peer relationships, conflict management skills, bully prevention, ingroup–outgroup issues). A counseling psychologist may also engage in crisis intervention in schools that have experienced a loss of a student or teacher, a shooting in the school, and any other traumatic situation. They facilitate groups for children and adolescents experiencing divorce, for those with single parents, and for depressed students and may supervise other school counselors and social workers. Some states require additional credentials or certification for work in the schools.

BUSINESS AND INDUSTRY

Kagan et al. (1988) noted at the Georgia Conference in Counseling Psychology that the skills and perspectives of counseling psychologists have been valued by business and industry for decades. More recently, psychologists in other applied areas, such as clinical psychologists, have come to see business and industry as a new setting for service provision. A corporation or organization might hire counseling psychologists on a full-time, part-time, or contract basis to provide services in three areas: counseling and psychotherapy, corporate consultation, and direct management (Kagan et al., 1988).

Counseling and Psychotherapy

Employee assistance programs provide employment opportunities for counseling psychologists. EAPs help with early identification and treatment of employee problems and provide in-house counseling and psychotherapy services, often short term. Counseling psychologists assess issues related to absenteeism, loss of productivity, substance abuse, and marriage and family problems and provide career development services regarding transitions, promotions, preretirement, and terminations. A colleague of mine works for a large urban police department, providing counseling services for police that include crisis intervention on an individual basis, as when a police officer shoots and kills an alleged perpetrator, or on a group basis, as when an officer is killed in the line of duty. At times, this psychologist provides the services directly; at other times, he refers clients to other practitioners in the community.

Consulting for Corporations

Companies who hire psychologist consultants include high technology, financial, and health companies and megaconglomerates, as well as large not-for-profit organizations. Consultants in business and industry offer assistance, usually to top management, on such matters as executive education, executive coaching, team building and effectiveness, supervisor–staff relationships, management assessment and development, diversity management, conflict resolution, and enhancement of communication within and across departments (Kagan et al., 1988; S. L. Shullman, personal communication, August 15, 2005). They may also conduct organizational research and evaluation or needs assessments or provide training to supervisors or managers in a variety of skills, including burnout prevention, stress management, time management, and personnel management. When consulting at the highest levels, counseling psychologists may facilitate processes for corporate decision making and for organizational change and performance management processes (Kagan et al., 1988; S. L. Shullman, personal communication, August 8, 2005). Most behavioral science consulting firms hire psychologists with specialties in industrial/organizational counseling and clinical psychology. Industrial/organizational psychologists tend to do test development, instrumentation, and research, whereas counseling and clinical psychologists tend to do more of the other activities described in this paragraph.

In a 2-year period, a colleague who co-owns a corporate consulting business traveled to several cities in the United States, as well as to Austria, Chile, Columbia, Germany, Hungary, India, Italy, Malaysia, Mexico, Switzerland, Turkey, and the United Kingdom (S. L. Shullman, personal communication, August 6, 2005). She finds the work highly stimulating, challenging, and rewarding, in terms of both productivity and income. This kind of work requires high energy and the ability to deal with diversity.

Recently, psychology consultants have begun providing performance consulting or executive coaching. Hays and Brown (2004), for example, described how performance consultants provide consulting in three domains: the performing arts (e.g., composers, dancers, actors, talk show personalities), business (e.g., attorneys, bankers, advertising executives, insurance salespeople, corporate executives), and high-risk professions (e.g., neurosurgeons, emergency room physicians and nurses, combat medics). Whether as full-time consulting work, as part of an independent practice, or as an extension of academic research, the knowledge, skills, and abilities of counseling psychologists enable them to deliver effective consultation to enhance the effectiveness of people in these domains. One colleague, former APA president Dick Suinn, has provided consultation to Olympic athletes, for example. The education and experiences provided in most doctoral programs provide excellent skills that are transferable and valuable in working with organizations or individuals in business and industry (Davis, 1997), including the sports arena!

Direct Management

Occasionally, counseling psychologists are employed in management roles in business and industry in positions involving employee relations. Hiring and firing, career development counseling, conflict resolution, interpersonal training skills, and health and wellness promotion may all be activities of psychologists in this role. They may be directors of the human resources division in a large company, or they may play key service roles.

Academic Preparation of Counseling Psychologists

The preparation of counseling psychologists begins in graduate school, preferably in a program accredited by the APA. Accreditation serves as a guide for quality control. A list of accredited doctoral and internship programs, curriculum requirements, and requirements of core faculty for programs are described in the *Guidelines and Principles for Accreditation of Programs in Professional Psychology* and are available online at http://www.apa.org/ed/accreditation/initial_accred.html (APA, 2005b). Most state licensing boards require that candidates for licensure have attended APA-accredited graduate programs and internship sites to sit for the licensure examination. The entire graduate school process usually takes 5 or more years from the beginning of studies to the awarding of the doctorate. Some students take longer to complete the dissertation.

Usually, after 2 or 3 years of coursework and applied supervised practice experience, students go through a formal examination process to advance to candidacy for the doctorate. Most programs prefer that the student have at least begun, if not completed, the dissertation research before obtaining the internship experience. Various attempts have been made in counseling psychology programs to modify training to meet market demands, particularly by increasing the availability of practice opportunities for graduate students with in-house training clinics and a variety of external practicum sites (Thorp, O'Donohue, & Gregg, 2005). Thorp et al. (2005) found that although the APA traditionally required graduate programs to provide students with at least 400 hours of practicum experience, students reported an average of more than 2,200 hours before starting the internship, with a wide range of 279 to 9,049 hours. It is through coursework and then practicum experiences that students begin to evolve their special interest areas.

The internship is usually a full year of supervised practice and occurs in a wide variety of settings (e.g., hospitals, university counseling centers, inpatient units, outpatient clinics). Internship training for counseling and clinical psychology doctoral students takes place in 578 separate internship programs throughout the country that have an average of 4.5 students per program (Thorp et al., 2005). The APA accredits internships, as it does graduate programs, thus providing quality control at the internship level as well. The Association of Psychology Postdoctoral and Internship Centers provides an online directory and facilitates the matching of students to internship programs. Most students travel to a setting in another city or state for their internship. The required internship experience culminates with the student's entry into the workforce, and he or she obtains licensure usually after 1 or 2 years of supervised experience. Stedman, Hatch, Schoenfeld, and Keilin (2005) examined the populations served in internship training and found that internships most often involve individual, adult, and outpatient therapy; others provide training with adolescent and child patient populations and brief, couples, and group psychotherapy. Stedman et al. called for more internships in specialty areas that might increase job opportunities, including substance abuse, forensics, behavioral medicine, and geriatric and ethnic minority clients.

Financial support throughout the process varies. The majority of doctoral programs in counseling psychology require that students attend full time and take the full curriculum, even if they have previously acquired a master's degree in psychology or a related field. Some programs provide research or teaching assistantships, and some fellowships or grants are available through the university or from other sources. During the internship, a minimal stipend is often provided, but not always; stipends for full-time (40 hours per week or more) internship positions in 2002–2003 averaged only $18,600 per year (Thorp et al., 2005). The training process thus involves significant financial costs to students. Many graduate students do not receive health care coverage or retirement benefits from the jobs that they engage in during their years in graduate school. Relocation to attend graduate school and fulfillment of the internship requirement can also involve substantial financial costs.

A master's degree may or may not be required before entering a doctoral program. Some students have found that obtaining a master's degree provides research experience that makes them more likely to be accepted into a doctoral program (Law, 2004). Obtaining a master's degree also provides a dissertation "practice run" (Law, 2004, p. 31), a point of progress, a chance for publication, and an employment edge before and during the doctoral program. Other students acquire the master's degree en route to the doctoral degree through the same program.

Although most students who enter graduate school in counseling psychology have undergraduate degrees in psychology, others have related undergraduate or master's degrees. Students with nonpsychology undergraduate degrees may need to take extra courses before or after entering the doctoral program to obtain a basic foundation in psychology.

Financial Compensation

The overall median salary in 2003 for counseling psychologists was $65,000 (APA, Research Office, 2005). Salaries vary by setting and years of experience. At 5 to 9 years of experience, counseling psychologists in university counseling centers reported a median salary of $46,000 while their colleagues in independent practice claimed median salaries of $55,000 at 5 to 9 years.

How I Became a Counseling Psychologist

I had no idea what a counseling psychologist was or what career opportunities were available when I first considered applying to a counseling psychology doctoral program. I am a first-generation college student. I obtained my undergraduate degree from my hometown university while living at home, Southwest Texas State University, which was then a Teacher's College (now Texas State University). I majored in English and political science and obtained secondary teaching certification. I taught at a New Braunsfels, Texas, middle school for 2 years while I worked on a master's degree in school counseling. Toward the end of the master's program, one of my professors, for whom I had worked as a work–study student throughout my undergraduate program, encouraged me to apply to the counseling psychology program at the University of Texas at Austin, 30 miles north of my hometown. She tried to describe what a counseling psychologist was and assured me that it would be a good fit. She was right. The opportunities for employment as a counseling psychologist have been abundant, and I thoroughly enjoy all the work I do, even when there is a bit of drudgery (such as sitting and writing).

I was told at the time that the program was a 4-year program. Because I did not have a psychology background, I had to take three "vestibule" courses, so I took summer classes every year of my program to catch up and finish the program on time. At the end of my first year in graduate school, I received an APA Minority Fellowship grant that provided partial financial support for the last 3 years of graduate school, which helped considerably. The directors of the APA Minority Fellowship program, Dalmas Taylor and then James Jones, also served as mentors and facilitated my entry into the profession by encouraging me to attend national conventions.

I consider myself fortunate to have had the opportunity to explore the career paths and opportunities of a counseling psychologist. I have found the doctoral degree in counseling psychology to open doors to a varied, diverse, outstanding, and highly rewarding career. I began my career as a university counseling center psychologist at Colorado State University (CSU), where I also held an assistant professorship in the psychology department. I taught graduate courses in the doctoral program in counseling psychology and also supervised doctoral practicum and intern students. In addition, I provided individual, group, and relationship psychotherapy to university students. I consulted with faculty and staff, served as advisor for student organizations, and conducted an ethnic minority needs assessment for the vice president of student affairs. I also provided numerous workshops on topics such as stress management, test-taking skills, communication skills, date rape, and death and dying. After 4 years at CSU, during which time I became training director of the APA-accredited training program, I took a similar position at the University of Texas at Austin, where I did virtually the same kind of work for 9 years.

Since 1991, I have been in full-time independent practice. Although I had considered exploring an administrative role as director of a university counseling center, I decided to try independent practice; I had had a small part-time practice an evening or two a week during my university counseling center years. I found that I love full-time independent practice. In addition to providing individual, group, and relationship psychotherapy, I have at times provided assessments for individuals entering various careers (e.g., police work, religious service). I have served as an expert witness in civil court on such issues as sexual harassment, workplace discrimination, sexual assault, and therapist violations (e.g., therapist–client sexual violations). I have provided consultation for various businesses, agencies, and nonprofit boards regarding personnel issues and conflict resolution and have provided skills training as well. I have been invited to serve as instructor at various universities, and although I may do so at some point, I have not had time to prioritize that activity. Instead, I have given talks to various classes each semester and have served as visiting professor for brief periods. Independent practice was much more lucrative financially than university counseling center work, although those salaries have increased in the past 15 years, and the gap between independent practice income and those in other settings may no longer be as great.

Although both my counseling center work and my independent practice are considered applied positions, and neither has required me to publish, I have authored and coauthored numerous journal articles and book chapters and a couple of books. I enjoy the role of scholar and consider my writing and conference presentation activities to be part of my passion for life-long learning. Most doctoral programs in counseling psychology produce *scientist–practitioners*, who have an identity as both scientist (or scholar, or researcher) and practitioner. I write in the areas of professional ethics, psychology of women, ethnic minority psychology, and supervision and training. I am invited to provide keynote addresses, workshops, seminars, and other presentations at commencement services, in state and national conferences, and for various groups across the country on topics in those related areas.

Another professional activity that I enjoy very much is my involvement with various professional associations. I was elected to serve as the 2006 president of the Texas Psychological Association, and I have served in various leadership roles in the APA, including as president of Division 17, Society of Counseling Psychology, and of APA Division 35, Society for the Psychology of Women. I have also served on several APA boards and committees.

Advantages and Disadvantages of Being a Counseling Psychologist

This chapter thus far describes the advantages of being a counseling psychologist. It provides a reasonably lucrative, interesting, varied, and diverse set of opportunities. One has only to trust the process of engagement and follow one's interests to apply a very general and productive set of skills. The personal development that goes along with the professional development, in my opinion, enhances one's quality of life; self-growth and self-care are ethical responsibilities, especially for those who work in practice on a daily basis.

The only disadvantage that I can think of is that clinical psychology used to be thought of as better training than counseling psychology for practice with individuals with serious mental illness. It used to be rare for medical settings, for example, to accept counseling psychology trainees into their internships. However, the situation has changed in recent years, and both academic and practice settings now provide training in counseling psychology to prepare students to see the full range of health and dysfunction in individuals, and that narrow perspective has dissipated somewhat. Even in university counseling center settings, the full range of normal and dysfunctional development is observed.

The rights and privileges of this esteemed field come with responsibilities to model being a contributing, positive citizen in society, in my opinion. Although this is mostly a positive thing, it can feel like a burden at times.

Professional Involvement and Volunteer Activities

One of the options and opportunities for all professionals in any field is to become involved with one's professional organizations. I strongly encourage this involvement because my experience is that there is a wonderful reciprocity in the process. Counseling psychologists have the opportunity to become involved with the APA, including its Division 17, Society of Counseling Psychology. APA members can affiliate with one or more divisions (I am a member of nine divisions, all of which reflect special interests of mine). Involvement in one's state psychological association and other local or regional psychological associations is also beneficial. Not only is it an opportunity to provide service to one's organization, but the benefits of involvement are numerous, including supporting the mission of the discipline of psychology and its application to society.

I believe it to be very important to engage in advocacy and political giving, as well as professional involvement. Advocacy for one's profession may involve sending letters or e-mails to legislators about some consumer protection or professional legislative concern or issue. Political giving to support the profession helps to direct the course that counseling psychology takes. Advocacy and political giving allow counseling psychologists to influence important professional issues such as scope of practice, licensure laws, full parity for mental health treatment, inclusion of psychologists in Medicare and Medicaid and other third-party payers, regulation of managed care and the insurance industry, hospital privileges, prescriptive authority, social justice advocacy, funding of postgraduate training, and government funding of research (Barnett, 2004). In fact, I would recommend that all students, both graduate and undergraduate, who are interested in psychology join American Psychological Association Graduate Students (APAGS), which represents and supports the interests of its approximately 40,000 members. More information about this very important group is available at http://www.apa.org/apags.

A Day in the Life of a Counseling Psychologist

On a typical workday, I get up at about 5:30 a.m. and exercise either before or after checking my e-mail. My exercise routine consists of stretches, lifting weights, and walking about 4 miles with a neighbor, my partner, or alone. I have breakfast and work on my writing projects, and then I see clients (and occasionally professionals who consult with me) from 9 or 10 a.m. straight through until about 6 p.m., 45 minutes apiece. I may have an hour or so off during the day, but not always. I sometimes have a conference call during the day or early in the evening (about every week and a half or so), usually with the Divisional Ethnic Minority Pipeline group that involves representatives from several divisions working on projects to increase the numbers of ethnic minorities in psychology (currently we are working on a national survey) or with some other board or committee.

I almost always take lunch with me and snack a couple of times during the day. I take calls and make calls between appointments, but I have chosen to not check e-mail or work on other projects unless I go home during the day (which is easy to do if I have at least an hour break, as I live 5 minutes from my office). I find that I go into an altered state while I see clients, and I prefer to keep distractions to a minimum. At the end of the day, I eat something light and then do more e-mail or writing. I spend an hour or two with my partner before bedtime.

On Fridays, I usually have breakfast with two friends with whom I consult on a regular basis or with the Austin Women's Psychotherapy Project, a group of five women who work together to put on conferences a couple of times a year that focus on women's psychological development. I see three or four clients on Fridays and sometimes schedule lunches with friends or business meetings. I also have a once-a-month feminist therapy study group that has been ongoing since 1991. I have dinner on Wednesdays or Thursdays with friends once or twice a month. On weekends, my partner and I walk or ride bicycles for a longer period in the mornings, often do yard or gardening work, and usually work 3 to 6 hours (on writing or other professional projects) each day of the weekend. I enjoy cooking, movies, theater, and socializing with friends or family. I thoroughly enjoy all the work that I do, despite the fact that there are times when I'd rather be at a movie or working in my yard. I have a lot of energy, but this work and lifestyle energize me even more.

In summary, I love the field of counseling psychology, and I believe that most people interested in human behavior would find it interesting, stimulating, and very rewarding. The perspectives, attitudes, skills, and knowledge that counseling psychologists develop as a result of their training make them very marketable in a number of different career paths. The role of counseling psychologist elicits respect, prestige, and power to some degree, as well as being reasonably financially rewarding.

References

American Psychological Association. (2004a). Accredited doctoral programs in professional psychology: 2004. *American Psychologist, 59,* 930–944.

American Psychological Association (2005a, May). *Committee of accreditation online newsletter.* Retrieved July, 30, 2005 from http://www.apa.org/ed/accreditation/coa_homemay05.html

American Psychological Association. (2005b). *Guidelines and principles for accreditation of programs in professional psychology.* Washington, DC: Author.

American Psychological Association. (2007). *Graduate study in psychology.* Washington, DC: Author.

American Psychological Association, Research Office. (2005). *Table 6: Direct human services positions (licensed only): Counseling psychology doctoral-level, 11–12 month salaries for selected settings: 2003.* Retrieved July 30, 2006 from http://research.apa.org/03salary/homepage.html#dhs_counseling

Barlow, D. H. (2004). Psychological treatments. *American Psychologist, 59,* 869–878.

Barnett, J. E. (2004, Winter). On being a psychologist and how to save our profession. *Independent Practitioner: Bulletin of Psychologists in Independent Practice, 24,* 45–46.

Brown, S. D., & Lent, R. W. (Eds.). (1992). Preface. In *Handbook of counseling psychology* (2nd ed., pp. xi–xiii). New York: Wiley.

Brown, S. D., & Lent, R. W. (Eds.). (2000). *Handbook of counseling psychology* (3rd ed.). New York: Wiley.

Clay, R. A. (2005). On the practice horizon. *Monitor on Psychology, 36,* 48–52.

Davis, K. L. (1997). Emphasizing strengths: Counseling psychologists. In R. J. Sternberg (Ed.), *Career paths in psychology: Where your degree can take you.* Washington, DC: American Psychological Association.

DeLeon, P. H., Giesting, B., & Kenkel, M. B. (2003). Community health centers: Exciting opportunities for the 21st century. *Professional Psychology: Research and Practice, 34,* 579–585.

Division of Counseling Psychology. (1985). Minutes of midwinter executive committee meeting. *Counseling Psychologist, 13,* 139–149.

Dobmeyer, A. C., Rowan, A. B., Etherage, J. R., & Wilson, R. J. (2003). Training psychology interns in primary behavioral health care. *Professional Psychology, Research and Practice, 34,* 586–594.

Fassinger, R. E., & Schlossberg, N. K. (1992). Understanding the adult years: Perspectives and implications. In S. D. Brown & R. W. Lent (Eds.), *Handbook of counseling psychology* (2nd ed., pp. 217–249). New York: Wiley.

Fowler, R. D. (1990). Psychology: The core discipline. *American Psychologist, 45,* 1–6.

Fretz, B. R., & Simon, N. P. (1992). Professional issues in counseling psychology: Continuity, change, and challenge. In S. D. Brown

& R. W. Lent (Eds.), *Handbook of counseling psychology* (2nd ed., pp. 3–36). New York: Wiley.

Gray, G., Brody, D. S., & Johnson, D. (2005). The evolution of behavioral primary care. *Professional Psychology: Research and Practice, 36,* 123–129.

Hays, K. F., & Brown, C. H., Jr. (2004). *You're on! Consulting for peak performance.* Washington, DC: American Psychological Association.

Heiby, E. M., DeLeon, P. H., & Anderson, T. (2004). A debate on prescription privileges for psychologists. *Professional Psychologist: Research and Practice, 35,* 336–344.

Heppner, P. P., Casas, J. M., Carter, J., & Stone, G. L. (2000). The maturation of counseling psychology: Multifaceted perspectives, 1978–1998. In S. D. Brown & R. W. Lent (Eds.), *Handbook of counseling psychology* (3rd ed., pp. 3–49). New York: Wiley.

Hesketh, B. (2000). Prevention and development in the workplace. In S. D. Brown & R. W. Lent (Eds.), *Handbook of counseling psychology* (3rd ed., pp. 471–498). New York: Wiley.

Kagan, N., Armsworth, M. W., Altmaier, E. M., Dowd, E. T., Hansen, J. C., Mills, D. H., et al. (1988). Professional practice of counseling psychology in various settings. *The Counseling Psychologist, 16,* 347–365.

Law, B. M. (2004, September). The en-route master's. *Gradpsych: The Magazine of the American Psychological Association of Graduate Students, 2,* 30–31.

National Center for Education Statistics. (2003). *Digest of education statistics, 2003, postsecondary education: Graduates, degrees and attainment.* Retrieved May 30, 2005, from http://nces.ed.gov//programs/digest/d03/

Newman, R. (2005, February). A foundation for change. *Monitor on Psychology, 36,* 51.

Norcross, J. C. (2000). Clinical versus counseling psychology: What's the diff? *Eye on Psi Chi, 5,* 20–23.

Norcross, J. C., Sayette, M. A., Mayne, T. J., Karg, R. S., & Turkson, M. A. (1998). Selecting a doctoral program in professional psychology: Some comparisons among PhD counseling, PhD clinical, and PsyD clinical psychology programs. *Professional Psychology: Research and Practice, 29,* 609–614.

Pope, K. S., & Vasquez, M. J. T. (2005). *How to survive and thrive as a therapist: Information, ideas, and resources for psychologists in practice.* Washington, DC: American Psychological Association.

Pope, K. S., & Vasquez, M. J. T. (in press). *Ethics in psychotherapy and counseling: A practical guide, third edition.* San Francisco: Jossey-Bass.

Seligman, M. E. P. (1998, April). Positive social sciences. *Monitor on Psychology, 29,* 5–6.

Stedman, J. M., Hatch, J. P., Schoenfeld, L. S., & Keilin, W. G. (2005). The structure of internship training: Current patterns and implications for the future of clinical and counseling psychologists. *Professional Psychology: Research and Practice, 36,* 3–8.

Thorp, S. R., O'Donohue, W. T., & Gregg, J. (2005). The predoctoral internship: Is current training anachronistic? *Professional Psychology: Research and Practice, 36,* 16–24.

Vasquez, M. J. T. (2003). Extending the ladder of opportunity: Breaking through the colored glass ceiling (2002 presidential address). *The Counseling Psychologist, 31,* 115–128.

Walsh, W. B. (1999). Toward a broader view of knowing (1998 presidential address). *The Counseling Psychologist, 27,* 120–127.

Paul L. Craig

Clinical Neuropsychology: Brain–Behavior Relationships

9

"I love neuropsychology!" When I heard Erin Bigler spontaneously proclaim his passion for clinical neuropsychology while being honored with the Distinguished Neuropsychologist Award at the 1999 annual meeting of the National Academy of Neuropsychology (NAN; Ruff, 2003), I realized that he was speaking for the entire profession. It is rare for a leader in any scientific or health care field to make such a spontaneous and genuine public declaration of love for his or her profession. But as Bigler spoke from his heart, silence spread throughout the audience, and I noted several affirming nods acknowledging that he was speaking for all of us in the field. Neuropsychologists love neuropsychology!

Bigler's declaration was followed by an erudite lecture concerning the pathophysiology of traumatic brain injury and its contextual relationship with neuroimaging and

Paul L. Craig, PhD, ABPP-CN, is an associate clinical professor at the University of Washington School of Medicine, Department of Psychiatry and Behavioral Sciences. He received a BS in biopsychology at Nebraska Wesleyan University in 1974 and a PhD in clinical psychology at the University of Wyoming in 1980 and completed postdoctoral fellowships at the University of Washington School of Medicine and the University of Oklahoma Health Sciences Center. He delivers neuropsychological services through his independent practice in Anchorage, Alaska.

neuropsychological functioning (Bigler, 2001). This invited lecture was not without controversy and stimulated further discussion and scholarly debate (Bigler, 2003; Lees-Haley, Green, Rohling, Fox, & Allen, 2003; Ruff, 2003). My passion for clinical neuropsychology has been fueled by the foundation of empirical research on which the profession has been built. As is the case in any burgeoning field of science and health care practice, intellectual debate provides the yeast to leaven the profession. Since I first became interested in neuropsychology in the 1970s, the field has been replete (I am thankful to report) with a variety of professional and scientific debates leading the profession down the path of growth and maturation (e.g., Adams, 2002; Ardilla, 2002).

In this chapter, I provide an overview of neuropsychology as a potential career. I am writing in 2005, and the amount of change I have witnessed in the field of neuropsychology during the past 30 years has been staggering. I suspect that the rate of change in the profession will increase exponentially as a result of advances in assessment technology, neurosciences, neurocognitive theories, and research, as well as developments in connate fields such as neuroimaging. If you choose to pursue a career in neuropsychology, you will need to be a lifelong learner, given the inevitable changes on the road ahead. In this chapter, you will be introduced to the profession of neuropsychology as it exists today. I can barely begin to speculate what the profession may look like after another 30 years. If you pursue training to become a clinical neuropsychologist, you can help create the future of the profession through your research, clinical practice, and involvement in professional activities and associations.

Neuropsychology as a Profession

What exactly is neuropsychology? I am frequently called on to explain the field of clinical neuropsychology to the public. For example, when I serve as an expert witness in the courtroom, one of my first tasks is to educate the jurors about the profession. I begin by saying, "Neuropsychology is the scientific study of brain–behavior relationships." Then I say, "Clinical neuropsychology is the application of this scientifically derived knowledge for purposes of evaluating and treating individuals with known or suspected brain disorders." I emphasize that clinical neuropsychologists, depending on their interests and training, may provide assessment and treatment services to children, adolescents, and adults.

Neuropsychological evaluation techniques typically involve observing and measuring the behavior of an individual with a known or suspected brain disorder, which may be developmental or acquired. In almost all circumstances, the psychologist completes an assessment by administering standardized neuropsychological tests, recording the patient's responses, and comparing his or her test performances with normative performances expected among similar individuals. To determine whether neuropsychological test results are normal or abnormal, the neuropsychologist must analyze not only the level of ability the patient evidences but also the patient's pattern of strengths and weaknesses among the various skills assessed. Moreover, the neuropsychologist should analyze the process the patient uses when responding to a task to better understand why he or she may be experiencing difficulty when attempting to function within a particular social setting such as school or work (Kaplan, 1990). A well-trained neuropsychologist must also use clinical judgment to make sure that an individual is not being incorrectly diagnosed or categorized strictly based on a test score. There are many reasons why individuals may perform poorly on one or more neuropsychological tests, including motivational deficits, cultural and linguistic factors, emotional disorders, and uncooperativeness. Brain dysfunction is one of many putative explanations for poor performance on neuropsychological tests.

The practicing neuropsychologist must be thoroughly familiar with human neuroanatomy, as well as with the neuropathology associated with various developmental and acquired brain disorders. However, neuropsychological assessment does not involve direct investigation of brain structures and neural pathways. Rather, a neuropsychologist uses behavioral assessment techniques to infer how well the patient's brain is functioning in relation to memory, problem solving, language and communication, visuospatial and constructional skills, and related mental abilities. The neuropsychologist can usually address the patient's neuropsychological prognosis by examining the patient's history and the neuropathological condition thought to be causing the patient's current deficits.

In addition to neuropsychological evaluation services, many neuropsychologists are involved in treatment. For example, some neuropsychologists provide cognitive rehabilitation, psychotherapy, and related psychoeducational services to patients experiencing neurocognitive deficits following a traumatic brain injury or some other acquired insult to the central nervous system (e.g., Prigatano, 1999; Prigatano, Gilsky, & Klonoff, 1996; Sohlberg & Mateer, 2001). Although debate has surrounded the efficacy of various approaches used to rehabilitate brain-impaired patients (e.g., Salazar et al., 2000), reviews of the outcome research generally have supported the clinical utility of specific cognitive rehabilitation techniques (Cope, 1995; National Academy of Neuropsychology, 2002; National Institutes of Health Consensus Development Panel, 1999; Park & Ingles, 2001). Certainly, more refined approaches to neuropsychological rehabilitation should be developed and researched so that the treatment needs of individuals who have survived a significant traumatic brain injury are appropriately and cost-effectively met.

Work Settings and Activities

Clinical neuropsychologists work in a broad range of settings, including medical–surgical hospitals, psychiatric facilities, rehabilitation programs, outpatient practices, and others. Some neuropsychologists have academic appointments at universities within psychology departments and/or within a medical school department (e.g., neurology or rehabilitation medicine), where they may be involved in training and supervising students, interns, residents, and postdoctoral fellows in clinical neuropsychology.

As a result of the tireless efforts during the past 15 years of Jerry Sweet and his colleagues (Sweet & Moberg, 1990; Sweet, Moberg, & Suchy, 2000a, 2000b; Sweet, Moberg, & Westergaard, 1996; Sweet, Peck, Abramowitz, & Etzweiler, 2002, 2003), much is known about the range of professional activities associated with the profession of clinical neuropsychology, including the economics of practice. If you are seriously interested in becoming a clinical neuropsychologist, you would be well advised to read each of Sweet's publications summarizing various surveys completed during the past two decades. Others have published the results of related surveys regarding the practice of clinical neuropsychology in the more remote past (e.g., Putnam & DeLuca, 1990). Reviewing historical trends in the profession may lead to some insight regarding what the future might hold for newly trained professionals during the next few decades.

The most recently published survey (Sweet et al., 2002, 2003) was cosponsored by the Division of Clinical Neuropsychology of the American Psychological Association (APA Division 40) and the National Academy of Neuropsychology. More than 1,400 neuropsychologists who were members of one or both organizations responded (33.5% response rate). This survey, distributed in 2000, revealed that the proportion of women in the profession of neuropsychology had increased rapidly; 37.6% of the respondents were women. Private practice has become a predominant employment setting for neuropsychologists. More than two thirds of the respondents reported some involvement in private practice, and 38.7% of the respondents reported that their entire livelihood was derived from private practice. At least four of five respondents classified themselves as working full time. Private practitioners, as compared with neuropsychologists employed by institutions, reported a more diverse set of weekly clinical activities, a lower likelihood to use nondoctoral assessment technicians for administration of neuropsychological tests (Brandt & Van Gorp, 1999), and a greater amount of time engaging in forensic activities such as serving as an expert witness.

On a more personal level, I have provided professional services in a variety of settings during my career as a neuropsychologist. In the past, I have consulted with a comprehensive outpatient rehabilitation facility as well as an acute inpatient rehabilitation program located within a medical–surgical hospital. I was one of two founders of a behavioral health practice that subsequently developed into a large multidisciplinary outpatient mental health clinic.

Since 1997, I have been in solo private practice and almost exclusively provide neuropsychological assessment services on an outpatient basis. During each stage of my career, a typical day in my professional life has varied significantly depending on my involvements and commitments. When I was providing services as a consultant to the outpatient rehabilitation program, I participated in group counseling sessions with patients with brain injury and consulted with the multidisciplinary rehabilitation team to ensure that the services were appropriately integrated and individualized on the basis of each patient's neuropsychological strengths and weaknesses. I provided similar services as a consultant to the acute inpatient rehabilitation program. In that setting, I found myself spending a significant amount of time meeting with family members to help them understand the neuropsychological consequences of the acute insult to the brain incurred by their loved one (e.g., traumatic brain injury or cerebrovascular accident).

In my current outpatient practice, I am actively involved almost every day in the assessment of individuals with known or suspected brain disorders. I spend about an hour interviewing each patient to obtain a thorough health and psychosocial history. If a family member is available, I prefer to have him or her participate in the clinical interview to augment the history provided by the patient. Likewise, I review any records that have been made available to me through the referral source. Depending on the current level of patient functioning and the clinical questions to be answered, test administration can be very brief (e.g., administration of a dementia screening instrument in the case of a patient with advanced dementia) or can last up to a full day when a comprehensive neuropsychological evaluation is requested. Consistent with the practice pattern of the majority of neuropsychologists (Sweet et al., 2002), I employ testing assistants in my practice.

Hence, a typical day at this point in my career might involve two or more clinical interviews, an hour or more of record review, and a few hours of dictating, proofreading, and finalizing one or more neuropsychological evaluation reports. I frequently meet with patients and family members to provide feedback about my findings, including the recommendations contained in the report. I also encourage the patient and family to discuss the neuropsychological findings and recommendations with the referral source (e.g., physician, vocational rehabilitation counselor). Sometimes I am asked to travel to a remote village in the Alaska bush to provide neuropsychological consultation services (Craig, 2005). Although I could easily decline this type of work, I accept these requests in the same spirit of adventure that brought me to Alaska in 1980.

On some days, I find myself sequestered in my office for a few hours with a court reporter and two or more attorneys, responding to their questions during a deposition. Likewise, I sometimes am asked to serve as a witness in the courtroom relative to civil or criminal cases. If I have seen a patient in the context of a clinical referral from a physician and, later, a neuropsychological issue arises that is pertinent to a legal matter before the court, I am typically called to testify as a fact witness. If my professional involvement was based on being retained by legal counsel to serve as an expert relative to a civil or criminal case, my role in the courtroom is significantly different. In either role (i.e., fact witness or expert witness), I must remain unbiased and base my testimony on objective data interpreted in the context of published neuropsychological research rather than expressing a personal opinion or a subjective impression. Attorneys function as advocates. Neuropsychologists must avoid advocacy and need to remain objective and scientific when providing testimony.

When I was actively involved in providing neuropsychological services to hospitalized patients at a medical–surgical hospital, my day frequently concluded with a couple of hours at the hospital evaluating patients with impaired mental functions at the request of neurologists, neurosurgeons, internists, and related health care providers. Since 1997, my outpatient practice has followed a fairly predictable weekly schedule, with each new patient scheduled for the next available evaluation appointment. However, when working in an inpatient setting, the flow of work is not unlike drinking from a water fountain connected to an antiquated plumbing system. One minute, you are gazing at the fountain with nothing but an occasional gurgle emerging from the spigot; a moment later, as you hold your mouth close to the fountain, water is gushing toward your face, and you wonder if you can drink fast enough to avoid aspiration! Making yourself available in an inpatient setting can be quite rewarding professionally but can also be taxing because of the unpredictable demands on your time.

In addition to the activities I have described, many university-affiliated neuropsychologists are actively involved in research, as well as teaching and supervision of graduate students, interns, postdoctoral fellows, and related trainees. Some private practice neuropsychologists also maintain very active research programs in association with their clinical practices. A few neuropsychologists have contracts with pharmaceutical companies to participate in clinical trials to objectively determine whether and how proposed drugs influence cognition. In summary, professional neuropsychologists are applying specialty knowledge regarding brain–behavior relationships in a broad range of settings.

Academic Preparation

Sweet et al. (2002) reported that among the respondents to their survey of neuropsychologists, 64.9% had completed doctoral programs in clinical psychology, suggesting that this has been the most common path toward a career in clinical neuropsychology. Consistent with this historical trend, I completed my doctorate at an APA-approved clinical psychology training program at the University of Wyoming in 1980. Although my undergraduate major at Nebraska Wesleyan University was biopsychology, I did not become aware of clinical neuropsychology as an area of professional specialization until my 2nd year of graduate school. In September 1977, a doctoral program classmate, Dean Delis, returned from a summer practicum completed at the Boston Veterans Administration Hospital bubbling with stories about clinical neuropsychology. My intellectual curiosity was piqued, and I began reading everything I could find on neuropsychology in the university library.

During the last year of my doctoral studies, I completed an internship in health care psychology at the University of Minnesota Health Sciences Center, where I had the privilege of being supervised in clinical neuropsychology by Manfred Meier. Thereafter, I completed a postdoctoral fellowship specializing in rural community mental health, an area of professional interest throughout my training and career, through the University of Washington, School of Medicine. During this fellowship, I primarily lived and worked in Ketchikan, Alaska. In retrospect, this adventuresome lark defined the rest of my career. Twenty-five years later, I am still living and working in Alaska.

After a 3-year stint as the program director and psychologist at the community mental health center in Homer, Alaska, I decided that I wanted to specialize in clinical neuropsychology. I applied for a fellowship in clinical neuropsychology at the University of Oklahoma Health Sciences Center and was delighted when I received notification of acceptance. After completing this fellowship I returned to Alaska. I have maintained a clinical faculty appointment at the University of Washington, School of Medicine, through the multistate regional health care training consortium known as WWAMI—an acronym for Washington, Wyoming, Alaska, Montana, and Idaho.

APA Division 40—Clinical Neuropsychology (1989) defined the training that is required to be a clinical neuropsychologist: doctoral-level training, including successful completion of didactic and experiential training in neuropsychology and neuroscience at a regionally accredited university; 2 or more years of supervised training applying neuropsychological services in a clinical setting; licensure to provide psychological services in the state or province in which services are being delivered; and review by one's peers as a test of these competencies. This definition states, "Attainment of the ABCN/ABPP Diplomate in Clinical Neuropsychology is the clearest evidence of competence as a clinical neuropsychologist, assuring that all of these criteria have been met" (p. 22). The American Board of Clinical Neuropsychology (ABCN) is one of several boards affiliated with the American Board of Professional Psychology (ABPP). As of August 2005, 526 neuropsychologists had achieved board certification by the ABCN/ABPP.

In 1992, I passed the ABCN examination and became board certified in clinical neuropsychology through ABPP—a credential I value quite highly. If you are serious about becoming a clinical neuropsychologist, I would strongly encourage you to pursue the necessary training and supervised experience to eventually obtain board certification. As is the case with board certification in medicine, very bright and talented professionals sometimes fail the ABCN examination. When I was examined, the pass rate was about 70%. Obviously, failing the ABCN examination can come as a significant blow to a newly trained neuropsychologist, who has probably never failed a test in his or her life. However, well-trained and qualified applicants who initially fail can use the feedback from the exam to continue to develop expertise within neuropsychology. Frequently, these promising new professionals are able to pass the examination if they persist and reapply. Ivnik, Haaland, and Bieliauskas (2000) published a very useful article regarding the steps involved in obtaining board certification through the ABCN/ABPP. This article may be of interest if you decide that a professional career in neuropsychology is consistent with your interests.

Similarly, if you want to learn more about how to become a neuropsychologist, you should read the proceedings from the Houston Conference on Specialty Education and Training in Clinical Neuropsychology (Hannay, 1998). You may also benefit from reviewing the list of training programs in clinical neuropsychology (Cripe, 1995). The electronic list of training programs posted on the APA Division 40 Web site provides the most current list of doctoral programs, internships, and postdoctoral fellowships in neuropsychology (http://div40.org/tprograms.html).

During the past several years, finding an appropriate internship has proved to be a bottleneck for doctoral students in psychology in general, and neuropsychology in particular. Mittenberg, Petersen, Cooper, Strauman, and Essig (2000) surveyed the clinical neuropsychology internship programs listed by Cripe (1995) and found that, "selection criteria reflect a vertically integrated model of education and training in accordance with the Houston Conference model" (Mittenberg et al., 2000, p. 1). When applying for a doctoral training program with the goal of becoming a clinical neuropsychologist, it would be to your benefit to apply to programs that adhere to the Houston Conference model.

Financial Compensation

Independent practice in clinical neuropsychology has provided me with a healthy income, allowing me to lead a comfortable middle-class lifestyle. I have worked hard but have been sufficiently rewarded financially throughout my professional career to be able to raise a family on a single income, enjoy the occasional fly-in fishing trip to various lakes and rivers in Alaska, and savor some family trips to international destinations, creating memories that will last a lifetime. I have not created the personal wealth enjoyed by my agemates who majored in business and pursued entrepreneurial goals since they were in their 20s. However, the quality of my life has been outstanding as a result of the intellectual and financial rewards associated with my professional activities in neuropsychology.

Survey data collected by the NAN and the APA Division 40 in 2000 (Sweet et al., 2003) suggest that during the past decade, managed care has significantly affected independent practitioners in clinical neuropsychology throughout the United States. Neuropsychologists reported difficulty gaining access to membership on managed care panels. For those who were included on such panels, managed care companies frequently limited provision of services to an extent perceived as having a negative impact on quality of patient care. Many neuropsychologists reported that they felt obligated to provide a more thorough service than can be rendered in the amount of time allowed per evaluation under managed care and Medicare. Typically, conscientious neuropsychologists needed to write off the additional professional time as uncollectible following completion of a more extensive evaluation. Survey results indicated that "professional income is influenced by year of licensed practice, practice setting, gender, types and amounts of non-clinical professional activities, and types and amounts of reimbursement sources within one's clinical practice" (Sweet et al., 2003, p. 558). As compared with data collected in 1993, neuropsychologists responding to the survey distributed 7 years later reported that they were engaging in more hours of clinical practice per week but that the average level of income had decreased. In the case of private practice incomes derived from all combined professional sources, Sweet et al. (2003) reported a 12.1% decline from 1993 to 2000. It appears that some of this reported decline in income is due to the impact of strictures imposed by managed care companies during the mid to late 1990s. In support of this conclusion, Sweet et al. reported a modest negative correlation between income level and provision of neuropsychological services to managed care patients as well as Medicaid, Medicare, and public aid recipients.

The 1,164 respondents in 2000 who stated they worked full time reported a positively skewed distribution of income (Sweet et al., 2003). Specifically, the average income was slightly over $100,000 per year ($M = \$104,132$), but half of full-time respondents reported that they earned less than $83,000 per year ($Mdn = \$83,000$). There were a few fairly dramatic outliers among the respondents (e.g., 4 reported income in excess of $400,000 per year). Likewise, the authors noted a very significant difference between the average income reported among neuropsychologists in private practice ($M = \$120,177$) and those in institutional settings ($M = \$78,089$ per year).

In an attempt to understand the outliers and the large mean differences between private practice and institutionally employed neuropsychologists, Sweet contacted five of his private practice colleagues and asked them how they interpreted the income question when they completed the survey. Only two of these five private practitioners had interpreted the survey question as the authors of the survey had intended—that is, as a request to report net income (i.e., after deducting practice expenses from gross revenue). The other three private practitioners thought they had been asked to report gross revenue collected annually by the private practice before deducting expenses. Sweet et al. (2003) concluded that misinterpretation of the income question may have resulted in somewhat inflated data for some of the private practitioners responding to the survey.

Sweet et al. (2003) reported a powerful gender gap, with men reporting much higher incomes than women. However, the survey (Sweet et al., 2002) also demonstrated that female neuropsychologists were significantly younger and had fewer years of licensed practice than did male respondents. As I stated in a previous section, women have recently been entering the profession of clinical neuropsychology in much greater numbers than in the past. Age and years of licensed practice were two factors that Sweet et al. (2003) reported as being significantly positively correlated with annual income. Perhaps the gender gap in income will diminish as beginning female neuropsychologists increase the number of years in which they have engaged in licensed practice.

It will be interesting to compare and contrast data from new surveys of neuropsychologists with the historical trends I have described. Despite the reported decline in income among neuropsychologists from 1993 through 2000, a well-trained, competent neuropsychologist can still earn a reasonable living in this profession. Viewed from a business perspective, selling your time by the hour is not a business model that leads to the incredible wealth that some enterprising entrepreneurs have achieved. But a career in neuropsychology certainly can be financially, intellectually, and professionally rewarding.

Attributes of a Successful Neuropsychologist

Many personal characteristics collectively contribute to a successful career in clinical neuropsychology. Certainly, learning to be a clinical neuropsychologist is very intellectually demanding. By way of example, the neuropsychological trainee must learn the nuances of neuroanatomy. In the case of dementia of the Alzheimer's type, it is helpful for the neuropsychologist to know about the substantia innominata, which is the tissue located in the basal forebrain below the anterior perforated substance and anterior to the globus pallidus and ansa lenticularis. In particular, the substania innominata is inclusive of the nucleus basalis of Meynert, which is thought to provide cortical cholinergic innervation and has been the focus of intense research in the field of dementia.

This information is not intended to intimidate prospective neuropsychological students; a multitude of individuals studying medicine, neuropsychology, neuroscience, and related fields learn neuroanatomy. However, learning neuroanatomy requires a lot of rote memory and three-dimensional spatial reasoning skills to conceptualize how various brain structures fit together and interconnect. One neuroanatomical structure may be known by two or more names, all of which are considered correct labels. Likewise, two or more adjacent or functionally connected brain structures may collectively be described by yet another name. In addition to mastery of the fundamentals of neuroanatomy, training in neuropsychology requires the student to learn about neuropathology, neuroimaging, neurophysiology, and related fields within the neurosciences.

Neuropsychologists must also have broader training in clinical psychology to practice competently. When observing and measuring behavior, it is very important to be knowledgeable about and attentive to the cornucopia of variables that can influence performance—for example, motivation, prior learning, emotional disorders, and personality and character structure, to name but a few. The brain is not a binary computer crunching algorithms; it is an incredibly complex organ subserving sensory functions, perception, cognition, emotions, and associated behavioral responses of the individual.

Cross-cultural and transcultural competence is becoming increasingly important in clinical neuropsychology. Participating in a neuropsychological evaluation is a culturally defined endeavor. Interpreting neuropsychological test results and providing patients with feedback and recommendations require the neuropsychologist to be familiar with the cultural context of both the tests and the patient. Although I was not formally providing neuropsychological services while on vacation in Thailand several years ago, an experience I had while trekking with my daughters in the mountains near Chang Mai opened my eyes to the importance of cultural factors in interpretations of neuropsychological phenomena. Through a series of unexpected circumstances, I found myself in a small mountain village communicating through a translator with a Thai gentleman who had obviously experienced a right hemisphere cerebrovascular accident about 1 month earlier. During the prior year, he reportedly had another much milder right hemisphere stroke, from which he had enjoyed an excellent recovery. Unfortunately, he was not faring as well following the more recent cerebrovascular event. After struggling to help him understand what had probably occurred to his brain (e.g., "The right half of your brain controls the left side of your body"), I stopped talking and began listening to the interpreter more carefully. I discovered that this man's explanation for each cerebrovascular accident was that one or more chickens had stolen half of his spirit. Following the first stroke a year earlier, he sacrificed a chicken in front of his hut, after which his symptoms began to improve quite rapidly. He had sacrificed several chickens during the month following his more recent stroke, but to no avail. As I pondered his interpretive model for his neurological condition, I wryly wondered how many of our current scientific models for understanding neuropathological conditions and remediating neuropsychological impairment will be viewed far in the future as equally primitive, if not absurd.

Each year, I have the pleasure of introducing the WWAMI medical students in Alaska to clinical neuropsychology. I typically begin the lecture with a caveat: "If anybody ever tells you they know how the brain works, hold them immediately suspect!" If you choose to pursue a career in clinical neuropsychology, it will be very important for you to be broadly trained in both psychology and the neurosciences. While studying neuropsychological research, a student inevitably learns how far knowledge has advanced with regard to understanding the structure and function of the human brain. But the more you learn, the more you begin to realize how much is not known regarding the conundrum of the brain.

In short, a successful clinical neuropsychologist must be bright in relation to verbal and spatial thinking and broadly knowledgeable about neurosciences and psychology, enjoy working with people, have good critical thinking skills, enjoy report writing, and be meticulous when dealing with details. A full-day neuropsychological evaluation contains a huge amount of data that must be correctly scored and interpreted. The professional neuropsychologist must attend to all of the details associated with completing a neuropsychological assessment. However, a competent neuropsychologist also needs to be able to rise above these details to think more abstractly about the context from which these data emerge for purposes of arriving at reliable and valid diagnostic and prognostic conclusions. Finally, a student who wants to become a clinical neuropsychologist must be both patient and tenacious. The number of years of training necessary to become a board-certified neuropsychologist can be daunting. But senior professionals in the field usually remember those years of training as some of the most intellectually rewarding years of their lives.

Opportunities for Employment

More than 4,000 psychologists in the United States and Canada have identified themselves as practicing within the profession of clinical neuropsychology (Sweet et al., 2002). By the end of 2004, more than 500 licensed professionals had become board-certified neuropsychologists through the American Board of Clinical Neuropsychology. The APA Division 40 (Clinical Neuropsychology) was created in 1979 with 441 founding members (Goodglass, 1979). As of 2005, Division 40's membership roster had grown to 4,006 psychologists, making it the third largest of the 55 various divisions within the APA.

Many other examples could be provided to support the notion that the profession of neuropsychology has grown exponentially in the past 25 years. Despite this growth, the academic arena and health care marketplace appear to have absorbed the ever-increasing pool of clinical neuropsychologists who have emerged from postdoctoral fellowships. During each of the past 20 years in which I have practiced, I have attended one or more professional meetings with my neuropsychological colleagues (e.g., APA Division 40, NAN, International Neuropsychological Society). Although I recall several colleagues describing anxiety caused by the vicissitudes of private practice and others lamenting the political battles that sometimes occur within institutions, I cannot recall ever hearing a board-certified or board-eligible neuropsychological colleague complain that he or she could not find work. I am not aware of any employment surveys specifically targeting recent graduates of postdoctoral fellowships in neuropsychology. However, on the basis of personal communication with colleagues, my impression is that these newly trained professionals are finding employment in their field of specialization.

Some neuropsychologists are primarily involved with grant-funded research projects, which are frequently housed at university-affiliated teaching hospitals. Others are employed institutionally and spend most of their time providing neuropsychological services to patients. Some enjoy a combination of grant-supported research commingled with clinical service delivery. Private practice neuropsychologists work with a variety of populations depending on their area of expertise, specialization, and referral sources. Pediatric neuropsychologists have received specialized training that allows them to evaluate brain disorders among children and adolescents in the context of the template of normal development. Other practitioners work primarily with adults, and some specialize in the assessment of older individuals. Some neuropsychologists exclusively evaluate and treat physician-referred patients. Others mostly evaluate and treat individuals who are referred by mental health professionals and who have a primary psychiatric diagnosis with no other neurological problems identified. Some neuropsychological colleagues have built private practices focused on serving as a forensic consultant and expert witness (Heilbronner, 2005). Each of these niches is unique, but they all have a common denominator—a clinical neuropsychologist who is trained and credentialed to practice in this field of professional specialization.

Resources

For those who want to learn more about the scientific underpinnings of neuropsychology, *Fundamentals of Human Neuropsychology* (Whishaw & Kolb, 2003) is an outstanding text. Likewise, if you want to learn more about assessment, *Neuropsychological Assessment* (Lezak, Howiesen, Loring, Hannay, & Fischer, 2004) is considered by many to be the definitive book in the field. The APA Division 40 has a student organization, the Association of Neuropsychology Students in Training (ANST), that you may want to join. Using an Internet search engine, you can quickly learn more about the various professional organizations relevant to training and practice in clinical neuropsychology (e.g., APA Division 40, NAN, International Neuropsychological Society, Association for Internship Training in Clinical Neuropsychology, and the Association of Postdoctoral Programs in Clinical Neuropsychology). The American Board of Clinical Neuropsychology has some very useful Web links on its page and may be a good starting point for the inquisitive reader (http://www.theabcn.org/links.html).

If you are an energetic student who wants to pursue a professional career in clinical neuropsychology, follow your passion. As anybody who has lived more than a handful of decades knows, life never follows the plan one envisioned during one's youth. However, if you are focused on the goal of becoming a clinical neuropsychologist and tenaciously work toward that goal, it is possible that you may one day address a group of your colleagues and find yourself proclaiming, "I love neuropsychology!"

References

Adams, K. M. (2002). The Houston conference: The road more traveled. *Neuropsychology Review, 12,* 131–133.

American Psychological Assocation, Division 40—Clinical Neuropsychology. (1989). Definition of a clinical neuropsychologist. *The Clinical Neuropsychologist, 3,* 22.

Ardilla, A. (2002). Houston Conference: Need for more fundamental knowledge in neuropsychology. *Neuropsychology Review, 12,* 127–130.

Bigler, E. D. (2001). The lesion(s) in traumatic brain injury: Implications for clinical neuropsychology. *Archives of Clinical Neuropsychology, 16,* 95–131.

Bigler, E. D. (2003). Response to commentary: Neurobiology and neuropathology underlie the neuropsychological deficits associated with traumatic brain injury. *Archives of Clinical Neuropsychology, 18,* 595–621.

Brandt, J., & Van Gorp, W. (1999). American Academy of Clinical Neuropsychology policy on the use of non-doctoral-level personnel in conducting clinical neuropsychological evaluations. *Journal of Clinical and Experimental Neuropsychology, 21,* 1.

Cope, D. N. (1995). The effectiveness of traumatic brain injury rehabilitation: A review. *Brain Injury, 9,* 649–670.

Craig, P. L. (2005). On the far edge of the last frontier: The Alaska experience. In R. L. Heilbronner (Ed.), *Forensic neuropsychology casebook* (pp. 167–184). New York: Guilford Press.

Cripe, L. L. (1995). Listing of training programs in clinical neuropsychology: 1995. *The Clinical Neuropsychologist, 9,* 327–398.

Goodglass, H. (1979). *Letter to the APA Division of Clinical Neuropsychology.* Retrieved July 10, 2005, from http://www.lib.lsu.edu/special/apa/corr1.htm

Hannay, H. J. (1998). Proceedings: The Houston Conference on specialty education and training in clinical neuropsychology. *Archives of Clinical Neuropsychology, 13,* 157–158.

Heilbronner, R. L. (Ed.). (2005). *Forensic neuropsychology casebook.* New York: Guilford Press.

Ivnik, R. J., Haaland, K. Y., & Bieliauskas, L. A. (2000). The American Board of Clinical Neuropsychology (ABCN), 2000 update. *The Clinical Neuropsychologist, 14,* 261–268.

Kaplan, E. (1990). The process approach to neuropsychological assessment of psychiatric patients. *Journal of Neuropsychiatric and Clinical Neurosciences, 2,* 72–87.

Lees-Haley, P. R., Green, P., Rohling, M. L., Fox, D. D., & Allen, L. M., III. (2003). The lesion(s) in traumatic brain injury: Implications for a clinical neuropsychology. *Archives of Clinical Neuropsychology, 18*, 584–593.

Lezak, M. D., Howiesen, D. B., Loring, D., Hanna, H. J., & Fischer, J. S. (2004). *Neuropsychological assessment* (4th ed.). New York: Oxford University Press.

Mittenberg, W., Petersen, R. S., Cooper, J. T., Strauman, S., & Essig, S. M. (2000). Selection criteria for clinical neuropsychology internships. *The Clinical Neuropsychologist, 14*, 1–6.

National Academy of Neuropsychology. (2002). *Cognitive rehabilitation: Official statement of the National Academy of Neuropsychology.* Denver, CO: Author.

National Institutes of Health Consensus Development Panel on Rehabilitation of Persons With Traumatic Brain Injury. (1999). Rehabilitation of persons with traumatic brain injury. *JAMA, 282*, 974–983.

Park, N. W., & Ingles, J. L. (2001). Effectiveness of attention rehabilitation after an acquired brain injury: A meta-analysis. *Neuropsychology, 15*, 199–210.

Prigatano, G. P. (1999). *Principles of neuropsychological rehabilitation.* New York: Oxford University Press.

Prigatano, G. P., Gilsky, E. L., & Klonoff, P. S. (1996). Cognitive rehabilitation after traumatic brain injury. In P. W. Corrigan & S. C. Yudofsky (Eds.), *Cognitive rehabilitation for neuropsychiatric disorders* (pp. 223–242). Washington, DC: American Psychiatric Publishing.

Putnam, S. H., & DeLuca, J. W. (1990). The TCN professional practice survey: Part I. General practices of neuropsychologists in primary employment and private practice settings. *The Clinical Neuropsychologist, 4*, 199–244.

Ruff, R. M. (2003). A friendly critique of neuropsychology: Facing the challenges of our future. *Archives of Clinical Neuropsychology, 18*, 847–864.

Salazar, A. M., Warden, D. L., Schwab, K., Spector, J., Braverman, S., Walter, J., et al. (2000). Cognitive rehabilitation for traumatic brain injury: A randomized trial. Defense and Veterans Head Injury Program (DVHIP) study group. *JAMA, 283*, 3075–3081.

Sohlberg, M. M., & Mateer, C. A. (2001). *Cognitive rehabilitation: An integrative neuropsychological approach.* New York: Guilford Press.

Sweet, J. J., & Moberg, P. J. (1990). A survey of practices and beliefs among ABPP and non-ABPP clinical neuropsychologists. *The Clinical Neuropsychologist, 4*, 101–120.

Sweet, J. J., Moberg, P. J., & Suchy, Y. (2000a). Ten-year follow-up survey of clinical neuropsychologists: Part I. Practices and beliefs. *The Clinical Neuropsychologist, 14*, 18–37.

Sweet, J. J., Moberg, P. J., & Suchy, Y. (2000b). Ten-year follow-up survey of clinical neuropsychologists: Part II. Private practice and economics. *The Clinical Neuropsychologist, 14,* 479–495.

Sweet, J. J., Moberg, P. J., & Westergaard, C. (1996). Five-year follow-up survey of practices and beliefs of clinical neuropsychologists. *The Clinical Neuropsychologist, 10,* 201–221.

Sweet, J. J., Peck, E. A., III, Abramowitz, C., & Etzweiler, S. (2002). National Academy of Neuropsychology/Division 40 of the American Psychological Association practice survey of clinical neuropsychology in the United States: Part I. Practitioner and practice characteristics, professional activities, and time requirements. *The Clinical Neuropsychologist, 16,* 109–127.

Sweet, J. J., Peck, E. A., III, Abramowitz, C., & Etzweiler, S. (2003). National Academy of Neuropsychology/Division 40 of the American Psychological Association practice survey of clinical neuropsychology in the United States: Part II. Reimbursement experiences, practice economics, billing practices, and incomes. *Archives of Clinical Neuropsychology, 18,* 557–582.

Whishaw, I. Q., & Kolb, B. (2003). *Fundamentals of human neuropsychology* (5th ed.). New York: Worth Publishers.

Brian P. Daly and Ronald T. Brown

Career Experiences of Clinical Psychologists Working in a Hospital

10

C linical psychologists deal with the causes, prevention, diagnosis, and treatment of individuals with psychological problems. Over the past 50 years, the treatment settings have broadened to encompass a number of specialties that include the work of clinical psychologists in hospitals. These psychologists are often referred to as *clinical health psychologists* because of their involvement in psychological, behavioral, and health matters.

Clinical health psychology is now recognized as a specialty within the practice of psychology; the American Board of Professional Psychology offers certification in clinical health psychology. The American Psychological Association's

Brian P. Daly received his PhD from Loyola University Chicago, his MA from Boston College, an MA from Boston University, and his BA from Boston College. At present, he is a postdoctoral fellow in the College of Health Professions at Temple University in Philadelphia receiving specialty training in pediatric psychology.

Ronald T. Brown received his PhD from Georgia State University and his BA from Emory University. At present, he is dean of the College of Health Professions and professor of public health, psychology, and pediatrics at Temple University in Philadelphia. He currently serves as editor of the *Journal of Pediatric Psychology* and holds the diplomate from the American Board of Professional Psychology in the specialty area of clinical health psychology.

(APA's) comprehensive definition of *clinical health psychology* is as follows:

> The specialty of Clinical Health Psychology applies scientific knowledge of the interrelationships among behavioral, emotional, cognitive, social and biological components in health and disease to the promotion and maintenance of health; the prevention, treatment and rehabilitation of illness and disability; and the improvement of the health care system. The distinct focus of Clinical Health Psychology is on physical health problems. The specialty is dedicated to the development of knowledge regarding the interface between behavior and health, and to the delivery of high quality services based on that knowledge to individuals, families, and health care systems. (American Psychological Association, Commission for the Recognition of Specialties and Proficiencies in Professional Psychology, 1997)

This description indicates that clinical psychologists in hospitals are skilled at and engage in multiple roles within the hospital. These roles include team-oriented and individual tasks and activities. Clinical psychologists in hospitals

- are collaborative members of multidisciplinary teams whose goal is to improve patient care and functioning;
- work as solo professionals providing assessment, prevention, intervention, and research to improve the field and practice of clinical health psychology;
- communicate psychological diagnosis to physicians, the treatment team, the family, and the patient;
- conduct psychological and health-related research to improve the general health and welfare of society;
- engage in teaching, training, and supervisory roles for psychology and medical students, psychology and medical interns, postdoctoral fellows, clinical staff, nurses, and other health care professionals;
- work in staff and leadership positions for clinics, inpatient and outpatient programs, and psychology training programs; and
- conduct program development and evaluation.

The nature of the career of clinical psychologists in hospitals is ever changing, and responsibilities and specializations continue to grow. Their clients hail from diverse cultural, ethnic, and socioeconomic backgrounds and statuses, and cover the life span from newborn to geriatric. It is not uncommon for clinical psychologists employed in a hospital to engage in prevention programs, intervention (or individual) psychotherapy, assessment or diagnostic testing, research related to evidenced-based practice, and consultation, all within the same week. They may work in generic settings, such as outpatient clinics in hospitals, where patients present a broad spectrum of psychological and health difficulties. Alternatively, they may work in a more specialized clinic, such as a sickle cell disease comprehensive treatment center with a pediatric population. Pediatricians in the clinic may request consultation from the clinical psychologist to evaluate for possible depression secondary to chronic illness. Thus, clinical psychologists in hospitals must be well versed in both psychological and medical literatures. They must also have a working knowledge of the medical diseases as well as the pathophysiology associated with these diseases. Clinical psychologists in hospitals are most commonly involved with treatment of diabetes, hypertension, cardiovascular disease, asthma, obesity, and gastrointestinal disorders (Gatchel & Oordt, 2003).

Patient care in a hospital often entails interdisciplinary collaboration. Clinical psychologists in hospitals commonly work in tandem with a variety of health care providers, including nurses, social workers, and physicians. This team atmosphere provides unique opportunities to learn from other professionals and to gain a more holistic understanding of patient care. Clearly, the work of clinical psychologists in hospitals is diverse and challenging, and new opportunities appear daily.

Activities Pursued in the Career

Clinical health psychologists may engage in a variety of activities, including prevention; intervention; assessment; consultation and liaison; supervision, teaching, and training; research and program development and evaluation; and administration.

PREVENTION

Clinical psychologists in hospitals are often involved in the development and administration of prevention programs. The three-tiered model of prevention includes primary, secondary, and tertiary prevention efforts. *Primary prevention* focuses on programs designed for the entire population with the goal of preventing the problem from happening at all. *Secondary prevention* programs are intended for individuals or groups who are at greater risk for the problem and wish to prevent the problem from occurring. *Tertiary prevention* programs are used with a population in which the problem already exists and requires treatment. However, some programs can be geared to more than one audience. Common prevention areas include obesity, smoking, drug and substance abuse, relapse, and disease management.

INTERVENTION

Clinical psychologists in hospitals provide individual, family, marital, and group psychotherapy to clients throughout the life span. For example, a clinical psychologist might use family therapy to provide a patient with social support during an acute illness. The length of therapy may range from short term to long term. An example of short-term therapy would be a 6-week course of treatment to help a client develop and apply relaxation techniques with the goal of reducing anxiety about a medical procedure. In contrast, long-term therapy may last for 3 months or longer; the client and therapist may set multiple outcome goals, such as amelioration of depressive symptoms, improved family relations, acceptance of a chronic disease, and enhancement of adherence to medication. Although both short- and long-term therapies are used in the hospital, most treatment that clinical psychologists provide in medical centers emphasizes brief, cognitive, or behavioral intervention approaches that are targeted to relieve specific symptoms (Johnstone et al., 1995). Short-term psychotherapy recently has become the standard of care for many clients because of declining reimbursement for mental health services.

Knowledge of multiple intervention approaches, including psychological, behavioral, psychiatric, biomedical, and biopsychosocial, is essential in work with patients whose primary problems are physical but for whom psychological intervention is useful or essential. Specific interventions in hospitals include relaxation therapies, biofeedback, stress management, psychoeducation about health and disease, and strategies to manage and cope with disease.

ASSESSMENT

Assessment approaches that clinical psychologists in the hospital use include the following:

- clinical interviews,
- self-report measures of psychological functioning,
- projective and objective testing,
- psychophysiological and neuropsychological assessment,
- demographic surveys, and
- clinical and research-oriented protocols.

Clinical interviews are an effective approach when the clinical psychologist needs to obtain a medical history and information for use in making a diagnosis. *Projective tests* (e.g., the Rorschach test) can be helpful in elucidating emotional themes and personality characteristics. *Objective tests*, such as cognitive (e.g., intelligence tests) and behavioral assessments, provide more quantifiable data with regard to an individual's functioning. *Psychophysiological assessment* investigates associations between the mind, behavior, and bodily mechanisms, whereas *neuropsychological assessment* attempts to pinpoint the pattern of cognitive strengths and impairments that occur with learning disabilities, aging, brain injuries, or other diseases. *Demographic surveys* are used to gather information on health, disease, and emotions in a population. Finally, *clinical and research-oriented protocols* are used to assess the safety, efficacy, and outcomes of treatments.

CONSULTATION AND LIAISON

Clinical psychologists in hospitals are often called on to provide consultation and liaison services. Referral sources for consultation include physicians, nurses, social workers, and other psychologists, and the services typically occur in both inpatient and outpatient settings. The goal of consultation and liaison services is to complete an evaluation, provide intervention as appropriate, refer as necessary, and disseminate results to the requesting consultant or health care provider.

SUPERVISION, TEACHING, AND TRAINING

Clinical psychologists in the hospital often provide clinical and research supervision to psychology practicum students, psychology interns, postdoctoral fellows, and medical residents in the area of behavioral medicine. Supervision may occur on an individual basis or in a group format. The goal of supervision is to provide professional expertise to students and psychologists in training to help them achieve appropriate levels of competence in their respective specialties.

Roles for teaching and training in hospitals have increased with the growing recognition of the importance of psychological interventions in the hospital. Clinical psychologists in a hospital may teach courses that reflect both basic and advanced principles of general, abnormal, and health psychology to medical students, physicians, and other health care professionals. Training opportunities are common across a number of activities, including grand rounds, interdisciplinary team meetings, and continuing education seminars and workshops.

RESEARCH AND PROGRAM DEVELOPMENT AND EVALUATION

Clinical psychologists working in hospitals frequently conduct research on psychological factors related to health and illness and ways to assist patients in coping and managing the stressors associated with their illness. Research activities include designing and implementing treatment, evaluating outcomes, and conducting program evaluation and quality assurance programs.

ADMINISTRATION

Clinical psychologists may also have administrative responsibilities in the hospital in addition to their roles as clinicians, researchers, or teachers. The administrative activities may be as minor as scheduling meetings or as major as assuming responsibility for the day-to-day functioning of an entire psychology department. Examples of high-level administrative positions for clinical psychologists in hospitals include dean of a school, chairman of a department, or director of a clinical program.

Career Settings

Hospitals that employ clinical psychologists are typically classified as public, private, Veterans Administration, or university hospitals. Frequently, these classifications are based on the source of the hospital's funding, the population served, and the types of health problems managed. For example, some hospitals treat only pediatric populations, whereas others focus on physical and cognitive rehabilitation following injury. Clinical psychologists work in medical and psychiatric settings and are usually members of psychology, psychiatry, or behavioral health departments. Clinical psychologists are found in a multitude of settings, including inpatient medical units, outpatient and partial (day) hospitalization treatment programs, primary care clinics, and specialized psychological and health care programs.

Patients on inpatient medical, neurological, and psychiatric units often require a more urgent level of care than that provided by outpatient and partial hospitalization programs. Because the level of care in an inpatient unit is significant, clinical psychologists may be on call and expected to respond quickly to a psychological emergency or crisis. For example, a clinical psychologist may be consulted about a patient who is suicidal after learning that he or she has a chronic illness. Therapeutic interventions in inpatient units tend to be brief because stays on these units are short.

Clinical psychologists who work in partial hospitalization settings provide intensive outpatient psychiatric care for patients who also require a structured day program. Alternatively, clinical psychologists in hospital outpatient programs tend to work with patients who are able to function more independently than those receiving their treatment in inpatient or partial hospitalization programs. In both settings, clinical psychologists provide services including diagnostic evaluations, assessment, and crisis intervention, as well as individual, family, and group therapy.

The application of clinical psychology is especially important in primary care settings because of the frequent relationship between psychosocial adjustment and physical illness (see, e.g., De Groot, Anderson, Freedland, Clouse, & Lustman, 2001) and the high prevalence of psychiatric disorders in primary care settings (Barrett, Barrett, Oxman, & Gerber, 1988). Clinical psychologists are of great value in primary care settings by screening, diagnosing, and treating mental health disorders that primary care physicians frequently miss.

In specialized psychological and health care programs in hospitals, clinical psychologists treat patients with psychological disorders who need assistance in coping with a chronic illness. Examples of such programs include clinics for mood and behavioral disorders, trauma, serious psychiatric illness, pain management, weight management, oncology, cardiac care, smoking cessation, diabetes, HIV, and rehabilitation.

Preparing for the Career

To become a clinical psychologist eligible to work in a hospital or medical setting, one must fulfill requirements mandated by the APA, which sets standards for specialty training in applied psychology, and by state licensure requirements. First, the student should obtain a bachelor's degree from a college or university. A major in psychology during college is preferred, although not necessary, for acceptance to most graduate programs in clinical psychology. Students should have completed at least some coursework in psychology; statistics; the humanities; and the social, physical, or biological sciences before applying to psychology graduate programs.

Following completion of the bachelor's degree, the next step is to obtain a master's degree in some area of psychology, such as clinical, counseling, school, or experimental psychology. Typically, the degree awarded is either an MA or an MS. Some students obtain this degree through a terminal master's program (a 1- or 2-year program) or as the first stage of a PhD or PsyD program in clinical psychology. Advantages of a terminal master's degree include increased flexibility should a student choose not to apply to a doctoral program; an added benefit to the student when applying to a PhD or PsyD program in clinical psychology because students who have attained good grades in a master's program can demonstrate competence in graduate studies; and experience in graduate work in psychology before committing to the doctoral degree. Disadvantages of a terminal master's degree include the need to apply and fulfill the requirements of a doctoral program, which may include repeating master's-level courses or a master's thesis or project; the cost of the master's program; and the length of time to complete a master's degree before beginning the doctoral program.

The program requires of each student a minimum of 3 full-time academic years of graduate study (or the equivalent thereof) and completion of an internship prior to awarding the doctoral degree. At least 2 of the 3 academic training years (or the equivalent thereof) must be at the institution from which the doctoral degree is granted, and at least 1 year of which must be in full-time residence (or the equivalent thereof) at that same institution (APA Committee on Accreditation, 2005). For the clinical psychologist interested in working in a hospital, practicum and internship requirements may be completed in a hospital or health care setting. Coursework in clinical psychology doctoral programs is typically divided into three main areas: (a) general psychology, including learning, motivation, development, and individual differences; (b) clinical courses in assessment and psychotherapy; and (c) research. Examples of general coursework include the following:

- biological bases of behavior,
- social–cultural bases of behavior,
- cognitive–affective bases of behavior,
- human development,
- history and systems, and
- ethics and standards.

Coursework in the clinical area may include assessment, psychotherapy, and personality and psychopathology. Finally, statistics and research design and methodology are two common examples of coursework required for the research domain.

Students enrolled in traditional PhD programs in psychology frequently must complete a number of research requirements. Most doctoral programs are arranged to allow students to complete the PhD or PsyD within 4 to 5 years. However, the average number of years to meet degree requirement completion varies from program to program and typically ranges from 5 to 7 years, including the final internship year, which is spent primarily in clinical activities away from the home institution.

In the process of fulfilling coursework, students are required to complete two field practicum placements that focus on clinical work, assessment, or some combination of both. Generally, students work for about 8 to 12 months in each placement and average approximately 20 hours of work per week, which might include direct patient contact and intensive supervision by both university faculty and the field or clinic supervisor. Students also frequently participate in seminars and trainings and receive a minimum of 2 hours of face-to-face supervision per week.

The predoctoral internship experience is more advanced and intensive than the practicum experience in that it emphasizes clinical service, research, supervision, and didactics and requires a greater time commitment (approximately 40 hours per week) for a period of 1 year. Clinical and assessment experiences in hospitals benefit students who wish to pursue a career as a clinical psychologist working in a hospital.

Postdoctoral fellowships represent the next step after successful completion of the internship, dissertation, and doctoral degree. The general goals of postdoctoral fellowships, which may range from 1 to 2 years, are to build on the foundation of general skills developed in the internship year and, if appropriate, focus on areas of specialization of interest to the fellow. Thus, postdoctoral fellowships exist in most specializations, including health psychology, forensic psychology, pediatric psychology, and child and adolescent psychology. The fellowship experience enables one to acquire the supervised training necessary for licensing eligibility in most states or the required experience and credentialing for employment in an academic health sciences center. Postdoctoral fellows receive 2 hours of individual supervision per week and may also participate in educational activities, seminars, grand rounds, and research experiences.

After the postdoctoral fellow has completed all supervision requirements, he or she is eligible to sit for the state licensing examination as a psychologist. The licensing examination includes a national board examination of 200 multiple choice questions and may include an essay or an oral examination that frequently involves the laws (applicable in that particular state) pertaining to psychology. The criteria to pass the examination are set by the state. The required passing score may be the national average for the cohort who completed the examination, or it may be a fixed percentage (e.g., 70% is the passing score in many states). A passing score on the state examination enables one to work as a clinical psychologist in a hospital.

The final milestone in clinical psychology is the diplomate status, which is frequently completed after the psychologist has practiced for approximately 5 years. This status frequently involves a series of work samples and oral examinations. Upon completion of this requirement, the successful candidate receives the diplomate status in a specialty field, including clinical, health, child clinical, forensic, school, hypnosis, or psychoanalysis. The individual is then a board-certified psychologist (distinguished by the letters "ABPP" [American Board of Profession Psychology]). The second author (Brown) holds board certification in clinical health psychology, denoting his particular expertise in the application of health psychology within an applied practice setting.

Why We Chose This Career

We chose the practice of clinical psychology in the hospital for a number of reasons. Perhaps most compelling was the satisfaction our family members received from working in the health profession. We also were influenced by concern for individuals less fortunate than ourselves and our families, including low-income individuals, and the ways such individuals adapt to their home and school environments. Brown was hospitalized as a child, at a time when there was little psychosocial intervention related to children's hospitalization and medical illness. During this time—approximately four decades ago—children were separated from their parents or caregivers, received little preparation regarding medical procedures, and were provided little information about their illnesses. The prognosis for many pediatric chronic illnesses, including congenital heart defects, cancer, and renal diseases, was quite guarded during this time, and these diseases now have a much more favorable prognosis.

Both of us were interested in how patients cope with the pain and stress that often accompany an illness and with the feelings of sadness and vulnerability that some individuals experience after receiving a diagnosis of a chronic disease. Other questions that interested us included how to improve a patient's mood during a hospital stay and how to answer their questions about what will happen to them after they leave the hospital. Both of us possessed strong language and quantitative skills, which were important for entering any psychology graduate program and have served us well throughout our extensive clinical and research training. In addition, both of us were especially interested in people.

When we entered college, our interest in psychology was sufficiently strong, and thus, we declared psychology as our majors. Brown was mentored by a faculty member in research during the course of undergraduate studies, which solidified a quest for graduate training in psychology. He also developed a number of friendships during undergraduate school with graduate students in psychology and eventually became interested in their work. And we both consulted with professors and friends before entering graduate school.

Like many other students who were close to graduating with a BA or BS in psychology, we were unsure about whether to apply for job positions where we could use the skills and knowledge we learned in undergraduate courses or whether to pursue graduate education. Our undergraduate universities had a number of students who were going on to professional schools and graduate programs. Ultimately, the factors that persuaded us to pursue opportunities in psychology graduate school were that we performed well in all of our psychology courses and that we were especially interested in the material that we learned in those classes. We realized, however, that the material in these courses and our experience with research in undergraduate school only scratched the surface of all there was to learn about the field of applied psychology.

The first author (Daly) was particularly interested in a clinical and research focus on ethnically diverse, low-income child and adolescent populations, Brown was especially interested in issues related to psychopathology and learning problems and how these were managed in a school setting. Both of us pursued graduate programs that matched our specific interests in children and that had faculty with interests in psychopathology and health and a commitment to cultural diversity and social justice.

During our graduate training, both of us had a number experiences working as mental health workers and research assistants at hospital psychiatric facilities. We collaborated with professionals from various disciplines such as social workers, psychiatric nurses, and psychiatrists, who exposed us to different frameworks in the conceptualization, diagnosis, and treatment of patients with various psychiatric disorders. The experience of interdisciplinary collaboration, as well as the challenging and fast-paced environment of patient care in a hospital, had us fully engaged in health care. During our later graduate training, our interest in working in a hospital continued in our practicum placements at public hospitals that served a primarily urban indigent population. Our activities included conducting outpatient therapy with children and adolescents and their families, completing diagnostic assessments for individuals presenting to the hospital emergency room and walk-in clinic, providing inpatient pediatric consultations, and coordinating with physicians at a hospital-based clinic to provide mental health services for adolescents receiving medical attention.

We completed our internships at academic medical centers where we developed skills in the assessment and treatment of children and adolescents with neurological and psychiatric disorders. We also developed skills in consultation and liaison with children and adolescents who had been hospitalized for medical disorders, in conducting traditional psychotherapy to manage depression and anxiety in adults, and in helping individuals cope with trauma and loss. Finally, we honed our skills in conducting family systems therapy while working with children and adolescents with behavioral problems associated with significant familial dysfunction.

Financial Compensation

The 2003 APA salary survey (APA, 2005) provided specific data regarding financial compensation for clinical psychologists in direct human services positions. As shown in Table 10.1, compensation varies depending on the type of hospital. The median salary for licensed clinical psychologists with 5 to 9 years experience was $63,000 in 2003. In comparison, the median salary for all licensed doctoral-level psychologists with 5 to 9 years experience was $60,500 in 2001 (APA, 2003). According to the Bureau of Labor Statistics (2005), clinical, counseling, and school psychologists (studied as a group) earned an average yearly income of $58,640 in 2003. This change is promising; this figure represents an increase from the 2002 median for clinical, counseling, and school psychologists of $51,000 (range $30,000 to $88,000).

Compensation is usually determined by the clinical psychologist's prior experience, type of hospital in which the psychologist is employed, geographic location, tenure, and the specific nature and responsibilities associated with the position. Clinical psychologists employed in a hospital whose primary responsibility is to provide clinical services receive a base salary but may have the capacity to generate additional income depending on the number of patients they treat or the amount of revenue they generate for the hospital. Clinical psychologists engaged primarily in research activities may also receive additional income if they generate revenues through clinical practice. Finally, teaching and training responsibilities may also provide additional sources of income,

TABLE 10.1

Salaries for Licensed Doctoral-Level Clinical Psychologists in Selected Settings: 2003

Setting	Experience	Mdn	Quartile 1	Quartile 3	M	SD	N
				Salary ($)			
Public general hospital	5–9 years	61,000	53,500	73,000	62,000	9,941	13
	20–24 years	69,500	61,000	110,000	89,167	55,130	6
Private general hospital	2–4 years	70,000	54,000	80,000	68,000	13,102	7
	10–14 years	75,000	65,000	76,000	73,714	14,032	7
	15–19 years	60,000	50,000	75,000	62,000	14,832	5
	20–24 years	69,000	59,000	80,000	69,400	11,437	5
Public psychiatric hospital	5–9 years	53,500	50,500	66,250	57,333	10,652	6
	10–14 years	62,000	46,500	70,500	58,111	14,641	9
	20–24 years	67,500	58,250	71,250	64,167	10,496	6
	25–29 years	67,500	65,000	72,750	69,333	6,218	6
Veterans Administration hospital	10–14 years	82,000	78,000	86,000	79,714	9,429	7
	20–24 years	85,000	83,000	87,000	85,571	2,936	7
	25–29 years	87,000	81,750	89,000	86,300	7,889	10
	30+ years	88,000	85,000	98,000	86,857	13,120	7
Rehabilitation facility	5–9 years	59,000	51,000	63,500	56,556	9,787	9
	15–19 years	70,000	66,500	71,500	69,200	3,271	5

Note. Gaps in experience ranges are due to the low level of responses for the specific ranges. From *Salaries in Psychology 2003*, by W. E. Pate, J. Frincke, and J. Kohout, 2005, Washington, DC: American Psychological Association. Available online at http://research.apa.org/03salary/table5.pdf. Copyright 2005 by the American Psychological Association.

although changes in health care delivery have restricted psychologists' activities primarily to revenue-generating activities.

Government economists predict job growth for clinical psychologists to be faster than the average (i.e., employment is projected to increase 21% to 35% between 2002 and 2012) because of the increased demand for psychological services in hospitals (Bureau of Labor Statistics, 2005). The reasons for this increased demand may include decreased stigma associated with receiving psychological treatment and the developing realization that prevention and treatment of unhealthy lifestyles and behaviors (e.g., obesity, smoking) are more cost-effective than paying for treatment of the illnesses frequently associated with these lifestyle behaviors.

Advantages and Disadvantages of the Career

The practice of clinical psychology in a hospital or medical center provides many advantages, including a diversity of experiences; the opportunity for interdisciplinary collaboration; access to educational enrichment and, in some cases, research activities; and expanded job opportunities.

The advantage in the diversity of experiences is the assortment of interesting job tasks; a disadvantage is the potential for stress and burnout. For example, clinical psychologists in a hospital may engage in consultation, administer a neuropsychological assessment, supervise practicum students, participate in a case conference seminar, and provide family therapy—all during the same workday. The availability of diverse experiences in the hospital offers a sense of flexibility and independence that is not always afforded in other careers and work settings. At the same time, the demands can be significant and, at times, overwhelming. For this reason, it is important that psychologists schedule work assignments carefully and take appropriate time for professional development as well as for family and recreation.

The opportunity to participate in an interdisciplinary treatment team in a hospital represents another advantage for several reasons. First, collaboration with professionals from fields such as medicine (e.g., pediatricians, neurologists, surgeons), social work, physical and occupational therapy, and nursing affords training in and exposure to new models of clinical care, research, and training (Drotar, 2002).

Mutual support and the exchange of ideas with other professionals are important benefits. Finally, interdisciplinary collaboration promotes an integrated services model that allows for a more coherent, efficient, and cost-effective response to the complex medical and psychological problems of patients in hospitals (Rice, 2000; Ruebling et al., 2000).

Hospitals and medical centers routinely offer diverse educational enrichment activities such as case conferences, grand round lectures, invited seminar speakers, and continuing education workshops. These activities are tremendous opportunities to enhance one's knowledge base. Most hospitals have libraries that make available leading journals in the field and emphasize continuing education and (in some cases) research to keep their staff up to date with cutting-edge practice.

Over the past decade, significant changes in the delivery of health care have put an emphasis on economic efficiency and justification of costs associated with patient care (Brown & Freeman, 2002). This emphasis has been partly due to the escalating costs in health care and insurance companies' efforts to control these high costs. For example, third-party payers have required that most services be delivered by primary care providers rather than by specialty providers because of the higher cost of the specialty care provider. Pediatricians are now asked to initially evaluate children and adolescents with psychological difficulties before referring these children to specialty care providers, such as developmental pediatricians or child psychiatrists. Thus, primary care providers have become the gatekeepers for children and adolescents with psychological disorders or with psychological factors that may influence their disease.

The rise in health care costs associated with unhealthy lifestyles such as smoking, alcohol use, poor eating habits, and lack of exercise has increased the importance of the role of clinical health psychologists in prevention. In addition, patients with substance abuse, behavioral, or psychological disorders frequently present to a hospital or medical center. For example, O'Donahue, Ferguson, and Cummings (2002) reported that at least half of visits to primary care medical providers were for problems associated with psychological issues. In addition to patient demands for clinical health psychology services, consultation and liaison relationships with medical teams flourish because of the high demand for clinical psychology input in settings such as the burn unit, oncology ward, and pain service. Many medical centers have few psychologists on staff, so these psychologists frequently fulfill a teaching or liaison role in which they provide instruction to primary care physicians or other providers about how to manage patients with psychological adjustment difficulties or identifiable psychopathology. This education also saves on the cost of services for patients as timely prevention and intervention may help reduce bed days and future hospital admissions. However, the extra teaching responsibilities can be very demanding for the clinical psychologists on staff.

One of the main disadvantages of performing clinical psychology activities in a hospital is that the psychologist is bound by hospital policies, guidelines, and job expectations. The hospital may determine such important issues as fee schedules, clinic hours, allotted office space, hiring decisions, and quotas for volume of service without considering input from the psychologist. A fee committee within the hospital often determines charges for various services, and psychological services are frequently reimbursed at a very low rate, and some services not at all. The result is that psychologists must provide services to more patients to meet revenue expectations. Although hospitals provide administrative support, navigating the bureaucracy of large hospital systems can be challenging and time consuming; there are many regulatory issues mandated by federal and state laws that guide hospital practices. Finally, because clinical psychologists in hospitals are in high demand and engage in so many activities, they often carry a large caseload and have multiple responsibilities that require a significant time commitment to their job.

Despite the demands on clinical psychologists in hospitals, working in such a setting as a clinical psychologist can be intellectually stimulating, fast paced, and gratifying. Although the disadvantages are tangible and at times frustrating, the intellectual stimulation, opportunities to enhance patients' quality of life, and contact with other health care providers, genuinely dedicated to patient care, are rich and rewarding experiences that have sustained psychologists in these settings for many years.

Attributes Needed for Success in the Career

Many clinical psychologists working in hospitals are trained in the scientist–practitioner model. This model represents an integrative approach to science and practice whereby psychologists seek to generate and integrate scientific and professional knowledge, attitudes, and skills to further psychological science, the professional practice of psychology, and human welfare (Belar & Perry, 1990). In short, clinical psychologists who subscribe to this model use clinical practice to guide their research questions and science to inform their clinical practice. Thus, clinical psychologists who are successful in their work usually possess characteristics that enable them to be proficient in scientific endeavors or inquiry, clinical endeavors, or a combination of both activities. Being informed in both practice and science is necessary for doctoral-level providers who must generate funds either through clinical reimbursement or research funding.

Intellectual attributes in science and practice for clinical psychologists working in a hospital include a strong fund of knowledge of psychological and medical disorders, critical reflection and reasoning skills, the ability to synthesize information succinctly, the capacity to draw inferences and implications from information, and an interest in clinical research that addresses the many practical issues that psychologists and physicians struggle with on a daily basis (e.g., how to enhance adherence to antibiotic or psychotropic medications). Additional qualities that are important, particularly when working directly with patients in a hospital, include empathy, sensitivity, compassion, strong interpersonal skills, and a desire to help others, including patients struggling with issues related to their illness and providers who are attempting to provide the best possible care to their patients. Psychologists conducting psychotherapy with patients should also possess a capacity for insight and personal awareness and for growth and development as a professional and individual. It is important for clinical psychologists to have interests outside the work setting, including family and friends, given that the stressors often associated with these jobs may include death and dying, difficult patients, and in some cases difficult colleagues.

Because multidisciplinary collaboration is critical in working within a hospital environment, clinical psychologists must be flexible and relate to and work well with other health care professions and allied health staff. Additionally, because collaborative efforts can be challenging (and frustrating) at times, emotional maturity and stability are valuable assets. The clinical psychologist is frequently called on to be a consensus builder because many professionals employed in hospitals place a premium on turf issues rather than being agreeable and amicable. Although collaboration is common in hospitals, at times clinical psychologists are required to work independently, especially when performing psychology-specific responsibilities such as psychological testing, program evaluation, or research related to psychological disorders. In such times, it is advantageous to have a clear sense of autonomy and responsibility as well as the necessary drive and ambition to complete assignments.

Personal qualities that help clinical psychologists perform their activities include motivation, persistence, initiative, a proactive attitude, time management abilities, problem-solving and organization skills, and a strong work ethic. However, the ability to care for oneself and to avoid becoming overextended is equally important. The ability to think and act ethically is imperative for all psychologists, regardless of the work setting. Finally, the ability to seek guidance from more senior individuals and to learn from others also is important. Clinical psychology is an art as well as a science; thus, experience and wisdom become precious commodities over the course of a clinical psychologist's career.

Opportunities for Employment

The range of opportunities for clinical psychologists working in hospitals is virtually limitless because clinical psychologists are trained in and skilled at activities including prevention, intervention, research, assessment, consultation, program development and evaluation, and supervision and teaching. Clinical psychologists trained to provide services in a health care setting may find employment in a variety of areas, including general and specialty care hospitals, health clinics, community mental health centers affiliated with medical centers, child and adolescent mental health services, and social service agencies. Finally, many clinical psychologists who work in health care settings provide some of their services in outpatient private practice settings.

Job opportunities are also determined by the type of hospital in which the psychologist is employed, the population served, and the area of treatment specialization. For example, clinical psychologists may

- teach and supervise the broad spectrum of health care professionals in a general hospital,
- participate in a research-based intervention program (e.g., for adolescents with eating disorders) in a hospital affiliated with an academic medical center,
- lead a social skills or family psychoeducational group for patients diagnosed with schizophrenia who are receiving their care on an inpatient psychiatric unit,
- engage in research activities related to posttraumatic stress disorder in military hospitals or provide treatment to military personnel with mental illness and their families, and
- conduct a neurocognitive assessment in a rehabilitation hospital for a patient who has suffered memory loss secondary to a stroke or a closed head injury.

Clinical psychologists in hospitals work with a broad range of patient populations, including individuals at various developmental stages, couples, families, groups, organizations, and even individuals employed in the hospital. Many clinical psychologists choose to focus their interests on special populations, such as children, minority groups, or older adults. There are many new and exciting opportunities for clinical psychologists to work with populations that have not been served well in the past because of a dearth of research or knowledge, including children, families, older adults, inner-city residents, and various ethnic groups.

Clinical psychologists who receive the appropriate training may work in specialized areas such as health or medical psychology, serious mental illness, clinical child or pediatric psychology, geriatric psychology, neuropsychology, neurorehabilitation, and clinical neuroscience. For example, clinical psychologists who specialize in health or medical psychology may work as a multidisciplinary team member on a transplant service conducting psychosocial assessments of appropriate organ transplant candidates. Clinical psychologists working in the area of clinical child or pediatric psychology may conduct research on issues related to childhood, developmental problems, or interventions with children, as such those designed to diminish the stressors associated with a chronic illness. Specialization in the area of geriatric psychology offers clinical psychologists opportunities to work with older patients experiencing emotional, cognitive, and behavioral symptoms associated with the aging process. Assessment, treatment, and research on conditions and disorders such as epilepsy, learning disability, attention-deficit/hyperactivity disorder, dementia, Parkinson's disease, head trauma, and metabolic disease represent opportunities for clinical psychologists working in the specialized areas of neuropsychology, neuro-rehabilitation, psychopharmacology, and clinical neuroscience. Clinical psychologists specializing in these areas are often employed in health science centers or schools of medicine to promote the highly specialized services provided at these facilities.

Typical Day of a Clinical Psychologist in a Hospital

Clinical psychologists in hospitals work in a variety of activities and collaborate with multidisciplinary teams, so they may be hard pressed to describe any day as typical. In this section we provide examples of the various activities we engage in as psychologists in a health sciences center, where we are responsible for clinical service, teaching and training of other psychologists, research, and administration.

We are both employed at an urban academic health sciences center. Daly's activities include assessment and treatment of pediatric patients referred by primary care pediatricians or nurse practitioners, weight management of pediatric clients, and consultation to a spina bifida clinic. In this spina bifida clinic, children and adolescents who have presented to the hospital outpatient clinic primarily for medical reasons are referred to me for evaluation, diagnosis, and management. Following an initial clinical evaluation, for example, the physician or nurse practitioner may refer the patient to me for psychotherapy, assessment, or some combination of both. After completing the assessment, I would consult with the referring provider about the findings of the initial evaluation and propose a follow-up plan for intervention. Multidisciplinary collaboration with other professionals is critical to ensure that the patient will receive the highest level of continuity of care.

Both of us are involved in clinical research, some of which includes the evaluation of psychological treatments for children who have survived cancer. We are also involved with research examining psychotherapy delivered by means of a telemedicine modality for adolescents with lupus. Both of us are regularly involved in writing projects that include articles, books, and chapters for publication in medical and psychology journals. For example, Daly is submitting a study for publication that examines the association between sleep loss and school engagement in a sample of inner-city African American adolescents. Both of us are involved in seeking ongoing support for our research projects, an activity that is highly valued at many health sciences centers, including the one where we are employed.

We are also involved in the teaching, training, and supervision of clinical psychology interns in the predoctoral psychology internship program in the academic medical center and hospital. We participate in seminar presentations, case conferences, and journal club meetings and in the selection of prospective internship applicants. Some of our colleagues provide direct supervision of the interns in psychotherapy and diagnostic assessment. Additionally, we attend many of the educational opportunities provided in the hospital, such as grand round lectures, invited seminar speakers, and continuing education workshops. We also present papers and attend lectures at national and international conferences. Finally, Brown is involved in administration in an academic health care setting that includes the training of health care professionals across a number of disciplines (including clinical psychology). In short, our experiences as psychologists in a hospital are exciting and rich. We provide a great deal of instruction, in both the classroom and the conference room, yet we learn a great deal from our colleagues each day.

Conclusion

Working as a clinical psychologist in a hospital is rewarding and stimulating. Opportunities are available to engage in clinical intervention, assessment, and treatment with patients and their families to help foster better physical and mental health. In addition, consultation and multidisciplinary collaboration occur frequently in hospitals and provide clinical psychologists with avenues for learning new perspectives on the holistic treatment of patients. Moreover, clinical psychologists employed in a hospital can make contributions to the scientific knowledge base through research activities. Finally, supervision, teaching, and training provide the stimulus for personal and professional growth. We are both privileged to work in settings where we learn on a daily basis. At the same time, we give much of ourselves in the interest of enhancing both our patients' quality of life and our students' knowledge. Our career experiences reflect the growth and prosperity of clinical psychologists' work in hospitals, with new and exciting opportunities ever present.

References

American Psychological Association. (2003). *2001 salaries in psychology*. Washington, DC: Author.

American Psychological Association. (2005). *2003 salaries in psychology*. Washington, DC: Author.

American Psychological Association, Commission for the Recognition of Specialties and Proficiencies in Professional Psychology. (1997). *Archival description of clinical health psychology*. Retrieved August 1, 2005, from http://www.apa.org/crsppp/health.html

American Psychological Association, Committee on Accreditation. (2005). *Guidelines and principles for accreditation of programs in professional psychology*. Retrieved July 11, 2006, from http://www.a-pa.org/ed/G&P052.pdf

Barrett, J. E., Barrett, J. A., Oxman, T. E., & Gerber, P. D. (1988). The prevalence of psychiatric disorders in a primary care practice. *Archives of General Psychiatry, 45*, 1100–1106.

Belar, C. N., & Perry, N. W. (1990) *Proceedings: National conference on scientist–practitioner education and training for the professional practice of psychology.* Sarasota, FL: Professional Resource Press.

Brown, R. T., & Freeman, W. S. (2002). Primary care. In D. T. Marsh & M. A. Fristad (Eds.), *Handbook of serious emotional disturbance in children and adolescents* (pp. 428–444). New York: Wiley.

Bureau of Labor Statistics. (2005). *Labor statistics occupational outlook handbook 2004–2005.* Retrieved August 1, 2005, from http://www.bls.gov/oco/ocos056.htm

De Groot, M., Anderson, R., Freedland, K., Clouse, R., & Lustman, P. (2001). Association of depression and diabetes complications: A meta-analysis. *Psychosomatic Medicine, 63,* 619–630.

Drotar, D. (2002). Reflections on interdisciplinary collaboration in the new millennium: Perspectives and challenges. *Journal of Developmental & Behavioral Pediatrics, 23,* 175–180.

Gatchel, R. J., & Oordt, M. S. (2003). *Clinical health psychology and primary care: Practical advice and clinical guidance for successful collaboration.* Washington, DC: American Psychological Association.

Johnstone, B., Frank, R. G., Belar, C., Berk, S., Bieliauskas, L. A., Bigler, E. D., et al. (1995). Psychology in health care: Future directions. *Professional Psychology: Research and Practice, 26,* 341–365.

O'Donahue, W. T., Ferguson, K. E., & Cummings, N. A. (2002). Introduction: Reflections on the medical cost offset effect. In N. A. Cummings, W. T. O'Donahue, & K. E. Ferguson (Eds.), *The impact of medical cost offset on practice and research: Making it work for you.* (pp. 11–25). Reno, NV: Context Press.

Pate, W. E., Frincke, J., & Kohout, J. (2005). *Salaries in psychology 2003: Report of the 2003 APA salary survey.* Retrieved August 1, 2005, from http://research.apa.org/03salary/

Rice, A. H. (2000). Interdisciplinary collaboration in health care: Education, practice and research. *National Academies of Practice Forum, 2,* 59–73.

Ruebling, I., Lavin, M. A., Banks, R., Block, L., Counte, M., Furman, G., et al. (2000). Facilitating factors for, barriers to, and outcomes of interdisciplinary education projects in the health sciences. *Journal of Allied Health, 29,* 165–170.

III

A Variety of Organizations

Tamara M. Haegerich and Lynn Okagaki

Careers in Public Service: The Intersection of Science and Policy

11

D o you like being challenged to learn about new fields of study? Do you enjoy collaborating with other people? Are you able to work on multiple projects and complete tasks at a rapid pace? If so, then a position in a federal research agency might be a good match for you. The federal government employs research psychologists from all areas of psychology, including social, cognitive, clinical, and educational psychology. These psychologists use their expertise in human behavior and social science research methodologies to plan, conduct, and disseminate research that answers policy-relevant questions. For example, a clinical psychologist with training in cognitive–behavioral therapy might direct a

Tamara M. Haegerich, PhD, was trained at the University of Illinois at Chicago and obtained an MA and a PhD in social psychology. She has been active in research on social–emotional development, youth violence, and child maltreatment. She is currently a research scientist at the Institute of Education Sciences, U.S. Department of Education.

Lynn Okagaki, PhD, is a developmental psychologist. She received a BS in applied behavioral sciences from the University of California, Davis, and a PhD from Cornell University. She is currently commissioner for education research at the National Center for Education Research in the Institute of Education Services. Dr. Okagaki has held appointments at Purdue University, Yale University, Cornell University, and the University of Houston. Her research has focused on parenting and minority children's school achievement and on the socialization of beliefs and values.

program of research at the National Institute of Drug Abuse in the National Institutes of Health on how to best intervene in adolescent substance abuse. A cognitive psychologist with expertise in visual perception might monitor cognitive neuroscience projects at the National Science Foundation. Psychologists in these types of positions have the opportunity both to advance the field of psychology and to fulfill a commitment to public service.

Although psychologists fill a variety of roles in the government system, in this chapter we focus on our experiences within a federal research agency, the Institute of Education Sciences (IES), which is only one of many federal research offices and agencies. IES was established in 2002 as the primary research office in the U.S. Department of Education. Its mission is to expand knowledge and provide information about the condition of education, practices that improve academic achievement, and the effectiveness of education programs. Psychologists fill many roles at IES, such as ensuring the quality of research funded on the development and evaluation of education programs and practices; overseeing research grant programs; and making certain that IES research, statistics, and evaluation reports meet the highest standards of scientific rigor.

Because we focus only on our experiences at IES in this chapter, we encourage readers interested in working for the government to contact psychologists in other federal agencies to obtain a broader perspective on the types of responsibilities and projects that are available in the government. After all, as psychologists in federal agencies, we are here to serve you, the public.

The Nature of the Career

Although many of the activities of a researcher in a federal agency are similar to those an academic researcher engages in, the nature of a career in government is quite different. When you choose a government position, you are assuming a responsibility to serve public needs and carry out the mission of the agency you work for. You are no longer an independent researcher with complete discretion over your topics of study; your work is constrained by the needs of the agency. Thus, as a government scientist, you have less flexibility in studying the topics that are of greatest interest to you personally. For example, I, Tamara, am interested in the etiology of behavior problems in children. The mission of IES, however, emphasizes applied research that addresses improving education practices and programs. Although I have not been able to develop a line of research at IES that purely investigates the development of aggressive behavior, I have been able to participate in the development of a research program that investigates the effects of school-based social–emotional learning and violence prevention programs on student behavior and academic achievement, which are quite related to research on the etiology of aggressive behavior.

In a federal research position, you are also much more likely to become a generalist than a specialist in a given area. Academic researchers may spend their career conducting a narrowly focused program of research and developing expertise in a well-defined domain. As a researcher in a federal agency, you are much more likely to take a broad perspective on a field of research and to be expected to be knowledgeable on a wide range of topics. For example, an academic researcher might spend an entire career investigating vocabulary acquisition as a component of reading. In contrast, a government researcher with a background in vocabulary acquisition might initially be assigned a project related to teacher training in reading and then might work on an evaluation of adult literacy programs or the development of programs for teaching young children prereading skills.

A multidisciplinary perspective is often required as a federal researcher. Because of the complexity of the problems that federal agencies address, the overlapping responsibilities of federal agencies, and constraints on financial resources, it is common for researchers in different federal agencies to collaborate with one another, bringing together different expertise and capitalizing on pooled resources. For example, developmental and social psychologists at IES with expertise in social and emotional development and the evaluation of school-based programs might collaborate with public health scientists at the Centers for Disease Control and Prevention (CDC) with expertise in youth violence prevention to develop a joint research program on violence prevention in schools. This type of collaboration not only results in a stronger research program but also provides an opportunity for the individual scientists to gain new skills and knowledge from their colleagues.

A research career in a federal agency also involves a strong focus on research methodology, design, and statistical analysis. Although there is a broad range of research topics investigated, the common element underlying those areas of research is the scientific method by which they are explored. Thus, much time is spent thinking about how to advance the methods and approaches used to understand and solve psychological problems.

Responsibilities of the Job

In research offices within federal agencies, psychologists fill many different types of positions that entail a large range of responsibilities. For example, psychologists might work in an intramural research program and conduct basic or applied research within the federal agency, oversee an extramural research program that offers federal funding to researchers outside the government to conduct psychology-relevant research, or coordinate the review of research grant applications or government-sponsored research reports.

Within IES, for example, psychologists hired in the role of research scientist hold a variety of responsibilities. Many of IES's social scientists have primary responsibility for directing a program of research in areas such as reading, mathematics and science education, social and character development, teacher professional development, early intervention and assessment for young children with disabilities, or special education programs for adolescents with disabilities. Research scientists are responsible for developing and monitoring these programs of research. Specifically, they review existing research in the context of the needs of education practitioners and policymakers, identify those needs for which there is little empirical evidence to guide the decisions and actions of education practitioners and policymakers, and develop the guidelines for a research grant competition to generate research to meet these needs. They provide technical assistance to researchers in the field who are interested in applying to the research grant competition. After the grants have been awarded, the research scientists are then responsible for working with the funded researchers; they monitor the progress of the research project, provide technical assistance, and help to ensure that the research conducted through the research program will ultimately meet the needs of education practitioners and policymakers.

Research scientists may be responsible for planning and directing research and evaluation projects that are carried out by private research firms via federal contracts. For example, IES might conduct an evaluation of interventions for struggling adolescent readers. A research scientist at IES would develop the research plan for evaluating the interventions. A private research firm would then be hired to carry out the research plan. IES's research scientist would be responsible for monitoring the work of the research firm and contributing to decisions about the design, methodology, and analysis, as well as to the research report that summarizes findings from the work.

Senior research scientists may have primary responsibility for reviewing the education research, evaluation, and statistics reports prepared by IES (e.g., an evaluation research report that culminates from work conducted by a private research firm on contract). These psychologists have duties that are similar to journal editors: soliciting manuscript reviews from external scientists, conducting their own reviews of manuscripts, and ensuring that the reports meet IES's standards for the quality of research.

Whatever their primary responsibilities might be, research scientists at IES are generally involved in many other activities that serve the mission of the agency. They are frequently asked to prepare research briefs that summarize existing research in an area. Scientists who are responsible for research grant programs typically present information about the grant programs at national research conferences, many times in collaboration with the researchers funded by the agency. Research staff frequently provide feedback on research and evaluation projects being developed or conducted by IES. Researchers at IES may also collaborate with representatives from other offices in the U.S. Department of Education or from other federal departments and agencies on a variety of projects. Such collaboration can be on particular grant programs or on more comprehensive, crosscutting federal initiatives. Given these multiple responsibilities, the daily life of a research scientist can include participation in a wide range of challenging activities.

A Day in the Life of a Research Scientist

What can a psychologist filling the role of research scientist expect during a day in the office? If you were to follow one of us through a day, here's what you might observe. I, Tamara, am primarily responsible for directing a research program on social and character development. Under this program, IES is collaborating with the National Center for Injury Prevention and Control at the CDC on a multisite, randomized field trial to investigate the efficacy of seven school-based interventions

aimed at promoting social development, preventing violence, and enhancing academic achievement in elementary schoolchildren. Teams
of researchers from seven academic research institutions were awarded
research grants to randomly assign schools to implement a schoolwide
intervention or continue with traditional education practice and to
conduct research on the efficacy of these interventions. In addition, a
research firm was awarded a contract to conduct a comprehensive
evaluation of all seven programs using a core set of measures. Collaborating with science officers from the CDC, I monitor and coordinate
the efforts of the seven research teams (the grantees) and the evaluation
firm (the contractor) as they conduct the research.

In a given day, I usually engage in a variety of research and administrative tasks. For example, I might provide recommendations to the
research firm about the preferred method for computing scale scores
on a student assessment instrument based on my examination of the
research literature and a review of preliminary analyses conducted by
the contractor. During periods of data collection, I review updates
from the contractor on the number of surveys collected from students,
parents, and teachers and engage in conference calls with the research
sites to coordinate data collection by the grantees and the contractor.
Methodological and design questions can surface: For example, a school
in one of our research sites closed during the middle of the project,
necessitating discussions with the investigators at that site and the
contractor about the implications for the research design. My job involves anticipating problems that might arise to prevent them and
making sure that any problems that do occur are resolved. I make
conference calls to collaborators from the CDC to discuss project progress, challenges, and timelines for completing the work. I complete
some of my administrative duties, such as documenting conversations
with grantees and contractors in official files or processing invoices for
payment. In addition, I may attend a research meeting for one of
IES's other evaluation projects because that team is seeking advice on
character education programs. These responsibilities may arise in one
day of my work at IES.

This hypothetical day illustrates that the responsibilities of research
psychologists in federal agencies involve multiple dimensions—
collaborating with colleagues, thinking critically about methodological
issues, problem solving, and always multitasking. Responsibilities of
research scientists within and across federal agencies can be quite varied, however. In some positions, psychologists conduct more hands-
on research activities, including data collection and statistical analysis.
In other positions, psychologists provide broad oversight for others who
are responsible for the research activities, such as research grantees in
academic institutions or private research firms. The roles and responsi-

bilities depend on an agency's structure, mission, and philosophy regarding the degree to which its scientists should be involved in the research it supports. Regardless of the responsibilities, working in federal agencies can be intellectually challenging and engaging and provides research psychologists with opportunities to learn something new every day.

Opportunities for Employment

There is a broad range of employment opportunities for psychologists in the federal government in both the executive and legislative branches. In addition, there are several mechanisms through which one can obtain a position. For individuals who want a taste of government service before deciding if this is the direction that they want their careers to take, many professional societies offer opportunities to experience working in federal agencies through fellowships, such as the American Psychological Association Science Policy Fellowship Program or the Society for Research in Child Development Congressional/Executive Branch Policy Fellowship Program.[1] In addition to providing fellows with an opportunity to work in a federal agency, fellowship programs have the advantage of exposing individuals, in a relatively brief period of time, to a variety of educational opportunities to help them learn about how different agencies work, how policies and legislation are developed, and how science can be used to inform public policy.

Psychologists can also obtain positions in the federal service system directly or can work for the government "on loan" from an institution of higher education. Government positions can be short term or long term. For example, hiring researchers for relatively short terms (e.g., 1–5 years) can be beneficial for the agency and the employee. For the federal agency, recruiting strong scientists for a 1- or 2-year term can bring new ideas and perspectives to a research area. After working at an agency for a couple of years, a scientist may return, for example, to an academic position with a better understanding of the way federal

---

[1] More information about the American Psychological Association Science Policy Fellowship Program can be found at http://www.apa.org/ppo/funding/scifell.html. For more information about the Society for Research in Child Development Policy Fellowship programs, see http://www.srcd.org/policyfellowships.html.

research granting agencies work and, of what makes research projects attractive to funding agencies.

Why Government Service?

Both of us have frequently been asked why we decided to work at IES. In part because we entered government service at different times in our careers, our paths to government service were very different. I, Tamara, have always been interested in applying research to answer policy questions—that is, in how to improve programs and practices in institutions serving children so that better outcomes could be realized (see Biglan, Mrazek, Carnine, & Flay, 2003, for an example of how psychological research can inform public policy and practice in prevention). In graduate school, my goal was to obtain a nonacademic position, yet one in which I would still be involved in research and use the skill set that I developed in graduate school. While completing my dissertation, I applied to the Society for Research in Child Development Executive Branch Policy Fellowship Program. Upon being accepted into this program, I was offered the opportunity to interview with federal agencies, including the U.S. Department of Education. Through the fellowship interview and acceptance process, I began my career working at IES, and I continued my work as a federal employee after the fellowship term ended.

In contrast, for me, Lynn, my current position at IES came as a total surprise. My career followed a traditional academic career path for 20 years. It was because of the work I did during that career that I was asked to take a senior position at IES. The opportunity to work at IES presented me with new challenges: to be a part of a team that was creating a new federal research organization, establishing the initial direction and standards of that organization, and shaping the field of education research. The work has been intellectually challenging, demanding, and intrinsically engaging. I have had to read broadly across areas of education research, covering topics from early intervention to adult literacy and from teacher professional development to education finance. I have had the pleasure of working with many competent and dedicated researchers and administrators across several federal agencies.

Working in a federal research office allows one to take a broad perspective on social science research, make linkages between different fields of study, and help shape a field of research. It can be a rewarding career or a stimulating sabbatical for a research psychologist.

Financial Rewards and Benefits of the Federal System

If you are looking for job security, a good salary, and great benefits, the federal government is the place to look. Although there is a wide range of positions available and mechanisms for hiring psychologists, psychologists beginning their careers with a PhD most often fill positions that range in salary from around $55,000 to $70,000, depending on amount of prior experience. Positions afford yearly pay increases and opportunities to obtain raises as you progress in your government career. In addition, the health insurance, life insurance, and retirement plans are generous. Vacation and sick leave are comparable to positions in the private sector, and alternative work schedules are often available (e.g., compressed schedules), although schedules are not as flexible in the government as they are in the academic environment.

Advantages and Disadvantages of a Career in Public Service

As with all jobs, there are advantages and disadvantages to working for the government. For those who enjoy developing a broad perspective on a field, working in a federal agency allows one to be more of a generalist than a specialist, to learn about multidisciplinary perspectives on a given topic, and to develop knowledge in multiple academic fields of research. When methodological and statistical innovations are discovered in a field of study or new research findings are unveiled, scientists in federal positions are often the first to learn about them. One of the opportunities that research scientists in federal agencies have is to meet leading investigators in a field of study. This contact may occur through the award of federal grants, collaboration on research programs, participation in expert panels, presentations at national conferences, or briefing sessions where researchers inform federal agencies about innovations in a field of research or ways in which research findings can be applied to policy decisions.

Of course, research scientists in federal agencies obtain a greater understanding of the role of the federal government in forming research agendas in a field of study, the funding mechanisms for researchers in academic or nonacademic settings, and the entire discretionary grant process from proposal submission to the review process to the award of funding. Psychologists who choose to enter academia after an employment experience in a federal agency may be able to capitalize on this experience when they seek funding for their research. Finally, for those who want to facilitate the process by which research contributes to policy decisions, working in a federal agency can put an individual in a position to communicate psychological science to decision makers.

Naturally, there are some disadvantages to a federal career. Researchers in federal agencies are not as free as those in academia to choose the topics that they study; the mission and needs of the agency drive the research programs. When government scientists contribute to the development of commercial products, such as educational products or research handbooks, or when they serve as technical consultants on workgroups, they are not permitted to earn consulting fees or royalties. When attending and presenting at national research conferences, research scientists in federal agencies are representing the agencies in which they work and must be cognizant of the messages they communicate to the audience. Finally, workflow can often be disrupted with changes in agency leadership and administrations that may, in turn, change research priorities.

Attributes Needed for Success

To be successful in federal research offices or agencies, researchers should have content expertise relevant to the field of study that is central to the agency's mission and must have the methodological and analytical skills to conduct high-quality research in that field. Researchers need to be able to critically review bodies of literature. For an agency like IES that has a legislative mission to serve education practitioners and decision makers, the research scientist should be able to identify the important research needs of that community and develop research programs to address those needs. Because research scientists are called on to represent the agency to the public, strong interpersonal skills and the ability to communicate clearly to both scientific and lay audiences are very important. Finally, research scientists must be able to be flexible, solve problems, work under pressure, meet short timelines, and skillfully handle multiple tasks at the same time.

Preparing for and Finding a Government Position

Those interested in working as a research scientist in a federal agency should have a doctoral degree in a behavioral science with a strong research background. When we interview recent graduates, we are looking for individuals who are good researchers, who know their field, who have strong methodological and statistical skills, and who have published in scientific journals. These are the some of the same attributes that are important to other employers, like academic institutions. Federal research agencies are interested in people who understand the mission of the agency. For IES, experience working in or conducting research in schools is very helpful. To find a federal position, one can begin by checking the U.S. Office of Personnel Management's job site (http://www.usajobs.opm.gov/), which lists federal employment opportunities. Troutman and Troutman (2004) have provided helpful, basic information about the intricacies of the federal hiring process.

Finally, we return to where we began: Those who are interested in working for the government on a short-term basis or as a long-term career should talk to scientists who are currently working in the agencies in which they have some interest. There is great variety across the federal research agencies in the types of jobs available for psychologists. Talk to researchers who are in the agencies; we are public servants. Who knows . . . you might get lucky and hear about an open position.

References

Biglan, A., Mrazek, P. J., Carnine, D., & Flay, B. R. (2003). The integration of research and practice in the prevention of youth problem behaviors. *American Psychologist, 58,* 433–440.

Troutman, K. K., & Troutman, E. K. (2004). *The student's federal career guide: 10 steps to find and win top government jobs and internships.* Baltimore: United Book Press.

Marc H. Bornstein

Scientific Careers in Psychology in Government Service

12

M any agencies in the federal government of the United States rely on psychological scientists. The military, for example, has a long history of employing psychologists in a wide array of roles from intelligence analysis to the study of ergonomics to the treatment of posttraumatic stress disorder. Likewise, many civilian areas of the federal government employ psychologists to work on an equally diverse array of problems

Marc H. Bornstein, PhD, is senior investigator and head of child and family research at the National Institute of Child Health and Human Development. He holds a BA from Columbia College and MS and PhD degrees from Yale University. Dr. Bornstein was a J. S. Guggenheim Foundation Fellow, and he received numerous other awards. Dr. Bornstein has held faculty positions at Princeton University and New York University as well as academic appointments in Munich, London, Paris, New York, Tokyo, Bamenda, and Seoul. Dr. Bornstein is coauthor of *Development in Infancy* (five eds.) and *Perceiving Similarity and Comprehending Metaphor*. He is general editor of the *Crosscurrents in Contemporary Psychology Series*, and the *Monographs in Parenting* series. He also edited dozens of other books. He is author of or consultant on several children's books, videos, and puzzles in *The Child's World* and *Baby Explorer* series. Dr. Bornstein is editor emeritus of *Child Development* and founding editor of *Parenting: Science and Practice*. His papers have appeared on experimental, methodological, comparative, developmental, cross-cultural, neuroscientific, pediatric, and aesthetic topics. Visit http://www.cfr.nichd.nih.gov/ and http://www.parentingscienceand practice.com/. I thank C. Varron for assistance with this chapter.

from basic biomedical research in human development through applied research in specific issues (e.g., traffic safety).

Psychologists are found in the Departments of Defense, Homeland Security, Veterans Affairs, and Transportation, as well as in the Department of Health and Human Services (DHHS). In several agencies of the DHHS—for example, the National Science Foundation and the National Institutes of Health (NIH)—psychologists play important roles in administrative sectors as well as in both basic and applied research. In this chapter, I describe scientific psychology within one agency of the DHHS, the NIH, and specifically in the Division of Intramural Research in the National Institute of Child Health and Human Development (NICHD).

Agencies of the Department of Health and Human Services

The Department of Health and Human Services (DHHS) oversees several agencies that sponsor basic biomedical research in the public interest. Many offer career paths for psychologists. One such agency, which is concerned in part with basic and applied psychological research, is the National Institutes of Health (NIH). The NIH, located in Bethesda, Maryland, is the nation's, and perhaps the world's, foremost biomedical research facility. The NIH consists of approximately 30 institutes and programs ranging in size from the National Cancer Institute (large) to the National Eye Institute (small).

One institute that offers diverse opportunities for psychologists is the National Institute of Child Health and Human Development (NICHD). Established by U.S. Congress and President John F. Kennedy in 1962, the NICHD supports and conducts research concerned broadly with human development. The NICHD is headed by a director, under whom two major divisions bifurcate. One division (accounting for approximately 90% of the NICHD budget), the Division of Extramural Research (DER), is devoted to funding research that is investigator initiated or requested by the agency and arranged by contract to institutions outside the NIH. Psychologists who work in the DER often contribute to decisions about and oversee grants and contracts to institutions outside the NIH and funded by the NIH.

The other division of the NICHD (to which approximately 10% of funds are allotted) is the Division of Intramural Research (DIR), which currently houses approximately 20 research branches and laboratories on the Bethesda campus. Within the DIR, there are perhaps 100 active protocols devoted to clinical intervention and basic research on topics related to the health of children, adults, families, and populations. One laboratory within in the DIR is the Laboratory of Comparative Ethology (LCE), and one of two existing research sections within the LCE is my laboratory of Child and Family Research (CFR).

The mission of Child and Family Research is to investigate dispositional, experiential, and environmental factors that contribute to physical, mental, emotional, and social development in human beings in the first two decades of life. The research goals of the CFR are to describe, analyze, and assess the capabilities and proclivities of developing children, including their genetic characteristics, physiological functioning, perceptual and cognitive abilities, and emotional, social, and interactional styles; the nature and consequences of interactions within the family and social world for children and their parents; and influences of children's exposure to and interactions with the natural and designed environments on their development. Laboratory and home-based studies in the CFR use a variety of approaches, including psychophysiological recordings, experimental techniques, behavioral observations, standardized assessments, rating scales, interviews, and demographic and census records in both longitudinal and cross-sectional designs.

More specifically, research topics of the CFR concern the origins, status, and development of biopsychological constructs, structures, functions, and processes in humans; effects of child characteristics and activities on parents; and the meaning of variations in parenting and in the family across different sociodemographic and cultural groups. Examples of sociodemographic comparisons under investigation include family socioeconomic status, maternal age and employment status, and child parity and day-care experience. Study sites include Argentina, Belgium, Brazil, Cameroon, Canada, Chile, England, France, India, Israel, Italy, Japan, Kenya, Peru, and the Republic of Korea as well as the United States; intracultural as well as cross-cultural comparisons of human development are pursued. In addition, the CFR studies three samples of families acculturating to the United States: Japanese Americans, South Americans, and Korean Americans.

Investigators in Child and Family Research also conduct a broad program of research in neuroscience and behavioral pediatrics that investigates diverse questions at the interface of child development, biological growth, and physical health and attempt to build bridges to more directly applied areas:

- fetal assessment and its developmental sequelae;
- the role of cardiac and vagal function, electroencephalographic cortical potentials, and eye movements in early psychological development;

- the role of deafness in child development and family life with samples that include hearing children and hearing parents, deaf children and hearing parents, hearing children and deaf parents, and deaf children and deaf parents;
- cancer and major surgery in infancy and their developmental outcomes;
- research in child development and early health care, including studies of children's knowledge, implementation, and evaluation of strategies for coping with stressful medical experiences; the development of children's understanding of health and health care; and relations among children's own health histories, pediatric health care utilization, and maternal health beliefs; and
- maternal depression and child development. (For more information, visit http://www.cfr.nichd.nih.gov.)

Within government laboratories (like the CFR) are a number of possible positions for bachelor's-level, master's-level, and PhD-trained psychologists. At all levels, psychologists in government service collaborate in, supervise, or engage in research; conduct literature reviews; and publish research articles on knowledge and practice in particular problem areas. Normally, senior investigators hold a PhD, control funding, and are responsible for the nature and design of scientific investigations conducted within their research program; they also supervise other investigators and contractors who carry out all phases of research projects. With some degree of freedom, program research must be consistent with the basic mission of the larger scientific unit and approved by laboratory and scientific directors. The support and endorsement of site visitors (described later in this chapter) to a laboratory are essential.

To gain insight into a government research career, one will find it beneficial to compare it with other similar situations, such as academia or business and industry. As in academia, senior investigators in government service often carry out research that they conceive, but many questions that occupy government researchers are also assigned to them, a situation that is common in business and industry. Normally, too, government work includes both basic research that follows avenues into understanding new areas and applied research devoted to addressing questions of policy. Likewise, research in business or industry often is concerned with the development of marketable products. Government research projects are also aimed at providing the public with information geared to solve problems. Government researchers conduct experiments and correlational studies in laboratory settings; because it frequently applies to matters of public policy, government research often also involves fieldwork.

Like academics, government researchers routinely belong to scholarly societies, attend conferences and present papers, write journal articles and reviews, and sit on journal editorial boards. The implementation of a government research plan is more often than not carried out by a team of researchers consisting of specialists from several different disciplines. Unlike academia, but similar to business and industry, becoming a specialist in alternative areas of psychology often proves difficult once one is on the job in a government research setting. Although opportunities for interagency collaborations present themselves from time to time, in practice these are rather difficult to effect in the government. By contrast, establishing collaborations with investigators outside government is comparatively easy and rewarding.

Unlike extramural scientists, intramural scientists at the NIH do not typically write grants or respond to requests for applications to support their research. Rather, the scientific director in an institute draws on the expertise of a consultant board of scientific counselors to recruit other senior extramural scientists from around the nation, who are experts in the research fields of each intramural laboratory, to site visit that laboratory and to prepare a critical appraisal about the past, current, and future activity of the laboratory. It is on the basis of site visit reports that intramural investigators compete for sources of support and personnel within the funding constraints of the DIR. Such site visits take place every 4 years and last for several days.

My Career

Government service attracts and retains people who want to do research full time as well as play other roles in public service. I am senior investigator and head of Child and Family Research. I received a BA from Columbia College and a PhD from Yale University, both in psychology. Before coming to the NICHD, I held positions at the Max Planck Institute in Germany as a visiting scientist, at Princeton University, and at New York University. While at New York University, I also trained as a Child Clinical Fellow at the Institute for Behavior Therapy. I have been in government service for nearly 20 years.

Before joining the government, I received support for my research from the J. S. Guggenheim Foundation, the W. T. Grant Foundation, and the Spencer Foundation, as well as the National Science Foundation and the National Institutes of Health. I have written or edited about three dozen books, including *Development in Infancy* (Bornstein & Lamb, in press), *Developmental Science* (Bornstein & Lamb, 2005), and the multivolume *Handbook of Parenting* (Bornstein, 2002a, 2002b, 2002c, 2002d, 2002e). I have authored hundreds of peer-reviewed scientific articles, and I have also contributed hundreds of chapters to scholarly collections and encyclopedias. I have served the field of developmental science at large as editor of the Society for Research in Child Development's flagship journal, *Child Development*, and am founding editor of *Parenting: Science and Practice* (http://www.parentingscienceand practice.com). My research contributions have spanned topics ranging from heart function in infants to parenting in different cultures, and I have contributed papers on experimental, methodological, comparative, developmental, cross-cultural, neuroscientific, pediatric, and aesthetic topics.

My Basic Science Work

By the way of illustration, I recount in this section how I entered government research and some of what I have derived from my experience in the government. I then illustrate what government research is about, and finally, I suggest issues to consider for those who contemplate working as a research scientist for the government, either in the short term or as a career.

My research has followed two intertwined directions. The first concerns children's physical, cognitive, and socioemotional development and the second, aspects of children's experiences with parents and family life. Results of my early work led to revelations about what infants know and the observation that measures of information processing in infancy predict language and cognitive competencies in later childhood. These findings challenged views about infancy and about human cognitive development as immeasurable, unstable, and not predictive. My studies were also among the first prospective efforts to document how parenting, together with infants' abilities, affects children's developmental trajectories.

My approach to the study of child development, parenting, and family process incorporates three major avenues. First, my observations are based in the naturally occurring interactions of parents and children during the daily routines of family life, as well as in laboratory-based experimental studies. Second, I take a longitudinal, ecological, dynamic systems approach to understanding phenomena in human development. Finally, I have extended my observations of child development, parenting, and family process to diverse cultures within and outside the United States, thereby advancing knowledge of universal and culture-specific aspects of each. Investigations of naturally occurring parent–child interactions offer a rich description of what parents do in rearing their young children and how specific parenting behaviors contribute to specific aspects of child growth and development. The longitudinal approach to the study of child development, parenting, and family process in natural settings is a prominent feature of my work, and any grounded observations feed back into theory building and guide the refinement of coding systems. On the basis of repeated assessments, I have demonstrated the specific and transactional nature of parent–child engagements and have attempted to offer a comprehensive framework for modeling their mutual influences across time. Parents provide specific experiences to their children, and those experiences affect specific childhood outcomes at specific periods of development in specific ways. This specificity principle is a logical extension of my work in understanding child development and parenting.

I have also geared my efforts to disseminate research on child development, parenting, and family process to multiple parenting communities, including researchers, practitioners, policymakers, educators, and parents themselves. These efforts are organized to make child development and parenting flourishing areas of scientific inquiry. For example, I am principal scientist for parenting and child well-being at the Center for Child Well-Being (http://www.childwellbeing.org), an organization dedicated to promoting the positive growth and development of children from birth to age 5 by supporting those most responsible for children—their parents (Bornstein, Davidson, Keyes, Moore, & Center for Child Well-Being, 2003).

Federal officials, policymakers, educators, practitioners, and parents alike are increasingly turning to applied developmental scientists to provide evidence-based research on how to promote positive development in children and on how society might best support positive parenting. This research directly addresses socially relevant issues, and my efforts to disseminate work on child development and parenting are intended to help bridge the gap between basic research and application.

Advantages of Government Service

Longitudinal developmental investigations are those in which children and their parents are studied repeatedly across development. They are labor intensive and time consuming, yet are unmatched in terms of the questions they can address. Longitudinal studies document life histories of parent–child relationships, thereby enabling researchers to identify the antecedents and later consequences of parenting and child behavior.

Much of my developmental research has been longitudinal. I have attempted to trace stability, change, and mutual influence in parent–child interactions from before birth and in the earliest months of infancy through childhood into adolescence and emerging adulthood. I have also extended my longitudinal research on families to well over a dozen societies. These longitudinal cross-cultural studies have produced an extensive archival database on child development, parenting, and family process, and they offer the field of developmental science a detailed portrayal of how broader cultural ideologies and customs suffuse everyday parenting practices and styles to shape human development.

Because funding depends on performance, past and promised, consistently productive and successful scientists within the DIR can usually count on a continuous (if not magnanimous) stream of funding, which permits their undertaking some kinds of research that are not supported in academia or business and industry. For example, from the perspective of developmental science, longitudinal research, and especially cross-cultural longitudinal research, is unique for its potential yield; normally, it is rare as well. The nature of the funding stream within the DIR supports this kind of high-risk/high-payoff approach. Almost no institution outside the federal government is in a position to promise continuing support of this kind. So, for example, at the time of this writing, I am undertaking the 18-year follow-up to a longitudinal research program begun when the infants in participating families were 5 months of age. Similarly, I have been able to engage in multiple collaborations to conduct parallel (at least short-term) longitudinal studies with colleagues in a variety of different cultures worldwide.

There are other benefits associated with a position of responsibility in a government agency such as the NICHD. For example, each year a small amount of available funds is set aside for travel to national and international scientific meetings and for intramural research scientists themselves to organize conferences on relevant scientific topics. I have competed successfully for such funds and, through NICHD sponsorship, have organized research conferences on topics of my choosing approximately every other year for nearly 20 years (Bornstein & Bradley, 2003; Borstein & Cote, 2006).

Disadvantages of Government Service

A position as a federal scientist has some distinct advantages, but it also has distinct disadvantages. The degree of academic and personal freedom that normally goes along with a tenured appointment within a university setting, for example, does not exist within the hierarchically structured and militarily regimented federal bureaucracy. Despite the good will and efforts of succeeding executive administrations interested in streamlining government agencies, the functioning of the U.S. government remains mired in a tight bundle of red-tape rules and regulations that constrain scientific action, ingenuity, and enterprise to the detriment of progress in science, personal careers, the functioning of research laboratories, and the efficient use of taxpayer dollars. Even considering the extraordinary productivity of the scientific community within the NIH, for example, scientific progress could be increased severalfold if the scientific staff were released (to the degree possible) from the bonds of that red tape.

The NIH and other similar government research institutions do not (normally) grant degrees, so there are no students—undergraduate or graduate—to mentor, collaborate with, and teach. The NIH do, however, train young people following their bachelor's degree and sponsor postdoctoral training.

One disadvantage for behavioral scientists is that there is often little or no recognition within the executive administration or general scientific staff that major afflictions in the population of the United States (and the world) have distinct and identifiable behavioral causes and are not solely or wholly genetic in their origin. That is, cancer, obesity, AIDS, traffic accidents, binge drinking, and lack of exercise often reflect fundamental behavioral choices and decision making. In 2005, nearly 1.5 million Americans learned that they had cancer, and more than 500,000 Americans died of it. Many of the cancer deaths that occurred in 2005 were related to poor nutrition, physical inactivity, obesity, smoking, and other lifestyle factors. According to the American Cancer Society, more than 60% of all those cancer deaths could have been prevented if people stopped smoking, exercised more, ate healthier food, and so forth. These healthy and positive behavioral choices are learned in childhood and are not reducible to DNA.

Nonetheless, the arrow of reductionism is very strong within the current of thinking and funding in the NIH and the government at large. For example, virtually all of the 20 or so branches and laboratories within the DIR of the NICHD are concerned with molecular or genetic function; several are theoretical in nature. Only one or two laboratories in the DIR are concerned with the organism as a whole, and one of those is concerned with primates. In short, on the contemporary federal scene, behavioral and social science research is ill esteemed and poorly supported.

Finally, government employment is often perceived as being secure and stable relative to business and industry; academia also has its tenure. There are other distinctions as well. Scientists in academia have much freer access to remunerative opportunities outside of work than does the typical government researcher; academics can write books, be expert witnesses in court, and consult. Scientists in business and industry are normally remunerated for their work at substantially higher levels than researchers in government service. Scientists who are federal civil servants have received a pay raise (on average, 2%) every year (but 2) since 1969, rising by about 400%, but average annual wages and salaries in the private sector grew by more than 500% in the same period, as did consumer prices. In the government, supplementary employment is possible, but permission to do so is required because of the potential for conflict of interest between outside employment and government work. Often the process of securing permissions is onerous (i.e., filling out forms, obtaining approvals and signatures of various executives). Consequently, most government researchers give up doing outside work, or they limit the amount of outside work they do. Federal service for many is a 9-to-5 job and has no sabbatical opportunities.

Conclusion

Combining science and government service can be rewarding but at the same time frustrating. It is possible for researchers who are employed by the federal government to obtain a steady stream of funding for their research, to engage in basic and applied science, and to have their findings affect policy. It is also possible that their science will be frustrated by rules and regulations beyond their control. Many psychologists have been employed directly or indirectly by the federal government; famously, B. F. Skinner once conditioned pigeons to peck at targets in the nose cones of bombs to increase missile precision. Since World War II, the federal government has supported psychological research at federal installations (such as the NIH) as well as through grants and contracts to psychological scientists in the nation and around the world. In his *Foundation* series, polymath Isaac Asimov (1974) cast psychologists (actually *psychohistorians*, scientific practitioners of predicting the future, developed by the Foundation's founder, Hari Seldon) as the rulers of government to the benefit of all humankind.

References

Asimov, I. (1974). *The foundation trilogy: Three classics of science fiction.* New York: Avon Books.

Bornstein, M. H. (Ed.). (2002a). *Handbook of parenting: Vol. 1. Children and parenting* (2nd ed.). Mahwah, NJ: Erlbaum.

Bornstein, M. H. (Ed.). (2002b). *Handbook of parenting: Vol. 2. Biology and ecology of parenting* (2nd ed.). Mahwah, NJ: Erlbaum.

Bornstein, M. H. (Ed.). (2002c). *Handbook of parenting: Vol. 3. Status and social conditions of parenting* (2nd ed.). Mahwah, NJ: Erlbaum.

Bornstein, M. H. (Ed.). (2002d). *Handbook of parenting: Vol. 4. Applied parenting* (2nd ed.). Mahwah, NJ: Erlbaum.

Bornstein, M. H. (Ed.). (2002e). *Handbook of parenting: Vol. 5. Practical parenting.* Mahwah, NJ: Erlbaum.

Bornstein, M. H., & Bradley, R. H. (Eds.). (2003). *Socioeconomic status, parenting, and child development.* Mahwah, NJ: Erlbaum.

Bornstein, M. H., & Cote, L. C (2006). *Acculturation and parent–child relationships: Measurement and development.* Mahwah, NJ: Erlbaum.

Bornstein, M. H., Davidson, L., Keyes, C. M., Moore, K., & Center for Child Well-Being. (Eds.). (2003). *Well-being: Positive development across the life course.* Mahwah, NJ: Erlbaum.

Bornstein, M. H., & Lamb, M. E. (Eds.). (2005). *Developmental science: An advanced textbook.* Mahwah, NJ: Erlbaum.

Bornstein, M. H., & Lamb, M. E. (in press). *Development in infancy: An introduction* (5th ed.). Mahwah, NJ: Erlbaum.

Mary Barringer and Adam Saenz

Promoting Positive School Environments: A Career in School Psychology

13

The present is a challenging time to be a school psychologist. Violent, delinquent acts by children and adolescents, school failure and dropout, bullying and sexual harassment, and substance abuse are now considered routine occurrences (Walker & Shinn, 2002). It has been estimated that as many as 20% of young adolescents experience symptoms of depression (Saluja et al., 2004), and suicide is the fourth leading cause of death among youths ages 10 to 14 years and third among those ages 15 to 24 years (President's New Freedom Commission on Mental Health, 2003). Family factors that contribute to a child's risk include family violence, negative interactions, abuse, criminality, substance abuse, parent psychiatric disorders such as depression, long-term parental unemployment, and poor supervision (Walker &

Mary Barringer, PhD, is a licensed specialist in school psychology. She is employed by Bryan Independent School District and is a partner in an educational and organizational consulting company. She earned a BS from the University of North Texas in 1985 and a PhD from Texas A & M University in 2000. Her interests include early childhood assessment and autism spectrum disorders.

Adam Saenz, PhD, earned his doctorate in school psychology from Texas A & M University and a postdoctorate from Brown University. He works as a school psychologist for the Bryan Independent School District in addition to his private practice and consulting.

Shinn, 2002). Community and cultural factors, including socioeconomic disadvantage, neighborhood violence and crime, media portray-
als of violence, and social and cultural discrimination, also contribute
to a child's risk for developing emotional and behavioral problems
(Walker & Shinn, 2002). These are the facts of daily life for 21st-century
students, and they bring these issues to school with them every day.
These problems can interfere with students' ability to benefit from the
educational process, and that is why schools need psychologists.

Now for the good news: Evidence that school-based mental health
programs are effective in preventing youth violence, drug abuse, and
mental disorders and in promoting positive youth development continues to accumulate (Graczyk, Domitrovich, & Zins, 2003). In fact, although up to 80% of children and adolescents with mental health
needs do not receive the services they require (Kataoka, Zhang, &
Wells, 2002), between 70% and 80% of those who do receive mental
health services do so through the education sector (Burns et al., 1995).

School Psychology as a Career

American Psychological Association (APA) Division 16, School Psychology, defines *school psychology* as "a general practice and health service
provider specialty of professional psychology that is concerned with
the science and practice of psychology with children, youth, families;
learners of all ages; and the schooling process" (APA, Division of School
Psychology, 2004). Most school psychologists work in special education
departments or psychological services departments for public and private school systems or in school-based and school-linked health centers
(Bureau of Labor Statistics, 2004–2005). Licensed doctoral-level school
psychologists also work in private practice providing evaluations, individual and family therapy, and consultation and training for school
districts. The juvenile correctional system employs school psychologists
to serve incarcerated youths. Doctoral-level school psychologists working within university systems conduct research and provide training for
undergraduate and graduate students. Reschly (cited in Fagan, 2002)
reported the following distribution of employment settings for school
psychologists: public schools (89.1%), private practice (3.6%), clinic/
hospital/other (3.9%), college or university (2.9%), and institutional/
residential (0.5%).

A Model of School Psychology Service Provision

Although school psychologists have been criticized for focusing their efforts primarily on the identification of individual student deficits and for devoting too much time to special education eligibility determination, the trend in school psychology is toward using data-driven problem-solving approaches to provide integrated prevention and treatment activities that reduce the risk for poor outcomes and improve social, emotional, and academic functioning of all students (Graczyk et al., 2003). The evolution of the role of school psychologists in our school district provides an example of this shift. In the 2004–2005 school year, Bryan Independent School District opened its first Department of Psychological Services, staffed by one bilingual, doctoral-level school psychologist (the second author, Saenz), one master's-level Licensed Specialist in School Psychology (LSSP), and the first author (Barringer), with a mandate to provide appropriate prevention and intervention services to all students. Although we continue to play a very active role in special education assessment and intervention, we now spend a larger portion of our time in prevention activities. We spend the most time in *primary prevention activities* (also referred to as "universal interventions"), which are those proactively provided to all students in a population and focused on creating healthy individuals, classrooms, schools, and communities. *Secondary* (also referred to as "selective") *prevention activities* are provided to students identified as at risk for negative outcomes such as school failure, and *tertiary* (also referred to as "targeted" or "indicated") *interventions* are intensive services provided to a very small group of students already identified as having disabilities or as exhibiting severe emotional, behavioral, or academic problems.

PRIMARY PREVENTION

A basic tenet of primary prevention is that all students do not arrive at school equally prepared or equipped for school success. If a student is to be held to any expectation, the skills for meeting the expectation must be taught directly. For this reason, a school system using a preventive model allocates the majority of its resources (time, money, staff) to primary prevention activities in an attempt to give all students equal opportunities for success and to prevent problems from emerging.

Establishing districtwide classroom management expectations for teachers and providing skills training to enable them to meet those expectations is an example of a universal or primary prevention activity. Others include establishing rules and routines for all students in the system and developing a positive behavior support system to teach them the rules and routines and the skills required to meet established expectations. Similar primary prevention activities include promoting effective instruction to prevent learning problems and establishing anti-bullying campaigns and teaching students mediation skills to prevent school violence.

So what is the role of the school psychologist in primary prevention? Because the goal of primary prevention is to provide positive interventions for all students in a system, and because school psychologists are in short supply, training campus-based staff to implement direct interventions is a critical and cost-effective activity. A small sample of the training school psychologists provided in our district in the past year include

- training in positive behavior support to all new employees in the district,
- training for parents of students with autism spectrum disorders in the basic concepts of behavior training,
- training for general education teachers in strategies for successful mainstreaming of students with Asperger's disorder,
- training for all teachers at an elementary campus in team building,
- crisis intervention training for more than 400 employees, and
- training for the district's counselors in functional behavior assessment.

We also trained more than 50 teachers and counselors to implement an intensive social skills and anger management intervention program for students identified as at risk for behavioral difficulties.

Another efficient method of service provision is consultation, which most often supports primary or secondary prevention but is also used at the tertiary level. School psychologists conduct system-level consultation at the request of administrators such as superintendents, principals, or directors of special programs. The "client" in system-level consultation is almost always a large organization or department, rather than an individual student. Consultation at this level may target, for example, development and implementation of new programs to increase parent involvement, improvement in services to students with limited English proficiency, or the promotion of effective teacher communication in a specific building. School psychologists also conduct program evaluations and needs assessments to help administrators identify the strengths and weaknesses of specific programs or departments, identify goals, develop plans for improvement, implement plans, and evaluate program processes and outcomes.

SECONDARY PREVENTION

Most students benefit significantly from primary prevention activities, but some do not benefit enough to prevent the emergence of emotional, behavioral, or academic difficulties. It is important to have a plan in place to monitor the primary prevention program and identify students who are not responding in the desired manner so that secondary interventions can be implemented, and the school psychologist can be instrumental in creating and supporting effective monitoring plans.

Secondary prevention involves intermediate-level prevention activities for students who continue to experience difficulties (academically or behaviorally) despite consistent implementation of primary prevention activities. The emphasis in secondary prevention is on early identification and intervention before problems become severe. Secondary interventions are provided to a much smaller population of students, usually in groups.

A typical secondary intervention for a student with persistent behavior problems is the development of an individual behavior improvement plan, which is based on a functional assessment of the problem behavior. A functional behavior assessment can be conducted either by the school psychologist or by a campus-based professional, such as a counselor, who has been trained by the school psychologist. The assessment consists of identifying a measurable behavior and collecting information about how, when, and where the behavior occurs to determine its function or purpose. Once the school psychologist has collected the information, he or she creates a plan to teach the student positive, effective replacement behaviors that serve the same function. School psychologists may assist a campus-based team in analyzing the information obtained through functional behavior assessments and identifying the key components of the behavior plan. Interventions may include additional training for the teaching staff, modifications to the classroom or school environment, and direct skills training for the student.

Other examples of secondary interventions include assigning adult or peer mentors for the student, changing instructional strategies, providing additional tutoring, and providing counseling groups for students with anger management difficulties or specific social skills deficits. Secondary interventions have been successful in improving the academic, emotional, and behavioral functioning of the majority of students referred. Again, monitoring the effectiveness of the intervention and making adjustments along the way are crucial components of secondary prevention activities that may require the support of the school psychologist.

TERTIARY PREVENTION

Tertiary prevention interventions build on, rather than replace, primary and secondary prevention activities for a very small group of students who exhibit severe, persistent academic or behavioral problems. Tertiary interventions are individualized and intensive. They can also be intrusive, expensive, and perceived by the student as stigmatizing, which is why schools must ensure that all primary and secondary prevention activities have been implemented appropriately before tertiary interventions are considered. As they relate to behavior, tertiary interventions are required when the student's emotional and behavioral difficulties are so extreme as to interfere with learning or threaten the safety of the student or others, and they usually include counseling and a more intensive behavior intervention plan. Tertiary interventions for behavior problems may also include services to the student's family and intensive case management to coordinate services provided at school with services provided in the community. Academically, tertiary interventions are indicated when the student fails to respond to research-based instructional interventions. Tertiary interventions focus on the student, rather than the classroom or the school, and some tertiary interventions require the removal of the student from the home campus to an alternative setting where the environment is more highly structured and behavior can be managed more safely. Students requiring tertiary interventions are often, but not always, identified as requiring special education support services.

PUTTING IT ALL TOGETHER: CRISIS PLANNING AND RESPONSE

Although for purposes of clarity, primary, secondary, and tertiary prevention have been explained as distinct entities; in reality they occur simultaneously throughout the system. An example is a school district's preparation for and response to crisis. Following a number of highly publicized school shootings, the U.S. Secret Service and the U.S. Department of Education emphasized the importance of threat assessment in public schools and published a document, *Threat Assessment in Schools: A Guide to Managing Threatening Situations and to Creating Safe School Climates* (Fein et al., 2002). The guide proposes a process for identifying, assessing, and managing students who may pose a threat of targeted violence in schools. School psychologists have assumed a leading role in the development and implementation of threat assessment programs in public school districts and in creating model programs at the national level.

Although threat assessment focuses on identifying threats to prevent crises, unpredicted crises do occur in schools. Schools must therefore have a plan for responding in a manner that protects the physical and emotional safety of everyone involved, including students, parents, and staff. School psychologists participate in the development of crisis response plans for districts and individual buildings (primary prevention) and provision of direct intervention to help groups of affected students, parents, teachers, and administrators cope in the immediate aftermath of a crisis, should one occur (secondary prevention). If adequate primary and secondary prevention activities are provided, most individuals involved can be expected to return to school relatively shortly after the incident. Some students and faculty, however, may be more severely affected. Students who develop ongoing mental health problems following a crisis may require tertiary interventions from the school psychologist, who may provide either direct services or a referral to a community agency.

Services to Students With Identified Disabilities

In most, but not all, school systems, school psychologists work directly with students who are identified as eligible to receive special education support services, so in addition to the skills and knowledge required of all psychologists, school psychologists must have a thorough knowledge of the federal and state laws protecting people with disabilities and regulating the provision of special education services in schools. In the past 30 years, the practice of school psychology has been influenced significantly by Public Law 94-142, the Education for All Handicapped Children Act of 1975 (now codified as the Individuals With Disabilities Education Act, or IDEA), which was created to ensure that all children with disabilities are provided a free appropriate public education and to protect the rights of these students and their families. The act specifically addresses eligibility, mandating that all states make an active effort to find and evaluate all students who may have a disability and be eligible for special education support services. Historically, school psychologists have been involved in the implementation of IDEA, primarily within the realm of identifying students who are eligible to receive special education services.

School psychologists assess students who are suspected of having a wide array of disabilities, including emotional disturbances, learning disabilities, mental retardation, traumatic brain injuries, and autism, as well as those who come from diverse cultural and linguistic backgrounds. School psychologists also participate on multidisciplinary teams to identify and provide interventions for these students.

ASSESSMENT

Although they may assess students for many different special education eligibilities, school psychologists almost always take the leading role in evaluations for emotional disturbances. The school psychologist's role in evaluation of these students typically includes reviewing referral information; consulting with teachers; planning and conducting assessments; interpreting results; and writing reports that include recommendations for planning, implementing, and evaluating interventions to meet the needs identified by the assessment (National Association of School Psychologists [NASP], 1993). Because there are five different types of emotional disturbance, the assessment procedures vary from student to student. Instruments are selected based on the specific referral question and the student's age and developmental level. Assessment procedures typically include parent and teacher ratings of the frequency of specific behaviors; interviews with parents and school staff; classroom observations of the student; and individual assessment of the student, including an interview, self-report measures, standardized measures of intelligence and academic achievement, measures of adaptive functioning, and projective measures when appropriate. A school psychologist has significant autonomy in selecting measurement tools and strategies and therefore must be diligent in selecting only the measures he or she has been trained to administer and is qualified to interpret.

Controversy surrounds the school psychologist's appropriate role in the assessment of learning disabilities. In contrast to the process for identifying mental disorders in clinical settings (where disorders are defined by a diagnostic manual), the definition of learning disabilities for the purposes of special education eligibility is legislated under IDEA. Although a thorough explanation of the controversy is far beyond the scope of this chapter, a very brief explanation will help to clarify the issues. Historically, learning disability has been defined in terms of the magnitude of difference between a student's ability (as measured by standardized tests of intelligence) and academic achievement (also as measured by standardized tests) in one of seven areas. School psychologists and professionals from other fields, such as education, have raised serious questions regarding the validity of the "formula" for determining whether a learning disability exists, the usefulness of data obtained through standardized evaluation, the link between the data and changes in instructional strategies, and the amount of time spent in standardized assessment (which might be better spent on other activities). Reschly and Ysseldyke (2002) reported that school psychologists devote approximately two thirds of their time to special education classification and placement, with slightly over half of that time devoted to individual assessment, including administration of standardized measures of ability and achievement. They further reported that "diagnosis of LD [learning disability] through determination of the size of the ability–achievement discrepancy, involving administration of one or more IQ tests and one or more achievement tests, is *the* single most frequent activity of school psychologists" (p. 8). Although the disproportionate allocation of school psychologists' time to diagnosis of learning disabilities does not exist in all school settings, it is common.

The 2004 reauthorization of IDEA may substantially change the process by which learning disabilities are identified and thus may substantially change the role of school psychologists in the assessment process. The reauthorization specifically states that the discrepancy model does not have to be used when determining whether a child has a specific learning disability. The revisions allow schools to use a process that determines whether the child responds to scientific, research-based intervention as a part of the evaluation procedures. This development may result in increased use of the school psychologist's expertise in identifying student strengths and weaknesses and learning styles, designing instructional interventions and environmental modifications that meet each student's unique needs, and assessing response to intervention, thus decreasing the time school psychologists spend in standardized testing. No matter what the outcome, the school psychologist will continue to play a key role in assessment, whatever its form.

INDIVIDUALIZED EDUCATION PLAN TEAM PARTICIPATION

As members of individualized education plan (IEP) teams, school psychologists contribute to the development of education plans for students identified as eligible to receive special education support services. The role of the school psychologist is to interpret assessment data and to assist the team in determining eligibility and the appropriate academic and behavioral supports, modifications, and interventions. IEP teams use assessment data to develop specific, measurable, annual learning objectives (including behavioral objectives) and then develop a schedule of services for implementing the IEP goals in the least restrictive environment (LRE). The LRE requirement emphasizes the importance of educating students with disabilities, to the maximum extent appropriate, with nondisabled peers to prevent their being isolated and stigmatized because of their disabilities. Multidisciplinary IEP teams include a parent or adult student, general education teachers, special education teachers, assessment professionals, administrators, and related service providers. Related service providers and other professionals providing services to students and serving on IEP teams include occupational and physical therapists, school nurses, music therapists, counselors, autism specialists, adapted physical education teachers, and assistive technology specialists, among others.

After the IEP is developed, the role of the school psychologist in its implementation varies considerably. For some students, the school psychologist may continue to be involved in providing individual psychological services, ongoing parent and teacher consultation and training, and implementation of the behavior intervention plan. For other students, all services in the IEP may be provided by campus-based professionals with little additional involvement by the school psychologist. Should problems arise, however, the school psychologist is usually called. For students with emotional disturbances in particular, problems may come in the form of disciplinary infractions requiring a *manifestation determination,* the process required when a student identified as needing special education support services engages in a behavior subject to certain levels of discipline. The IEP team meets to determine whether the behavior is linked to (or a manifestation of) the identified disability. The school psychologist's role is to interpret assessment data and to help the team understand the disability and how it could interfere with the student's ability to understand the consequences of the behavior or to refrain from the behavior even if the student did understand the consequences.

Opportunities for Specialization

Because early identification of disabilities is essential to positive outcomes, public schools are required by IDEA to find and assess children with disabilities and offer school-based services for eligible students beginning on their 3rd birthday. This requirement has created a demand for school psychologists who specialize in developmental disabilities and early childhood evaluations and interventions. At the other end of the childhood-to-adolescent spectrum, schools serve adolescents and young adults with severe disabilities through the school year in which they reach the age of 21. In meeting the needs of these students, school psychologists work with IEP teams to facilitate the transition from school-based services to life after public school. Transition activities include identifying student and parent expectations for how and where the student will live, work, and socialize and providing training to support the transition process. School psychologists support transition by providing counseling to students and parents, consulting with teachers, and monitoring the implementation of the behavior plan to help strengthen the student's ability to perform appropriately in vocational settings.

Opportunities for school psychologists to specialize are abundant. Currently there is a burgeoning population of students identified with autism spectrum disorders, and this area is becoming a specialization for many within the field. School psychologists who are fluent in American Sign Language and familiar with deaf culture are in short supply and are needed to provide appropriate assessment and interventions to the very sizeable population of students with auditory impairments. Rapid developments in the field of neuroscience have produced a growing subset of school psychologists who specialize in neuropsychology, particularly the neuropsychology of learning disabilities.

Providing Culturally and Linguistically Competent Services

School psychologists who are fluent in Spanish are in great demand across the country to meet the mental health needs of the growing population of bilingual and monolingual Spanish-speaking students enrolled in public schools in the United States. Demographic, legal, and ethical factors have played a significant role in shaping the delivery of psychoeducational services to culturally and linguistically diverse students. Hodgkinson (1992) examined demographic changes between 1980 and 1990 and projected data for 1990 to 2010. He predicted that in 2010, four states—New York, Texas, California, and Florida—will have about one third of the nation's minority youths. Furthermore, over half of students in Texas, California, and Florida will be non-White, and about 19% of the teaching staff in California, 15% in Florida, and 22% in Texas will be non-White. After 2010, Hodgkinson predicted, the size of the U.S. population will stabilize, and after 2030, immigration will be the primary source of population increase in the

United States, which will continue to attract two thirds of the world's immigrants; 85% of these immigrants will come from Central and South America.

The legal system has played a critical role in extending educational services to the general public (U.S. Department of Education Office of Civil Rights, 1992). Legal intervention, however, has a relatively short history in public schools, and much of the legislation that has influenced policy in the schools has arisen through litigation by parents on behalf of their children (Bersoff & Hofer, 1990). As Baca and Cervantes (1989) noted, the Supreme Court case *Brown v. Board of Education of Topeka*, in which the U.S. Supreme court ruled that segregation of children by race prohibited equal educational opportunity among the races, played a significant role in influencing educational policy. *Brown v. Board of Education of Topeka* opened a floodgate of subsequent legislation extending equal educational opportunity to a variety of specific populations.

The ethical guidelines and policy of the governing agencies for providers of psychological services play a large role in shaping the standards by which practitioners must deliver services. Regarding general practitioner competence, the APA (1993, 2002) has published guidelines relevant to the general practice of psychology. The NASP (1992) has also published guidelines regarding more specific issues related to the practice of school psychology with linguistically and culturally diverse populations.

In providing culturally and linguistically appropriate services to students, best practice involves a service delivery process that establishes client rapport, identifies the presenting problem, and recognizes the role of the family system in a manner sensitive to the client's acculturation process (Ortiz & Flanagan, 2004). Tseng and Hsu's (1991) review of family systems from a cross-cultural perspective provides an excellent overview of critical issues. Developing cross-cultural competence is vital to the school psychologist's ability to effectively deliver culturally sensitive services. Miranda's (2004) discussion of basic considerations such as culture, race, ethnicity, social class, and assimilation and acculturation lays an appropriate foundation on which to build knowledge and skills in developing cross-cultural competence.

Academic Preparation for the Career

The APA School Psychology division (Division 16) sets the minimum standards for the doctoral-level preparation of school psychologists.

NASP, another professional organization for school psychologists, awards the Nationally Certified School Psychologist (NCSP) designation. In contrast to Division 16 of APA, NASP allows certification at the specialist as well as the doctoral level. According to the *Occupational Outlook Handbook* (Bureau of Labor Statistics, 2004–2005), although most specialties (e.g., clinical and counseling psychology) require doctoral degrees, school and industrial/organizational psychologists need only a master's degree.

DOCTORAL TRAINING AND LICENSURE

Most doctoral programs in school psychology follow the scientist–practitioner model. A doctoral degree usually requires a minimum of 4 years of full-time (or the equivalent) graduate study, a dissertation based on original research, and a full-time internship of at least 10 months. In keeping with their practice standards, the APA accredits doctoral training programs in school psychology and institutions that provide internships for doctoral students in school psychology. The National Council for Accreditation of Teacher Education and NASP are also involved in the accreditation of advanced degree programs in school psychology. NASP requirements for doctoral programs include a minimum of 4 years (90 graduate semester hours) of full-time study (or the equivalent) at the graduate level, at least 78 hours of which are exclusive of credit for the supervised internship and dissertation, and a minimum of 1 academic year of doctoral supervised internship experience consisting of a minimum of 1,500 clock hours (NASP, 2000).

Doctoral-level licensure is required for the independent practice of psychology. Licensure is regulated by state agencies, and requirements vary by state. All states require a written examination. In addition to passing the required written (and in some states oral or essay) examinations, applicants for doctoral-level licensure must have completed an approved internship and have 1 to 2 years of professional (postdoctoral) experience. Continuing education credits are required for license renewal in some states.

SPECIALIST-LEVEL TRAINING AND CREDENTIALS

NASP requirements for specialist-level training include a minimum of 3 years (60 credit hours) of full-time study (or the equivalent) at the graduate level and a minimum of 1 academic year of supervised internship experience consisting of a minimum of 1,200 clock hours

(Harrison, 2002). Academic preparation includes training in data-based decision making and accountability; consultation and collaboration; effective instruction and development of cognitive and academic skills; socialization and development of life skills; student diversity in development and learning; school and systems organization, policy development, climate; prevention, crisis intervention, and mental health; home/school/community collaboration; research and program evaluation; school psychology practice and development; and information technology (NASP, 2000). Eighteen states now accept the NCSP as one avenue to obtaining the state credential. Requirements for the NCSP include completion of 60 graduate semester hours in school psychology; a 1,200-clock-hour internship, 600 hours of which must be completed in a school setting; and a passing score on the National School Psychology Examination.

Financial Compensation

In 2001, the mean 11- to 12-month salary for licensed doctoral-level school psychologists responding to an APA survey was $77,000 (Singleton, Tate, & Randall, 2003). Results of a 1999 NASP national survey indicated a mean salary of $49,086 (Thomas, 2000). The lower average annual salary reported in the NASP survey likely reflects the inclusion of master's-level professionals. The *Occupational Outlook Handbook* reported 2002 median annual earnings of school psychologists employed in elementary and secondary schools as $54,480 (Bureau of Labor Statistics, 2004–2005).

Do You Want To Be a School Psychologist, Too?

The advantages of choosing school psychology as a profession are many. The outlook for employment opportunities is particularly good. Citing the growing awareness of how students' mental health and behavioral problems affect learning, the *Occupational Outlook Handbook* (Bureau of Labor Statistics, 2004–2005) predicted that among the specialties in psychology, school psychologists may enjoy the best job opportunities.

School psychologists typically have control over their daily schedules and practice with a significant level of autonomy. They may move between several settings within a day, interacting with a diverse population of individuals and engaging in a broad array of activities from individual assessment and intervention to developing and evaluating programs for system change at the highest level.

School psychologists have the opportunity to collaborate with other professionals, including occupational and physical therapists, speech therapists, counselors, and other psychologists in private practice or clinics. They can serve as the critical link between pediatricians and psychiatrists providing pharmaceutical interventions and school-based teams providing educational interventions for the same student. Because medical professionals rarely have a thorough understanding of the provision of services under the educational model, and because school staff rarely understand the medical model, school psychologists can provide consultation with both types of professionals to coordinate services to produce the best outcomes for the student.

Continuing education, in addition to being required for annual renewal of the psychologist's license in most states, is strongly encouraged in most employment settings. School districts and departments of special education usually budget for psychologists and other professional staff to attend local, regional, state, or national conferences to obtain specialized training, which allows school psychologists to obtain required continuing education credits at reduced personal expense.

Another advantage of the profession is that many school psychologists employed in school districts have contracts that roughly approximate the number of days students are in attendance. Annual contract lengths between 180 and 210 days are common and allow the freedom either to enjoy substantial vacation time or to engage in other professional activities during summer breaks.

On the down side, school psychologists who work within departments of special education often find their daily activities driven by timelines preestablished by federal regulations and state boards of education. They may find that they spend an inordinate amount of time completing evaluations for learning disabilities, managing paperwork, and conducting IEP team meetings. The first author (Barringer) has worked under these circumstances and found it stressful and frustrating because it required good clerical skills (which I do not possess) and allowed for only very limited use of my professional expertise. Some school psychologists are assigned large special education caseloads, with significantly limited time to devote to each student. School psychologists must have good training, strong skills, and the confidence to advocate both within their school districts and at the state and national level to protect the integrity of their work and define their roles.

PERSONAL ATTRIBUTES REQUIRED FOR SUCCESS

To complete a training program in school psychology, you need to have strong writing skills and you will have to develop skills in organizing your time. Self-discipline in time management and organization will serve you well. Personality characteristics are equally important. Successful completion of the training program will require you to have the self-confidence to hear constructive criticism from faculty without becoming defensive.

Once you are on the job, you must have patience and flexibility. Being effective in a school system requires that you understand that children's problems are often symptoms of system problems, and systems do not change easily or quickly. Believe it or not, some staff and parents will not immediately jump at the opportunity to act on your recommendations. Persistence is crucial. Given the size and complexity of most school systems and the increasingly multicultural aspect of many communities, your ability to communicate effectively and respectfully with individuals of different ages and developmental levels and from a broad range of cultures, socioeconomic strata, and educational backgrounds will in a large part determine your effectiveness.

Why Did I Become a School Psychologist?

The first author (Barringer) has had an interest in psychology since my senior year of high school, when I stumbled on an article about autism while trying to find a topic for a research paper. Later, as I considered my options for a major field of study in college, I chose psychology. As I worked toward an undergraduate degree, I assumed that I would work predominantly with adults and in private practice. I was unaware of the existence of school psychology as an area of specialization. In 1985, I earned a bachelor of arts degree from North Texas State University (now the University of North Texas), and in 1990 I completed my master's degree in counseling psychology at Texas A & M University (TAMU).

Because the Department of Educational Psychology at TAMU offers master's and doctoral training programs in both counseling psychology and school psychology, I had the opportunity to learn about school psychology as a career option. The possibility of working with children and adolescents became more appealing when I volunteered for Family

Outreach (a national child abuse prevention program) and served as education chair on their local board of directors. Volunteer work with a local literacy program piqued my interest in education and in factors that interfere with academic achievement.

After earning my master's degree, I took a position as undergraduate counselor in an academic department within the university, and my supervisor encouraged me to continue my education. A visit with one of the professors in the school psychology program convinced me that this was a career path that would allow me to pursue a wide variety of activities and to practice in many different settings. Well into my doctoral training, however, I continued to assume that I was preparing for work in private practice or a clinical setting. My internship at Fort Worth Independent School District's Department of Psychological Services introduced me to the realities of full-time work in a public school setting and revealed one of the advantages of practicing within a school setting, which would eventually lead me to my current job: Practicing in a public school allows the psychologist to work with children and adolescents who may have a significant need for intervention but, for reasons related to their socioeconomic status or culture, are unlikely to present for treatment in any other setting.

As I write this chapter, I am enjoying my 8th year practicing in Bryan Independent School District in Bryan, Texas. My experience has been that a career in school psychology is, like most things in life, what you make of it. Over the past 8 years, my role in the school district has changed considerably, and my career evolution has mirrored, in some ways, the evolution of school psychology. When I was hired in 1997, psychologists and Licensed Specialists in School Psychology in the district worked almost exclusively as assessment staff within the Department of Special Education, and our jobs were essentially the same as that of an educational diagnostician. My role was to meet all of the special education assessment needs of three elementary campuses, schedule and conduct IEP team meetings for students in special education, and ensure that paperwork was completed and submitted within timelines. Referrals to special education were numerous, and I completed more than 80 evaluations at one kindergarten through 2nd grade campus in 1 year.

As I entered the field, I found it crucial to advocate, continuously and at multiple levels, for the development of roles for school psychologists in the district that use our expertise appropriately. Although not always easy, persistent advocacy has been productive. The role of school psychologists in our district has changed considerably. In recent years, I have enjoyed the opportunity to supervise and train specialist-level trainees and interns and doctoral students completing school-based practicum placements; I particularly enjoy this part of my work. I have also enjoyed working toward systemic change; developing strong working relationships with administrators, counselors, and teachers; and working with hundreds of children and adolescents and their families.

In addition to my work within the school district, I have recently added a partnership in an educational and organizational consulting firm to my professional activities. I have also had the privilege of teaching a practicum in assessment for school psychology doctoral students at TAMU. I enjoy all of my professional roles enormously, but if I were forced to choose, I would work exclusively in the school system, because school is the only environment in which I can work with all of the children in my community, from those with the most profound disabilities to those who are the most gifted, and from a variety of cultures and socioeconomic backgrounds. I have the freedom to work with any children or adolescents for whom parents and teachers seek help, and I do not have to refuse to serve any of them because they do not have insurance or the ability to pay. American public schools provide a unique opportunity for psychologists who want to work with children and adolescents.

A Day in the Life of a School Psychologist

On one typical day, I began work at 7:30 a.m. by answering e-mails and telephone calls. At 8:30 a.m., I conducted a play-based developmental evaluation of a 2-year-10-month-old child who was referred by the Early Childhood Intervention program to determine whether she was eligible to receive special education services through the public school at age 3. Other members of the assessment team included a speech therapist, a Preschool Program for Children With Disabilities teacher, an occupational therapist, and a teacher with experience and training in autism and assistive technology.

At 10:30 a.m., I began a classroom observation for a functional behavior assessment of a 2nd-grade boy who exhibited intermittent aggressive behaviors such as hitting and kicking classmates and teachers. The classroom observation was one component of the functional behavior assessment being conducted to assist the IEP team in developing a behavior improvement plan for this student.

At 11:30, an IEP team meeting and manifestation determination was held for a high school student who received special education support services for mild mental retardation and other health impairment (attention-deficit/hyperactivity disorder [ADHD]). She had been involved in a fight on campus. While being questioned in the assistant principal's office, the student had revealed that she had a box cutter in her backpack. The IEP team met to review the student's assessment reports and determine whether the behaviors subject to discipline were related to the disabilities for which she received special education support services. My role was to interpret the assessment results for the IEP team and to help them determine whether the student's level of mental retardation and/or factors related to ADHD interfered with her ability to understand the consequences of her behaviors (both fighting and bringing a weapon to school) and to refrain from engaging in the behavior even if she did understand the consequences.

At 1:00 p.m., I held a parent consultation regarding a requested evaluation for emotional disturbance. The parent of a kindergarten student had requested an evaluation for emotional disturbance for her son, who was diagnosed by his pediatrician as having bipolar disorder. School staff had reported that the student exhibited appropriate behaviors at school and was making good academic progress. This initial parent interview focused on identifying the parent's concerns about her child's behaviors at home and at school and her perception of his bipolar disorder as affecting his ability to benefit from instruction in the general education setting.

At 2:30 p.m., I provided consultation to a 6th-grade teacher concerned that one of her students might be experiencing school phobia. Beginning in August, the student was frequently tardy, and absences had increased each month. The student's mother reported that he physically fought with her to avoid getting out of the car at school each morning. The consultation focused on obtaining more information regarding the student's emotional and academic difficulties before the onset of school avoidance, providing the teacher with information about research-based interventions for school avoidance or phobia; giving the teacher handouts for the parent, and scheduling a conjoint consultation with both the parent and teacher for later in the week.

At 3:45 p.m., I provided campus training on how to use timers to increase time on task. This 1-hour training was provided, at the request of the building principal, for all teachers at an elementary school. The training combined a didactic presentation about how and why timers help students remain on task with a discussion of case studies and demonstration of a variety of timers that can be used with students with different needs, disabilities, and developmental levels.

At 5:00 p.m., I had scheduled a consultation with a middle school principal on campuswide behavior improvement planning. This consultation focused on how the administrator could motivate his staff to meet the needs of students, most of whom came from low-income families. The campus had been designated as low performing for the past 2 years, and staff appeared demoralized and isolated. Staff perceived students as being "out of control." This was the principal's 1st year in the building. Ongoing consultation had focused on team building for the staff, identification of specific concerns from parents and staff, and support for the administrator in managing his own stress. Consultation and interventions were expected to continue for the duration of the school year.

Conclusion

Like most people who have found a career that matches their strengths, personality, and values, I find immense pleasure in my work. My job offers me variety, autonomy, and personal satisfaction. No career path is without challenges, and school psychology is no exception to this rule. If you would like to explore it further, your first stop might be to volunteer in a public school. Many children need additional adult support, and even if you decide not to pursue a career in school psychology, your time will have been well spent.

References

American Psychological Association. (1993). Guidelines for providers of psychological services to ethnic, linguistic, and culturally diverse populations. *American Psychologist, 48*, 45–48; also available at http://www.apa.org/pi/oema/guide.html

American Psychological Association. (2002). Ethical principles of psychologists and code of conduct. *American Psychologist, 57*, 1060–1073; also available at http://www.apa.org/ethics/code2002.html

American Psychological Association, Division of School Psychology. (2004). *Goals and objectives*. Retrieved November 8, 2004, from http://www.indiana.edu/~div16/G&O.htm

Baca, L. M., & Cervantes, H. T. (1989). *The bilingual education interface* (2nd ed.). Columbus, OH: Prentice Hall.

Bersoff, D. N., & Hofer, P. T. (1990). The legal regulation of school psychology. In C. R. Reynolds & T. Gutkin (Eds.), *Handbook of school psychology* (2nd ed., pp. 939–963). New York: Wiley.

Brown v. Board of Education, 347 U.S. 483 (1954).

Bureau of Labor Statistics. (2004–2005). *Occupational outlook handbook, 2004–05 edition, psychologists*. Retrieved November 8, 2004, from http://www.bls.gov/oco/ocos056.htm

Burns, B., Costello, E., Angold, A., Tweed, D., Stangl, D., Farmer, E., & Erkanli, L. (1995). Children's mental health service use across service sectors. *Health Affairs, 14(3)*, 147–159.

Education for All Handicapped Children Act of 1975, 20 U.S.C. § 1400 (1975).

Fagan, T. (2002). Trends in the history of school psychology in the United States. In A. Thomas & J. Grimes (Eds.), *Best practices in school psychology IV* (pp. 209–221). Bethesda, MD: National Association of School Psychologists Publications.

Fein, R., Vossekuil, B., Pollack, W., Borum, R., Modzeleski, W., & Reddy, M. (2002). *Threat assessment in schools: A guide to managing threatening situations and to creating safe school climates*. Washington, DC: U.S. Department of Education, Office of Elementary and Secondary Education, Safe and Drug-Free Schools Program, and U.S. Secret Service, National Threat Assessment Center.

Graczyk, P. A., Domitrovich, C. E., & Zins, J. E. (2003). Facilitating the implementation of evidence-based prevention and mental health promotion efforts in schools. In M. D. Weist, S. W. Evans, & N. A. Lever (Eds.), *Handbook of school mental health: Advancing practice and research* (pp. 301–318). New York: Kluwer.

Harrison, P. (2002). Executive summary: NASP standards and guidelines for the training and credentialing of school psychologists [Electronic version]. *NASP Communiqué, 30*(7). Retrieved June 1, 2005, from http://www.nasponline.org/publications/cq307training.html

Hodgkinson, H. L. (1992). *A demographic look at tomorrow*. Washington, DC: Institute for Educational Leadership, Center for Demographic Policy.

Individuals With Disabilities Education Act, 2 U.S.C. § 1400 (1975).

Individuals With Disabilities Education Improvement Act of 2004, 20 U.S.C. § 1400 (2004).

Kataoka, S., Zhang, L., & Wells, K. (2002). Unmet need for mental health care among US children: Variation by ethnicity and insurance status. *American Journal of Psychiatry, 159*, 1548–1555.

Miranda, A. H. (2004). Best practices in increasing cross-cultural competence. In A. Thomas & J. Grimes (Eds.), *Best practices in school psychology IV* (pp. 353–362). Bethesda, MD: National Association of School Psychologists Publications.

National Association of School Psychologists. (1992). *Principles of professional ethics*. Washington, DC: Author.

National Association of School Psychologists. (1993). *Position statement on students with emotional/behavioral disorders*. Silver Spring, MD: Author.

National Association of School Psychologists. (2000). *Standards for training and field placement programs in school psychology: Standards for the credentialing of school psychologists* [Electronic version]. Retrieved June 1, 2005, from http://www.nasponline.org/certification/Final Standards.pdf

Ortiz, S. O., & Flanagan, D. P. (2004). Best practices in working with culturally diverse children and families. In A. Thomas & J. Grimes (Eds.), *Best practices in school psychology IV* (pp. 337–352). Bethesda, MD: National Association of School Psychologists Publications.

President's New Freedom Commission on Mental Health. (2003). *Achieving the promise: Transforming mental health care in America*. Retrieved June 1, 2005, from http://www.mentalhealthcommission.gov/reports/FinalReport/toc.html

Reschly, D. J., & Ysseldyke, J. E. (2002). Paradigm shift: The past is not the future. In A. Thomas & J. Grimes (Eds.), *Best practices in school psychology IV* (pp. 3–20). Bethesda, MD: National Association of School Psychologists Publications.

Saluja, G., Iachan, R., Scheidt, P. C., Overpeck, M., Sun, W., & Giedd, J. N. (2004). Prevalence of and risk factors for depressive symptoms among young adolescents. *Archives of Pediatrics and Adolescent Medicine, 158*(7), 60–65.

Singleton, D., Tate, A., & Randall, G. (2003). *Salaries in psychology 2001: Report of the 2001 APA salary survey*. Retrieved June 1, 2005, from http://research.apa.org/01salary/

Thomas, A. (2000). School psychology 2000: Average salary data [Electronic version]. *NASP Communiqué, 28*(6). Retrieved June 1, 2005, from http://www.nasponline.org/publications/cq286Index.html

Tseng, W. S., & Hsu, J. (1991). *Culture and family: Problems and therapy*. New York: Haworth Press.

U.S. Department of Education, Office of Civil Rights. (1992). *The provision of an equal education opportunity to limited English speaking students*. Washington, DC: ED Publications.

Walker, H. M., & Shinn, M. R. (2002). Structuring school-based interventions to achieve integrated primary, secondary, and tertiary prevention goals for safe and effective schools. In M. R. Shinn, H. M. Walker, & G. Stoner (Eds.), *Interventions for academic and behavior problems: Vol. 2. Preventive and remedial approaches* (pp. 1–26). Bethesda, MD: National Association of School Psychologists Publications.

John J. Pass

Industrial/Organizational (I/O) Psychology as a Career: Improving Workforce Performance and Retention

14

S o, you are thinking about pursing a career in the field of industrial/organizational (I/O) psychology. The following are two examples of what you might end up doing as an I/O psychologist:

1. A large company is experiencing high turnover in its sales department and needs to stop losing its top salespeople. The company decides to hire the consulting company that you work for as an I/O psychologist to determine the reasons for the turnover and make recommendations for improvements. You are asked to be a part of a consulting team with other members who specialize in information technology, finance, and business strategy to help solve this company's problem.

2. You work for a large company as an I/O psychologist, and the company needs to design a hiring

John J. Pass, PhD, is on the faculty of Iona College in New Rochelle, New York, and is the industrial/organizational (I/O) program coordinator and assistant chair of the psychology department. He has a PhD in I/O psychology from North Carolina State University and has extensive leadership and consultative experience in I/O psychology in the public and private sectors. His primary interest is in employment selection and human resources organizational consulting.

and selection procedure for a new call center that is being opened in 6 months. The center will need to have 450 call takers hired before the opening. You are asked to join a team to help design a Web-based system that uses the best selection tools, such as cognitive-ability tests, personality inventories, and interviews, to select the most qualified people for the call taker jobs. And one other item: The call center is in India.

Sound interesting? If so, I/O psychology may be for you. If you have an orientation to business and a drive to implement programs that affect organizations and large groups of people, then industrial/ organizational psychology will be a rewarding professional area for you to pursue.

Industrial/ Organizational Psychology: What Is It, Anyway?

I/O psychology is the application of psychological concepts and research findings to the workplace to improve workforce performance and retention. I/O psychology is an applied field of psychology, yet it is still based on the scientist–practitioner model; I/O psychology depends on sound research and theoretical frameworks to form the basis for the design of programs and systems that enable organizational improvements. An I/O psychologist can be either more of a practitioner, applying research findings to solve organizational problems, or more of a scientist or researcher. I/O psychologists who hold faculty positions are typically more focused on research, but the boundary between the roles is often blurred, so that I/O psychologists often pursue both.

In the research area of I/O, you might focus on developing and validating new assessment tools or evaluating the effectiveness of different types of leadership development programs. If you lean toward the practitioner side, you might work as an internal consultant, designing and developing programs while working as an employee of an organization, or you might be an external consultant, working for a consulting firm and designing and developing programs for other companies. External consultants can also be faculty members, or they can work solely for a consulting firm.

The primary objective of both the internal and external I/O consultant is to design programs that improve workforce performance and retention. The programs that I/O psychologists analyze, design, or improve are typically human resource programs and include hiring and selection, training and development, performance appraisal, and employee satisfaction and retention programs. You may be involved in executive coaching or even in market research, determining what parts of the market may offer opportunities for your company.

I/O psychologists frequently work as part of a team. Sometimes the team is rather static, as in a company department, or the team may be temporary, convened to solve some acute problem. Typically, the team analyzes a problem that needs to be worked on, makes recommendations to management, implements the recommendations, and follows up on the implementation. One of the last team problems that I worked on at IBM was to develop an online workforce skills inventory system that would identify the current skills of hundreds of thousands of employees. This type of system is used for several purposes, including enabling employees to move to jobs that are in high demand as reflected by the market or by organizational strategy changes.

Because most of the programs or systems that I/O psychologists design and implement affect employees' careers, legal and fairness issues are usually a major concern. As an I/O psychologist, you must pay attention to these concerns to avoid possible lawsuits. And while you do this type of work, your performance will be evaluated in terms of the value your implemented recommendations add to the company in saving money, producing revenue, or improving performance or productivity. You will likely have an opportunity to work on a global team. Many companies are multinational and so, more and more, the work that I/O psychologists do involves working with associates in other countries.

Preparation for the Career

You need a graduate degree to be successful in I/O psychology. A PhD will definitely lead to more opportunities and better compensation (see the Financial Compensation section later in this chap.). And if you want to be an I/O faculty member, you definitely will need a PhD. But this does not mean that if you have an MA degree in I/O psychology, you will not be able to find good I/O or human resources jobs. With a PhD, you will be more likely to conduct research and/or to design programs and improvements in large organizations, but many organizations, such as local government agencies, require only an MA degree for their I/O work. Although some states require I/O psychologists to be licensed, a license is typically required only if you are working in your own business and offering your individual services as an I/O psychologist. Nonetheless, it is a good idea to investigate any license requirements in the state in which you wish to work.

A few other points about your graduate education: First, be sure to develop some level of expertise in the basic areas of I/O (selection, training and development, performance evaluation, compensation administration, consulting skills, and statistics). Second, be sure to gain some knowledge about global issues and applications, as this area is taking on greater and greater importance. Finally, a relevant internship will definitely improve your competitiveness in the job market; employers look for an internship that has provided you with actual work experience in a relevant I/O area.

Potential Work Opportunities

What does the future hold for I/O psychology in regard to opportunities for employment? Because most I/O jobs are focused on improving, in one way or another, human-resource-related functions such as selection or hiring, training and development, or workforce satisfaction and performance, these functions will obviously continue to be needed as long as there are organizations of people. But the number and types of opportunities depend on many factors such as the overall economy and the economic health of different sectors in the economy such as secondary education, the government, and the private sector.

The Bureau of Labor Statistics (see, http://www.bls.gov) estimates opportunity growth for all occupations in their *Occupational Outlook Handbook*. According to the Handbook, the growth of employment opportunities for psychologist positions, including I/O psychologists, will be faster than the average rate of growth when compared to all other occupations. The Bureau of Labor Statistics predicted average growth through 2012:

> Industrial/organizational psychologists will be in demand to help to boost worker productivity and retention rates in a wide range of businesses. Industrial/organizational psychologists will help companies deal with issues such as workplace diversity and antidiscrimination policies. Companies also will use

psychologists' expertise in survey design, analysis, and research to develop tools for marketing evaluation and statistical analysis. . . . Psychologists with extensive training in quantitative research methods and computer science may have a competitive edge over applicants without this background. (U.S. Department of Labor, 2006)

Financial Compensation

The Web site of the Society for Industrial and Organizational Psychology (SIOP; http://www.siop.org) shows the results of a salary survey of SIOP members that was conducted in 2003 (Medsker, Katkowski, & Furr, 2005). I/O psychologists with a doctorate make substantially more over the course of their careers than those with only a master's degree. Recent PhD graduates earn a median income of about $65,000, with a range of about $70,000 to about $140,000, and private sector jobs pay substantially more than university or public sector jobs. Master's degree graduates earn about one third less, on average, than their PhD counterparts. (See American Psychological Association [2005] for salary data as well as data on new doctorates from the Doctorate Employment Survey.)

My Career

My own career in I/O psychology reflects the opportunities and types of jobs that I/O psychologists have. I highlight some important tips that helped me and could well improve your opportunities and chances of success in the I/O field.

My career as an I/O psychologist has spanned some 30 years. I have worked in many different organizations, from a small consulting firm to some of the largest public and private organizations in the world. So how did I get started? First of all, after obtaining a BA in psychology, I went on to graduate school in I/O psychology for my PhD, and I was fortunate to have an excellent North Carolina State graduate advisor who had obtained a grant that provided me with invaluable experience in the area of job analysis. *Job analysis* refers to the systematic analysis of jobs and their constituent knowledge, skills, and abilities. The results of such analysis inform all the major human resources programs of organizations, namely hiring and selection, training and development, performance evaluation, and compensation administration. For example, if you need to hire software engineers, you need to know what types of skills and abilities the applicants for the job need and how to assess those skills and abilities.

The experience I had in graduate school and the area I specialized in led to my first job as an I/O psychologist working for the U.S. Navy Personnel Research and Development Center in San Diego. In this first job, I helped evaluate the effectiveness of the Navy's job analysis procedures that determined the responsibilities and requirements for more than 100 enlisted military jobs, from clerk to jet engine mechanic. I heard about this position because of the contacts of my graduate advisor, Bill Cunningham, an expert in the area of occupational analysis, whose own graduate advisor was Ernest McCormick, known as the father of job analysis. The Navy contacted McCormick, who contacted Cunningham, who recommended me. *Tip 1:* As with many careers, the key to success is to develop a specialty area and to have associations with key people in your field.

After about 6 years at the Navy Personnel Research and Development Center and having worked with several different Navy organizations in job analysis, an opportunity opened up for me to be the technical director of the Navy Occupational Development and Analysis Center. It was a lucky break for me because it was a terrific job in which I had a primary role in the technical and personnel leadership of an organization of 80 people that conducted job analyses for all the jobs in the Navy. This job analysis information was used to develop promotional exams and to identify required training for different Navy jobs. To get this job, I had to relocate across country and leave San Diego for Washington, DC. Although I did relocate to Washington, I kept a house in San Diego because I hoped to be able to move back there one day. *Tip 2:* Being willing to relocate will greatly improve your career opportunities.

During my 3 years as technical director in Washington, I honed my leadership and organizational skills and this experience proved to be critical for my future career. In this position, I was responsible for motivating and promoting some individuals as well as for demoting others—the tough side of a leadership position. I also had a multimillion-dollar budget to oversee and had to make sure that the money we spent to improve our procedures added significant value to the Navy. I often had to present our proposed recommendations for improvements to the management level above and convince them that our improvements would yield substantial benefits and that the job analysis information we collected would be very useful for developing promotional exams and training programs.

I was able to make many improvements for the Navy's job analysis procedures because I knew something about statistics. I was able to analyze and evaluate different procedures and make improvements that led to more effective and less expensive ways to do the organization's work. For example, we analyzed the statistical reliability (or consistency) of job analysis data collected using our survey procedures and as a result developed better survey methods that improved reliability. *Tip 3:* A sound knowledge of statistics is a relatively rare commodity in many organizations. It will enhance your ability to succeed and will always be a good selling point for opportunities that you might want to pursue.

Because I was interested in going back to San Diego, I contacted my associates back at the Navy Personnel Research and Development Center in San Diego. Again, through contacts and luck, I found myself the director of personnel systems at that organization. Through this job, I was introduced to the realm of government contractors and many well-known I/O psychologists who worked for the government in different capacities. While in this position, I started to focus more on procedures for hiring or selecting people into the Navy; this focus on selection was to become my new specialty area over the course of my remaining career.

After working for quite a few years with the Navy, which is, of course, a public sector organization, I wanted to try the private or corporate side of life as an I/O psychologist. I thought it would be more exciting and perhaps more profitable for me as well. I got my chance when, through a friend, I learned of an opportunity that led to an offer to work as an I/O psychologist in the area of selection for one of the major telephone companies in Denver, Colorado. This job provided me with the corporate experience I was looking for, and it led to one of the best jobs a corporate I/O psychologist could have: working as the head of a global selection team for IBM, one of the largest companies in the world. This was a very exciting job, and our team instituted global interviewing procedures, global on-line testing for analytical skills, and on-line assessment of personality attributes such as customer orientation skills. Our team's programs affected thousands of applicants who were hired by IBM. *Tip 4:* Getting the job you want is based on relevant experience, your reputation, your resume, and how well you interview. Work on improving these for increased success.

As my career demonstrates, there are many different and varied opportunities for I/O psychologists. Perhaps one or several of these appeal to you.

Resources

One of the best sources for additional information on the field of I/O psychology is the Society for Industrial and Organizational Psychology. The SIOP Web site (http://www.siop.org) and the Web site of American Psychological Association Division 14 (http://www.apa.org) provide information on graduate schools, license requirements, salary information for master's and PhD graduates, and job opportunities. The SIOP annual conference includes a job placement center where SIOP members can interview with many employers. If you want to pursue a career in I/O psychology, you should become a member of SIOP. According to the SIOP Web site, as of 2002, the society's membership totaled 6,117.

Let me make one other point about opportunity: As indicated, I/O psychology is closely aligned with human resource functions. As such, it provides those who go into this field with knowledge of the functions that all managers need to know. This knowledge also makes I/O psychologists competitive for general management positions, either inside or outside of the field.

Conclusion

I hope that you now have a better idea of what you might be able to do as an I/O psychologist. You can work in many types of organizations, including private, public, and global organizations, and the activities that you can choose to engage in are indeed varied and potentially rich in satisfaction.

References

American Psychological Association. (2005, May). *Salaries in psychology 2003*. Retrieved July 6, 2006, from http://research.apa.org/

Medsker, G. J., Katkowski, D. A., & Furr, D. (2005). *2003 income and employment survey results for the Society for Industrial and Organizational*

Psychology (Unpublished report). Alexandria, VA: Human Resources Research Organization.

U.S. Department of Labor, Bureau of Statistics. (2006). *Psychologists.* Retrieved August 3, 2006, from http://www.bls.gov/oco/ocos 056.htm#outlook

Judith S. Blanton

In the Halls of Business: Consulting Psychology as a Career

15

When I was in graduate school, I had no idea that psychologists did what I ended up doing—consulting to organizations. Most of my colleagues in the field also came to this work in a roundabout way. In Leonard's (1999) article describing how a number of senior people ended up consulting, he reported that they had moved into this area from many directions. For example, in my own career, when I completed my doctorate in social–developmental psychology within an educational psychology department, I took a job evaluating a large government program within the Bureau of Indian Affairs. This job required site visits to various tribal schools across the country, where I clarified program objectives, identified measures, and attempted to assess the impact of the program on academic performance and other variables. Very quickly, I became interested in trying to make

Judith S. Blanton is senior consultant and director of professional affairs for RHR International, a management consulting firm of psychologists. She received her doctoral degree from the University of Texas at Austin and worked in private industry and academia before beginning her consulting career. She has served as president of the Society of Consulting Psychology (Division 13 of the American Psychological Association) and received its Outstanding Service Award in 2005.

The author thanks Ken Ball for his comments on a draft of this chapter.

the programs better rather than merely documenting what was wrong, and this interest evolved into action research. My colleagues and I involved tribal councils, Native American parents, and Bureau of Indian Affairs employees, encouraging these very different groups to work together to develop useful programs. Over time, I moved from evaluating programs to broader kinds of consulting. My focus shifted from working with education and social service organizations to consulting with businesses and corporations.

What Is Consulting Psychology, and Where Do Its Practitioners Work?

Is consulting a particular application of psychology skills or a separate and distinct profession or discipline? The question is controversial, and debate continues. Lent (cited in Boyce, 2004) suggested that it is not a distinct field at all, but more a matter of context: "It is easier," she observed, "to describe the activities and settings where consulting psychology takes place" than it is to categorize it. Regardless of how it is classified, as the field matures, we learn more about the methods, techniques, and skills that make consulting effective, and a growing body of knowledge and literature in this area has emerged.

I think of it this way: Occasionally, most psychologists consult with colleagues, clients, and patients by providing technical assistance and information. However, for consulting psychologists, consulting becomes the primary focus on their work. The consulting psychologist is not so much a content expert (although content about the client and business helps) as an expert on facilitating a client's own ability to identify key issues and to implement needed change.

A report of the 2001 Future's Task Force commissioned by American Psychological Association (APA) Division 13 (Society of Consulting Psychology) offered this formal definition of the consulting psychologist's role:

> [T]he function of applying and extending the special knowledge of a psychologist, through the process of consultation, to problems involving human behavior in various areas. A Consulting Psychologist shall be defined as a psychologist who provides specialized technical assistance to individuals or organizations in regard to psychological aspects of their work.

Such assistance is advisory in nature and the consultant has no direct responsibility for its acceptance. Consulting Psychologists may have as a client, individuals, institutions, corporations, or other kinds of organizations. (APA's Society of Consulting Psychology, n.d.)

In short, consulting psychologists use their knowledge and skills to increase organizational effectiveness and improve individual performance. Careers in consulting psychology cover a wide range of activities within a broad range of environments. They may specialize in an industry (e.g., provision of services to retail companies) or provide a specific service (e.g., assessment, coaching, team building). Others consult to government agencies, not-for-profit organizations, and educational institutions.

Consulting psychologists also work independently as solo practitioners. They may, however, join forces when a project demands multiple consultants, an arrangement that seems to be an increasing trend. An additional option is to work in a small boutique consulting company or as part of a larger firm that may involve professionals from outside the field of psychology (e.g., MBAs, human resource professionals). Consulting psychologists can also work internally within an organization providing services to individuals, teams, or functional units within that company, university, or agency.

A consulting career can be a part-time or full-time profession. A substantial number of academics consult part time as an adjunct to their teaching and research. Psychologists may also combine a consulting and a clinical practice. For example, a colleague of mine sees clinical patients but also works with corporations doing team development and coaching of senior executives. Substantial numbers of consulting psychologists work part time as a consultant to supplement their "day job" (e.g., teaching). This method can provide a solid professional base while one is building a practice.

What Do Consulting Psychologists Do?

The practice of consulting requires not only skills in doing the work but also skills in getting the work, managing the work and clients, and (for those in independent practice) managing the consulting business. The following sections discuss these four clusters of skills with an emphasis on the work itself.

SKILLS IN DOING THE WORK

In the late 1990s, the Society of Consulting Psychology (Division 13 of APA) began to clarify competencies for the organizational side of consulting psychology. This ambitious project culminated in the creation of the "Principles for Education and Training at the Doctoral and Postdoctoral Level in Consulting Psychology/Organizational" (Lowman et al., 2002). The competencies were clustered into three broad domains of expertise: individual, group, and organizational. Clearly, these are not neatly separate categories; they overlap and interact. Effective practice often requires work at all three levels simultaneously. Certain areas of competencies are critical at all levels—for example, assessment, process skills, research, and evaluation. Still, this division into three domains can be useful in discussing the kinds of work and kinds of skills needed. The following subsections provide examples of work that consulting psychologists do at the individual, group, and organizational levels. The examples are merely that; they are weighted in terms of my own experience. My hope is that they will provide a picture of the broad scope of the field. (For another view, see Kasserman, 2005.)

Work With Individuals

Employee Selection and Appraisal

Many consulting psychologists in the business community focus their work in the areas of employee selection and appraisal. This activity involves assessing a candidate's suitability for a particular job. The consultant generally begins with a careful analysis of the kinds of knowledge, skills, and attitudes related to success in that job. For lower or midlevel jobs, the consultant may assess a number of employees who have been highly successful and compare their scores or performance with those who have had average- or below-average success. Candidates whose profiles are more like successful employees would presumably be better hires. A number of standardized tests are available that can be used to rate applicants on specific skills or additional dimensions related to the job. Consulting psychologists also construct and run assessment centers in which a candidate performs tasks that simulate activities he or she would perform on the job.

For a more senior level executive position, the consulting psychologist also needs to understand the knowledge, skills, and attitudes necessary for that job in that business at that point in time. For senior positions, however, it is usually not possible to norm the tests on incumbents or predecessors because the numbers are too small and because future job requirements are likely to be different from earlier job demands. Caution should also be exercised in using standardized tests because the culture and requirements of a company can be very distinctive. Typically, for higher-level positions, interviews supplement any tests that are given. A good interview can focus on the unique demands of a particular company and job and get at nuances that a standardized test cannot. In most cases, the consulting psychologist provides a written report. In addition, he or she may discuss the strengths and weaknesses of the individual with the potential boss (and/or human resources person). Generally, the consulting psychologist also provides the candidate with feedback, which, if he or she accepts an offer, can be used to plan his or her integration into the company to improve the likelihood of successful "on-boarding." Such a program would typically involve coaching.

Executive Coaching

Executive coaching is one of the fastest growing areas within the consulting psychology field. Although many nonpsychologists are executive coaches, consulting psychologists who can combine their deep knowledge of human behavior with knowledge of the business culture can be particularly effective when working with business or corporate executives. Executive coaching is different from therapy or counseling in a number of ways. Most of the people receiving coaching are high-functioning individuals. Executives may receive coaching because they are valued employees but are plateaued or are having difficulties because of a specific behavior, such as abrasiveness or communication problems. Coaching is also used when accelerated development is the goal for individuals identified as high potential. In both cases, the focus is on professional development within the workplace rather than on dealing with personal problems, as is usually the case in counseling or therapy. The company typically pays for coaching and expects a return in the form of improved or accelerated job performance. Coaching can be short term but generally lasts from 3 to 6 months, although some coaches require a commitment of a year.

360-Degree or Multirater Surveys

The *360-degree survey* is designed to obtain feedback from all those "around" an individual and entails gathering data from the individual, his or her boss, subordinates, and peers. Sometimes customers or representatives from key constituencies with whom the subject of the survey interacts are also involved. The consultant may use any one of many standardized surveys. Alternately, he or she might create a customized survey or gather the data through interviews. The consultant compiles the results and presents them graphically in a way that shows the similarities and differences in the responses of the various groups. The consultant debriefs the individual about the findings and, typically, creates a development plan based on the feedback. Often, the 360-degree survey process is included as part of an executive coaching effort.

Process Consultation and Being a "Trusted Advisor"

Consultants often develop a strong personal relationship with a senior executive or manager and may have an ongoing relationship that is more like serving as a trusted advisor or sounding board than doing formal coaching. "It's lonely at the top" may be a cliché, but it is also true, and some executives use consulting psychologists as an honest and objective source of feedback and as a sounding board to try out ideas or just discuss difficult topics.

Work With Teams and Groups

Consulting psychologists do not work only with individuals. They can also work with the executive team (the chief executive officer and his or her direct reports), a departmental team, or other kinds of groups. This work can take a number of directions, and the following paragraphs provide a few examples.

Assessment and Development of Teams

On occasion, consulting psychologists work with new teams, helping them cohere and get direction, or with existing teams to help them plan and work together more effectively. For example, as part of my work with the leaders of an information technology department, I interviewed each member individually to gain background information about the managers and to identify what was working and what was not. I also used a questionnaire that measured various team dimensions. Using this information, I planned a retreat where we addressed issues that had been identified, set goals, and did exercises to clarify values that would be helpful in reaching those goals. We then held follow-up meetings after 3 and 6 months to assess progress. In one follow-up meeting, my colleague and I helped the team clarify its roles and responsibilities and addressed a few residual conflicts.

Team Conflict

Group members do not always work well together. As part of team building, I have had group members take a test that measured how they dealt with conflict. I summarized the data from the instrument and presented it graphically as a way of kicking off a discussion of conflict management. In coaching, I have sometimes had joint meetings with the coachee and his or her boss to discuss how they could deal with their conflicts.

Recently, I was asked to intervene when two engineers from different departments had stopped speaking to each other although they needed to work together to develop a product. At that point, they were communicating only by e-mail and this was affecting their work and slowing down product development. They were from different countries and cultures, which complicated their communication. Each was convinced that the other was the total cause of the problem. My task was to get them focused on the way their behavior was affecting the work. I was able to convince them that they did not need to be friends but did need to behave in a more professional manner and to fully share information.

Teams can also get into difficulty when they suppress conflict. I have worked with groups to develop "rules of engagement" to help them develop a culture that surfaces and deals with problems in a direct and constructive manner.

Family Businesses

A number of consulting psychologists specialize in working with family businesses. It is a particularly challenging area because it requires an understanding not only of business issues but also of family dynamics. The consulting psychologist needs to have a good understanding of the individuals and of how they interact within this particular setting and how their personal relationships affect their business goals. Issues of sibling rivalry, long-standing resentments, and favoritism can greatly complicate a business. One of my colleagues who practices in this area said that although he is not doing family therapy, his earlier training in this area has been an asset.

Intergroup Management in an Organizational Context

Race, gender, and ethnic group membership can have a powerful impact on how a group works (or does not work) together. Certain consulting psychologists focus on helping diverse groups work effectively together. I have a particular interest in organizations that span time zones, countries, and languages. As organizations become global and diverse, they need to find better ways of communication. One of my colleagues specializes in working with global companies and cross-national teams. He described the difficulty a cross-national team with members from Japan, France, and the United States had coming to decisions and then implementing them. He found that when the Japanese did not verbally object to an idea or statement, the Americans were assuming that they agreed. However, it never occurred to the Japanese that their silence represented a commitment to a course of action, and they were surprised when the Americans were upset when their Japanese colleagues did not implement their suggestions after the meeting. My colleague used his facilitation and team-building skills to have the group agree on what *agreement* meant. Both morale and follow-up action improved.

Consulting psychologists also help organizations improve their "virtual teams." Such teams involve a group of geographically dispersed people that rely primarily or exclusively on electronic forms of communication to work together. I have worked with managers who were trying to develop skills in supervising employees who were nine time zones away and with whom they mostly interacted through e-mail, phones, teleconferencing, and various computer technologies. More and more managers now supervise groups of individuals who seldom or never meet but must solve problems and develop products as a team. This is a challenging and exciting new area for research, technology, and consulting.

Work With Organizational Systems

Survey Development and Analysis

Consulting psychologists (along with industrial/organizational psychologists) often develop and implement attitude, satisfaction, or climate surveys for organizations. A company may want to know about their employees' concerns and what they like or dislike about their working situation. Many standardized instruments have been created for use in this area, and consulting psychologists need to identify what tools might be appropriate and how to interpret findings. Alternatively, they may customize or develop a new survey from scratch. The skills needed to develop a new survey are complex and require substantial effort to ensure that the tool is both reliable and valid for its purpose. Consulting psychologists usually don't merely administer the survey or supply summary data but, instead, work with the organization to understand the findings and, often, to develop strategies for dealing with problems that surfaced in the process. Although survey development and analysis is an important and complex skill, most consulting psychologists see this activity as a means to an end (organizational improvement) rather than an end in itself.

Management of Change and Transitions

Consulting psychologists may take on a broad variety of organizational issues under the heading of managing change, including helping a company implement a new system or initiative, deal with the need to downsize, adapt to rapid growth, or smooth the merger or acquisition process. For example, consulting psychologists may get involved early in the "due diligence" process of an acquisition, in which they assess the management or senior leadership team in the business being acquired. Other tasks might involve the development and implementation of a communication plan. Surveys or interviews are often used to understand the cultures of the companies that are merging. After the merger or acquisition, the consulting psychologist can help the two organizations address the differences in their cultures or operating procedures.

The boundary between individual and organizational systems work is fluid. For example, I have been involved as part of a consultant team in the selection of the new management team following a merger. The work was on the individual level (executive assessment) but deeply linked to the organizational transition. Initially, I was concerned that employees would be threatened by being interviewed and evaluated by an outside person. I was surprised to find that most of the managers and executives were supportive of the process because they saw our consultant team's involvement as providing an objective third-party perspective and clarifying criteria for positions. Employees were scattered over multiple states, and some were in another country. They had been concerned that the senior executives would pick only managers they knew from the acquiring company. With our involvement, all appropriate managers had an opportunity to be considered in terms of clear criteria based on the needs of the new merged company. We did not make the decisions, but our assessments provided key data and were instrumental in the identification of qualified individuals. In the merger process, we were also involved in coaching key executives as they moved through this challenging process.

The book *Big Change at Best Buy* (Billings & Gibson, 2003) described a complex management-change process implemented in this well-known retail firm. The company had spent a great deal of time and money developing standard operating procedures but found that the various stores were not implementing them. The book provided a case study of actions taken to engage employees and managers in making and sustaining the needed changes. It also demonstrated how a team of consulting psychologists worked together and how they partnered with an internal team of Best Buy employees assigned to this project.

The consulting psychologists not only helped with the change process, but also built the internal capacity of the organization to do this.

Human Resource Systems Development

Consulting psychologists also get involved in developing and implementing various human resource systems, such as a performance management or succession planning system, a leadership or high potential development program, or an employee retention plan. The objective might be to increase internal capacity, provide input on best practices, or evaluate the organization's current program and make recommendations for improvement. To implement such initiatives successfully, a consulting psychologist would need to partner with internal human resources or a variety of company employees.

SKILLS IN GETTING AND MANAGING THE WORK

To do the work, you must first get the work, particularly important if you are in a solo practice. You need skills in networking, developing marketing materials, and promoting sales. In addition to being able to write a good proposal, you need to be able to develop a realistic time frame and estimate the costs of doing the work. How many days will it take? What sort of materials or tests will be needed, and what will they cost? These generally are not skills one learns in graduate school, and early in my career, I found that I consistently underestimated time and costs. I forgot that there were always unforeseen interruptions and problems. I might be ready to go, but I might have to wait on someone else to do their task before I could proceed. Luckily, I had a knowledgeable colleague who would add 20% to whatever my initial estimate was, and that was generally on target.

Then, once you have the project, you must manage it and the client as well. If you have a complex project, particularly one that requires you to direct other consulting psychologists, skills in project management are necessary. Our firm believes this skill set is so important that it developed an internal course in this area. Numerous software programs now exist that are useful in project planning and management—for example, helping to construct Gantt charts.

SKILLS IN MANAGING THE BUSINESS

Business management skills are not important if you are an employee, but if you want to create your own private practice, it would be useful to cultivate the kinds of business skills needed by anyone starting and running a small business. If you plan to go it alone, be prepared to wear the following hats in addition to being a consultant: secretary, receptionist, controller, health benefits administrator, accountant, accounts receivable clerk, accounts payable manager, tax auditor, insurance agent, office manger, travel agent, information technology help desk, marketing vice president, director of sales, event planner, retirement fund administrator, president, chief executive officer, and chief financial officer. For those who plan to employ other consultants on a part-time or full-time basis, additional challenges arise. You need to deal with issues of selection, salaries, bonuses, performance management, and quality control.

Obviously, the decision to enter private practice takes careful consideration. I have had colleagues who started their own firms but vastly underestimated the time it took to manage the business itself and were frustrated because they wanted to concentrate only on consulting.

Preparation Needed for the Career

The "Principles for Education and Training at the Doctoral and Postdoctoral Level in Consulting Psychology/Organizational" developed by APA Division 13 (Lowman et al., 2002) provide an excellent and highly detailed description of the training required to be a consulting psychologist. Currently, one doctoral program is specifically focused on training consultants; Alliant University began this program in 1999. Most people in the field still receive their education from doctoral programs in industrial/organizational, counseling, clinical, social, or other psychology and then broaden their skills through self-study, on-the-job experience, mentoring, continuing education courses, and internal training offered by various consulting firms.

As I noted in a previous section, the APA Division 13 guidelines stress training in the individual, group, and organizational or systems levels. In addition, they stress the necessity for knowledge in research and evaluation:

> The behavioral sciences are most clearly distinguished from fad and "pop" psychology by their discipline of research and evaluation. Consulting Psychologists need to learn methods of evaluating their organizational interventions to assure that clients are maximizing their return on investment. (Lowman et al., 2002, p. 222)

In addition to an understanding of both quantitative and qualitative evaluation methods, the guidelines suggest that consulting psychologists have practical experience in "real-life" research projects. A final area of training has to do with practical professional issues such as ethics, confidentiality, license requirements, and legal issues. Because consulting psychologists operate in the turbulent world of organizations, these practical professional issues are particularly salient.

Two organizations provide excellent resources for those interested in learning more about consulting and improving their skills in that area. The Society of Consulting Psychology (Division 13 of APA) has formal programs for psychologists who want to move into consulting. The society has a midwinter meeting that offers continuing education courses and opportunities for dialogue with experienced consultants. *The Consulting Psychology Journal: Practice and Research*, the official journal of the division, has many articles that provide theory and case examples useful to both newcomers and senior consultants. The Society for Industrial and Organizational Psychology (SIOP; Division 14 of APA) is another excellent resource. Its annual meeting offers a wide range of sessions on topics relevant to consulting, including the latest research in related areas and workshops that offer continuing education credit.

In terms of the training needed for consulting work, my own postdoctoral experience and training provide an example. I did (and continue to do) a great deal of independent reading in the area of process consultation, organizational change, and business. In addition to reading the psychological literature, I read the *Wall Street Journal*, *Harvard Business Review*, and other business magazines. Because I had grown up in an academic and not-for-profit world, early in my consulting career I enrolled in a program in the Business School at the University of Southern California that offered a certificate in management with a "mini-MBA"-type curriculum. This program enabled me to understand not only the business jargon but also the way that business people think about things. Just learning a few buzz words of business and expecting that you can work in this environment is like just learning words like *id, ego,* and *superego* and thinking that you can provide psychoanalysis. One must learn not only a new language but a new conceptual system.

Furthermore, I was fortunate enough to join a consulting firm that invested a great deal of time and money in training its consultants. When I joined the firm, I took a number of internal courses taught by my senior colleagues. I shadowed fellow consultants as they worked and sought out feedback and advice on projects in which I was involved. Even today, I have coworkers read drafts of reports and question my assumptions. In my office, we have regular meetings regarding key clients. In this review of our work, we discuss such issues as whether we are addressing the genuine needs of the client, how we can evaluate our progress or success, the quality and impact of our current efforts, and what we might need to do differently to add more value. Another excellent learning tool we use is to debrief an intervention when it is completed. We call this a "postmortem" and use it as an opportunity to learn from our successes and failures. Whatever one's training, as a consulting psychologist, it is critical to continue to hone one's skills.

Why I Chose Consulting as a Career

Because consulting is a multifaceted field, I can offer many reasons why I chose this work. Let me give just five.

First, I find the work itself inherently interesting and intellectually stimulating. Even what may look like a routine assessment of a job applicant can be enormously challenging if you take seriously your assignment to understand the complexity of the individual and his or her fit with a new role. This variety presents an opportunity (even a necessity) to apply everything you have learned in school (and elsewhere).

Second, consulting also provides a great opportunity to learn about new things. Like an anthropologist, the consulting psychologist enters into many different cultures. In my career, I have worked with Fortune 100 companies, small family businesses, Native American tribal councils, and college administrators. By working within them, I have learned about the operations of newspapers, the TV and movie industry, and the challenges in developing spacecraft. I found out that it is much more difficult than one would imagine to manufacture what looks like a simple bolt. I've had back-room knowledge of scientific laboratories, insurance companies, and electronic equipment retailing.

Third, I like the fact that, at times, one must improvise and operate without a safety net. Often I have planned a clear agenda for an intervention, such as a team-building retreat, with a specific timetable and maybe even a PowerPoint presentation, only to throw it out to take a completely different direction because I sensed that the group needed to probe more deeply into a topic or found that a new issue surfaced that needed to be addressed quickly and directly. In spite of the initial dizziness that this kind of challenge creates, successfully negotiating the difficulties allows for creativity and is personally rewarding.

Fourth, I enjoy working with very smart, competent people. Many of our clients are highly impressive people who have accomplished a great deal professionally, and I have had the honor of learning about the life histories of those I assess and coach. I usually work not at the remedial level, but rather at helping effective people become even more so. It is also stimulating to work with bright colleagues who are psychologists and with whom I can share and learn.

Finally, I derive great satisfaction from helping to make situations, individuals, and organizations better. Seeing an executive who was struggling with his or her boss feel positive about that relationship, having a dysfunctional team begin to work together collaboratively, or helping smooth a difficult organizational change provides enormous satisfaction, because I have made a positive difference.

Financial Compensation

Financial compensation in consulting psychology ranges wildly. It can be one of the highest paying areas of psychology, yet many need to supplement their consulting with other work because they are unable to develop a solid practice. For people who are used to getting a regular salary, the compensation structure for consultants can arouse anxiety. One's ability to do the work is not the same as one's ability to get the work within a highly competitive environment. And typically, it is billing for the work that drives compensation. Many in the field build a solid independent practice that provides much more income than would be possible in academia or a salaried position. Entrepreneurial individuals can often make well into the six figures but just as many probably struggle or leave the field. The consulting psychologist with a substantial level of billing must still consider overhead expenses; he or she may enter a state of shock when comparing gross income with net profit after the checkbook is balanced.

As an example of how income may fluctuate, a consulting psychologist might be dependent on a major client, and when his or her contact within that company leaves, the entire contract evaporates. The psychologist's billing can go from hundreds of thousands of dollars to zero almost overnight, and it may take time to find an equally lucrative client.

Even the salaries of those who work within a consulting firm can vary a great deal from year to year, depending on the individual's billing and the overall success of the firm. The 2003 APA salary survey (Pate, Frincke, & Kohout, 2005) reported that salaries can be $84,000 to over six figures. Consulting firms generally pay a moderate base salary but provide opportunities for bonuses that can double (or more) that income if the individual is highly productive; the *if* is the issue. Within a single firm, coworkers' remuneration may vary by more than $100,000. In consulting, variability is probably related more to productivity than to seniority.

Disadvantages of the Career

Consulting provides a number of advantages, which I mentioned when I described why I chose the profession. However, the field has disadvantages as well. Travel can be fun and glamorous but also very fatiguing. You might be on the road from 50% to 80% of your time. Such schedules can put strains on family life. The high-functioning clients are exciting to work with, but can also be quite challenging and demanding. Few are in awe of the doctoral degree, and they can be intimidating to a novice consultant.

Because most consultants are self-employed or work for a consulting firm, the pressure of business development is always present. The independent consultant who does not sell, does not eat. In a consulting firm, your bonus, your promotion, and even your job itself are affected by the degree to which you can generate work for yourself and your colleagues.

Attributes Needed for Success in the Career

Your personal characteristics are at least as important as your competence as a psychologist. Students often ask, "What specific classes should I take to be successful?" As I noted earlier in this chapter, certain knowledge areas are very important, but this is only the ticket for admission. I believe that, in the long run, personal style, professional presence, and interpersonal abilities are the elements that differentiate the highly effective consulting psychologist. You need to be able to relate to and have credibility with your client group. For example, if working with line staff, consulting psychologists cannot be seen as too academic or theoretical, or they will be dismissed as "ivory tower." If you want to work with senior executives, you must be able to interact comfortably and credibly with assertive, demanding, fast-paced executives. Those intimidated by such individuals do not do well. The ability to establish rapport and trust rapidly is a necessity. Communication skills are important; business people are not patient with long, complex, jargon-laden explanations. Both verbally and in writing, the consulting psychologist needs to be articulate without being pretentious. He or she needs to be crisp, focused, and to the point.

Stamina and energy are critical. I have seen excellent people leave the field because they found the pace to be too fast or grueling. A consulting psychologist is likely to spend substantial time in a car driving to meet a client or in an airport waiting for a plane to go home. It is not necessary to be an extravert when doing consulting, but if you are an introvert, you need to find ways to replenish your energy after long periods when you need to be "on." For example, if you are facilitating an off-site retreat, you would probably be expected to have dinner (and perhaps drinks) with the participants late into the evening. Then, when the participants have gone to bed, you might be up late with your colleagues debriefing and revising plans for the next day's events. Even informal social activities are work for the consultant. Because everything is data, you are on duty even during recreational activities such as golf. It is in these less-structured times that you can learn a great deal about the dynamics of the group and the operating styles of its members.

In terms of intellect, good consulting psychologists must not only be smart but have high learning agility. That is, the successful consulting psychologist is a sponge who absorbs useful ideas and skills rapidly but can also switch gears with ease. Good work requires the ability to think systemically—that is, the capacity to view an organization as an interconnected system where intervention in one place affects functioning in others. Flexibility in thinking is important to incorporate different perspectives as needed. My colleagues and I talk about successful consulting psychologists having "helicopter thinking": That is, they are able to operate at both a conceptual and a very practical level—to see the big picture—but then to drop down to examine and handle the details.

Highly successful consulting psychologists are very achievement motivated, set high standards for themselves, and are competitive. Those who work within a firm also need to be able to work well as part of a team and not always be the star. Good colleagueship requires individuals to have an interesting blend of self-sufficiency and independence while also being highly collaborative. Tenacity and drive are important, particularly in doing business development. Successful consulting psychologists generally have a strong customer service orientation and take great pride in going the extra step for their client. At the same time, they should not have a high need for approval. Often the job of the consulting psychologist is to speak the truth to a powerful individual who may not be pleased with the information. It is OK to want to be liked, but if you need to be liked, you should get a springer spaniel rather than go into consulting.

The best consulting psychologists I know are self-aware: They are attuned to their impact on others. They are also perceptive, able to pick up subtle cues from those around them, and skilled in applying their understanding of individuals when dealing with varied situations and styles. The consulting psychologist needs to be able to read the audience and adjust to diverse situations and people.

Personal qualities such as follow-through and good organization are critical. A lack of attention to detail, such as misspelling a key executive's name or making a mistake on a bill, can be deadly. I have had colleagues falter because they were unable to juggle the multiple demands, the constantly changing schedules, and the torrent of phone calls and e-mails. The use of technology (e.g., laptop computers with sophisticated office management software packages, Palm Pilots, Blackberries) has made handling the logistics easier, but the consulting psychologist must still organize and prioritize a flood of information.

A Typical Day in the Life of a Consulting Psychologist

One of the things I like about consulting psychology is that I never have a "typical" day. Everyone's practice is different, and my own has changed from year to year and even day to day. Those who work internally, those who work for government groups, those who work independently, and those who work as part of a large firm have quite different experiences from mine. For example, for me, business development might take up entire days; related activities could include taking a potential client to lunch, giving a talk to raise awareness about my work, or developing marketing materials.

Although no day is typical, I give an example of a day that is not unusual. I start early, checking my e-mails and voice mail before breakfast to make sure I have not had a cancellation or a major change in schedule. I will be assessing a candidate for chief operating officer for a client company this morning, so I spend a few minutes reviewing notes I made last week after interviewing the chief executive officer and senior staff members about success factors for that job. While I drive across town to a client's office, I make calls on my cell phone, returning a call I had received on my voice mail and checking in with my assistant about some administrative work. When I arrive at the client's office, I enter a conference room, where I meet the candidate and get a last-minute briefing from the human resource vice president about areas where they would like me to probe. (Although this meeting was in the client's office, we might well have met in my office or in an airport lounge.)

After the interview, I check my voice messages again and perhaps return a call or two. On the way back to the office, I pick up a sandwich that I eat while I check my e-mail. In the afternoon, I meet in our office conference room with a colleague to finalize the plan for an off-site retreat scheduled for the coming weekend for a dozen members of a marketing department. When we are done, I meet with my assistant, who is putting together materials for the off-site retreat to make sure that everything has been copied. I decide to add one more handout, and I photocopy it while my assistant makes packets for the participants. I reschedule a meeting that has been canceled (for the second time) with a potential client. I begin to fill out my expense form, which is due tomorrow (my least favorite part of the job). I score an instrument that I gave this morning as part of the assessment interview and begin work on the assessment report, because I want to get back to the client tomorrow to give verbal feedback. Depending on my schedule tomorrow, I might work on the report tonight on my laptop. Before bedtime, I check e-mail and voice mail and my schedule for tomorrow one last time. It looks as if I have breakfast on the other side of town at 8:00 a.m. with an executive I have worked with before and who has just taken a job at a new company. This means I will have to set the alarm early.

Conclusion

A career in consulting psychology offers the option of part- or full-time work that is varied, stimulating, and demanding. Becoming a consulting psychologist is a professional option for a wide range of psychologists who are willing to broaden their initial training in another area of psychology. At least one graduate institution now offers training specifically in this field, and many other graduate programs provide coursework in various areas of consulting. The consulting field is growing as psychologists seek to apply their skills outside of the mental health and health fields. Consulting provides the opportunity to use one's psychological skills to make a difference in a broad range of settings, including businesses, corporations, government agencies, academic institutions, and the not-for-profit world.

Suggested Web Resources

American Society for Training and Development: http://www.astd.org/
Center for Creative Leadership: http://ccl.org/
Human Resources Planning Society: http://hrps.org/
Leader to Leader Institute (formerly the Peter F. Drucker Foundation for Nonprofit Management): http://pfdf.org/
Society for Consulting Psychology: http://apa.org/divisions/div13/
Society for Human Resources Management: http://shrm.org/
Society for Industrial Organizational Psychology: http://siop.org/

References

APA's Society of Consulting Psychology (n.d.). *The Society of Consulting Psychology home page.* Retrieved July 19, 2006, from http://www.apa.org/divisions/div13/InsideIndex.htm

Billings, A., & Gibson, E. (2003). *Big change at Best Buy.* Palo Alto, CA: Davis-Black.

Boyce, J. (2004). New dog, old tricks: Defining consulting psychology for the new professional. *The Consulting Psychologist, 6*(2). Retrieved July 19, 2006, from http://www.apa.org/divisions/div13/Update/2004Fall/SpotlightOldDog.htm

Kasserman, J. (2005). Management consultation: Improving organizations. In C. J. Habben, T. L. Kuther, & R. D. Morgan, (Eds.), *Life after graduate school in psychology: Insider's advice from new psychologists* (pp. 183–195). New York: Psychology Press.

Leonard, H. S. (1999). Becoming a consultant: The real stories. *Consulting Psychology Journal: Practice and Research, 51,* 3–13.

Lowman, R., Alderfer, C., Atella, M., Garman, A., Hellkamp, D., Kilburg, R., et al. (2002). Principles for education and training at the doctoral and postdoctoral level in consulting psychology/organizational. *Consulting Psychology Journal: Practice and Research, 54,* 213–222.

Pate, W., Frincke, J. L., & Kohout, J. L. (2005). *Salaries in psychology: 2003 report of the 2003 APA Salary Survey.* Retrieved July 19, 2006, from http://research.apa.org/03salary/homepage.html

IV

Diverse Areas of Psychology

Debra L. Dunivin and M. Victoria Ingram

Military Psychology: A Dynamic and Practical Application of Psychological Expertise

16

O ne of the most fascinating and rewarding careers in psychology is that of the military psychologist. Psychologists in the military are dual professionals; they are both psychologists (research or clinical) and military officers. Both are honorable, demanding professions with long histories of tradition, integrity, and community respect. Psychology and the military have been intertwined for about a century and during this time psychologists have found opportunities for training, teaching, research, practice, and consultation in military

Debra L. Dunivin, PhD, ABPP, is chief of the Department of Psychology at Walter Reed Army Medical Center. She earned a PhD in clinical psychology from St. John's University and is a graduate of the Department of Defense Psychopharmacology Fellowship program. Dr. Dunivin is currently a Lieutenant Colonel in the U.S. Army. Before entering military service, she worked in the public sector as a school psychologist, in the private sector as a general family practitioner, and on Capitol Hill as an American Psychological Association Congressional Science Fellow.

M. Victoria Ingram, PsyD, ABPP, is the program director at Walter Reed Army Medical Center's Clinical Psychology Internship program. She received her PsyD in clinical psychology from the Florida Institute of Psychology and is currently an Army Major who has spent the past 10 years serving in various roles within the Army's predoctoral and postdoctoral training programs.

Opinions expressed in this chapter are the private views of the authors and should not be construed as official views of the Departments of the Army, Navy, Air Force, or Defense.

settings. Some of the earliest applied research and clinical practice by psychologists was conducted in the military.

Assessment and selection of military personnel and treatment of war casualties around the time of the world wars marked the emergence of the professional practice of clinical psychology. Very few other career paths in psychology have the potential to place one so squarely in harm's way, and few offer such an incredible diversity of professional activities, opportunities for leadership, and cutting-edge contributions to the science and practice of psychology, as well as the ability to serve the country. In this chapter, we describe many of the training opportunities and follow-on assignments for those choosing careers as military psychologists, including internships, fellowships, and other professional development activities, as well as research and clinical positions for active duty and reserve psychologists in the U.S. Army, Navy, and Air Force. We also include several personal accounts of psychologists in uniform, many of whom served during times of war.

Beginning a Military Psychology Career

Many, but not all, military psychologists start out in a predoctoral internship at one of the large military medical centers. Some enter the military after completing a civilian internship; a few attend graduate school as active duty military officers at the Uniformed Services University for the Health Sciences, and others through scholarships at civilian universities. Whether entering military service as an intern, after completion of a civilian graduate school program, or as a licensed psychologist ("direct accession"), some requirements are the same. Both interns and direct accessions must meet service-specific physical health standards as well as age and citizenship requirements. The military does not discriminate on the basis of sex, race, religion, ethnicity, or national origin. (Current Department of Defense policy does not allow homosexuals to serve openly in the U.S. military.)

All military officers must also meet standards of personal conduct, judgment, and reliability to acquire a secret-level security clearance. Many military psychology jobs in Special Operations or Military Intelligence require higher standards necessary for a top-secret clearance. In addition to these requirements, psychologists serving on active duty must complete certain types of military education required of other military officers. This education differs somewhat from service to service. For example, before starting an internship or one's first assignment as a direct accession, the Navy and Air Force require attendance at a 6-week officer indoctrination school and a 4-week commissioned officer training course, respectively, whereas the Army requires attendance at a 10-week officer basic course. There are many other military colleges, schools, and courses that one may attend later, depending on assignments and length of service; these schools often focus on increasing knowledge of military and defense strategy, for example, and developing leadership and other skills required for positions of increased responsibility.

INTERNSHIPS

Graduate students wishing to apply for military internships must be enrolled in an APA-accredited clinical or counseling psychology program. Internships for all three branches participate in the Association of Psychology Postdoctoral and Internship Centers National Computer Match program so that prospective interns have the opportunity to prioritize their preferred internship sites. The Army, Navy, and Air Force have different programs for scholarships and loan repayment, and some of these programs may be unavailable for periods of time. Calling a training director at one of the internship sites is an excellent way to secure more specific information and a referral to a medical or health care recruiter. Each branch of service has recruiters who specialize in the recruitment of health care personnel; health care recruiters are responsible for processing applications for training programs as well as applications for joining the military. The following paragraphs provide some general information that was current at the time of this writing but is subject to change, so check the Web sites in Exhibit 16.1 for the most updated information available.

The Army attracts qualified students to their internships through the Health Professional Scholarship Program (HPSP). This program offers 2- and 3-year scholarships that pay for all graduate school tuition and books and provide a stipend for living expenses during the scholarship. (The internship year is included as one of the scholarship years.) The scholarships are open to all students who are currently enrolled in an APA-accredited doctoral program in clinical or counseling psychology, and the applications are due the December before the start of the scholarship. HPSP scholarships are competitive, and applications are processed through the Army health care recruiter, so interested students should contact their Army recruiter. Students who accept the scholarship are obligated to enter the Army for their internship year and have a 3-year obligation for service following internship, the same obligation as for nonscholarship students. Scholarship recipients are also required to complete some active duty training during graduate

EXHIBIT 16.1

Online Resources for Military Psychology

Title of Web site	Web address
APA Monitor online articles	
A chance to serve: Psychology's military division places a premium on training the next generation of military psychologists. Vol. 36, No. 1, January 2005	http://www.apa.org/monitor/jan05/closer.html
Primary-care paths. Vol. 35, No. 10, November 2004	http://www.apa.org/monitor/nov04/paths.html
Psychology and the soldier. Vol. 34, No. 11, December 2003	http://www.apa.org/monitor/dec03/soldier.html
Unforgettable training. Vol. 33, No. 2, February 2002	http://www.apa.org/monitor/feb02/ unforgettable.html
Military psychologists respond to attacks. Vol. 32, No. 10, November 2001	http://www.apa.org/monitor/nov01/ militarypsych.html
Navy to put more psychologists on board. Vol. 30, No. 7, July/August 1999	http://www.apa.org/monitor/julaug99/nl3.html
Military research psychology	
Military Operational Medicine Research Program	http://www.momrp.org
Naval Submarine Medical Research Laboratory	http://www.nhrc.navy.mil/nsmrl/
Walter Reed Army Institute of Research	http://wrair-www.army.mil/default.asp
Naval Medical Research Center	http://www.nmrc.navy.mil
Air Force Toxicology	http://www.hes.afrl.af.mil/hest/toxicology.htm
Navy Aerospace Experimental Psychology	http://www.navyaep.net
Military health care recruiters	
Air Force	http://www.airforce.com http://www.airforce.com/careers/healthcare/ index.php
Army	http://www.goarmy.com http://www.goarmy.com/amedd/m_service/ index.jsp
Navy	http://www.navy.com http://www.navy.com/healthcare/medicalservices

(continued)

EXHIBIT 16.1 (Continued)

Online Resources for Military Psychology

Title of Web site	Web address
Other related Web sites	
2006 Regular Military Compensation chart	http://www.defenselink.mil/militarypay/pay/index.html
American Psychological Association Society for Military Psychology, Division 19	http://www.apa.org/about/division/div19.html
Uniformed Services University of the Health Sciences	http://www.usuhs.mil/mps/Psychology/index.html
Society of Air Force Psychologists	http://www.usafpsychologists.org

school. The HPSP scholarship for clinical psychology is offered only through the Army and is not available through the other military branches.

The Air Force and Navy attract applicants by offering loan repayment programs that become available after several years of service; in this sense, they are used as tools for retention beyond the initial service obligation after the internship. These programs are very competitive and not guaranteed to be available every year. Once their initial commitment is completed, Air Force and Navy psychologists may apply for the Health Professional Loan Repayment Program and, if awarded, will incur an additional service obligation. Eligibility requirements vary between services in the amount of the loan to be repaid by the service (up to $100,000) and in the obligation incurred by the psychologist (2–4 years).

Psychology interns enter the military as junior officers at the rank of lieutenant in the Navy and captain in the Air Force and Army; Although these are equivalent ranks, the difference in terminology is an example of the many differences between the branches. In recent years, the predoctoral internship programs in the Army and Air Force have been called *residencies* and the students are called *residents* to help define their training level in the context of the environment with medical interns and residents. Although the Army has resumed use of the terms *intern* and *internship,* the Air Force continues to use the terms *resident* and *residency;* the Navy has always used *intern* and *internship.* (Throughout this chapter, the terms *intern* and *internship* will be used.) The military clinical psychology internship programs are based in major medical centers throughout the country (see Table 16.1). All of the internship programs are APA accredited and are among the oldest

TABLE 16.1

Military Clinical Psychology Internship Programs

Branch of service	Location	Web site
Air Force	Malcolm Grow Medical Center, Camp Springs, MD	http://www.mgmc.af.mil/res_site/index.htm
	Wilford Hall Medical Center, San Antonio, TX	http://www.whmc.af.mil/clinics/psychology/residency.asp
	Wright Patterson Medical Center, Dayton, OH	http://wpmc1.wpafb.af.mil/psychology/index.htm
Army	Brooke Army Medical Center, San Antonio, TX	http://www.bamc.amedd.army.mil/mededu_new/GME/GME%20RES%20Prog%20Description/Clinical_psychology.htm
	Dwight D. Eisenhower Army Medical Center, Augusta, GA	http://www.ddeamc.amedd.army.mil/clinical/MentalHealth/Psychology/psych_intern.htm
	Madigan Army Medical Center, Tacoma, WA	http://www.mamc.amedd.army.mil/new_bhd/dept_psychology/residency/psycres.html
	Tripler Army Medical Center, Honolulu, HI	http://www.tamc.amedd.army.mil/residency/mchk-ph/cprp.htm
	Walter Reed Army Medical Center, Washington, DC	http://www.wramc.amedd.army.mil/departments/psychology/residency.htm
Navy	National Naval Medical Center, Bethesda, MD	http://www.bethesda.med.navy.mil/careers/navy_psychology_internship/NNMC_internship.aspx
	Naval Medical Center, San Diego, CA	http://www.bethesda.med.navy.mil/careers/navy_psychology_internship/NMCSD_internship.aspx

continuously accredited programs in existence. At the time of this writing, the programs begin in July for the Navy, August for the Air Force, and September for the Army.

Each of the internship programs has the same overarching goal: to train generalist psychologists to provide a variety of services to active duty service members, their family members, and retirees. Each program provides training in psychological assessment, intervention, consultation, and military education. In addition, however, each program has unique characteristics and offerings. Some of the programs have specialty rotations in primary care psychology, health psychology, child psychology, consultation and liaison, inpatient psychiatry, neuropsychology, military psychology, and substance abuse, as well as opportunities for research activities. The psychology training programs are well supported, both financially and administratively, and each program has nationally recognized distinguished visiting professors who provide workshops in their specialty areas. Psychologists such as Roger Greene (Minnesota Multiphasic Personality Inventory), Phil Erdberg (Rorschach), Dennis Turk (pain management), Frank Andrasik (biofeedback), and Erin Bigler (neuropsychology) are regular presenters at military training programs.

Military interns earn some of the best salary and benefits packages offered by psychology training programs throughout the country. (Financial compensation is discussed in the section Benefits of Military Life.) Not only does completing a military internship program guarantee a job immediately after the internship, it also allows the graduate to collect the year of supervised postdoctoral hours required for licensure in most states. Often support is available for licensure preparation courses. Military psychologists may select any state or U.S. territory for licensure and may then practice within the military setting wherever they are stationed, regardless of the state of licensure. After completing a 1-year internship program, graduates incur a 3-year active duty service commitment during which they gain additional experience and supervision. Mission requirements sometimes preclude the availability of supervisors, but efforts are being made to ensure licensure as soon as possible following the internship.

FELLOWSHIPS

Military psychologists also benefit from significant opportunities for continuing professional development, including specialization fellowships. Postdoctoral fellowships vary from service to service and from year to year. Location also varies from prestigious civilian universities to major military medical centers, or other military facilities (see Table 16.2). The military fellowships were among the first postdoctoral programs in the United States to receive APA accreditation. Specialization fellowships offered by the military in the recent past include neuropsychology, clinical health psychology, child or pediatric psychology, aviation psychology, forensic psychology, and clinical psychopharmacology. Fellowships in Special Operations and Information Operations have recently been offered to military psychologists. In 2005, the Navy implemented a postdoctoral fellowship in Special Operations that includes training at several Department of Defense and civilian agencies involved in the Global War on Terrorism. In addition, all branches of service provide financial support to pursue diplomate status from the American Board of Professional Psychology and an annual bonus for achieving this recognition.

TABLE 16.2

Military Psychology Postdoctoral Fellowship Programs

Branch of service	Specialization	Location
Air Force	Aviation psychology	Civilian site placement[a]
	Clinical health psychology	Wilford Hall Medical Center
	Forensic psychology	Civilian site placement
	Neuropsychology	Civilian site placement
	Pediatric psychology	Civilian site placement
	Special Operations psychology	Air Force Intelligence Agency
Army	Child or pediatric psychology	Madigan Army Medical Center
		Tripler Army Medical Center
	Health psychology	Tripler Army Medical Center
	Neuropsychology	Tripler Army Medical Center
		Walter Reed Army Medical Center
Navy	Health psychology[b]	Tripler Army Medical Center
	Neuropsychology	Civilian site placement
	Pediatric psychology	Civilian site placement
	Special Operations psychology	Various civilian and Department of Defense locations

[a]Fellowships have been completed in the past at prestigious civilian universities. [b]This 2-year fellowship in health psychology includes training in psychopharmacology.

MILITARY GRADUATE SCHOOL PROGRAM

In 1994, the U.S. Congress mandated the establishment of a doctoral program in clinical psychology at the Uniformed Services University of the Health Sciences (USUHS), F. Edward Hebert School of Medicine. The program integrates theory and skills in the areas of clinical psychology, health psychology, and organizational psychology to train military clinical psychologists as providers of health care in public health contexts. The American Psychological Association (APA) has accredited the program since 1997.

The USUHS program follows a scientist–practitioner model of training. Although the program strongly values the development of knowledge and skills in applied clinical psychology, it equally acknowledges the importance of developing critical thinking skills in psychology and related areas and applying them to real-world situations, particularly in the military, public health, and medical environments. Basic and applied approaches to clinical psychology, health psychology, and behavioral medicine are emphasized, focusing on the study of psychosocial, behavioral, and psychobiological variables.

The program's curriculum includes graduate and medical school courses, relevant research activities, clinical training, and some teaching experience. The clinical practicum is directed and supervised by experienced licensed clinical psychologists. The completion of the doctoral program requires independent scholarly work that contributes to the professional knowledge base and a 1-year clinical internship. Graduates of the program have held leadership positions in military heath care, many have received awards and commendations for their work, and several have published papers in the clinical literature.

The program in Medical and Clinical Psychology at USUHS is open to civilians as well as military service members, both officers and enlisted. Each branch of service has different application criteria and processes, and service obligations vary. For example, Air Force members may apply directly to USUHS and must have the approval of their commander to release them to attend; they incur a 7-year service obligation after graduation. The Navy billets may be filled by civilian selectees as well as military service members; prior service officers may lose rank, and enlisted service members become commissioned officers on acceptance into the program. They also incur a 7-year service obligation. Army applicants must submit an application packet both to USUHS and to an Army board that is convened for long-term health education training programs; they incur a 6-year active duty service obligation. This information is by no means exhaustive, and interested persons should contact the school, education manager, or health care recruiter for details about current application procedures.

Opportunities for Active Duty Military Psychologists

The military offers a broad spectrum of opportunities for psychologists—in training, teaching, administration, research, practice, and consultation. The focus of this chapter is on those opportunities available to uniformed service members, however there are many positions in military settings open to psychologists as civilian employees and contractors. The Navy and Army have two categories of psychologists—clinical psychologists and research psychologists. The Air Force does not have a separate category for research psychologists. Nevertheless, some Air Force, Navy, and Army clinical psychologists conduct research in addition to their clinical duties.

DUTIES OF MILITARY RESEARCH
PSYCHOLOGISTS

Military research psychologists are far fewer than military clinical psychologists; however, their numbers and contributions are significant. Their backgrounds include industrial/organizational, social, and experimental psychology, and the areas they study are quite diverse. Military research psychologists study training and personnel selection, human factors and safety, modeling and simulation, and knowledge acquisition, as well as conduct basic behavioral and medical research. They study human performance and human factors engineering (i.e., enhancing the human–machine interface to improve the functioning of systems and equipment). They also conduct research in environmental medicine and on the impact of adverse and extreme environments on performance. Other research topics include leadership and team effectiveness, executive-level policy making, tactical decision making, and communication among multinational forces. Military research psychologists also conduct field and laboratory research in such areas as combat stress, returning prisoners of war, hostage negotiations, military intelligence, and reserve readiness, as well as performance during wartime, peacekeeping, and humanitarian missions.

Military research psychologists, like clinical psychologists, are assigned throughout the United States and abroad. Many Army research psychologists are assigned to the Walter Reed Army Institute of Research in Washington, DC, and a field office in Heidelberg, Germany. Other assignments include the Aeromedical Research Laboratory in Fort Rucker, Alabama; the U.S. Army Medical Research and Material Command in Fort Dietrich, Maryland; and the Industrial College of the Armed Forces in Fort McNair, Washington, DC. Naval aerospace experimental psychologists, whose specialized training is described in the following paragraph, are assigned to a variety of billets, including the Office of Naval Research in Ballston, Virginia; Naval Health Research Center in San Diego, California; Naval Research Laboratory in Washington, DC; Naval Air Systems Command in Orlando, Florida; NASA Ames Research Center in Moffett Field, California; Defense Advanced Research Projects Agency in Arlington, Virginia; Naval Aerospace Medical Research Laboratory in Pensacola, Florida; and the Naval Operational Medicine Institute, which has various locations throughout the country.

The Navy offers its specialized training for aeromedical experimental psychologists at the Naval Operational Medical Institute at the Pensacola Naval Air Station in Florida. The first phase of the course is operational psychology and operational medicine, which exposes students to the physical stresses associated with flying and provides an understanding of the broad mission of the Navy Medical Department. The second phase of the course focuses on aerospace psychology and such topics as human factors engineering and performance. The third phase includes aviation preflight indoctrination at the Naval Aviation Schools Command and flight instruction at the Aviation Training Command Wing in Whiting Field, Milton, Florida. The flight training exposes students to the hazards and stressors of flight from the perspective of the aircrew. The Naval officers completing this 6-month course are known as aerospace experimental psychologists; they are maintained on flying status and play a critical role in naval aviation medicine. The Army and Air Force offer much briefer courses in aeromedical psychology and aviation psychology for clinical psychologists.

DUTIES OF MILITARY CLINICAL PSYCHOLOGISTS

Job assignments vary among the services and over time; however, there are many similarities in the type of work military clinical psychologists do early in their career. The duties assigned to junior psychologists are primarily clinical and usually are carried out at some type of military medical treatment facility. Clinical duties may include psychotherapy, testing and assessment, forensic evaluations, program development, consultation, and teaching. The specific population served may vary; Navy psychologists tend to work with Navy and Marine personnel, whereas Army and Air Force psychologists usually work with personnel associated with their own branch of service. Military clinical psychologists work primarily with active duty service members, retirees, and their families in a wide variety of settings.

It is not unusual for military psychologists to move directly from the internship into positions with levels of responsibility and autonomy that exceed those typical in other contexts. Initial assignments might include that of a chief psychologist at a small mental health clinic or specialty service chief at a larger military treatment facility, both of which require participation in service delivery as well as planning and oversight for other psychological services.

A psychologist at a military installation not only provides direct clinical care but also conducts evaluations of fitness for duty and consults with installation leadership on programs and policies to improve the community's capacity to manage stress. Installation psychologists are often responsible for providing programs on suicide prevention, alcohol and drug abuse prevention, and redeployment (i.e., return home and reunion with family after deployment), illustrating the kind of public health perspective that a military psychologist must maintain in promoting the health of the military community.

Military psychologists still provide traditional mental health services, although there is a trend for these kinds of services to decrease and other kinds of services to increase. Increasing emphasis is placed on prevention, early intervention, and integration of behavioral health with other medical disciplines, notably primary care and internal medicine. At the larger medical centers, military psychologists may work in pediatrics, oncology, and cardiology. Military psychologists in the future are less likely to be assigned continuously to mental health clinics and hospitals than they have been in the past. They are more likely to be deployed or attached to operational units in which the emphasis is on enhancing personnel readiness by providing high-quality psychological services focused on prevention of situational and psychological disorders.

Military psychologists currently have many opportunities to provide behavioral health care in settings outside of the traditional outpatient mental health clinic. For example, the Air Force Behavioral Health Optimization Project places psychologists and other trained mental health care providers in primary care clinics, where they work in a consultative role with primary care physicians to more effectively identify and treat a wide range of behavioral health care concerns. The primary care behavioral health consultant can also assist in the implementation of behavioral interventions directed by the patient's treatment plan and can facilitate referrals to traditional mental health care services, if required.

UNIQUE OPPORTUNITIES FOR MILITARY PSYCHOLOGISTS

As they gain experience, military psychologists have the opportunity to work in various academic positions and jobs that are not typically available to civilian psychologists. For example, psychologists may work aboard aircraft carriers and hospital ships and in special operational units (e.g., Navy SEALS, Marine Corps unit, Army Stryker Brigade Combat Team, Joint Special Forces Task Force). Military psychologists find many opportunities for academic positions as training directors, supervisors, and instructors in the military internship and postdoctoral fellowship programs and as faculty members at the military academies (i.e., West Point, Annapolis, Air Force Academy) and war colleges (e.g., the National Defense University). Psychologists at the U.S. Army Center for Health Promotion and Preventive Medicine provide concrete guidance for how to cope with deployment separation, exposure to casualties, and stress during military operations. A psychologist serves as director of the U.S. Army Physical Fitness Research Institute at the U.S. Army War College in Pennsylvania. This psychologist heads up a multidisciplinary program and research protocol that targets the life-style and health-related changes needed to reduce cardiovascular disease risk among the nation's key strategic leaders in the department of defense. A Navy clinical psychologist currently works at the U.S. Navy Bureau of Medicine and Surgery; there are even military psychologists who work at the White House and in the Congressional offices.

Military psychologists are very active within the Special Operations Forces (SOF) and aviation communities. Within SOF, psychologists are heavily involved in the assessment and selection of personnel for high-stress jobs. They also help develop SOF leaders using multirater assessments, individualized feedback, and performance enhancement training with interventions designed to enhance functioning under adverse and extreme conditions. As internal consultants, they also provide operational psychology support, including crisis negotiation, behavioral profiling, mental health support, and reintegration support. Individuals filling these positions must be trained for deployment from the air; they attend the Army's jump school and learn to parachute from a military aircraft.

Improving pilot performance and reducing flight crew error are primary concerns in aviation psychology. Aviation psychologists offer services including initial selection, education and training in human performance issues (e.g., concurrent task management, counterfatigue, situational awareness, and cockpit resource management), critical incident responsibility (i.e., response to a major disaster, emergency, or national threat), and support to operations and to families of pilots and aircrew. Aviation psychologists work to prevent aircraft mishaps and investigate them when they do occur. Prevention activities include providing consultation and education to pilots, aircrew, and other members of the aviation profession on the human and psychological factors associated with mishaps. For example, aviation psychologists may teach skills to improve communication and problem solving between crew members, methods for identifying situations in which visual illusions or other disorientation may occur, and techniques for combating air sickness.

Military psychologists conduct aircraft mishap investigations in all branches of service. Such psychologists have completed either a post-doctoral specialization in aviation psychology or a specific course such as the Aircraft Mishap Investigation and Prevention Course. Because human factors are involved in the vast majority of aircraft mishaps, a psychologist may be included as a member of the Aircraft Mishap Investigation Board or Safety Investigation Board, which conducts a 30-day process to identify causes and make recommendations to prevent future mishaps. The psychologist's role is to assist the flight surgeon in evaluating the human factors that may have played a role in the mishap. During the course of the investigation, the psychologist works with a team of diverse aviation professionals, including pilots, navigators, maintenance personnel, aircraft designers, engineers, safety personnel, air traffic controllers, and weather personnel. The military offers a formal course in aviation psychology, and graduates can qualify for aircrew status and some forms of flight pay.

An additional area of practice that is exclusive to military psychology involves Survival, Evasion, Resistance, and Escape (SERE) activities. Military personnel and Department of Defense employees are at risk for capture by unfriendly forces, whether a recognized military force, terrorists, or criminals. Under the auspices of the Joint Personnel Recovery Agency, the Air Force, Army, and Navy provide academic training and practical experience designed to provide service members with skills necessary for survival should they become prisoners of war, hostages, or be otherwise isolated from friendly forces. SERE psychologists, who have received specialized education and guidance in the psychology of isolation, capture, and detention, provide psychological oversight of these training environments.

When these individuals are released, are rescued, or escape, they enter the phased process of reintegration (also referred to as *repatriation*). The focus of reintegration is on returning the individual to his or her family, friends, and military unit in the best possible physical and psychological health. Currently conceived in three phases, the process can last anywhere from several days to a year; not all returnees require all phases. Ideally, the one constant throughout reintegration is the SERE psychologist. Although medical care and psychological support are essential components of reintegration, the primary goal of the first phase of the process is to gather time-sensitive tactical and operational information from the returnees. The SERE psychologist's role is to ensure that the process does not overwhelm returnees and to allow them sufficient time to begin the recovery process and develop an effective action plan for dealing with the inevitable and intense media pressure and with changes in their relationships and, often, career paths.

Psychologists in the National Guard and Reserves

A psychologist interested in serving in the military but not wishing to make it a full-time career may find that joining a guard or reserve unit is an attractive alternative. The skill set needed by psychologists in the National Guard and Reserve component is essentially the same as that needed by psychologists in the active duty component. Often psychologists in National Guard and Reserve units are former active duty psychologists who want to maintain their connection with the military and work toward a military retirement but maintain civilian employment. National Guard and Reserve psychologists are generally required to attend 2 days per month of drills and 2 weeks per year of annual training. However, some reservists are in a category designated as *individual ready reserve* and are not required to drill or serve on active duty unless called to duty for contingencies such as Operation Iraqi Freedom.

Before September 11, 2001, National Guard and Reserve psychologists often did not have opportunities to deploy or serve on extended active duty. But these positions no longer require only weekend drills and annual training; reservists and guard members are increasingly deployed to combat zones or locations that are quite austere. This trend is likely to continue for years to come. Guard and reserve psychologists must be prepared to deploy, sometimes with very little notice. They must maintain the physical fitness and height and weight requirements of their particular branch and be ready to serve as a military psychologist.

Typically, National Guard and Reserve psychologists do not provide clinical services during a weekend drill; rather, the time is spent completing training requirements that maintain military and medical readiness standards (e.g., common soldier skills training; nuclear, biological, and chemical defense training; CPR certification). They may perform additional duties such as becoming a subject matter expert in a particular area and teaching classes that meet training requirements. Some psychologists may be assigned to a reserve unit in another capacity, such as company executive officer or commander.

The National Guard and Reserve components are vital and active parts of the U.S. military. The opportunities to serve periods of active duty have become numerous and may at times be problematic for those who have a private practice to maintain. Sometimes reserve psychologists have the support of their civilian employer in substantial ways, such as making up the difference in pay during periods of active duty. Other employers are less supportive, but several federal laws are designed to prevent discrimination against military reservists.

The benefits and opportunities for National Guard and Reserve psychologists are worthwhile. The may choose between a part-time and occasional full-time commitment, and they perform some of the most exciting and rewarding work available in the clinical psychology field. They are eligible for a pension with medical benefits after 20 years and full medical benefits, and they have the opportunity to serve their country and make a difference in the lives of others at time of great need. As long as one understands the commitment and responsibilities of a National Guard or Reserve psychologist and accepts the challenge, the payoffs are great.

Benefits of Military Life

The benefits military personnel receive include space-available free travel to destinations worldwide; access to base facilities such as supermarkets, retail stores, officer's clubs, free or discounted movie theaters, state-of-the-art fitness centers, and libraries; annually funded continuing education; full health coverage (including pharmacy and dental coverage) for the service member and his or her family; 30 days of paid vacation every year; and a retirement option at 20 years of service with life-long health coverage. Financial compensation is highly competitive and consists of both taxable pay (base pay) and nontaxable allowances that vary depending on rank, time in service, geographic location, and number of family members.

The Regular Military Compensation chart combines the taxable base pay, two nontaxable allowances, and the tax advantage of those allowances to produce the average annual salary earned by military service members. According to the 2006 figures, the typical military predoctoral intern, a commissioned officer at the 3rd-level pay grade (O-3) and less than 2 years of service, earns just over $62,000 annually. Military psychologists with 10 years of service earn approximately $94,000 annually, and those toward the end of a 20-year career earn as much as $115,000 per year if promoted to the 5th-level pay grade or $127,000 per year if promoted to the 6th-level pay grade.

Military service often includes assignments in different locations in other countries as well as throughout the United States, usually entailing a move every few years. Many military psychologists consider the chance to live and work abroad to be one of the most exciting opportunities available; those assigned to overseas installations provide services to military personnel and their families. Assignments to countries such as England, Germany, Italy, Japan, Korea, and Turkey provide a rich cultural experience and serve as a base for traveling prospects. The military pays the costs for these moves, including the costs of moving family members, household goods, and a personal vehicle, although some assignments (generally those lasting 1 year or less) may not permit family members to accompany the service member.

A typical overseas tour usually lasts 3 years. Housing arrangements vary; some people choose to live in military housing, and others prefer to live in the local community. A cost-of-living adjustment is provided to account for differences in exchange rate. The camaraderie and shared values of the military community help to ease relocation to a foreign country. In many ways, a military assignment abroad provides the best of both worlds: access to such comforts of home as stores, schools, theaters, and radio and television programming offered on the larger military installations, on the one hand, and exciting opportunities to visit historic and cultural sites and other places of interest throughout the world, on the other.

Psychologists are often given temporary assignments that carry them away from duties at their usual duty station. Air Force psychologist Travis Adams described one such experience as follows:

> Temporary duty assignments provide some of the most unique and challenging opportunities for a military psychologist. In the spring of 2002, I was part of a three-person team of Air Force psychologists assigned to visit the "top of the world," Thule Air Base in Greenland. Thule is situated about 700 miles north of the Arctic Circle, right next to the polar ice cap. Thule has 6 months of sunlight, 6 months of darkness, and 12 months of cold. The purpose of our mission was to conduct a quality of life assessment and provide training on seasonal affective disorder and critical incident stress management. We were given 8 days to complete the assignment, which included a written summary report with recommendations to the base commander, so we had to hit the ground running. Skills that were essential for successful completion of our mission included public speaking, writing skills, statistical analysis, cultural competence, leadership, and organizational abilities. My personal highlights were working with the Danish firefighters, watching massive glaciers drifting in the bay, hiking on the polar ice cap, and witnessing midnight sun. The pace was swift, the work was stimulating, and the 8 days passed quickly. Overall, it was a wonderful experience and an adventure that I will never forget. (T. Adams, personal communication, April 23, 2005)

Psychologists in Wartime: Personal Accounts

Whatever else military psychologists may do, the health and safety of uniformed service members is their greatest and primary responsibility, and this is never so apparent as during times of war. Some military psychologists treat Soldiers, Sailors, Airmen, and Marines returning from combat, whereas others deploy forward with troops to care for them in theaters of war. Female psychologists in the U.S. military are given all the same duty assignments as their male counterparts, including deployments to combat zones and tours aboard aircraft, hospital ships, and aircraft carriers. Recent conflicts have had an impact on both psychology training programs and duty assignments. Following the terrorist attacks on the Pentagon on September 11, 2001, residents, fellows, and staff alike mobilized in response to the disaster. Under close supervision, military psychology interns in the Washington, DC, area obtained focused on-the-job training in disaster response and preventive psychological interventions. (Some of these activities are described in the *APA Monitor* articles listed in Exhibit 16.1.)

Following declaration of the Global War on Terrorism, many military psychologists have deployed to support Operation Enduring Freedom (military name of U.S. war in Afghanistan 2001–present) and Operation Iraqi Freedom (military name of U.S. war in Iraq 2003–present). We thought that the best way to illustrate these experiences is to provide descriptions from some of these psychologists. The first three accounts are from Army psychologists and the next two from Navy psychologists.

ADDRESSING BATTLE FATIGUE

Josh Friedlander deployed to a combat zone less than 2 years after completing his psychology internship at Walter Reed Army Medical Center. His first assignment after the internship was a 1-year tour in Korea; from there, he returned to Walter Reed, and within a few months he was deployed to Iraq in support of Operation Iraqi Freedom. He described his experiences as follows:

> During my assignment to Walter Reed Army Medical Center, I was tasked with supporting the 85th Combat Stress Control Medical Detachment out of Fort Hood, Texas, at the beginning of Operation Iraqi Freedom. In this assignment I served as a coteam leader in a Combat Stress Control unit. Combat Stress Control units have a specialized mission during wartime—the prevention and treatment of battle fatigue. The aim of combat stress control is to identify and treat soldiers with battle fatigue early to prevent symptoms from progressing to debilitating levels. Depending on his or her rank, the clinical psychologist is the team leader or second in command. Combat Stress Control units comprise prevention and restoration teams. I was on both, although typically clinical psychologists are assigned to prevention teams, which are composed of a clinical

psychologist, a social worker, and two mental health technicians.

On the prevention team, clinical psychologists assess and treat soldiers with battle fatigue. They may provide individual therapy; group therapy for anger management, stress management, and communication skills training; suicide prevention classes; unit cohesion evaluations; consultation to commanders; organizational psychology, personnel management, and psychological testing; and evacuation of soldiers when necessary. The clinical psychologist also must demonstrate solid military leadership skills in maintaining the discipline of his team, organizing supplies, and coordinating convoys to outlying camps when necessary. In this capacity, the psychologist has two roles—team leader and clinical psychologist.

If soldiers do not respond to care at the prevention team level, they are managed at the next higher echelon of care—the restoration team. Soldiers are typically removed from their unit for about 3 days to an area with fewer environmental stressors to allow for a brief reprieve from the stressful environment. In the restoration setting, the soldier has the opportunity to restore his or her basic physical and psychological needs for safety, adequate food and water, and regular bathing; has minimal work demands; and receives classes in anger management, communication skills, and stress management. When indicated, a psychiatrist conducts a thorough psychological assessment. Soldiers who respond positively to this level of intervention are returned to their unit, with follow-up provided as needed.

If a soldier's symptoms become debilitating, he or she is managed at the next level of care, which can include further assessment at a psychiatric facility in the theater of operation or evacuation out of the theater, with the possibility of future return to duty should their symptoms respond to treatment.

Serving side by side with soldiers in a wartime environment is a rare opportunity and privilege, and it requires expertise in two roles, as an officer in the U.S. Army and as a clinical psychologist. Although it can be challenging to balance these roles, the benefits are tremendous for the soldier with battle fatigue, who receives the best care possible, and for the clinical psychologist, who in helping soldiers serves his or her country. (Friedlander, 2005, 130–150)

WORKING IN A COMBAT ZONE

David Dodd was serving in Iraq in support of Operation Iraqi Freedom at the time of this writing. When asked what it is like to practice psychology when one is constantly on alert for physical attack, he offered the following perspective:

Working as a psychologist in a combat zone is rewarding but can be the most challenging work a psychologist will ever do. The psychologist must be not only proficient in clinical and consultation skills but also competent performing as a solider. One learns to live within an unpredictable, ever-changing, and potentially explosive environment that for many individuals causes physical harm and psychological difficulties.

Psychologists are not assured of safety and can be exposed to danger and trauma themselves. During moments of battle, psychologists experience the same fears and reactions as anyone involved in combat. They experience within themselves, and see in others, intense emotions, most typically fear. They feel the ongoing desire to run away and avoid the events that cause the distress. Yet they learn how to stay and cope, even though the threat continues day after day.

Whatever the psychologist's personal weaknesses are (e.g., depression, anxiety, limited attention, insomnia), they will be magnified on the battlefield. Managing psychological weaknesses requires a focus on basic human needs such as food, water, security, freedom from fear, and social affiliation. In stressful circumstances, people tend to be selfish and to look out only for themselves, and yet they also feel a competing need to be with others. Serving as a psychologist in a combat environment provides an often uncomfortable, but still valuable, opportunity to learn about and serve people in the most unfortunate and costly circumstances. (D. Dodd, personal communication, April 13, 2005)

SHOWING SOLIDARITY IN HARSH CONDITIONS

Samantha Boyd's first assignment after her internship was with the 10th Mountain Division (10th MNT DIV), based in upstate New York. Shortly after arrival, she deployed to Afghanistan in support of Operation Enduring Freedom. She described the initial interaction with her commanding officer (i.e., her boss) and the two noncommissioned officers (NCO; i.e., enlisted personnel) who worked for her as follows:

"Captain Boyd doesn't know this yet," my new Battalion Commander said, clapping a hand on my shoulder as I surveyed the 30 unfamiliar 10th MNT DIV officers and NCOs who were hailing me that night, "but in just a few short weeks, we're going to be suiting her up, putting her on a plane, and giving her a turn to play in the sandbox." Now, one of the skills that every psychologist has to have is the ability to suppress the shock response. Thankfully, I got that one down pat by the time I earned my diploma. Internally, I was thinking,

"OK, so that was my first test to see how hoo-ah[1] I am. He couldn't have informed me of that privately?" Externally, I exercised my military bearing, got a firm grip of the Battalion Commander's hand, and stated, "Sir, I would be honored to represent your battalion in Afghanistan. I'll keep my bags packed."

When I arrived in Afghanistan, my unit had been in place for 6 months already. The soldiers shielded their eyes when they saw me, "blinded" by my spotless, new uniform. I saw money being exchanged, and when I inquired about it, a soldier confessed they all had bets on whether I would get pregnant to avoid the deployment. I used my don't-show-the-shock-face and realized that I was going to have to work very hard to earn my respect out there. Five days into the deployment, I was tasked to fly with two male NCOs to a firebase and deliver mental health briefings, administer a psychological screening to the soldiers stationed there, and further screen and provide therapy to soldiers in need of treatment during the course of a week. During the week, I learned that the task was to be administered to a total of six other firebases across the next month, meaning that we had another 5,000 soldiers to screen. At that point, the NCOs sat me down and said, "Ma'am, we are going to put you back on a flight back to Kandahar tomorrow." I became concerned and asked if there was a crisis back at the home base in Kandahar where there was another NCO and a major running the clinic. The NCOs looked at each other and then back at me. "No, everything there is fine. We just thought you would be more comfortable there." Comfortable? "Yes, comfortable. You puke on all the Chinooks, and you've been losing weight out here. You haven't seen another female since we left, and you probably won't see another one until we get back to Kandahar. This is the highest functioning of all of the firebases. It is going to get rougher as we go. Is that really what you want? You have the opportunity to get on a plane tomorrow and go back to the home base."

I sighed and sat down in the dust. I lay my M16 across my lap. I looked my well-intentioned NCOs square in their faces. I was going to have to let them know exactly who I am and what I am made of if we were going to do this together and build trust in one another. "I suggest you stock up on some black garbage bags for the Chinook flights and secure some extra protein bars from the cooks, because you are stuck with me. I did *not* come to a combat zone to worry about breaking a nail. When I sit down with my patients, I want to be able to relate to them in

---

[1] *Hoo-ah* is a word that Army people use for building esprit de corps; it is used to express motivation and encouragement, much like the word *amen* is used in a tent revival. Marines say *"oo-rah,"* which is similar in meaning to the Army word and, like the Army *hoo-ah*, is often used as a greeting and farewell. Navy personnel sometimes also say *oo-rah*, especially those assigned to a Marine unit.

their own element. If that means going a month without a shower, losing weight, getting rocketed, or puking in helicopters, those are small sacrifices I am willing to make. Now, which one of you is going to call back to Kandahar to tell the Major there's been a misunderstanding?" Over the next months, the three of us completed countless tasks and missions together. Although I had to do everything short of standing on my head to prove myself to them, I also learned to trust those NCOs with my life, and we all came home safely. (S. G. Boyd, personal communication, May 23, 2005)

SERVING ON AN AIRCRAFT CARRIER

Within 2 days of reporting to the USS *Theodore Roosevelt*, Kirsten Betak was deployed for Operation Iraqi Freedom. She told us about her experience aboard this vessel and about the history, rationale, and typical duties for psychologists serving aboard aircraft carriers:

Ding. Ding. Ding. Ding. "Reveille! Reveille! All hands heave out, trice up, and carry out the plan of the day." The ringing of bells and overhead announcements mark the start of the day at 5:30 a.m. and carry on throughout the day until taps at 9:00 p.m. Calls for sweepers to man their brooms, spills in the reactor, medical emergencies, and power outages occur, calling us to our duties. Drills and General Quarters interrupt the performance of routine work, both in port and while under way. We learn how to brace for impact, put out fires, and prevent or control flooding. Amid these activities, the medical department operates an outpatient clinic, inpatient ward, surgical unit, physical therapy unit, and mental health unit.

Psychologists were first placed on ships in 1996 as a test to determine whether it would be more cost-effective to provide psychological services at sea rather than on shore. At that time, medical evacuations for mental health disorders were common. Any sailor not coping well with sea duty would be loaded on a helicopter or airplane and flown to a shore station for assessment and treatment. They would fly with an escort for safety, as well as with the aircrew and pilots. The loss of manpower and expense of the transportation was estimated at about $45,000 per medical evacuation. On an average deployment, three to five soldiers were evacuated in this way. By placing psychologists on the aircraft carriers, the Navy was able to significantly reduce medical evacuations not only from the aircraft carriers, but from the entire battle group. Today, there are psychologists on each of the Navy's 12 aircraft carriers located around the world.

On average, an aircraft carrier has more than 3,000 permanent members attached to the ship for duty. While under way, the air wing brings on another 2,000 air specialty members, including pilots and flight crews. The battle group has another 5,000 sailors and officers on smaller ships assigned to guard the aircraft carrier. Each carrier has one psychologist and one psychiatric technician assigned to it. They work directly for the Senior Medical Officer, Executive Officer, and Commanding Officer of the ship and are responsible for the mental health and well-being of the personnel attached to the entire battle group.

Enlisted sailors range in age from 18 to 45 years old, and officers are slightly older. Most sailors are in their 20s. As a result, much of the psychology practiced is adolescent psychology, with a focus on healthy life skills, coping skills, and anger and stress management. The psychologist also acts as the licensed independent practitioner for the Substance Abuse Rehabilitation Program (SARP) and supervises the SARP counselors, who are specially trained enlisted personnel. (K. Betak, personal communication, May 28, 2005)

Tara Smith was at sea at the time this chapter was written, and she described the following experiences serving as a ship psychologist:

I am currently completing a tour on the USS *Kitty Hawk,* the country's only forward-deployed aircraft carrier. This tour is very different from my initial experiences at the hospital during my internship and the following assignment, which felt no different than any other hospital, except that everyone wore uniforms. Onboard the ship, I know that I am definitely in the Navy. From wearing men's coveralls and steel-toed boots daily, to sleeping in cramped berthing, to learning shipboard firefighting, this is not the typical job of a clinical psychologist. Our ship is out to sea most of the year; therefore, all sailors, but particularly the psychologist, must be able to handle the everyday stressors of being out at sea. These stressors, which usually become routine, include mild seasickness; aching knees, feet, and back (from the steel decks and ladderwells); loud noises (made by launching and recovering planes); extreme weather conditions; long working hours; unusual smells from a variety of sources (e.g., jet and diesel fuel, the huge shipboard septic tank); variable food quality (it's typical to run out of fresh fruits and vegetables); and, of course, work with 5,000 different personalities.

As the Ship Psychologist, I am responsible for the mental health of the 5,000 sailors onboard and those on the ships deployed with us. I must first set the example for appropriate coping by avoiding alcohol, eating healthy, exercising, building a support network, and using diplomacy when dealing with difficult people. It's common for tempers to flare and personalities to clash when under way together for long periods of time. Most of my work involves administrative evaluations. Sailors wanting to work in security, intelligence, and other special fields must have a psychological evaluation. The rest of my work involves evaluating sailors for a variety of complaints, such as depression, anxiety, homesickness, and relationship problems. On rare occasions, sailors feel suicidal and make gestures or attempts, and my job is not only to evaluate and treat these sailors but to also make recommendations to the command about the sailor's suitability for continued service. Many times I am essentially a human lie detector; a few sailors know that they can get out of the Navy if the Ship Psychologist makes the recommendation, and they try their best to malinger. A great education in psychology is often not enough; immersing oneself in the military and understanding the inner workings of the ship help the psychologist make the correct call.

The best part about being a Ship Psychologist is learning about what sailors actually do. Treating sailors in a hospital is nothing like treating them on the "front line," where I often face the very same stressors. I have more credibility when I can show that I, too, am homesick and get tired of being out at sea but that I can model appropriate coping. It is also exciting to learn about maintaining the material readiness of the ship, being equally responsible for fighting fires and stopping flooding, and learning about everything from navigation to engineering. As an undergraduate, I never imagined that I'd be doing these things, but it's been a great experience.

Regarding leisure, there isn't much. The ship is designed for transporting planes and weapons, not for the comfort of the crew. The Navy has made improvements in many newer ships, but in general the racks (beds) still tend to be small and the berthing cramped. The food is not terrible, but it's mostly frozen or canned and therefore not optimally nutritious. E-mail is a luxury. The ship has to use satellite connectivity, and it often goes down. Using the Internet is also a luxury and cannot be relied on. We watch movies, because cable television is also unreliable. (This is especially demoralizing during March Madness or the Superbowl.) It is difficult to stay aware of world news without Internet or television. Many of us have family and friends mail newspapers and magazines. (I have a subscription to *Newsweek*). There are 27 church services onboard our ship and three chaplains. There are also three gyms; a library with games, books, and movies; and two stores with DVDs, CDs, food, and gifts to mail home. Although it's not home, most take pride in doing something as meaningful and difficult as being on an aircraft carrier. (T. Smith, personal communication, June 4, 2005)

Conclusion

As the personal accounts in this chapter demonstrate, attributes needed for success as a military psychologist include a positive attitude, flexibility, creativity, the desire to work as a team member, patriotism, and a sense of adventure. Military psychologists are often given levels of responsibility and independence very early in their careers that would be rare in other contexts. As seniority increases, there are increasing opportunities to serve in leadership roles involving both clinical and military knowledge. The advantages of such a career include the opportunity not only to become a respected professional with an outstanding breadth of clinical and research experience but also to acquire a great diversity of cultural and life experiences. At the same time, one is serving one's country and caring for the individuals who place themselves in harm's way and their family members who sacrifice so much in the process. The Web sites listed in Exhibit 16.1 and Table 16.1 provide more information on careers in military psychology. If you are adventurous and interested in a rich and rewarding experience, a tour or a career as a military psychologist may be for you. The authors gratefully acknowledge the contributions of the following military psychologists in the development of this chapter: Travis Adams, Morgan Banks, Paul Bartone, Kirsten Betak, Samantha Boyd, Paul Byrd, Bruce Crow, David Dodd, David Fennell, Joshua Friedlander, Marshall Goby, Glenn Goldberg, Carroll Greene, Sally Harvey, Larry James, Brad Johnson, Wendy Law, John Ralph, Rose Rice, Bob Roland, Ken Rollins, Morgan Sammons, William Satterfield, Russell Shilling, Tara Smith, Gary Southwell, Mark Staal, Melba Stetz, Wayne Talcott, and Donna Waechter. We also acknowledge the many men and women who serve in uniform daily so that families and individuals everywhere enjoy the comforts of peace, freedom, and safety.

Reference

Friedlander, J. N. (2005). An Army clinical psychologist. In R. D. Morgan, T. L. Kuther, & C. J. Habben (Eds.), *Life after graduate school in psychology: Opportunities and advice from new psychologists* (pp. 130–150). New York: Psychology Press.

Kelly D. Brownell and Peter Salovey

Health Psychology: Where Psychological, Biological, and Social Factors Intersect

17

H ealth psychology, although relatively new compared with other specialties such as clinical, developmental, and social psychology, has become an established, vital, and growing field of global importance. The primary aims of the field are to identify the links between the way people think, feel, and behave and their physical well-being; to understand the impact of physical factors on human behavior; and to improve health and prevent illness with psychosocial interventions. Fulfilling these aims promises to have an impact on the major diseases of modern life.

Kelly D. Brownell, PhD, is professor and chair of the Department of Psychology, professor of Epidemiology and Public Health, and director of the Rudd Center for Food Policy and Obesity at Yale University. He served as president of several national organizations, including the Society of Behavioral Medicine and the Division of Health Psychology of the American Psychological Association. He was elected to the Institute of Medicine and was named by *Time* magazine as one of the World's 100 Most Influential People.

Peter Salovey, PhD, is the Chris Argyris Professor of Psychology and dean of Yale College, Yale University, where he served previously as dean of the Graduate School of Arts and Sciences and chair of the Department of Psychology. He is also professor of Management and professor of Epidemiology and Public Health at Yale. He has been awarded the William Clyde DeVane Medal for Distinguished Scholarship and Teaching and the Lex Hixon Prize for Teaching in the Social Sciences at Yale.

TABLE 17.1

Leading Causes of Death in the U.S. Population, 1900

Cause of death	Percentage of all deaths
Pneumonia	11.8
Tuberculosis	11.3
Diarrhea and enteritis	8.3
Heart disease	6.2
Liver disease	5.2
Injuries	4.2
Cancer	3.7
Senility	2.9
Diphtheria	2.3

Note. From Healthy People 2000: National Health Promotion and Disease Prevention Objectives, by U.S. Department of Health and Human Services, 1991, Washington, DC: U.S. Government Printing Office. In the public domain.

The primary causes of death in the United States changed dramatically over the past century. Tables 17.1 and 17.2 show the leading causes of death in 1900 and in 1997. In 1900, infectious diseases were most prominent killers, with pneumonia and tuberculosis the leading causes of death. Today, the leading causes of death are chronic rather than infectious illnesses, and the combination of heart disease and cancer accounts for 54.7% of deaths, compared to 9.9% in 1900. These changes are the result in part of advances in preventing and treating infectious diseases, but there are other contributors as well. Longer life

TABLE 17.2

Leading Causes of Death in the U.S. Population, 1997

Cause of death	Percentage of all deaths
Heart disease	31.4
Cancer	23.3
Stroke	6.9
Chronic obstructive pulmonary disease	4.7
Unintentional injuries	4.1
Pneumonia and influenza	3.7
Diabetes	2.7
Suicide	1.3
Kidney disease	1.1
Chronic liver disease and cirrhosis	1.1

Note. From Healthy People 2010: Understanding and Improving Health (2nd ed., p. 22), by U.S. Department of Health and Human Services, 2000, Washington, DC: U.S. Government Printing Office. In the public domain.

spans expose people to diseases that may take decades to develop. Moretroublesome, however, are conditions of modern living that promote lifestyle habits such as smoking, poor diet, and physical inactivity, which in turn have a serious impact on both longevity and quality of life.

The contribution of lifestyle to the major modern diseases has been known for decades. A landmark event was the release of a report in 1964 by Surgeon General Luther Terry describing clear links between smoking and cancer (U.S. Department of Health, Education and Welfare, 1964). In the intervening years, countless calls have been made for people not to smoke, and also to eat better, exercise more, and engage in preventive and screening behaviors. As an example, the U.S. Department of Health and Human Services (1991) released the *Healthy People 2000* report in 1991, which contained specific health objectives for the United States to be reached by the year 2000 and stated that to reach the objectives, the nation must "depend heavily on changes in human behavior" (p. 8). The release of this report was followed by an explosion of research on behaviors such as diet, exercise, smoking, alcohol consumption, and preventive actions such as screening mammography, Pap smear testing, sunscreen and seat belt use, and stress reduction.

The magnitude of potential benefit from behavior change is staggering. If every smoker in the United States quit, there would be a 25% reduction in cancer deaths and 350,000 fewer fatal heart attacks each year. A mere 10% weight loss in middle-aged men would lead to a 20% decrease in coronary heart disease and would have a significant impact on diabetes, stroke, and some cancers.

Following *Healthy People 2000* by a decade was a similar report by the U.S. Department of Health and Human Services (2000) called *Healthy People 2010: Understanding and Improving Health*. It focused less on the leading causes of death and more on the causes of the causes—what the report called "health indicators." This focus was based on the belief that messages about the ultimate causes of death, like heart disease and cancer, did not lead to obvious action but that emphasizing the behaviors contributing to these diseases would be more useful. The report listed these leading health indicators:

- physical activity,
- overweight and obesity,
- tobacco use,
- substance abuse,
- responsible sexual behavior,
- mental health,
- injury and violence,

- environmental quality,
- immunization, and
- access to health care.

With a few exceptions, the list of leading indicators from 2000 was much the same as the list of recommendations from 1990. Tobacco use in the United States had decreased, obesity had increased, and the links between physical activity and health had become clearer, thus raising its priority, but overall, relatively little had changed.

In recent years, awareness of the global importance of these problems has increased (World Health Organization, 2004; Yach, Hawkes, Gould, & Hofman, 2004). The dramatic reduction of smoking in the United States has been more than offset by heavy promotion by the tobacco industry in other countries, particularly in developing nations. In addition, virtually every nation on earth is reporting increased obesity among its citizens. Stated simply, the conditions that place Americans at risk are spreading around the world. Major increases in chronic diseases and staggering health care costs are likely to follow.

Tackling such powerful and disquieting social trends requires an interdisciplinary focus, a cardinal feature of health psychology. Understanding how behavior affects health demands breadth of knowledge and collaborative relationships with researchers in multiple disciplines. As an example, Murali and Chen (2005) conducted a study to examine the physiological impact of exposure to violence. In the study, 115 high school students were monitored for systolic and diastolic blood pressure, heart rate, heart rate variability, and cortisol levels in a baseline phase and during exposure to a laboratory stressor. The individuals with the greatest history of exposure to violence showed pervasive physiological changes in response to stress. Such a study requires knowledge of psychology but also medical expertise on blood pressure variability, stress, and the impact of stress on cortisol.

Another important advance in health psychology is the consideration of broad determinants of behavior, risk, and disease. Health-related behaviors themselves have determinants. Whether a person has the opportunity and resources to be physically active, is in a demographic group targeted by the tobacco industry, can afford healthy foods, has an overly stressful life, or has good medical care, he or she is affected by economics, politics, and the environment.

Income and social class are key drivers of psychological and physical health, leading to important work on health disparities (Adler & Newman, 2002). Poverty affects access to health care, quality of care, the availability of preventive services, knowledge of health issues, exposure to environmental risks such as pollution, dangerous work conditions, and much more. Poverty is linked strongly to access to healthy foods, the frequency of unhealthy food choices, and diseases such as diabetes and obesity (Drewnowski & Darmon, 2005), leading to specific economic proposals to deal with these problems (Brownell & Horgen, 2004; Nestle, 2002).

At the beginning of the 21st century, it is no longer novel or surprising to note that human behavior is associated with the etiology of and recovery from disease. The strength of these associations is impressive and shows the vital role health psychology can play in health and well-being. Consider the following examples:

- Epel et al. (2004) examined the association of chronic stress with a measure of cellular aging (telomere length). Women with the highest levels of perceived stress, compared to those with lowest stress, had shortened telomeres the equivalent of a decade or more of aging.
- An analysis of diet, physical activity, and body weight in the United States predicted that today's children will be the first generation in the nation's history to lead shorter lives than their parents (Olshansky et al., 2005).
- Whether a person is depressed after having a heart attack is as strong a predictor of mortality 6 months later as is a history of previous heart attacks and extent of physical damage from the heart attack itself (Frasure-Smith, Lesperance, & Talajic, 1993).
- Ornish et al. (1990) randomly assigned men with severe coronary artery disease to receive their usual medical care or an intensive lifestyle intervention program involving a low-fat vegetarian diet, moderate aerobic exercise, smoking cessation, and stress management. The men in the lifestyle intervention group showed greater drops in overall cholesterol and low density lipoprotein cholesterol and had a 91% reduction in the frequency of angina (compared with a 165% increase in the control group). Most impressive was that the average diameter of blockages in the coronary arteries decreased in the lifestyle intervention participants and increased in the individuals assigned to the control group.
- Another study of Ornish et al.'s (2005) intensive lifestyle program found significant reductions in markers for prostate cancer in men participating in the program.
- Phillips, Ruth, and Wagner (1993) documented a profound effect of beliefs on health: They examined deaths in 28,169 Chinese Americans and 412,632 randomly selected persons listed as "White" on death certificates. The Chinese Americans died significantly earlier than the White Americans when their disease

and birth year were combined in a way that Chinese astrology and medicine consider ill fated. The effect was particularly strong among individuals most strongly attached to Chinese traditions.

These examples highlight the present and continuing need for health psychologists and the diversity of areas for potential involvement. In the remaining sections of this chapter, we examine how health psychology is defined, the history of the field, training and career paths, financial compensation, and a day in the life of a health psychologist.

Definition of Health Psychology

A number of terms have been used over the years to describe the association of psychology with health. One of the first was *psychosomatic medicine*. This term and the field with the same name were born from the supposition that people could make themselves sick or, more consistent with the popular understanding of the term "psychosomatic," that people could experience a number of maladies for which there were no discernable physical causes. Examples were headache, irritable bowel syndrome, and chronic pain.

Health psychology is a more recent term. Various definitions have been proposed, the core features of which are nearly identical. Two prominent definitions are those of Matarazzo (1980) and Taylor (2003):

> Health psychology is the aggregate of the specific educational, scientific, and professional contributions of the discipline of psychology to the promotion and maintenance of health, the prevention and treatment of illness, the identification of etiological and diagnostic correlates of health, illness, and related dysfunction, and the improvement of the health care system and health policy formation. (Matarazzo, 1980, p. 815)

> Health psychology is the field within psychology devoted to understanding psychological influences on how people stay healthy, why they become ill, and how they respond when they do get ill. Health psychologists both study such issues and promote interventions to help people stay well or get over illness. (Taylor, 2003, p. 3)

Another term used to describe the study of health and behavior is *behavioral medicine*. As we describe in the section on the history of the field, behavioral medicine predated health psychology:

> Behavioral medicine is the interdisciplinary field concerned with the development and integration of behavioral and

biomedical science knowledge and techniques relevant to health and illness and the application of this knowledge and these techniques to prevention, diagnosis, treatment, and rehabilitation. (Schwartz & Weiss, 1978, p. 149)

For most purposes, the various definitions of health psychology, behavioral medicine, and psychosomatic medicine are indistinguishable. The same is true to some extent of the professional organizations dedicated to promoting the study of connections between health and behavior, which include the Division of Health Psychology of the American Psychological Association (APA), the Society of Behavioral Medicine, and the American Psychosomatic Society. Each has a slightly different emphasis, but many professionals, including the authors, belong to more than one association. Although the potential for fragmentation exists because of different definitions and professional organizations, we interpret the growing number of organizations and journals (e.g., *Health Psychology, Psychology and Health, Annals of Behavioral Medicine, Psychosomatic Medicine*) as signs of a field with considerable social importance and strong potential for career opportunities (Chesney, 1993; Stone, 1990; Taylor, 2003).

A Condensed History of Health Psychology

Hippocrates believed that imbalances in bodily fluids (what he called *humors*) caused both psychological and physical problems. Too much blood made people sanguine but predisposed them to epilepsy; too much yellow bile led to angry feelings and risk for malaria or genital rot. Although the particulars are incorrect, Hippocrates's beliefs show that the idea that psychological states like anger and physical illnesses might share common underlying mechanisms has a long history.

Two thousand years later, in the 19th century, writings on *psychosomatic medicine* (a term coined in 1818) developed the notion that internal mental conflicts can express themselves as physical diseases. Modern health psychology places much less emphasis on mental conflict but still emphasizes the role of attitudes, beliefs, emotions, and behavior in physical illness. The first clear delineation of health psychology as a field was an article by Schofield (1969) that motivated the APA to appoint a task force on health research, chaired by Schofield, 4 years later. Schofield noted that psychology as a field was preoccupied with mental illness and had largely ignored physical health. The task force issued a report calling for attention to health, noting the strong potential for psychology to apply to health maintenance, illness prevention, and care delivery and calling for related graduate training (APA, 1976). At about that time, the psychology faculty at the University of California, San Francisco, established the first program designed to train health psychologists. Around 1974, George Stone, a faculty member, was likely the first person to use the term *health psychology* (Stone, 1990).

Later in the 1970s, Gary Schwartz and Judith Rodin at Yale mounted a significant effort capped by a 1977 conference on *behavioral medicine*, defined as the interdisciplinary field concerned with integrating behavioral and biomedical sciences to prevent, diagnose, treat, and rehabilitate illness. The Yale conference galvanized the field of behavioral medicine and marked the beginning of a formal training program at Yale.

Shortly thereafter, in 1978, the APA formed the Health Psychology division (Division 38), and the division's founders agreed that the new effort should represent both basic research on psychological factors in physical health and the application of principles based on research to the prevention and treatment of disease itself. The division's journal, *Health Psychology*, appeared in 1982. By the next year, 2,000 psychologists had joined the division, and a formal conference established guidelines that could be adopted by the growing number of departments of psychology wishing to establish formal training programs. The APA Division of Health Psychology now lists more than 40 training programs (APA, 2005).

Currently, numerous books have delineated the field; predoctoral internships for clinical students specializing in health psychology exist; training programs have begun to emerge worldwide, especially in Sweden, Finland, Germany, the United Kingdom, Italy, and Spain (Richards, 1992); and the tension between those focusing on basic research and those interested in clinical intervention has largely been resolved (Richards, 1992; Stone, 1990). The field is nurtured by many factors, not the least of which is the rising cost of health care and an emphasis on less expensive alternatives to traditional treatment (e.g., behavioral interventions). Both *Healthy People* reports (U.S. Department of Health and Human Services, 1991, 2000) noted that health promotion and disease prevention objectives depend on changes in behavior—more so than the discovery of new antigens or antibodies—to reduce morbidity and mortality from the major chronic diseases (Taylor, 2003). Today's health psychologists are trained in a variety of areas and enter many different settings, as we discuss in the following sections.

Training in Health Psychology

Training opportunities in health psychology have multiplied over the years. One can now find excellent programs at undergraduate, graduate, internship, and postdoctoral levels.

UNDERGRADUATE PREPARATION

Being admitted to graduate programs in psychology is a competitive process. At Yale, for instance, students wishing to specialize in health psychology are admitted through the clinical or social psychology programs. In a typical year, we select three or four clinical psychology students from a pool of about 350 applicants and three or four social psychology students from a pool of about 100 applicants. The odds of admission vary considerably among universities, and the Yale numbers are among the most exclusive, but in all programs, one's undergraduate record is important in gaining admission.

Successful applicants to the Yale doctoral program have often majored in psychology or, if they majored in a different field, have taken a sampling of psychology courses from across the discipline (e.g., abnormal, social, behavioral neuroscience). Courses in statistics and research methods are especially helpful. Of course, if your college offers an undergraduate course in health psychology or behavioral medicine, you should certainly take it. Other useful courses of study outside of psychology include some exposure to human biology, on the one hand, and the study of illness in other social sciences such as medical sociology and medical anthropology, on the other.

At least as important as coursework, however, is some kind of research experience as an undergraduate, one of the keys to admission to many graduate programs. Typically, research experience constitutes helping a professor or graduate student with his or her research. Some undergraduates also complete an independent honors thesis describing a study that they designed themselves. It is not necessary that research experience be in health psychology; it is more important simply to have research experience in general. We often advise students to begin some kind of research collaboration no later than the junior year. Volunteer work with patients in hospital or other medical settings can be helpful for individuals who desire additional training in health psychology, but it cannot substitute for research experience. Even doctoral programs in clinical psychology rank undergraduate research experience as the most important component of undergraduate preparation (Eddy, Lloyd, & Lubin, 1987).

Summers are an excellent time to gain experience in the field. We receive many inquiries from undergraduates around the world who wish to work or volunteer with us for a summer. Such experience provides new contacts, experience in research, and a glimpse into the day-to-day life of a health psychologist, as least in one setting. Scanning the Web sites of departments of psychology or relevant medical school departments will yield names and contact information for faculty with varying interests.

A comprehensive listing of graduate programs in psychology is available in the book *Graduate Study in Psychology* published by the APA (2005; http://www.apa.org). An excellent guide titled *A Directory of Doctoral Programs Offering Health Psychology Programs* has been prepared by the Health Psychology division (Division 38) of the APA. It lists various programs and contains a great deal of information pertinent to graduate training and is available to download from the Web site of APA's Health Psychology division (http://www.health-psych.org/downloads/guidebook.pdf).

GRADUATE TRAINING IN HEALTH PSYCHOLOGY

For the past 25 years, individuals who identified themselves as health psychologists generally received their graduate training in clinical or social psychology and then applied their knowledge to problems in the health area (Taylor, 2003). In recent years, however, there has been a growing enthusiasm for more specialized training in health psychology at the graduate level. Doctoral training in health psychology can be found within traditional clinical psychology and social psychology programs, occasionally within other specialized programs such as behavioral neuroscience, and at times as a major field of specialization in its own right. The label of the program is less important than the kinds of research and practical opportunities it provides. Many graduate programs emphasize research in collaboration with faculty more than coursework, so the match between an applicant's interests and those of the faculty at potential graduate schools is critical. Students should examine carefully the rosters of faculty members to find the best fit.

An important decision is whether a student desires training that will lead to licensure as a clinical psychologist and, hence, the opportunity to deliver psychological services to clients. Many health psychologists do not desire such training; they are involved in university-based research and teaching, for example. But if you wish to pursue a career that combines research and clinical practice, you should consider health psychology programs embedded within doctoral programs in clinical psychology. Also, if you imagine a career as a professor in a medical school or as a researcher in a hospital setting, clinical training can be advantageous.

There is no standard doctoral program in health psychology. Rather, programs vary in their emphasis on coursework versus research and practical experiences, mentoring by a single faculty member versus opportunities to work with multiple faculty members, and an explicit structure versus a more self-designed format. There are excellent programs that vary in these dimensions (e.g., the program at Yale emphasizes research, generally with multiple faculty members, in a self-designed sequence with few departmental requirements; other excellent programs are much more structured). It is important to identify the learning environment that most fits your strengths. These differences may be clear from a department's application packet or can be learned through discussions with faculty or graduate students.

A central criterion in choosing a program is the availability of faculty members who can provide mentoring in your areas of interest. It is important to identify programs where, for instance, there is more than one professor engaging in research relevant to health psychology, which signals a commitment by the program to the area of health psychology and also leaves opportunities for guidance when a faculty member retires, moves, or is otherwise unavailable. Moreover, if a student wishes to work with particular patient populations (e.g., women with breast cancer, people with AIDS, children with birth defects), it is important that treatment facilities for such individuals are located in the school's community. It is easier for you to be engaged with such programs if a faculty member has already established collaborative ties.

Doctoral training in health psychology typically lasts 4 to 6 years. Whether you desire a career in academic research, practice, or research and practice combined, it is helpful to develop more than one area of specialization. As we mention later in the section on career tracks, either health psychologists specialize in particular psychological processes (e.g., social comparison, control, emotion) and then investigate how they are related to physical diseases, or they specialize in a particular disease or disease process (e.g., cancer, heart disease, chronic pain, obesity) and study the related psychological variables that seem important. The first approach to specialization is more likely to characterize social psychologists working in health psychology, and the second approach is more typical of clinical psychologists.

Internship

Individuals who desire licensure as clinical psychologists need to complete an internship before obtaining the degree. Many clinical internships have developed special tracks for trainees in clinical health psychology, and there are many such specialized clinical internships sites in the United States and Canada. A guide to available programs can be downloaded from the Web site of APA's Division of Health Psychology (http://www.health-psych.org/pub.htm).

Internships in clinical health psychology may emphasize work with either individuals who seek help for physical health problems or those with mental health issues who also have physical problems. Many individuals have problems with depression, sexual dysfunction, anxiety, or other psychological issues, but they enter the medical system because of physical health complaints. It is not surprising that clinical health psychology interns often work as part of a medical team organized around patients' physical health problems (e.g., cardiac rehabilitation, chronic pain management, psychosocial adjustment to cancer). They are less likely than traditional clinical interns to spend time in psychiatric inpatient wards or mental health centers. Interns may be involved in consultation and liaison work in which they are called on by physicians or other health care professionals to provide assistance in understanding and treating psychological problems in a medical patient (e.g., adherence to a prescribed treatment regimen, substance abuse issues, coping with a disability). This role often involves work with the family of the designated patient to deal with issues caused by the patient's illness and to facilitate the creation of a home environment more conducive to recovery. Finally, health psychology interns may administer programs, often to groups, concerning the modification of health-relevant behaviors like smoking, weight control, and physical exercise.

Postdoctoral Training

The technical knowledge required to conduct research in health psychology has increased exponentially. Often, individuals who have obtained a PhD in an area of psychology (or even in a specialized health psychology program) find continued specialized training to be helpful. Such individuals may apply for a postdoctoral training grant from the National Institutes of Health to work for 2 to 3 years with a designated mentor, usually at an institution other than where the PhD was completed. Postdoctoral positions sponsored by institutional training grants or individual research grants are also advertised. Because the market for academic jobs is competitive, recent PhDs may seek out these positions before applying for professorships. Some institutionally sponsored post-doctoral positions are designed especially for individuals whose training has not been in health psychology but who now desire this specialization.

Postdoctoral experience varies widely from program to program. Under the supervision of a professor, postdoctoral trainees work on research projects of their own design or participate in a program of research funded by a grant to the professor. Because the funding often comes from a grant to the senior scientist, the trainee specializes in the designated area of study. There may or may not be opportunities for clinical practice. A postdoctoral fellowship provides a person with advanced training, contacts in the field, and the opportunity to publish the results of research projects.

A few institutions offer "respecialization" programs that are generally oriented toward psychologists who completed the PhD in a nonclinical field but now desire some clinical training, often with licensure as a desired outcome. Unlike most postdoctoral positions, respecialization programs may not pay a salary and may require tuition of some sort, and they are often designed for individuals who wish to work as practitioners rather than researchers. APA's Health Psychology division has information available on postdoctoral opportunities in the field at http://www.health-psych.org/pub.htm.

Career Tracks in Health Psychology

Individuals trained in health psychology have many potential career paths. We have grouped these into three broad categories: research careers, practitioner careers, and combined research and clinical careers. However, two people in the same category may differ widely in the nature of their work, types of colleagues, and specific specialty area.

Our own careers serve as examples of this diversity. Although we teach in the same department of psychology (at Yale), we pursue different activities. The first author (Brownell) is a clinical psychologist and does research on obesity, eating disorders, nutrition, and public policy. Part of this work involves directing the Rudd Center for Food Policy and Obesity and the Yale Center for Eating and Weight Disorders, places where both basic and applied research are conducted and where interests range from the fundamental control of eating to legislation and regulation that can affect public health. Colleagues outside the department and the university include psychologists and experts in endocrinology, epidemiology, economics, and public policy.

The second author (Salovey) is a social psychologist (although clinically trained) and conducts research on the relationship between emotions and health and on the framing of public service announcements and educational programs to encourage preventive health behaviors. Although there is no clinical intervention involved in this research, there is intervention at the level of the individual, workplace, and community. Studies include tests of messages to promote mammograms and sunscreen to reduce the risk of breast cancer and skin cancer, respectively. Colleagues include other psychologists, especially those interested in attitude change and persuasion, and experts in oncology, dermatology, communications, and public health. This approach also involves participation in interdisciplinary networks of investigators such as the Yale Transdisciplinary Tobacco Research Center and the Center for Interdisciplinary Research on AIDS, for which the second author (Salovey) serves as the deputy director.

As our experiences show, careers in health psychology vary widely. This diversity is a positive feature of health psychology as a field, as there are many options for partitioning duties between research, teaching, training, and practice, even within the same institution.

RESEARCH CAREERS

Health psychologists have a wide array of research opportunities. In some cases, these opportunities are specific to a disease, as with research on cancer, heart disease, diabetes, alcoholism, eating disorders, obesity, diabetes, AIDS, and arthritis. Other health psychologists focus on a general area of psychosocial functioning that may span many issues (e.g., social support, coping). Yet others emphasize some aspect of lifestyle (e.g., diet, smoking, exercise) or a specific population (e.g., women's health or health in minority populations). The opportunities are as vast as health itself.

There are research opportunities in both basic and applied areas. At the basic end, some researchers study behavior genetics and even molecular biology. Other basic research might include studies with laboratory animals on issues such as the effects of stress or diet on the development of cancer or heart disease. Controlled clinical trials to test different interventions are an example of more applied work. Research that tests different messages to promote health behavior would have both basic and applied implications.

Although many individuals in the field of health psychology are engaged in research, relatively few do research exclusively. In university settings, research is combined with teaching and training graduate students and sometimes with administrative appointments. In a medical school, research may be the exclusive task, especially if a person is hired by a more senior investigator to work on specific research projects. More often, individuals in a medical school setting combine research with teaching or clinical activity. Some research opportunities are available in the corporate world or with a government agency (e.g., National Institutes of Health, National Center for Health Statistics).

PRACTITIONER CAREERS

Practice in the field of health psychology, like research, can take many forms. Clinical psychologists work in private practice or in mental health settings and specialize in the treatment of people with health-related problems. Others work with clients with alcoholism, eating and weight disorders, or chronic pain. Psychologists may work in conjunction with other health professionals to deliver clinical service. For example, psychologists work with physicians to screen people for surgical procedures such as plastic surgery, gastric bypass surgery for obesity, or organ transplantation. Groups of clients may need counseling as a result of a medical crisis (e.g., mastectomy, primary caregiving for a chronically ill person).

Some psychologists provide services in the form of consulting, a burgeoning area of health care delivery and preventive services. With the advent of managed care, psychologists are involved in decisions on the delivery of both mental health and physical health services. Preventive services have become more important, and psychologists are central to the delivery of prevention programs, managing such issues as recruitment and retention in these programs, adherence to prescribed treatment regimens, and relapse prevention (Brownell, Marlatt, Lichtenstein, & Wilson, 1986; Witkiewitz & Marlatt, 2004).

Corporate health settings provide additional opportunities for health psychologists. Many businesses, both large and small, encourage employees to make use of health promotion services such as weight loss, stress management, exercise, and smoking cessation programs. Larger businesses may have an on-site facility, and a psychologist, especially one with additional training in an area such as nutrition or exercise science, is an attractive candidate to direct a corporate health program.

COMBINED RESEARCH AND CLINICAL CAREERS

Clinical psychologists trained in health psychology may combine clinical work and research. The most obvious example is a person who does work with a clinical population where some means of assessment or intervention is the focus of the research. Many others work with individuals with clinical problems in research but are not involved in intervention. For example, research on breast cancer has identified genetic markers of risk for the disease. A psychologist may study coping and the impact of learning that one's risk is high, but he or she may not be involved in clinical service.

The variation in combined research and clinical careers is enormous. The nature of the clinical work varies greatly depending on the target population and employment setting, and the same is true for research. Adding even more to the flexibility in careers is that health psychologists vary in the proportion of time they allot to research and clinical work. As a result, the field of health psychology can accommodate many different interests and lifestyles.

Financial Compensation

Figures on salaries for health psychologists have not been assembled in a systematic way. The chapters in this book on clinical psychology and social psychology are good guides to what an individual might earn with a background in these two areas. Salaries in university departments of psychology (or related areas) will not be affected by whether the person specializes in health psychology or in another area. Work in government settings is likely to pay about the same as academic departments, and work in corporate settings might pay more. Salaries in medical schools are generally higher than in arts and sciences departments at the assistant professor and sometimes the associate professor levels, but at the level of professor, the gap closes considerably, and approximately equivalent pay is the rule. Compensation for private practice or consulting may be small or large depending on the amount of work available, the reputation of the professional, and the amount of time devoted to this work.

A Day in the Life of a Health Psychologist

What follows is a description of a typical day in the life of the first author (Brownell), although the activities the two of us engage in are quite similar. As is clear from the preceding section, various combinations of research, clinical work, teaching, and administration are available to a person with a background in health psychology, so it is difficult to define a "typical" day in the life of a health psychologist.

A typical day might begin with a research meeting, known in our department as a "lab meeting." Attended by 15 to 20 graduate students, undergraduate students, postdoctoral fellows, research assistants, and faculty members, in these meetings individuals or groups of individuals present their work. The work can range from studies in the earliest stages of planning to articles nearly ready for publication. This format provides valuable opportunities for participants to prepare and practice delivering scientific presentations and to acquire feedback on ideas. Participants frequently discuss new and controversial work and identify emerging trends in the field. I work hard to encourage creativity and to establish an environment in which people feel part of an interdisciplinary team. (The work of our center is described at http://www.Yale RuddCenter.org.)

Following the research meeting, I teach classes. Graduate classes with 8 to 20 students take the form of seminars with lively class discussions, presentations, and critical review of a particular field. Research articles from the literature form the reading list. Undergraduate classes in health psychology may draw 70 to 120 students and involve lecture and some discussion. Teaching is important to the work of health psychologists employed in college and university settings. Courses in health psychology can be specific to a topic as well (e.g., stress, nutrition, emotions and health). An example is a class I teach called "Psychology, Biology, and Politics of Food" (see http://research.yale.edu/psyc123a/).

My next activity involves the supervision of graduate students, postdoctoral fellows, and undergraduate students involved in research. I hold individual meetings to discuss both conceptual and practical aspects of specific research projects. The aim is to generate new knowledge and to communicate this via publication to other professionals. The joy of being a research mentor lies in working with trainees to nurture their scientific skills, sharing the wonder of discovery, and watching new careers take shape.

Our group does clinical supervision in both individual and group meetings. Trainees present case studies of the clients they are seeing and receive feedback from both the professor and fellow students. Once each week, a clinical forum is held in a group setting, called the "team meeting." Participants analyze the existing literature on the clinical problem in one of their cases, present the case, and participate in a general discussion of the case.

Another feature of my day's work usually involves professional activities at the national or international level. Such activities might involve writing scholarly papers, editing books, reviewing articles for journals, preparing a lecture for a professional meeting, conversing via telephone or computer with collaborators or colleagues in different cities or countries, planning a national meeting, or working with officials in other countries on health policy. There is a strong global emphasis to my work.

Securing research funding is important for many researchers, and hence considerable activity, particularly for medical school faculty, is oriented around writing grants. Research that involves large populations, costly equipment or tests, or heavy personnel commitment usually requires grant funding. Being creative about securing funding typically involves contact with traditional funders like the National Institutes of Health or the National Science Foundation, but also with private foundations and, increasingly, industry of some sort (although this raises conflict of interest issues).

Psychologists in all settings often rise to leadership positions that require them to spend more time on administrative duties. In academic settings, such individuals might serve as director of undergraduate or graduate studies, department chair, dean, provost, and even university president.

A day in the professional life of a health psychologist is characterized by a diversity of activities and interaction with individuals at different stages of their careers. Health psychologists are likely to engage in each activity to a certain extent; those with training in clinical psychology might perform more clinical work. Because the field is developing rapidly and important discoveries occur frequently, being in a setting involving teaching, research, and training can be both stimulating and rewarding.

Advantages of the Career and Attributes Needed for Success

There are many advantages of a career in health psychology. Some professionals treasure most the growing and vital nature of the field, as well as the fact that the necessary expertise to understand problems such as cancer, heart disease, AIDS, stress, and addiction lies at the intersection of several disciplines and areas of study. Others value the opportunity to help people in an area as important as health and well-being. Still others find the scientific challenges to be most interesting, as there are many important unanswered questions in the field (e.g., Is there a cancer-prone personality? Is there a best means of coping with stress? Can food be addictive? By what means does social support protect a person from disease?). The field is large enough, is growing in so many directions, and has such a bright future that professionals with diverse interests can be accommodated.

Little is known from a scientific perspective about attributes needed for success in health psychology (or other areas of psychology, for that matter). Because so many career paths are available (e.g., teaching, research, clinical work, consultation), different personal attributes will be necessary, depending on the specific job demands.

What is common across all career paths are the rewards of practice in a field in which new information becomes available at a striking pace and in which the future of not only the information itself but also the sources of information is difficult to foresee. As an example, 2 decades ago, few would have predicted that molecular biology and genetics research would have such a profound impact on the understanding of both wellness and disease. The AIDS epidemic drew a number of researchers and clinicians into an entirely new field and exposed them to new information on epidemiology, public health models of disease, and immunology. Being open to and excited by rapid developments in the field and being open minded about the contributions of many other disciplines is a prerequisite for competence in health psychology.

Conclusion

We began this chapter by claiming that health psychology is a field with considerable vitality and opportunities for professional growth. These opportunities exist across many topic areas and with many combinations of professional activities. With the ongoing changes in the health care system, the growing recognition that behavior is central to the nation's health, and increased emphasis on prevention, the prominence of the field will only increase with time.

References

Adler, N. E., & Newman, K. (2002). Socioeconomic disparities in health: Pathways and policies: Inequality in education, income, and occupation exacerbates the gaps between the health "haves" and "have-nots." *Health Affairs, 21,* 60–76.

American Psychological Association. (1976). APA Task Force on Health Research: Contribution of psychology to health research: Patterns, problems, and potentials. *American Psychologist, 312,* 263–274.

American Psychological Association. (2005). *Graduate study in psychology.* Washington, DC: Author.

American Psychological Association, Division 38. (April, 2000). *A directory of doctoral programs offering health psychology training.* Retrieved July 6, 2006, from http://www.health-psych.org/downloads/guidebook.pdf

American Psychological Association, Division of Health Psychology. (2005). *Directory of health psychology programs.* Retrieved October 20, 2005, from http://www.health-psych.org

Brownell, K. D., & Horgen, K. B. (2004). *Food fight: The inside story of the food industry, America's obesity crisis, and what we can do about it.* New York: McGraw-Hill/Contemporary Books.

Brownell, K. D., Marlatt, G. A., Lichtenstein, E., & Wilson, G. T. (1986). Understanding and preventing relapse. *American Psychologist, 41,* 765–782.

Chesney, M. A. (1993). Health psychology in the 21st century: Acquired immunodeficiency syndrome as a harbinger of things to come. *Health Psychology, 12,* 259–268.

Drewnowski, A., & Darmon, N. (2005). The economics of obesity: Dietary energy density and energy cost. *American Journal of Clinical Nutrition, 82,* 265S–273S.

Eddy, B., Lloyd, P. J., & Lubin, B. (1987). Enhancing the application to doctoral professional programs: Suggestions from a national survey. *Teaching of Psychology, 14,* 160–163.

Epel, E. S., Blackburn, E. H., Lin, J., Dhabhar, F. S., Adler, N. E., Morrow, J. D., & Cawthon, R. M. (2004). Accelerated telomere shortening in response to life stress. *Proceedings of the National Academy of Sciences, 101,* 17312–17315.

Frasure-Smith, N., Lesperance, F., & Talajic, M. (1993). Depression following myocardial infarction. *Journal of the American Medical Association, 270,* 1819–1825.

Matarazzo, J. D. (1980). Behavioral health and behavioral medicine: Frontiers for a new health psychology. *American Psychologist, 35,* 807–817.

Murali, R., & Chen, E. (2005). Exposure to violence and cardiovascular and neuroendocrine measures in adolescents. *Annals of Behavioral Medicine, 30,* 155–163.

Nestle, M. (2002). *Food politics: How the food industry influences nutrition and health.* Berkeley: University of California Press.

Olshansky, S. J., Passaro, D. J., Hershow, R. C., Layden, J., Carnes, B. A., Brody, J., et al. (2005). A potential decline in life expectancy in the United States in the 21st century. *New England Journal of Medicine, 352,* 1138–1145.

Ornish, D., Brown, S. E., Scherwitz, L. W., Billings, J. H., Armstrong, W. T., Ports, T. A., et al. (1990). Can lifestyle changes reverse coronary heart disease? The Lifestyle Heart Trial. *Lancet, 336,* 129–133.

Ornish, D., Weidner, G., Fair, W. R., Marlin, R., Pettengill, E. B., Raisin, C. J., et al. (2005). Intensive lifestyle changes may affect the progression of prostate cancer. *Journal of Urology, 174,* 1065–1069.

Phillips, D. P., Ruth, T. E., & Wagner, L. M. (1993). Psychology and survival. *Lancet, 342,* 1142–1145.

Richards, J. C. (1992). Training health psychologists: A model for the future. *Australian Psychologist, 27,* 87–90.

Schofield, W. (1969). The role of psychology in the delivery of health services. *American Psychologist, 24,* 565–584.

Schwartz, G. E., & Weiss, S. M. (1978). Behavioral medicine revisited: An amended definition. *Journal of Behavioral Medicine, 1,* 249–252.

Stone, G. (1990). An international review of the emergence and development of health psychology. *Psychology and Health, 4,* 3–17.

Taylor, S. E. (2003). *Health psychology* (5th ed.). New York: McGraw-Hill.

U.S. Department of Health and Human Services. (1991). *Healthy people 2000: National health promotion and disease prevention objectives.* Washington, DC: U.S. Government Printing Office.

U.S. Department of Health and Human Services. (2000). *Healthy people 2010: Understanding and improving health* (2nd ed.). Washington, DC: U.S. Government Printing Office.

U.S. Department of Health, Education, and Welfare. (1964). *Smoking and health: Report of the Advisory Committee to the Surgeon General of the Public Health Service* (Public Health Service Document No. 1102). Washington, DC: U.S. Government Printing Office.

Witkiewitz, K., & Marlatt, G. A. (2004). Relapse prevention for alcohol and drug problems: That was Zen, this is Tao. *American Psychologist, 59,* 224–235.

World Health Organization. (2004). *Global strategy on diet, physical activity and health.* Geneva, Switzerland: Author.

Yach, D., Hawkes, C., Gould, C., & Hofman, K. J. (2004). The global burden of chronic diseases: Overcoming impediments to prevention and control. *Journal of the American Medical Association, 291,* 2616–2622.

Bruce L. Bobbitt

A Psychologist in Managed Care: An Unexpected Career

18

When I was approached by the editor to provide a chapter on my career in managed health care for this volume, I was obviously flattered but also a bit surprised. My surprise resulted from the some of the controversies that surround managed health care and the fact that managed care has not been well represented in the core psychological literature. Managed health care has been particularly troubling to many in psychology and certainly to the field of organized psychology. However, as I reflected on this invitation, I realized that my own career path is more typical of careers in psychology than I had originally thought, and much of what I have

Bruce L. Bobbitt, PhD, LP, received his undergraduate degree in human development and family studies from Cornell University, his PhD from the Institute of Child Development at the University of Minnesota in 1979 and completed postdoctoral studies in the Psychology in the Schools Training Program, also at the University of Minnesota. A licensed psychologist in the state of Minnesota since 1983, Bruce has worked in community mental health, hospital psychology, private practice, and has served the profession as American Psychological Association Council Representative from Minnesota and served 16 years on the Executive Council of the Minnesota Psychological Association. At United Behavioral Health, he has held various management positions in the clinical and quality improvement area since 1993 and has given numerous conference presentations on psychology and managed care.

learned may be of value to you as you think about your career in this most exciting but continually changing discipline.

Early in my life, I realized I was fascinated with history and with stories about how things happened—and later, why they happened and, more important, how psychology as a discipline and profession can improve matters for Americans and their culture. When I read autobiographies, I was particularly struck by how the stories often seemed "inevitable"—the authors described their lives and decisions as rational responses to changing circumstances, and they always seemed to have a clear idea of where they were headed.

My own story and the depiction of the current health care environment that I describe alongside it are not like this. If someone had told me 20 years ago that I would be working for a Fortune 50 company and writing about how psychology can better contribute to the health care field, I would not have believed it. At that time, I had a very different vision of what I was doing and what I thought was important. I have come to believe that, with few exceptions (an academic career in research and teaching is perhaps the best example of relative stability), careers in psychology will be defined by ever-increasing change. As a result, those who enter this field need to be prepared to be flexible and to embrace new opportunities when they arise. Fortunately, the field of psychology provides the requisite intellectual rigor, knowledge base, and skills to succeed, regardless of the changes that occur in the broader health care field.

Managed Health Care Described

The terms *managed care* and *HMO* are now firmly rooted in U.S. culture and are used both accurately and inaccurately in the popular press. The major U.S. newspapers—for example, *The New York Times* and the *Wall Street Journal*—have articles on topics related to managed care and health care delivery and costs nearly every day; this was not the case a mere 20 years ago. Unfortunately, these accounts rarely describe the core meanings of these often-used terms. To make these meanings clear and relevant for someone preparing to become a psychologist, I recount two parallel histories—that of health insurance and that of the professional practice of psychology.

EVOLUTION OF HEALTH INSURANCE

Insurance allows one to protect assets by paying a premium to a company that will then compensate him or her if the asset is lost. The most common examples are house and car insurance; most everyone who owns a house or car also owns insurance that will pay for replacement in the case of catastrophic loss, such as a house fire or car accident. Some policies pay for portions of the loss, such as roof replacement if damaged by hail or a storm. Insurance does not pay for regular maintenance, such as painting the house or changing the car's tires. Most people who own houses and cars do not want to file claims; they prefer that the asset remain undamaged. In contrast, current health insurance policies provide a wide array of benefits and services, and people are encouraged to access their benefits, especially preventive health benefits. Current plans often provide payment for routine physicals and other preventive activities such as mammograms. However, current health insurance plans reflect a developmental history that dates back to the mid-part of the last century.

Before the 1930s, there was no private health insurance in the United States. Toward the end of that decade, the first policies were developed and were designed to pay for limited "catastrophic" health problems, such as the cost of major surgery or recovery from an accident. Then as now, as with house insurance, most people have enough money for routine medicines or a few visits to a doctor to treat a short-term illness. But few have the cash in the bank to pay for the replacement value of a house or for a major health event that could cost in the hundreds of thousands of dollars. The billing codes health professionals currently use are based on the language first used in the 1930s—they are called "procedure codes," as in surgical procedures. Today, if you see a psychologist for psychotherapy and the psychologist bills a health insurer, the therapy session is called a "procedure" (e.g., "individual psychotherapy" has its own procedure code).

Since the advent of health insurance policies, the benefit set, or the list of diagnoses and procedures that the insurance company will pay for, has expanded. Mental health and substance abuse treatment were generally not a covered benefit in the early plans, and many states still do not require health insurance plans to include them. As with all insurance, individuals can purchase a health insurance plan. However, one of the twists of health insurance is that it is usually purchased by employers, who cover most of the cost of the premium, and this fact has had (and continues to have) a profound impact on the health care industry. In most cases, employer-purchased health insurance does not require the individual employee to demonstrate that he or she has good health; all employees and their dependents can be covered. The assumption is that the risk for any one person's filing a claim for payment (a claim usually submitted by a doctor or a hospital) is distributed among all of the employees and their dependents—called the "covered lives." Thus, some of the employees will use many services, and some will use none. With the employer negotiating and purchasing the policy, there are four entities involved in the health insurance relationship: the purchaser (a company), the employee (or individual), the provider of services (the doctor or psychologist), and the payer (the insurance company). The tension among these different entities, which sometimes have different interests, is one of the pervasive aspects of all health insurance, especially that which is administered through managed care arrangements.

In addition to the expansion of benefits included in health plans, the other major change in health insurance, which emerged in the late 1960s and became pervasive in the late 1970s and early 1980s, was the dramatic increase in health care premiums charged to businesses to cover their employees. It was this pressure that led to the development of health insurance that is referred to as *managed care*. The federal government passed legislation in 1973 that enabled insurers to develop managed care products. One goal of these new insurance products was to end, or at least reduce, the premium increases that purchasers were being charged. The *Managed Health Care Handbook* (Kongstvedt, 2001) provides a good introduction to managed care operations and processes.

Before managed care, a licensed psychologist could receive payment for a service by submitting a bill, which the insurance company then paid at some specified rate. For example, the policy may have paid 80% of the charged fee, and the psychologist would then charge the patient the remaining portion. The arrangement of managed care plans differs in a number of important ways. Managed care companies develop networks of clinicians and enter into a contract with them in which a set fee is paid for each type of service. Moreover, not all clinicians in a particular region may be included in a network (sometimes called "panels"). Managed care companies also developed care management centers in which professionals (usually licensed master's-level clinicians) review cases according to a set of criteria called *medical necessity criteria* or *level of care guidelines*.

One of the unique aspects of managed behavioral health care is that a number of large managed care organizations either developed or contracted with separate companies to administer the mental health and substance abuse benefit. These companies, sometime called "carve outs" (because the mental health benefit was administered by a different group than the group managing the medical benefit), developed rapidly during the 1990s and are still a significant part of the health care environment. The company that I work for, United Behavioral Health (UBH), is one of these organizations.

Managed behavioral health organizations (sometimes referred to as *MBHOs*) focused on two aspects of behavioral health care. The first was to find ways to help patients receive appropriate care in the appropriate setting, which had the added benefit of reducing unnecessary expense. One of the major outcomes of this effort has been a reduction in the use of long-term inpatient treatment for patients with mental health conditions. Managed care organizations have care management programs designed to help patients move to outpatient care soon after inpatient discharge and to encourage patients to remain in needed outpatient treatment.

A second aspect of managed behavioral health care is the focus on improving overall health care for populations of individuals covered by the health plans. This aspect has been of crucial importance to health care organizations and advocates for better health care. The National Committee for Quality Assurance has been accrediting health care organizations for many years and has developed a series of measures for desirable medical care (called the Health Plan Data and Information Set, or HEDIS for short). Health plans assess and report these measures annually, and a number of these measures pertain to behavioral health.

As I write, in the middle of the 1st decade of the 21st century, the managed behavioral health care industry is quite a bit different than it was 20 years ago. The industry has consolidated substantially, and there is a greater emphasis on promoting wellness, measuring outcomes, and reducing unneeded administrative procedures. Health plan benefit designs have expanded to include a wide array of medical and behavioral health conditions and treatments. Most large organizations also include employee assistance programs that provide direct information on a variety of conditions and refer people for short-term counseling for routine problems in life. All major organizations are developing sophisticated Internet resources and encouraging enrollees to learn as much as possible about their problems both before and during treatment. Finally, new types of insurance plans are being developed called "consumer-driven health plans." These plans have larger deductibles and encourage individuals to take more responsibility for their health care choices.

A BRIEF HISTORY OF PROFESSIONAL PSYCHOLOGY

There are many aspects to the history of professional psychology, a number of which are covered in other chapters in this volume. I focus only on key highlights that relate to the current managed care environment. Before World War II, professional psychology was not organized or developed as a defined profession or discipline. Following that war, the practice of psychology expanded rapidly, and many subfields of professional psychology were formed; the best known are clinical, counseling, school, and industrial/organizational psychology. Psychologists who complete training in the first three receive specific clinical training in different settings that ultimately can lead to independent licensure to practice psychology. The states, which regulate the practice of psychology, began to license psychologists in the 1950s, and all states now have some type of licensing law. Shortly after World War II, there were few mental health providers, and the psychology profession contributed both to the growth in the number of professionals and, just as important, to the scientific underpinnings of good mental health treatment. In the early days of psychology practice, insurance policies did not cover mental health treatment—as with other outpatient procedures, if you wanted psychotherapy, you had to pay for it.

The situation today is quite different. The multiple disciplines of professional psychology have grown dramatically. In addition, in 1973, the American Psychological Association approved the doctor of psychology (PsyD) degree that could be granted either by traditional universities or by independent schools of professional psychology. Thus, in 2005, there are many more psychologists than there were some 30 years ago. Two other historical changes have had a major impact on mental health treatment. The first is the development and now widespread use of psychotropic medications to treat the symptoms of mental disorders. In the past 15 years, more and safer antidepressants and antipsychotics have been developed and are widely prescribed by physicians. Over the past few years, there has been an increase in overall treatment for mental health, which appears to be accounted for by increased use of medication treatment.

The second development is the rapid expansion of master's-level clinicians who provide individual, group, and family psychotherapy. Most states license these clinicians (most are clinical social workers and marriage and family therapists) for independent mental health practice. Many states are also licensing professional counselors, who provide a mixture of guidance activities and mental health treatment. Many insurance companies include these practitioners in their networks, and there is reason to believe that they outnumber doctoral-level psychologists in many cases.

In summary, the field of professional psychology has expanded both in quality and in quantity since World War II. At the same time, the use of medications to treat mental health disorders has increased, as has the number of master's-level clinicians. Psychologists are one of many types of professionals who provide psychotherapy, which is by far the most widely used mental health treatment other than prescribing of medication.

These brief histories of managed care and professional psychology provide the context necessary to understand the roles that psychologists play both within managed care organizations and in organizations that deal with managed care companies. Psychologists who provide primary mental health treatment also have to deal with managed care on an ongoing basis. Managed health care companies are not isolated from other health care sectors in U.S. society, and thus their evolution and context are important to understand as you think about your future career opportunities. Bobbitt (in press); Bobbitt, Marques, and Trout (1998); and Feldman (2003) have addressed some of the challenges managed care poses for psychology. In addition, Sanchez and Turner (2003) provided a useful discussion of the issues facing practicing psychologist in the era of managed care.

The changes in the health care arena have also changed the opportunities for psychologists who are interested in managed health care. In the early generation of managed behavioral health care, psychologists played major and significant roles in the development of the industry, and the business leaders in these companies were often psychologists. These psychologists combined administrative skills with strong clinical backgrounds. With the industry consolidation that has occurred in the past decade, there are fewer companies, and they are all becoming more sophisticated as their size and complexity has grown. The entrepreneurial phase is clearly over, and the management ranks are now being filled with MBAs in addition to psychologists and other health care professionals.

Preparation and Activities of Psychologists in Managed Care

In this section I address the roles and activities that psychologists play in managed care companies and in other health care organizations that deal with managed care companies. I also review some of my background and note how my training in academic and professional psychology prepared me for this career. The large managed care organizations are now mature businesses; they have the structures and functions that define any business in addition to those unique to the health care business. These core functions include business operations, finance, product development, sales and marketing, research and development, account management, information technology and Web site development, process and quality improvement, human resources, and corporate administration. The functions that are unique to managed behavioral health care include clinical care management and its oversight, improvement in clinical performance, accreditation, health sciences applied research, actuarial analysis, clinical network development, identification of best practices, and qualitative and quantitative analysis of cases and provider performance, as well as collaboration with other health care professionals.

At UBH there are doctoral-level psychologists in virtually all areas of the company, with perhaps the exception of finance, actuary, and information technology. Unlike other health care organizations and academic institutions, there is no department of psychology as such. Rather, psychologists work in disparate areas and are brought together on specific projects. UBH has field offices that provide care management services (i.e., helping members locate appropriate clinicians in the network, reviewing inpatient cases, monitoring outpatient treatment) and corporate support operations. Over the years, UBH has had doctoral-level psychologists in key positions in the field offices. UBH also has a department that does applied collaborative research with university partners and private organizations such as the Rand Corporation. This group has doctoral-level psychologists, as well as professionals from related fields such as statistics. In my current position, I oversee all accreditation operations and work on the development of clinical management programs. In the following paragraphs I describe a couple of projects to illustrate how psychologists contribute to both operations and the development of the company's capabilities.

Each year UBH completes both enrollee and provider satisfaction surveys to make sure that managers fully understand operations and identify ways to improve them. Although the company usually hires an outside firm to administer these surveys, the results are analyzed internally. Psychologists usually either complete or collaborate on these analyses because they have the requisite skills in understanding survey research.

A second project involves improving the identification of depression and other mental health problems in patients who have medical illnesses such as cancer and diabetes. My department developed an innovative approach involving the training of medical nurses in a sister company to administer a brief behavioral health screening (not a diagnostic instrument) to identify patients who may be helped by behavioral health interventions. These nurses make follow-up calls to patients who are discharged from medical facilities and interview them to identify service gaps, including gaps in behavioral health care. Many patients with medical illnesses also experience emotional distress, depression, and anxiety, and by collaborating in this way, my department hopes to increase referrals to behavioral health clinicians. When psychologists discuss service gaps with patients, they do not diagnose them, but rather try to make sure that patients are getting full access to necessary care. The actual treatment, including the diagnostic process, is completed by the treating provider.

In both of these examples, I found that my background in psychology was helpful in formulating the issues and also in developing the program. It is gratifying to work with other health care professionals and to bring psychological expertise to the table. Some of the psychologists at UBH work on identifying creative outpatient mental health programs to recommend to network development staff. Still others work on the review of clinical best practice guidelines and psychological testing guidelines.

During my work in managed care for the past 12 years, I have reflected on the types of background that lead to success in large managed care organizations. One of the reasons that psychologists have been influential and successful in these complex organizations is that they generally have a broad and deep background in both the science and practice of psychology. The training provided by most psychology graduate schools does not focus solely on one function (e.g., therapy) but focuses on depth of skill and understanding in addition to technique.

In the positions I describe earlier in this section, differing ranges and levels of expertise are required for success. Doctoral psychologists who complete reviews and requests for psychological testing must have a background and experience in testing and usually have extensive experience in doing psychological assessments and evaluations. They may also provide other types of care management services and work on development projects. For senior psychology positions, a broader range of experience and expertise is required. Many psychologist senior executives at UBH had experience in the administration of mental health services before joining the company. Of the current group of psychologists who hold leadership positions, almost all have had some experience in community mental health, which provides an appreciation of context, teamwork, and the multiple needs of patients.

I entered corporate managed care somewhat by accident. In 1993, I was running a nonprofit collaborative mental health program for the Wilder Foundation in St. Paul, Minnesota. Before that, I worked for a number of years in the community mental health center in Washington County, Minnesota, and for a year and a half in the University of

Minnesota Hospital and Clinics and in the Department of Pediatrics. I decided I wanted to return to more direct mental health work and accepted a position at United Behavioral Systems (owned by United Healthcare; now UBH). In the early 1990s, this company ran staff model mental health clinics as part of its overall clinical model; staff model clinics were common in the early days of managed behavioral health care, but they are rare now. In my first position, I was a senior psychologist and provided direct treatment, did assessments, and supervised staff—pretty traditional for a professional psychologist. In 1994, I took a job in the corporate office as the company's first quality improvement specialist. To make a long story short, there was much on-the-job learning because I did not have formal training in that area.

Over the years, I have held multiple positions, all focusing on clinical services and how to improve them. The theme that has run through my work has been the blending of mental health administration with direct practice. The most interesting work has been in the area of population-based health care improvement. This area was not part of my formal training, although my training in psychology prepared me well to learn what I needed to learn to do well.

As I thought about writing this chapter, I wondered how much of my own experience could serve as a model for others who are interested in pursuing a career in organized health care and specifically in the current iterations of managed health care. My psychology training provided an excellent background, given the professional demands and changes of the past 20 years. There were no formal courses of graduate study within psychology that focused exclusively on managed care when I went to graduate school at the University of Minnesota's Institute of Child Development or when I completed my postdoctoral fellowship in professional psychology in the Psychology in the Schools Training Program, also at the University of Minnesota. I have found that the intellectual climate and my clinical experiences at the University of Minnesota, along with my 10 years of work as licensed psychologist, prepared me well for my work at UBH. However, all of my learning about managed care came from on-the-job learning and reading during off hours.

Things have changed. Managed care is now a sophisticated industry that continues to change rapidly and evolve as the business climate changes. When I discussed managed care with psychologist colleagues in the mid-1990s, some said that they would consider employment in managed care only if other options did not work out. This strategy might have worked back then; after all, early in the industry many psychologists advanced through on-the-job training. At present, however, it would be extremely difficult for a psychologist to enter the business with no background in managed care. With industry consolidation, there are fewer companies and, thus, fewer positions. There are well-qualified applicants with excellent academic credentials and experience for most positions.

To prepare for a position in managed care and related areas, I still believe that psychology provides one of the best core educations imaginable. However, this preparation simply is not sufficient to move to high levels within managed care at the present time. Many of my colleagues have pursued MBAs to augment their training in psychology. Those who are more interested in research have opted for training in public health along with their psychology training. I recommend considering this type of dual course as part of your graduate training if you are interested in working in managed health care organizations, hospital delivery systems, or consulting firms or other organizations that deal with managed care.

Financial Compensation

My comments on the topic of financial compensation are based on nonscientific and informal discussions with individuals across the industry and are not based on direct information about any one company, including UBH. Psychologists usually come to managed care organizations with other experience, regardless of role. Care managers may make $45,000 on the low end and $70,000 on the high end. People who advance into the management ranks make more, and some make well over $100,000; senior executives make even more than that. Advancement and compensation tend to be tied not to profession or time in position, but rather to actual work performance. Like other private sector organizations, managed care companies have a variety of ways of providing additional performance-based compensation, including bonuses and stock option awards.

Factors for Success in the Current Health Care Environment

As I completed my studies and worked in my first jobs, I sometimes wondered what path my career ultimately would take. Initially, I thought I would have an academic career; later, I believed I would have a clinical career. My career is in neither. I found my way to a career in mental health administration and managed care by being open to new experiences and taking advantage of opportunities when they arose.

When I reflect on the other psychologists I have known who have worked in this industry, a number of themes emerge. First and foremost, these are people with tremendous energy and intelligence. I have been fortunate to attend two outstanding academic institutions—Cornell University and the University of Minnesota—both of which introduced me to people of outstanding intellect and accomplishment. The people I have met at UBH are different in only one way: The private sector, especially in a competitive environment like health care, places an enormous premium on rapid action and quick yet incisive decision making. The tasks my colleagues and I accomplish are inherently practical, not theoretical. You need to be able to integrate theory and practice in a subtle and effective way while working with many people under time pressure. For example, meetings are always focused on deliverables and outcomes. If there is no purpose to a meeting, it does not occur. Off-target discussions, although interesting and educative, are not reinforced unless they are demonstrably related to the task at hand. There are few standing committees; those that exist are related to a business function, regulatory requirement, performance guarantee, or accreditation activity.

In short, this business rewards individuals who have a broad and clear understanding of their areas of expertise and who can take these attributes and skills and turn them into effective actions that make a difference. I have found that psychologists are superb at this once they get the hang of it. The environment and the challenges change quickly, and you have to be nimble to adapt. This is not a good industry for people who want to do one or two things over a long period of time.

Advantages and Disadvantages of the Career

Earlier in this chapter, I discuss a number of the advantages of work in the managed care industry. It is important work, and it offers opportunity for growth and advancement for people who are ambitious, energetic, and skillful. The intellectual climate is stimulating. There are always new opportunities for those inclined to take advantage of them.

The negatives of this career choice have come primarily from certain peers in the field and at times from the APA itself. Managed care has generated controversy. In the mid-1990s, there was an attempt to form a Division of Managed Health Care and Psychology that failed to get the APA Council's approval. I was on the APA Council at that time (representing the Minnesota Psychological Association [MPA]) and was disappointed that this effort failed. However, this did not deter me or my colleagues in Minnesota. We started our own division within the MPA, and to my knowledge, this is the only division of its type in the country. In Minnesota, we took what looked like a negative outcome and turned it into a positive one. This experience led me to realize that one of the most important attributes to nurture if your are considering a career in managed care is the gumption to keep working at something if you believe that it is the right thing to do—even when some people around you disagree. Working in organized health care requires the ability to deal with a variety of conflicts, some of which arise from unexpected sources.

Future Opportunities in Managed Care

The current organized health care and insurance environment will surely change and evolve. I believe that there will be exciting opportunities for psychologists in the future, even though it might not be possible to predict what they are now. You should try to receive the broadest and most rigorous fundamental training that you can, including experience in areas outside of traditional psychology such as business and public health. Try to develop a mindset and skills that will allow you to succeed even if circumstances change. I have no reason to believe that the pace of change in the managed care field will slow; it is more likely to accelerate. If past performance is predictive of future performance, psychology should serve you well—if you are thoughtful about what you are learning and willing to continue to learn throughout your career.

References

Bobbitt, B. L. (in press). The importance of professional psychology: A view from managed care. *Professional Psychology: Research and Practice.*

Bobbitt, B. L., Marques, C. C., & Trout, D. L. (1998). Managed behavioral health care: Current status, recent trends, and the role of psychology. *Clinical Psychology: Science and Practice, 5,* 53–66.

Feldman, S. (2003). (Ed.). *Managed behavioral health services: Perspectives and practice.* Springfield, IL: Charles C Thomas.

Kongstvedt, P. R. (2001). (Ed.). *The managed health care handbook* (4th ed.). Gaithersburg, MD: Aspen Publishers.

Sanchez, L. M., & Turner, S. M. (2003). Practicing psychology in the era of managed care: Implications for practice and training. *American Psychologist, 58,* 116–129.

Wayne J. Camara

Improving Test Development, Use, and Research: Psychologists in Educational and Psychological Testing Organizations

19

A typical student takes many standardized tests before entering college. Many children first encounter educational testing around the age of 4, when they are assessed for kindergarten readiness. At that early age, educators often complete structured social and developmental history inventories with parents, assess children's motor and social skills with structured ratings, and assess cognitive skills with other tests. As students progress through elementary school, they typically complete a norm-referenced achievement test every couple of years that compares them to other students in their school, the state, and the nation. With the advent of No Child Left Behind Act (NCLB) legislation (2001), students are now

Wayne J. Camara, PhD, is vice president for research and analysis at the College Board. He is responsible for managing research, psychometrics, and development for a wide number of assessments, including the SAT and AP (Advanced Placement) programs. He is a fellow of the American Psychological Association (APA Divisions 1, 5, 14), past president of Division 5, chair elect of the Association of Test Publishers, and chair of the U.S. Department of Defense's Technical Advisory Committee. In the past 20 years, he has also had leadership positions in APA, Society for Industrial and Organizational Psychology, and National Council on Measurement in Education (NCME) governance. His primary areas of research include validity and fairness in admissions and selection, professional practice and ethical issues in testing, and predictor development.

faced with mandatory testing in grades 3 through 8 in reading, math, and science, in addition to state or local mandated testing. Beginning in middle school, career interest tests may be administered to help students explore careers and college majors.

The pace of educational testing continues unabated in high school, particularly for students who plan to attend college. In addition to NCLB requirements, college-bound high school students generally take preadmissions tests in their sophomore and junior years to qualify for scholarships and to prepare for the SAT or ACT. The majority of those students take the SAT or ACT (or both) at least twice. In addition, increasing numbers of students are taking Advanced Placement Exams and SAT II Subject Tests, and in 2005 students in 38 states were required to take high school accountability tests, with 20 states requiring them for graduation (Center for Education Policy, 2004). Finally, many students also complete various psychological assessments to evaluate for learning or emotional disabilities. Even students who don't complete high school eventually take a high school equivalency test or other assessments to qualify for a vocational program or a credential for employment. Many students also complete the Armed Services Vocational Aptitude Battery during high school, which is used both to gather career information and to identify students who may qualify for military service.

Just as the use of educational testing has increased dramatically, so have opportunities and demand for psychologists who have solid graduate school training in research, statistics, testing, and measurement. Different types of psychologists, as well as other professionals, spend much of their careers working in organizations that develop and administer educational and psychological assessments and in organizations that conduct educational research. This chapter describes my own career path in educational testing, the different paths leading to this career, attributes and training required for success, the work settings and environment in educational testing organizations, and career opportunities and financial compensation for psychologists.

My Career Path in Educational Testing

Like many undergraduate students, I entered college without a clear choice of a major or a career goal. I was soon drawn to the study of human behavior and chose psychology as a major (my fourth!) during my freshman year at the University of Massachusetts at Dartmouth. In my sophomore year, I completed the typical sequence of courses in statistics and research methods that is required of nearly every undergraduate psychology major; data analysis, statistics, and research methods are fundamental for psychologists who work in educational testing and research organizations.

In my junior year, I enrolled in an elective course, Psychological Testing, which used the classic text authored by Anastasi (1976). It became evident to me that psychological and educational tests attempt to provide empirical evidence to support clinical or educational judgments that psychologists make each day. I came to understand how information from standardized tests, when used appropriately, could supplement professional judgment and provide a means of comparing individuals to other individuals (a normative purpose), to themselves (a longitudinal purpose), or against a set of established criteria or standards (a criterion-related purpose). In addition, tests serve important descriptive and inferential purposes. Anastasi (1976) also demonstrated how tests could be used in a variety of settings such as industrial, clinical, vocational, counseling, and education settings.

I earned a master's degree in educational measurement and then a certificate of advanced graduate study in school psychology and worked for 2 years as a school psychologist in West Bridgewater, Massachusetts. I administered a large variety of cognitive, personality, and projective tests to students; developed individualized education plans; and provided psychosocial diagnostic reports for school-age children who were referred for assessment because of educational or behavioral issues. Although I enjoyed the testing, measurement, and diagnostic aspects of the work, I quickly experienced the barriers that face anyone who does not possess a doctoral degree, and I decided to continue my education.

In 1987, I completed a PhD program at the University of Illinois at Champaign–Urbana. My course of study included a unique combination of foundation and quantitative courses in both industrial/ organizational psychology (I/O psychology) and educational measurement. Again, my primary interests were the efficacy and validity of tests and assessment in decision making. My master's thesis evaluated a variety of predictors used in employment selection, and my dissertation involved developing an adaptive screening assessment for applicants to the state civil service. I completed as many graduate courses related to tests and measurement in education and I/O psychology as I could. Courses that focused on personnel selection, validation, educational testing, computer-based testing, and measurement theory formed the core of my graduate program. However, I also completed a number of required courses in statistics and quantitative psychology, and I became proficient with a variety of statistical software programs outside of formal coursework.

I began my career at the Human Resources Research Organization (HumRRO), where I worked on a number of extremely interesting research projects, including performing job analysis studies, identifying personality and other noncognitive factors that were associated with success in entry-level managers, and examining the validity of the military's testing program for a variety of uses in schools and for military entrance. As an entry-level research scientist, I was responsible for working with several small teams on different research projects, each of which was managed by a more senior research scientist. I devoted a substantial amount of time to writing responses to federal and state government requests for proposals, which are the primary sources of funding for educational research organizations. I gained an enormous amount of practical experience in budgeting, staffing, and pricing of research and technical services, areas that are not taught in most graduate programs. However, my training in research design, sampling, and research methodology were invaluable for this type of work.

The primary deliverables of all educational research organizations are written reports and oral presentations. Psychologists and psychometricians who work in such organizations must communicate clearly to a wide range of audiences. Efficiency in writing is just as important as clarity in communication, and it is not unusual to be expected to produce lengthy technical proposals in a few weeks while managing large research studies. Unlike graduate students, researchers may work on several different problems with several different teams of researchers under very tight deadlines. The ability to present the technical material in oral presentations and to handle questions under fire is essential for success.

My next employment was in the Science Directorate of the American Psychological Association (APA). I held a variety of positions, including director of testing and associate executive director of the Science Directorate. During that time, I was responsible for developing a testing policy within the APA and influencing federal policies on testing provisions of the Civil Rights Act, the Americans With Disabilities Act, and the Polygraph Protection Law. In my current position as vice president of research and psychometrics at the College Board, I am involved in the scientific, educational, public policy, media relations, and business aspects of large-scale testing programs such as the Advanced Placement (AP) program, PSAT/NMSQT, and SAT.

Different Paths Leading to the Career

Psychologists who work in educational and psychological testing organizations (or other educational research organizations) typically have advanced graduate training in quantitative psychology, psychometrics, or educational psychology. However, individuals who have graduate training in counseling, I/O psychology, or social psychology and have strong and demonstrable competencies in statistics, research design and methodology, measurement, evaluation, and testing may also find employment in such organizations. There are generally two career paths: one for doctoral professionals and one for master's-degree professionals. As in most other areas of applied psychology, professionals who have master's degrees do not normally compete for the same positions as doctoral-level psychologists; however, individuals who have accumulated a great deal of experience and recognition of their work despite the lack of a doctoral degree are exceptions to this rule.

Psychologists who consider positions in testing or research organizations often compete directly with nonpsychologists who possess similar training in research, psychometrics, evaluation, and testing. In fact, the majority of professionals working in educational testing companies are not psychologists; instead, they have doctoral degrees in educational measurement programs or other disciplines (e.g., sociology, economics, mathematics) that require strong research and statistical skills.

Only approximately 1% of the doctoral-level psychologists who are members of the APA indicate that their primary areas of specialization are in quantitative psychology, psychometrics, or statistics (APA, 1999). Seven doctoral-level programs in psychology offer a specialization in psychometrics, nine in quantitative psychology, and five in quantitative methods. These programs rewarded only 21 doctorates in 1997. Six master's degree programs awarded 17 degrees during the same time (APA, 2005). Kolen and Tong (2005) identified 67 doctoral programs in educational measurement in the United States, but fewer than half appeared to offer the specialized training in psychometrics and educational evaluation that would be required for entry-level positions in most educational testing and research organizations.

The field of psychometrics is intertwined with educational measurement and quantitative psychology and may be located in education departments. Programs that provide comparable graduate preparation may be called "research and statistics" or "research and evaluation" or may be within another specialty in graduate psychology programs (Sireci, 1996). Professionals who develop and conduct research on tests are commonly referred to as "psychometricians." *USA Today* (Toppo, 2004, p. D1) described them as "a small but growing group of elite researchers who do little else but think about standardized tests. . . . Trained in both psychology and statistics [they] make sure standardized tests actually test what kids know, quickly, fairly, and accurately." Psychometricians are concerned with measuring educational and psychological characteristics such as achievement, abilities, skills, personality traits, attitudes, and other factors. Other psychologists, working as research scientists, may evaluate educational programs, conduct research on educational problems such as literacy and gender differences in learning, or design and analyze surveys. They often attempt to answer educational questions that strive to improve teaching and learning. For example, they may examine issues such as test anxiety, gender differences in science achievement, or the types of instruction that result in greater reading achievement among elementary students.

The competencies required to be successful are common to most professionals working in the field of educational testing. Students interested in pursuing careers in this field must have strong quantitative skills and prior exposure to psychology, education, statistics, and testing. Coursework in advanced mathematics, such as calculus and matrix algebra, can be helpful in understanding the advanced statistical coursework required in psychometrics and quantitative psychology. Graduate coursework typically involves experimental methods, data analysis and interpretation, research design, test theory, and measurement. In addition, individuals pursuing a doctoral degree in psychometrics or quantitative psychology should have coursework in advanced statistical methods, computer programming, statistical software, and measurement theory (Illinois State University, 2005; Sireci, 1996). An informal review of job descriptions from the leading educational testing organizations indicated that nontechnical competencies are also essential for success, including attention to detail, precision, the ability to work independently and in groups, and the ability to explain and communicate statistical information and technical concepts to nontechnical audiences.

There are a number of important "softer" skills" associated with success among psychologists working in educational testing and research organizations. In addition to oral and written communication skills, psychologists working in educational organizations need to be able to work on different projects simultaneously and to balance priorities, deadlines, and demands among multiple projects. These work environments also require a high degree of personal organization, planning, and logic to develop project plans required for testing and research. Professionals who can speak to and write for a wide variety of audiences, including students, teachers, parents, educational administrators, and other researchers, are highly valued because much of the work involves communication and interdisciplinary groups.

Roles and Responsibilities

Psychologists often assist in developing educational tests that are used in schools. The SAT, the ACT, the Graduate Record Examination (GRE), and the Law School Admissions Test (LSAT) are examples of admission tests that are developed, administered, and scored by psychologists and psychometricians working in educational organizations such as the College Board, ACT, Educational Testing Service, and the Law School Admissions Council. Educational testing companies also produce hundreds of other educational and psychological tests of career interests and guidance, psychodiagnostics and personality, special education, speech and language, intelligence, and achievement. Psychologists and psychometricians working in educational testing and research companies are involved in designing, developing, and conducting research on all of these types of tests.

In 1997, the National Board of Educational Testing and Public Policy estimated educational tests sales at $267 million annually, and estimates by the Public Broadcasting Service (2002) ranged from $400 million to $700 million before the implementation of NCLB. The General Accounting Office (2003) estimated that states may spend an additional $3.9 billion to $5.3 billion on tests mandated under the federal NCLB requirements alone between 2002 and 2008. All of this translates into an enormous amount of testing in schools and a demand for more psychologists and psychometricians with the appropriate skills to produce, score, and report results on the increased number of tests. Many testing professionals have joked that the NCLB legislation also leaves no psychometrician behind, as the amount of testing conducted in public schools has at least doubled. States generally contract with large educational testing companies to develop tests that are specifically designed to assess educational standards for each subject (e.g., math, science) at various grade levels. Testing is tailored to the state's standards, unlike national testing programs such as the SAT, where many test forms are developed each year and used across the country, or "off-the-shelf" career interest or intelligence tests that may use the same one or two test forms for several years.

Psychologists and psychometricians who work in test development create a test blueprint that is similar to an architectural blueprint. They consider the construct being measured (e.g., mathematical reasoning, chemistry, career interests), the number and types of questions required to cover the knowledge or skill domain that is being assessed, and other psychometric features that are important in producing a fair, valid, and reliable test. For example, they are concerned with the reliability of tests and with ensuring that when humans score essays or open-ended items, they apply consistent and reliable standards across readers and student responses. Often psychometricians work directly with teachers to review items and to develop test blueprints and scoring rubrics. They conduct statistical analyses once tests scores have been produced; for example, they examine individual test items on achievement tests to ensure that they represent a range of difficulty for each skill or subject and that students have the appropriate amount of time to complete a test without taking more time from classroom instruction than is necessary. On tests such as the SAT, psychometricians equate each form to ensure that scores from all test forms are comparable. They may also work with educational administrators and counselors to ensure that score reports are accurate, clear, and easily understood by schools, students, and parents.

Test publishers have R&D units that examine a wide range of research questions concerning assessments and gather evidence of validity to support the use of test scores and results for students and schools. Psychologists and psychometricians do statistical analyses of test results after tests are administered, conduct research to ensure the quality of test results, and evaluate the effectiveness of the testing programs. Psychologists and psychometricians also conduct research on the tests, evaluate educational programs and interventions, investigate individual differences in terms of teaching and learning, and study the influence of a variety of different factors (e.g., background, social, cognitive, school, and teacher factors) in these areas. Educational organizations such as the American Institutes for Research (AIR), HumRRO, McREL, the RAND Corporation, and many others are involved in conducting research in these areas.

Master's-level psychologists are employed in test development, psychometric, and research units in these organizations. They typically begin their careers coordinating research tasks, such as contacting schools to coordinate data collection from students, writing test instructions, or conducting routine data analyses for doctoral-level professionals. Eventually, with substantial experience and training, some master's-level psychologists are given considerable responsibility in project management and research efforts.

There is no typical day for a research scientist or psychometrician. Each day brings different tasks, different challenges, and different duties depending on the type of organization one works for, the tests one works on or the programs one evaluates, and the specific responsibilities one has. One commonalty is that research scientists and psychometricians across organizations, programs, and jobs work independently on their own projects and analyses, but that work is always incorporated into a group product and team environment.

Developing a test and reporting scores for a small program many involve a handful of staff, whereas developing the new SAT and reporting scores has literally involved several hundred staff across three organizations (College Board, Educational Testing Services [ETS], and Pearson Educational Measurement), as well as thousands of educators who administer the tests, score the essays, and review scores with students in schools and at colleges. Psychometricians assist organizations and content experts (e.g., reading, math, science) in determining the number and types of items to place on a test. They ensure that items measure all major areas of a construct without overemphasizing one or two areas. They are similarly concerned that the test is not speeded and that students have an appropriate amount of time to complete the test. In addition, they ensure that no item differentially favors a group of students because of irrelevant factors. For example, items that contain terms or focus on content that is not widely known will not appear on national achievement tests, because they could favor a particular group of students on the basis of regional, ethnic, or cultural differences.

Before including items on tests, psychometricians try them out to determine how students will perform on the items. If the majority of items on a test are very easy, the test will not do a good job of differentiating students who are high performers from those who are low performers. Most achievement tests not only cover a wide variety of content and skills in an area (e.g., geometry, biology) but also include a mix of items that are considered easy, medium difficult, and hard. Psychometricians also oversee the scoring of tests. Many tests include essays or open-ended tasks that require human scorers to be trained to grade them consistently. Psychometricians also examine the difficulty of tests and equate scores from different forms of a test so that scores from one test administration are statistically comparable to scores from an earlier administration.

Research scientists are often concerned with examining a number of ways that irrelevant factors can affect scores. They conduct validity studies that gather evidence of how test scores can be appropriately used. At the College Board, psychologists and psychometricians conduct hundreds of validity studies with colleges that examine how accurately the SAT and high school grades predict student achievement in college. Some studies focus on group differences (e.g., ethnic, gender) on tests and demonstrate that the same differences often exist on the performance that is being predicted (e.g., college grades, graduation, retention). Other studies examine the effects of coaching, a more rigorous high school curriculum, or family education and wealth on test scores and college performance.

In some organizations, research scientists also spend a great deal of time on proposal development. One of the things I never learned in graduate school was how to write clear, concise proposals to obtain funding for research in the real world. When I began my career at HumRRO, I was part of a team that responded to government calls for research proposals. Proposal writing often required many long days, and some long nights, because I was working on three or four other projects full-time and had to find additional time to respond to these calls.

Psychologists in educational organizations may experience limitations on the types of research they can conduct, limitations that may not exist in academia. Educational companies bid for test development or research contracts, and employees work on the projects that the company is successful in winning. These projects become the priority, and although many professionals conduct some independent research or consultation, it is generally a last priority. Psychologists in an educational organization are also likely to work with many teams, and they need to be willing to compromise and to understand that marketing, business, and customer demands may be just as important to the success of a project as the scientific or statistical expertise they represent. Psychologists trained in research programs value objective information and empirical facts. They are trained to have a healthy dose of skepticism about conclusions or diagnoses that are based solely on professional judgment. These differences will often put such psychologists at odds with many of their colleagues who have worked in clinical and educational settings and who rely on expert judgment as the foundation for much of their interventions. The most successful researchers and psychometricians I have worked with in testing companies combined superb technical skills and organizational abilities, amazing amounts of drive and personal motivation, and an ability to communicate with nonresearchers and explain technical and complex issues in clear and simple language. In addition, they enjoyed solving problems in a practical and applied environment and could balance a large number of projects and responsibilities.

Employment Opportunities

Olson (2004) reported that CTB/McGraw Hill, ETS, Harcourt Assessment, Pearson Educational Measurement, and Riverside Publishing accounted for about 70% of state testing contracts. Several smaller organizations now account for the remainder of the state testing market, which is growing rapidly. However, there are many other large-scale educational testing programs that are developed by not-for-profit organizations such as the College Board, ACT, ETS, National Board of Medical Examiners, and additional organizations that conduct research on tests (e.g., AIR, HumRRO, McREL, WestEd). In 2005, more than 50 positions were advertised in measurement, testing, and research at the placement center during the American Educational Research Association's annual convention. All positions required a doctoral degree, but some employers would consider master's-level professionals with experience. More than two thirds of these positions were in not-for-profit educational testing and research organizations.

Not captured in those figures are the increased numbers of testing and psychometric positions open in state and federal government, as well as positions in licensing, credentialing, and psychological testing organizations. An estimate of 80 to 150 vacancies for psychometricians, statisticians, and measurement and testing professionals in a year is probably quite accurate. It has become common practice for headhunters to recruit experienced professionals among the major testing companies. Salaries, signing bonuses, and greater flexibility in work locations have become more common, although not the norm, for psychometricians and measurement professionals working in testing organizations. For example, some companies have opened up satellite offices specifically to recruit and retain researchers and psychometricians in more attractive and less costly geographic areas. In addition, several major testing organizations have opened small offices in states where they hold a major contract, and others have negotiated arrangements for senior staff to primarily work out of their homes.

Financial Compensation

Compensation is difficult to determine across educational testing organizations. A proprietary compensation survey of 20 educational testing and research organizations (Nina Fleiss, personal communication, February 7, 2005) reported a median starting salary between $67,000 and $70,000 for new PhDs in 2004, with increases to approximately $85,000 for professionals with 3 to 8 years of experience. Median salaries for research scientists and psychometricians with more than 8 years of experience were between $101,000 and $115,000. These figures do not include managerial and executive-level salaries in these fields, which may range from $150,000 to beyond $300,000, or the salaries given to top graduates from the most competitive graduate programs. After interviewing testing company officials, Toppo (2004) reported that "new psychometricians can often command $100,000 salaries, more than twice as much as in most other academic disciplines" (p. 3). Toppo noted that many psychometricians have competing offers from firms before they complete their coursework; he quoted testing officials who noted that the high demand for psychometricians and researchers, combined with the limited supply of new PhDs, has resulted in many positions that cannot be filled in the foreseeable future.

Conclusion

One's choice of career should rest not only on the intrinsic properties of the career but also on the broader social context to which the career contributes (Vroom, 1997). In this chapter I discuss the role of psychometricians and researchers who develop, administer, score, and conduct research on tests. The job tasks may appear to be statistical, but the challenges are broader and more complex than those associated with accounting or many other quantitative arenas. Tests are samples of human behavior or performance, and they never tell the entire story. Psychologists are one of the few professions that may spend as much time cautioning the public and customers about the limitations of their products (tests) and the tentativeness of their reports (test scores) as they do in advocating for their use.

Psychologists who work in educational research and testing organizations understand and use scientific principles, research methods, and advanced statistical and programming skills in test development and research. However, at the end of the day, they are attempting to predict future behavior or explain current behavior. These professionals understand that behavior is driven by many factors, several of which are not measured on a test or in similar fashions. Psychologists apply their skills to solve problems in education while keeping in mind the range of social, cultural, academic, and other influences that influence achievement and success in education; this is one way their work is fundamentally different from that of many other quantitative professionals.

Psychologists bring a perspective and skill set that are somewhat different than those of psychometricians and research scientists trained in educational measurement programs. Quantitatively trained graduates from both fields bring similar skills in measurement and statistics, but the context of their training may differ. Quantitative psychologists bring the knowledge of human behavior and are more likely to question the impact of individual and organizational interactions, such as those that may affect student achievement in schools or differential performance on tests.

References

American Psychological Association. (1999). *1999 APA directory survey.* Washington, DC: Author. Retrieved April 28, 2005, from http://research.apa.org/1999profiles.pdf

American Psychological Association. (2005). *Special analysis from RO using data from the 2005 graduate study in psychology.* Washington, DC: Author.

Anastasi, A. (1976). *Psychological testing* (4th ed.). New York: Macmillan.

Center for Education Policy. (2004). *State high school exit exams: A maturing reform.* Washington, DC: Author.

General Accounting Office. (2003, May). *Title I: Characteristics of tests will influence expenses: Information sharing may help states realize efficiencies* (GAO Report No. 03-389). Washington, DC: Author.

Illinois State University. (2005). *Preparing for graduate study in quantitative psychology.* Retrieved May 11, 2005, from http://www.ilstu.edu/~mshesso/quant_grad_prep.htm

Kolen, M. J., & Tong, Y. (2005). *Programs in educational measurement and related areas: 2005 update.* Washington, DC: National Council on Measurement in Education.

No Child Left Behind Act (NCLB) of 2001, Pub. L. No. 107–110, 11 Stat. 1425 (2002).

Olson, L. (2004, December 1). NCLB law bestows bounty on test in try. *Education Week.* Retrieved May 11, 2005, from http:// edweek.org/ew/articles/2004/12/01/14tests.h24.html?qu =nclb%20bounty%20on%20test%20industry&print=1

Public Broadcasting Service. (2002). *Frontline: The testing four.* Retrieved May 20, 2005, from http://www pages/frontline/shows/schools/testing/companie

Sireci, S. G. (1996, August). *Psychos and psychometrics: Careers in quantitative psychology.* Paper presented at the annual meeting of the American Psychological Association as part of the Psi Chi/Division 2 Symposium Nonclinical Degrees and Careers in Psychology, Toronto, Ontario, Canada.

Toppo, G. (2004, October 12). An answer to standardized tests. *USA Today.* Retrieved May 4, 2005, from http://usatoday.com/news/education/2004-10-12-tests-usat_x.htm

Vroom, V. H. (1997). Teaching the managers of tomorrow: Psychologists in business schools. In R. J. Sternberg (Ed.), *Career paths in psychology: Where your degree can take you* (pp. 49–68). Washington, DC: American Psychological Association.

Robert J. Sternberg

Epilogue: Preparing for a Career in Psychology

M any of the readers of this book are college students contemplating a career in psychology, whereas others are people who are already employed and considering switching fields, either from a field other than psychology or from one area of psychology to another. This chapter is addressed primarily to those who are not already in the field of psychology, but who are considering entering it.

As you have seen from the chapters of this book, different fields of specialization within psychology require slightly different preparation. But there is a common core of college coursework that will prepare you for just about any career in psychology.

Ideally, you will choose to major in either psychology or a closely related discipline, such as cognitive science, biology, or child development. The psychology major will generally give you the most flexibility for whatever career in psychology you might want to pursue. But for those who know the particular subfield in which they want to specialize, other majors may work just fine. For example, someone who wants to be a behavioral neuroscientist would probably do quite well majoring in biology.

Whatever your major, a solid and broad background in psychology will be a definite plus if you want to go on to graduate school. Most graduate schools do not want their graduate students to have to take undergraduate psychology courses, nor do they want to repeat, at the graduate level, training that students are presumed to have had as undergraduates. Moreover, some graduate programs require for admission the Graduate Record Examination (GRE) in psychology, an advanced test that is difficult to master without a solid background in psychology.

At the very least, potential candidates for graduate school should have taken the introductory psychology course, a course in statistics, and courses in most or all of the traditional basic areas of psychology, such as biological (or physiological) psychology, clinical (or abnormal) psychology, cognitive psychology, developmental psychology, social psychology, and personality. Most students also should have some advanced courses, such as learning, experimental design, thinking, adult development, or social cognition. Success in advanced courses shows that you will be able to handle the more rigorous challenges of the graduate school curriculum.

If you do not major in psychology, consider minoring in it. In this way, you will at least have the fundamentals of the field. And whether you major in psychology or not, many graduate schools consider a broad background outside psychology to be important. Courses in the natural sciences, mathematics, and computer science are often especially highly regarded. In addition, courses in sociology, anthropology, linguistics, and other social sciences will give you a broader perspective on the nature of human beings.

I strongly urge college students to get as much training and experience in writing and even effective speaking as they can. It is difficult to overstate the importance of communication in psychology. Psychologists frequently find themselves writing case reports, articles for publication, grant proposals, and even books. Strong writing skills are essential. Psychologists also frequently find themselves speaking in front of audiences of other psychologists, students, parents, educators, businesspeople, and others. Public speaking skills are thus a big plus for psychologists to have.

Many professors at the graduate level strongly urge college students to get research experience beyond that provided in lab-based courses. Such research experience can be had by working in a professor's laboratory, on an independent project supervised by a professor or advanced graduate student, or for a nonuniversity organization that conducts psychological research. Many applicants to graduate school have good credentials. Research experience, perhaps more than any other single attribute, is what often separates out the most successful applicants to graduate school.

Research experience has another advantage. When you apply to graduate school, you typically need three letters of recommendation, preferably from psychologists. Working with someone in a laboratory provides an excellent way to get to know one or more psychologists, who will then be in a better position to write letters for you. One of the saddest things I encounter as a professor is when a student reaches the senior year, has not gotten to know any psychology faculty members well, and then is scrounging at the last minute for people to write letters.

Research experience is not the only way to get to know faculty well, of course. Taking small seminars from them or working with them on student–faculty committees provides another opportunity to get to know faculty. But coursework and committee participation often do not give faculty members the same level of insight into your research skills as does research experience, and many graduate schools are particularly eager to attract students with such skills and experience.

Many graduate programs require applicants to take the GRE for admission. One session (the general test) assesses verbal, quantitative, and analytical skills, and another session (the subject test) tests for subject matter knowledge. In some schools, the general test is required and the subject test is optional. It is best to prepare for this test over the long term by getting an excellent, broad education. The Educational Testing Service provides information about the test, and books and courses are available that help one prepare for the examinations. The preparation materials may or may not raise scores, but they may give you the confidence you need to do your best on the tests.

Admissions offices seeking a diverse and interesting student body sometimes value extracurricular activities, but such activities typically count much less at the graduate level, unless they are related in some way to the graduate education for which you are preparing yourself. Examples are work in a psychological clinic or hospital, participation in psychological research, and membership in a psychology club. Occasionally, though, other kinds of life experiences are valued for their contributions to students' maturity. Many psychologists believe, for example, that successful work experience of almost any kind can bestow a kind of maturity that one cannot obtain merely from being a student. Some students take a year or two off to get such experience. This experience can be helpful, especially if it relates to one's career orientation, such as being a research assistant for a psychologist.

You should remember one other thing: When you fill out the application for graduate school, the essay you write will be considered very seriously. Graduate school admissions committees look for signs of understanding of, commitment to, and purpose in the field. Thus, merely saying you want to study psychology because you are interested in human nature is more likely to hurt you than to help you. Showing an understanding of what a particular program has to offer and of what the faculty members in a particular program do can help you gain admission to the program of your choice. No one expects you to know exactly what you want to do in graduate school. However, admissions committees do expect you to have formed at least some tentative interests.

Perhaps the single most important thing you can do is to get advice from faculty members, especially those working in the area of psychology you are interested in pursuing. College students are often shy about seeking advice. They shouldn't be: That's what faculty are there for. Seek out advice, and you will find that a lot of your preparations will go much more smoothly than you might have thought possible.

When you consider going to graduate school, remember that graduate school is not a continuation of the same kinds of activities you engaged in as an undergraduate. Coursework will generally be less emphasized, especially after the 1st or 2nd year. At that point, research, teaching, and in some cases clinical experience typically are emphasized more. In graduate school, you make the transition from being merely a consumer of psychological knowledge to being a producer or a user of psychological knowledge.

Some people who decide to enter careers in psychology majored in a field other than psychology as undergraduates and then decide, whether immediately on completing college or some years thereafter, that psychology is the field that truly interests them. Students can be and regularly are admitted to graduate programs whose main undergraduate concentration was in another field. The field need not even be a closely allied one, such as biology, sociology, or anthropology. Our program, from time to time, accepts students who majored in English literature, French, or mathematics.

If you are switching fields, however, you should make sure to complete coursework that gives you the equivalent of a college minor or, preferably, a college major in psychology. Graduate schools generally assume that enrolled students have undergraduate training in psychology, and their programs cannot repeat all the material of the undergraduate program. Many local colleges offer returning students opportunities to pick up the courses they need through part time, summer, or other special programs. You may even be able to achieve much of the training on your own through independent reading.

A high score on the GRE Advanced Test in Psychology may convince some programs that you have mastered the basic material of psychology, regardless of course preparation. Moreover, some graduate programs admit students for a master's degree who majored in other fields, despite the students' minimal background in psychology, and decide later whether the students are qualified to pursue the doctorate.

Again, gaining some research experience, such as by working as a research assistant, can also be invaluable.

Remember, though, that graduate schools differ widely in what they view as acceptable background for entrance into their programs. Some schools, for example, may view an undergraduate major in computer science or biology as being every bit as useful as an undergraduate major in psychology. Other schools may view relevant work experience as a decided advantage. You need to discuss the issue of your background with the appropriate official (usually a director of graduate studies) in each program to ascertain the program's expectations for admission.

You can start preparing for a career in psychology at almost any time. I hope you do seek out a career in psychology and that you are as happy with such a career as I am. But whatever you decide to do, good luck!

Index

About the Editor

Robert J. Sternberg, PhD, is dean of the School of Arts and Sciences and professor of psychology at Tufts University. Previously he was IBM Professor of Psychology and Education in the Department of Psychology, professor of management in the School of Management, and director of the Center for the Psychology of Abilities, Competencies, and Expertise (PACE Center) at Yale University. He continues to direct the PACE Center from Tufts. Dr. Sternberg also was president of the American Psychological Association (APA) in 2003. He has served on the board of directors of APA (2002–2004) and on the board of trustees of the APA Insurance Trust (2004) and is currently on the board of trustees of the American Psychological Foundation (2005–2009). He also is president elect of the Eastern Psychological Association.

Dr. Sternberg is the author of more than 1,100 journal articles, book chapters, and books and has received over $18 million in government and other grants and contracts for his research. The central focus of his research is intelligence, creativity, and wisdom, and he also has studied love and close relationships, as well as hate. This research has been conducted on five different continents. He has received seven honorary doctorates.

Dr. Sternberg is a fellow of the American Academy of Arts and Sciences and several other societies. He has won many awards from APA, the American Educational Research Association, the Association for Psychological Science, and other organizations. Dr. Sternberg has been listed in the *APA Monitor on Psychology* as one of the top 100 psychologists of the 20th century and is listed in the ISI as one of its most highly cited authors (top 0.5%) in psychology and psychiatry. He also was listed in the *Esquire* register of outstanding men and women under 40 and was listed as one of 100 top young scientists by *Science Digest.* He is currently listed in *Who's Who in America, Who's Who in the World, Who's Who in the East, Who's Who in Medicine and Healthcare,* and *Who's Who in Science and Engineering.*

Dr. Sternberg is best known for his theory of successful intelligence, investment theory of creativity (developed with Todd Lubart), theory of thinking styles as mental self-government, balance theory of wisdom, and wisdom-intelligence-creativity, synthesized (WICS) theory of leadership, as well as for his duplex theories of love and hate.